W9-BVZ-250

American Women Poets

Titles in the CRITICAL COSMOS series include

AMERICAN FICTION
American Fiction through 1914
American Fiction, 1914–1945
American Fiction, 1946–1965
American Fiction, 1966 to the Present
American Jewish Literature
American Women Novelists and Short
 Story Writers
Black American Fiction

AMERICAN POETRY, DRAMA,
 AND PROSE
American Drama to 1945
American Drama 1945 to the Present
American Poetry through 1914
American Poetry, 1915–1945
American Poetry, 1946–1965
American Poetry, 1966 to the Present
American Prose and Criticism to 1945
American Prose and Criticism, 1945 to
 the Present
American Women Poets
Black American Poetry

BRITISH LITERATURE THROUGH 1880
British Drama: 18th and 19th Centuries
Eighteenth-Century Fiction and Prose
Eighteenth-Century Poetry
Elizabethan and Jacobean Drama
Elizabethan Poetry
Elizabethan Prose and Fiction
English Romantic Fiction and Prose
English Romantic Poetry
Medieval Literature
Seventeenth-Century Poetry
Seventeenth-Century Prose
Victorian Fiction
Victorian Poetry
Victorian Prose

FRENCH LITERATURE
French Drama through 1915
French Fiction through 1915
French Poetry through 1915
French Prose and Criticism through 1789
French Prose and Criticism, 1790 to the
 Present
Modern French Drama
Modern French Fiction
Modern French Poetry
Modern French Prose and Criticism

GERMAN LITERATURE
German Drama through 1915
German Fiction through 1915
German Poetry through 1915
German Prose and Criticism through 1915
Modern German Drama
Modern German Fiction
Modern German Poetry
Modern German Prose and Criticism

MODERN BRITISH AND
 COMMONWEALTH LITERATURE
Anglo-Irish Literature
British Prose, 1880–1914
British World War I Literature
Canadian Fiction
Canadian Poetry and Prose
Commonwealth Poetry and Fiction
Contemporary British Drama, 1946 to the
 Present
Contemporary British Fiction, 1946 to the
 Present
Contemporary British Poetry
Contemporary British Prose
Edwardian and Georgian Fiction,
 1880–1914
Edwardian and Georgian Poetry,
 1880–1914
Modern British Drama, 1900–1945
Modernist Fiction, 1920–1945
Modern Poetry and Prose, 1920–1945

OTHER EUROPEAN AND LATIN
 AMERICAN LITERATURE
African Anglophonic Literature
Dadaism and Surrealism
Italian Drama
Italian Fiction
Italian Poetry
Jewish Literature: The Bible through 1945
Modern Jewish Literature
Modern Latin American Fiction
Modern Scandinavian Literature
Modern Spanish Fiction
Modern Spanish and Latin American
 Poetry
Russian Drama
Russian Fiction
Russian Poetry
Scandinavian Literature through 1915
Spanish Fiction through 1927
Spanish Poetry through 1927

THE CRITICAL COSMOS SERIES

American Women Poets

Edited and with an introduction
by *HAROLD BLOOM*
Sterling Professor of the Humanities
Yale University

CHELSEA HOUSE PUBLISHERS ◇ 1986
New York ◇ *New Haven* ◇ *Philadelphia*

© 1986 by Chelsea House Publishers, a division of Chelsea
House Educational Communications, Inc.
  133 Christopher Street, New York, NY 10014
  345 Whitney Avenue, New Haven, CT 06511
  5014 West Chester Pike, Edgemont, PA 19028

Introduction © 1986 by Harold Bloom

Printed and bound in the United States of America

∞ The paper used in this publication meets the minimum
requirements of the American National Standard for
Permanence of Paper for Printed Library Materials,
Z39.48-1984.

Library of Congress Cataloging-in-Publication Data
American women poets.
  (The Critical cosmos)
  Bibliography: p.
  Includes index.
  1. American poetry—Women authors—History and
criticism—Addresses, essays, lectures.   2. Women
in literature—Addresses, essays, lectures.
I. Bloom, Harold.   II. Series.
PS147.A39 1986   811'.009'9287   86-2579
ISBN 0-87754-960-5

Contents

Editor's Note   ix

Introduction   1
Harold Bloom

ANNE BRADSTREET
"No rhet'ric we expect": Argumentation in Bradstreet's
"The Prologue"   9
Jane Donahue Eberwein

EMILY DICKINSON
Emily Dickinson: A Voice of War   17
Shira Wolosky

"Ransom in a Voice": Language as Defense in Dickinson's Poetry   23
Joanne Feit Diehl

Et in Arcadia Ego: Representation, Death, and the Problem
of Boundary in Emily Dickinson   41
Sharon Cameron

GERTRUDE STEIN
Two Types of Obscurity in the Writings of Gertrude Stein   77
Randa K. Dubnick

H. D. (HILDA DOOLITTLE)
The Concept of Projection: H. D.'s Visionary Powers   97
Adalaide Morris

MARIANNE MOORE
The "Feminine" Language of Marianne Moore   117
Bonnie Costello

Emphatic Reticence in Marianne Moore's Poems   133
David Bromwich

LOUISE BOGAN
The Problem of the Woman Artist: Louise Bogan, "The Alchemist"   145
Diane Wood Middlebrook

"The Repressed Becomes the Poem": Landscape and Quest
in Two Poems by Louise Bogan   151
Sandra Cookson

ELIZABETH BISHOP
Elizabeth Bishop: Domestication, Domesticity,
    and the Otherworldly   161
        Helen Vendler

The Geography of Gender: Elizabeth Bishop's
    "In the Waiting Room"   175
        Lee Edelman

MAY SWENSON
May Swenson: "Turned Back to the Wild by Love"   189
        Richard Howard

GWENDOLYN BROOKS
Gwendolyn Brooks's *A Street in Bronzeville*, the Harlem Renaissance
    and the Mythologies of Black Women   205
        Gary Smith

DENISE LEVERTOV
Denise Levertov: A Poetry of Exploration   217
        Paul A. Lacey

ANNE SEXTON
Anne Sexton: Somehow to Endure   237
        J. D. McClatchy

ADRIENNE RICH
Adrienne Rich: A Feminine Tradition   259
        Margaret Homans

SYLVIA PLATH
Sylvia Plath: Enlargement or Derangement?   273
        Barbara Hardy

AUDRE LORDE
Audre Lorde: The Severed Daughter   289
        R. B. Stepto

AMY CLAMPITT
Amy Clampitt: "The Hazardous Definition of Structures"   295
        Richard Howard

VICKI HEARNE
Tremors of Exactitude: Vicki Hearne's *Nervous Horses*   299
        John Hollander

JAY MACPHERSON
Jay Macpherson: Poetry in Canada, 1957   301
        Northrop Frye

Jay Macpherson: *Poems Twice Told*   307
    Margaret Atwood

MARGARET ATWOOD
Atwood's Haunted Sequences: *The Circle Game, The Journals
of Susanna Moodie,* and *Power Politics*   311
    Judith McCombs

Biographical Notes   327

Contributors   339

Bibliography   343

Acknowledgments   351

Index of Names and Titles   355

Editor's Note

This volume gathers together what in its editor's judgment represents the best criticism yet published upon the principal American and Canadian women poets, from Anne Bradstreet to the present moment. The editor is grateful to Karin Cope for her erudition and insight, which helped him in locating and choosing the essays included here. Three essays have been devoted to Emily Dickinson and two each to Marianne Moore, Louise Bogan, Elizabeth Bishop, and Jay Macpherson. The remaining poets each receive one essay in criticism.

Anne Bradstreet, the first considerable American poet, is shrewdly analyzed by Jane Donahue Eberwein as a master of rhetoric who, like Emily Dickinson, "contrived to sound meek and vulnerable, even in the act of choosing among crowns." Dickinson herself is introduced here in an essay by Shira Wolosky that advances our apprehension of the poet's spiritual agon "with and against God . . ., the clash between his language and her own." Another aspect of this agon is illuminated by Joanne Feit Diehl in her study of language as defense in Dickinson, as the poet "explores the possibilities for a poetics that yields nothing to forces beyond the self." A trinity of Dickinsonian critiques is completed here by Sharon Cameron's analysis of the tangled relationships in the poetry between problematical representation, death, and the trope of boundary.

Gertrude Stein's poetry (and fictive prose) is examined by Randa K. Dubnick, who distinguishes between two modes of obscurity in Stein, one not unwillful, and one which "was a necessary consequence of the nature of her innovative experiment with language." H. D. (Hilda Doolittle), Stein's younger contemporary, receives consideration of a kind she would have welcomed, in Adalaide Morris's essay that relates Freud's mechanism of defense, projection, to the poet's visionary powers. On Marianne Moore, one of the major poets of H. D.'s generation, two very different but complementary essays are offered here. Bonnie Costello's innovative investigation of what Eliot, Jarrell, and Blackmur had termed Moore's "feminine" language concludes rightly that: "No container will hold her gusto." Humility, affection, and reserve are thus judged not to be "feminine" or passive qualities "but dynamic and vital modes of response." David Bromwich concentrates on Moore's affinities with the early Stevens and the early Eliot, like her explorers of the border between the visual and the visionary.

Two essays on Louise Bogan present very different emphases. Diane Wood Middlebrook analyzes Bogan's private mythology that "expresses a felt contradiction between writing and living a woman's life." Sandra Cookson, investigating quest images in Bogan, uncovers a pattern of repression in Bogan in which, as Bogan puts it, "the repressed becomes the poem." Elizabeth Bishop, the principal American poet after Dickinson, receives an illuminating overview from Helen Vendler, who ponders the intricate balance of the familiar and the uncanny in Bishop's poetry. Lee Edelman, in a detailed explication of Bishop's "In the Waiting Room," demonstrates a way in which the poem indisputably does involve us in the question of "female textuality."

Richard Howard gives an eloquent appreciation of an extraordinary poet, May Swenson, who in the editor's judgment is, in proportion to her merits, the most undervalued woman poet of our own or any other time. Howard celebrates her as being both magician and naturalistic dramatist, and sees the two modes as being unified in her later work.

The noted black poet Gwendolyn Brooks is sensitively discussed by Gary Smith, who sees her as exposing and combating the mythologies to which black women have been subjected. Paul A. Lacey's essay on Denise Levertov emphasizes her contribution to an enlarged social consciousness, in a kind of countermovement towards mythologizing.

J. D. McClatchy's tribute to Anne Sexton praises her for honesty and courage, qualities also ascribed to Adrienne Rich in an analysis of Rich's ideological stance by Margaret Homans. In an appreciation parallel to these, Barbara Hardy sees Sylvia Plath as having created a persona in her poems capable of "resisting narcissism and closure, right to the death." R. B. Stepto's high estimate of Audre Lorde also discourses on a poet's courage but refreshingly emphasizes Lorde's apt knowledge of West African culture and religion.

Richard Howard, reviewing Amy Clampitt's elegant *The Kingfisher*, salutes it as the best "first book" of American poems since A. R. Ammons, while noting Clampitt's precision throughout. John Hollander, in a similar review of Vicki Hearne's first book, *Nervous Horses*, emphasizes this young poet's remarkable combination of fresh *materia poetica* and profound philosophical insight.

The remainder of this book is devoted to the two leading Canadian women poets, Jay Macpherson and Margaret Atwood. Macpherson is described by the great critic Northrop Frye as an authentic mythological poet, very much in Blake's tradition. Margaret Atwood, in an overview of Macpherson's work, usefully compares her to Coleridge, another of this magnificent poet's authentic precursors. Atwood herself is studied by Judith McCombs in the final essay here and interestingly is compared to Coleridge the poet, also. Atwood, like so many of the women poets examined in this book, is a poet very much still in the process of development, and her imaginative vitality, like that of many of the others, makes certain a continued achievement in what has now become a distinguished tradition.

Introduction

A tradition of poets that includes Emily Dickinson, Marianne Moore, and Elizabeth Bishop has a palpable distinction, but it may be too soon to speak or write of a canon of "American Women Poets." The sixteen American and two Canadian poets studied in this volume are not chosen arbitrarily, yet considerations of the book's length as well as of the poets' canonical probability have entered into my selection. I regret the omission of Léonie Adams, Muriel Rukeyser, Sandra McPherson, Grace Schulman, Josephine Miles, Maxine Kumin, Mona Van Duyn, and several others, while various critics and readers might have included Amy Lowell, Sara Teasdale, Elinor Wylie, Edna St. Vincent Millay, and a large group of our contemporaries. But the eighteen poets studied here do seem a central grouping, and the canonical process is always an ongoing one anyway. Future editions of this book may be relied upon to correct emphases and clarify choices.

Two distinguished critics of literature by women, Sandra M. Gilbert and Susan Gubar, have taught us to speak of "the tradition in English," yet with characteristic fairness they quote the great poet Elizabeth Bishop's denial of such a tradition:

> Undoubtedly gender does play an important part in the making of any art, but art is art and to separate writings, paintings, musical compositions, etc., into two sexes is to emphasize values in them that are *not* art.

Bishop, a subtle intellect, makes clear that gender is a source of *values* in the genesis of art, but asserts that such values are not in themselves aesthetic. Though my inclination is to agree with her, I am wary of arguing against the tendency of origins to turn into ends or aims in the genealogy of imagination. Since I myself am frequently misunderstood on this point by feminist critics (though never, I am happy to say, by Gilbert and Gubar) I have a certain desire to illuminate the matter. Most Western poetry has been what Gertrude Stein called "patriarchal poetry," and most Western criticism necessarily has been patriarchal also. If Dr. Samuel Johnson, William Hazlitt, Ralph Waldo Emerson, and Dr. Sigmund Freud are to be considered patriarchal, then I as their ephebe presumably must be patriarchal also. So be it. But such a coloring or troping of critical stance is descriptive rather than prescriptive. Most strong Western poets, for whatever reasons, have been male: Homer and the Yahwist presumably, and certainly Virgil, Lucretius, Horace, on through Dante, Petrarch, and Chaucer to Shakespeare, Spenser, Milton, Pope, Wordsworth, Goethe, Shelley, Leopardi, Hugo, Whitman, Baudelaire, Browning, Yeats, Rilke, Stevens, and so many more. To this day, the only woman poet in English of that stature is Dickinson. Not every poet studied in this book seems to me of proven achievement; I have grave reservations about Plath and one or two others. Moore and Bishop, while hardly comparable to Dickinson, seem to me beyond dispute, and so do Jay Macpherson, May Swenson, and Vicki Hearne, but there are problematic aspects to many of the others.

However, there are values also, in nearly all the others, that seem to me rather different from the qualities of their strongest male contemporaries, and some of those differences do ensue from a vision, an experiential and rhetorical stance, that has its origin in sexual difference. To locate the differences in stance seems to me the admirable enterprise of the best feminist literary criticism. That polemic and ideology should be so overt in much feminist literary criticism is understandable, and unfortunately aesthetic considerations sometimes are submerged in political and programmatic designs, but nothing is got for nothing, and I foresee that the emphases of feminist criticism will be modified by the success of that criticism. Though I will attempt to isolate differences in vision from male precursors in the three poets I will discuss in this introduction, I am aware that I am a patriarchal critic, and I will not attempt to mask my own sense of the dilemmas confronted by women poets and poetry in what follows.

II

It is appropriate that the first considerable American poet should have been a woman, Anne Bradstreet, who addressed her own book with a charming sense of the difference involved in being a woman poet:

> If for thy father asked, say thou hadst none;
> And for thy mother, she alas is poor,
> Which caused her thus to send thee out of door.

A comparison of Bradstreet with Quarles, her indubitable if unexciting precursor, would reveal his greater skill at craft and her far more interesting poetic and human personality. Whether one wishes to believe, with the feminist critic Wendy Martin, that Bradstreet's poetry constitutes a mode of "subversive piety" may depend upon the ideological perspective of the individual reader. But she certainly had more wit, vitality, and humanity, in herself and in her poems, than Quarles possessed.

No American poet, except Walt Whitman, to this day is Emily Dickinson's peer, so that in moving from Bradstreet to Dickinson we enter upon the mystery of what will always remain, beyond all ironies, the American Sublime. Attempts to find women precursors for Dickinson are not likely ever to prove persuasive. Her agon, immense and capable, is with Emerson and with the High Romantic poets, and ultimately with the Bible itself. To undertake such a struggle is beyond the capacity of any American poet except for Dickinson and Whitman, even of Wallace Stevens. Whitman's subtle inventiveness, his uncanny mastery of figuration and nuances of diction, above all his astonishing powers of regenerating multiple selves out of his own abyss of being, more than compensate for his relative lack of cognitive strength. Dickinson is cognitively so endowed, and so original, that her only peers among poets writing in English might be Shakespeare, Milton, and Blake. Like them, she reconceptualizes very nearly every idea she considers, and more in the overt mode of Milton and of Blake than in Shakespeare's extraordinary and deftly misleading manner. Like Milton and the High Romantics, she excels at the difficult art of making herself prior to what genetically precedes her. Consider the remarkable poem 290:

> Of Bronze—and Blaze—
> The North—Tonight—
> So adequate—it forms—
> So preconcerted with itself—
> So distant—to alarms—
> An Unconcern so sovereign
> To Universe, or me—
> Infects my simple spirit
> With Taints of Majesty—
> Till I take vaster attitudes—
> And strut upon my stem—
> Disdaining Men, and Oxygen,
> For Arrogance of them—
>
> My splendors, are Menagerie—
> But their Competeless Show
> Will entertain the Centuries
> When I, am long ago,
> An Island in dishonored Grass—
> Whom none but Beetles—know.

This overtly is "about" the northern lights, but actually is mediated by Emerson's essay, "The Poet" (1843):

> For it is not metres, but a metre-making argument, that makes a
> poem,—a thought so passionate and alive, that, like the spirit of a

plant or an animal, it has an architecture of its own, and adorns nature with a new thing. The thought and the form are equal in order of time, but in the order of genesis the thought is prior to the form. The poet has a new thought: he has a whole new experience to unfold; he will tell us how it was with him, and all men will be the richer in his fortune. For, the experience of each new age requires a new confession, and the world seems always waiting for its poet. I remember, when I was young, how much I was moved one morning by tidings that genius had appeared in a youth who sat near me at table. He had left his work, and gone rambling none knew whither, and had written hundreds of lines, but could not tell whether that which was in him was therein told: he could tell nothing but that all was changed,—man, beast, heaven, earth, and sea. How gladly we listened! how credulous! Society seemed to be compromised. We sat in the aurora of a sunrise which was to put out all the stars. Boston seemed to be at twice the distance it had the night before, or was much farther than that. Rome, —what was Rome? Plutarch and Shakespeare were in the yellow leaf, and Homer no more should be heard of. It is much to know that poetry has been written this very day, under this very roof, by your side. What! that wonderful spirit has not expired! these stony moments are still sparkling and animated! I had fancied that the oracles were all silent, and nature had spent her fires, and behold! all night, from every pore, these fine auroras have been streaming.

Emerson is frolicking here, and yet his thought is so passionate and alive, his meter-making argument so compelling, that his little fable of the youth has its darker side also. The image of the aurora begins here as dawn, indeed an apocalyptic sunrise that might dim all the stars for good, but by a marvelous crossing is transformed into the aurora borealis proper, streaming from every pore of the night. The northern lights therefore represent, for Emerson, a reversal of belatedness into earliness, executed here with superb irony, since the belatedness belongs to Shakespeare and Homer, and the earliness to "a youth who sat near me at table."

Dickinson, frequently deft at taking hints from Emerson and then swerving away from them (in a process ably studied by Joanne Feit Diehl), seems to have taken the hint with more than usual dialectical agility in "Of Bronze—and Blaze—." I no longer agree with Charles R. Anderson's strong commentary upon this poem, which interprets its teaching as being that "the mortal poet corrupts his true nature if he attempts to be divine" and that "the poet must remain earth-bound." That tends to negate Dickinson's subtler ironies, which dominate the poem. The North, meaning the night sky and the auroras streaming through it, is *so* adequate as to overwhelm what might seem adequate desire to Dickinson, and infects her "simple spirit" with sublime longings. Her own bronze and blaze becomes the rhetorical stance of her poetry, which rises to the heights ("vaster attitudes") in order to manifest a sovereign unconcern all her own. Certainly the crucial irony is in "And strut upon my stem," which is a negative or downward metamorphosis, but only of the natural woman, as it were, and not of the poet. To say that her Splendors are Menagerie is indeed to admit that she is a performer, but the ancient Pindaric assertion of canonical renown and poetic survival follows with enormous authority. To be a "Competeless Show," able to entertain the centuries, indeed is to be preconcerted with oneself, to be distant to alarms, even to the prophecy of one's organic fate.

Why do we apprehend, beyond error, that "Of Bronze—and Blaze" was written by a woman? In a way more singular and persuasive than any other woman poet has managed (at least since Sappho), Dickinson in scores of her strongest poems compels us to confront the part that gender plays in her poetic identity:

> The Tint I cannot take—is best—
> The Color too remote
> That I could show it in Bazaar—
> A Guinea at a sight—
>
> The fine—impalpable Array—
> That swaggers on the eye
> Like Cleopatra's Company—
> Repeated—in the sky—
>
> The Moments of Dominion
> That happen on the Soul
> And leave it with a Discontent
> Too exquisite—to tell—
>
> The eager look—on Landscapes—
> As if they just repressed
> Some Secret—that was pushing
> Like Chariots—in the Vest—
>
> The Pleading of the Summer—
> That other Prank—of Snow—
> That Cushions Mystery with Tulle,
> For fear the Squirrels—know.
>
> Their Graspless manners—mock us—
> Until the Cheated Eye
> Shuts arrogantly—in the Grave—
> Another way—to see—

"Of Bronze—and Blaze" does not quite name the auroras, which is a typical procedure for Dickinson. "The Tint I cannot take—is best" goes further and avoids naming anything. American male theorists and poets from Emerson and Whitman through Stevens and W. C. Williams are programmatic in urging an unnaming upon us, and Stevens in particular achieves some of his greatest effects in that mode:

> This is nothing until in a single man contained,
> Nothing until this named thing nameless is
> And is destroyed. He opens the door of his house
>
> On flames. The scholar of one candle sees
> An Arctic effulgence flaring on the frame
> Of everything he is. And he feels afraid.

This is the crisis of "The Auroras of Autumn," where "this named thing" is the aurora borealis, which flames forth to frighten the poet or scholar of one candle and so undoes his attempt to enact the program of unnaming. But Dickinson, shrewdly exploiting her identity as woman poet, chooses another way to see, a way that unnames without defiance or struggle. The best tint is what she cannot take, too remote for showing, impalpable, too exquisite to tell, secret, graspless. Such a tint seems unavailable to the eye of the male poet, even to a Keats or a Shelley, even to Wordsworth's extraordinary mediation between the visual and the visionary. No woman poet since Dickinson has had the power to teach us so urgently and intuitively that women need not see as men see, need not will as men will, need not appropriate for themselves as men perhaps need to do. Freud, when he sadly admitted that women were a mystery, echoed the bafflement of Milton, and might have been echoing Blake. Only three men who wrote in English—Chaucer, Shakespeare, Samuel Richardson—seem able to convey the sense of a difference between women and men in a way comparable to the greatest women writers in the language, Jane Austen, George Eliot, Dickinson. If Austen is comparable to Chaucer as a craftsman in irony and George Eliot comparable to Richardson as a moral psychologist of the Protestant temperament, then Dickinson is quite comparable to some of the subtlest aspects of Shakespearean representation. Without Shakespeare, our sense of reality would be much diminished. Without Dickinson, our sense of reality might not be diminished, but we would know far less than we do about the sufferings and the satisfactions of a really isolated consciousness at its highest powers, particularly if it were the consciousness of a woman.

III

Dickinson sets a standard that no twentieth-century American poet, man or woman, not even Stevens or Frost or Hart Crane, can endure as measurement. Her influence upon our century's women poets is profound and more than a little dangerous. Rather than trace it from poet to poet, I want to observe it at play in the most powerful of Dickinson's descendants, Elizabeth Bishop, who engagingly employed Dickinson as a countervailing force and presence against Wallace Stevens, a more immediate influence upon Bishop's work. There are many instances of this beautiful interplay in Bishop, but perhaps the most remarkable is in the final verse paragraph of her magnificent and very American shore-ode, "The End of March":

> On the way back our faces froze on the other side.
> The sun came out for just a minute.
> For just a minute, set in their bezels of sand,
> the drab, damp, scattered stones
> were multi-colored,
> and all those high enough threw out long shadows,
> individual shadows, then pulled them in again.
> They could have been teasing the lion sun,
> except that now he was behind them
> —a sun who'd walked the beach the last low tide,
> making those big, majestic paw-prints,
> who perhaps had batted a kite out of the sky to play with.

The lion sun is Stevens's, and in some sense represents Stevens here, while the long shadows are Dickinson's, and represent her teasing and gentling effect upon the Stevensian trope of the lion. Bishop intends us to remember Dickinson's lyric 764:

> Presentiment—is that long Shadow—on the Lawn—
> Indicative that Suns go down—
>
> The Notice to the startled Grass
> That Darkness—is about to pass—

We are to remember also several Stevensian intertwinings of sun, lion, and male poet or Stevens, and perhaps these in particular among them, though there are others:

> It is
> For that the poet is always in the sun,
>
> Patches the moon together in his room,
> To his Virgilian cadences, up down,
> Up down.
>
> > The lion sleeps in the sun.
> > Its nose is on its paws.
> > It can kill a man.
>
> In the metaphysical streets of the physical town
> We remember the lion of Juda and we save
> The phrase . . . Say of each lion of the spirit
>
> It is a cat of a sleek transparency
> That shines with a nocturnal shine alone.
> The great cat must stand potent in the sun.

The second of these passages is from a poem candidly entitled "Poetry is a Destructive Force." Perhaps it is and must be, to and by men; I do not know. Dickinson valued the presentiment of mortality over even the lion sun of male poetic tradition. Bishop's high, momentarily multicolored stones throw out Dickinsonian long shadows of presentiment that are also the individual shadows of female poetic temperaments, say of Dickinson and Marianne Moore and of Bishop herself. Indeed they could have been teasing the lion sun, Stevens, that great cat standing always potent in the light of imagination, not the mere sun of common day. Except that Bishop, nearly as subtle as Dickinson, gently intimates that even so great a male precursor has at last been evaded, if not overcome: "except that now he was behind them." In a loving trope of closure, Bishop reminds us that, in how they play, all men are different from women:

> —a sun who'd walked the beach the last low tide,
> making those big, majestic paw-prints,
> who perhaps had batted a kite out of the sky to play with.

Even great poets, when they are men, play as if they were children again. In the teasing shadows of presentiment, Bishop gives us a mode of play that belongs to women poets, a mode that is neither childish nor childlike. Like Dickinson, Bishop teaches us that the strongest women poets can possess: "Another way—to see."

"No rhet'ric we expect": Argumentation in Bradstreet's "The Prologue"

Jane Donahue Eberwein

For an acknowledgment of a poet's simple capacities and modest literary goals, Anne Bradstreet's "The Prologue" elicits strangely varied responses—especially in regard to voice and tone. Is the poet humbly submissive or bitterly angry? Is she self-deprecating and self-denigrating, as some readers find, or a prefeminist champion of her sex? Both extremes find textual justification, depending on the weight one accords her admittedly blemished muse or her anticipated parsley wreath. Perhaps, as Elizabeth Wade White and Robert Arner have suggested, the poem divides structurally and tonally at stanza five, with the first half lamenting the poet's inferiority to male writers and the second half asserting, nonetheless, her right as a woman to express herself in verse. The tension between Bradstreet's modest disclaimers and her spirited self-defense runs through the poem, however; it may be found implicitly in the first stanza and explicitly in the last, and it permeates the language and logic of all "The Prologue." Only by reading the poem as consistently ironic can we hope to appreciate Bradstreet's conscious artfulness in deploying both sides of the argument: inviting both male and female champions (and the vast majority of more tolerant readers) to approach her writing with respect.

As the name indicates, this is a prologue designed to introduce the author to her readers while whetting their interest in the more substantive poems to follow. She proceeds by negation, telling what she cannot hope to do:

> To sing of wars, of captains, and of kings,
> Of cities founded, commonwealths begun,
> For my mean pen are too superior things.

From *Early American Literature* 16, no. 1 (Spring 1981). © 1981 by University of Massachusetts.

But, if we expect her to anticipate Barlow in turning from lofty historical themes to choose "a virgin theme, unconscious of the Muse," we will be unprepared for the succeeding poems. "The Prologue" was never meant to introduce Bradstreet's love poems or meditations; it was written directly for "The Four Monarchies" and was then prefixed to the four quaternions as well as the historical surveys in the opening section of *The Tenth Muse*. Despite her disclaimer, then, Bradstreet proceeded directly to write on the subjects she so pointedly reserved for poets and historians. The opening lines introduce an ironic counterpointing of claimed incapacity and demonstrated command which would enliven the whole poem.

The key to Bradstreet's strategy in preceding her lengthy, laborious, learned scholarly poems with this engaging prologue comes in the opening of stanza three: "From schoolboy's tongue no rhet'ric we expect." Like so many parts of the poem, this line has dual implications. We do not, in fact, count on hearing eloquent orations from schoolchildren, but we must recall that Bradstreet's contemporaries expected, in the sense of looked forward to, such skill as a probable outcome of the boy's education. From grammar, the student would proceed in course through the rest of the trivium: logic and rhetoric. In likening herself to the schoolboy, the poet suggests her own capacity to advance in the verbal arts—especially the art of persuasion. When we do not expect rhetoric, we may not even notice it; but we can be influenced by it, despite ourselves. As Henry Peacham wrote in the 1593 *Garden of Eloquence*, "By the benefit of this excellent gift, (I meane of apt speech given by nature, and guided by Art) wisedome appeareth in her beautie, sheweth her maiestie, and exerciseth her power, working in the minde of the hearer, partly by a pleasant proportion . . . and partly by the secret and mightie power of perswasion after a most wonderfull manner." Bradstreet praised apt speech given by nature and guided by Art in "The Prologue" and demonstrated it as well, keeping a pleasant proportion between instruction and delight to achieve a secret but significant power of persuasion. By recognizing her dexterity in manipulating logic and rhetoric, by remembering Rosamund Rosenmeier's caution that we must read Bradstreet as "someone accustomed to thinking figurally," and by responding to her varied cultural allusions, we can appreciate the complexity and sophistication of her apparently simple argument.

Like most of Bradstreet's successful poems, "The Prologue" is an argument: an attempt to articulate and reconcile opposition by emphasizing discrepancies while hinting at unity. As Ann Stanford has noted, the histories which "The Prologue" introduces fail as literature partly because they lack the tension the poet knew how to achieve when she engaged an I-narrator in vigorous argumentation. Unlike the quaternions, in each of which the four speakers demonstrate a different argumentative method, "The Four Monarchies" proceeds by discursive, impersonal narration. Bradstreet may have needed the chance to spar off against assumed sexist opponents in order to release the energy and excitement her familiar readers would anticipate in a new grouping of her poems.

With whom is Bradstreet actually arguing here? Certainly not with Thomas Dudley and the circle of admiring friends among whom she circulated her manuscripts. Textual analysis shows no direct personal address until stanza seven, when she says, "Preeminence in all and each is yours" to an inclusive audience of the whole male sex; but the apostrophe in stanza eight addresses a different you, limited to the great poets: "ye high flown quills that soar the skies." Her debate, however, seems to be with other antagonists—each "carping tongue" who belittles "female wits." Who those carping tongues might be remains a question. Although Jeannine Hensley, Elizabeth Wade White, and Ann Stanford all assume the reality of such criticism, they offer no specific examples. Those who sympathize with the poet's presumed cultural isolation as a frontier woman artist speak of the pain she "must have" felt and the insults she "must have" endured—linking her with Anne Hutchinson and Anne Hopkins, two well-documented examples of Puritan women who suffered for their intellectual aspirations. Yet Hensley admits that "we have no contemporary reference to her or her poetry which is not somewhere between admiration and adulation." There is simply no evidence of the attacks to which she retorts in "The Prologue."

The carping tongues, probably imagined, offered a useful opportunity for forceful, witty expression in this ironic battle of the sexes. Straw men, they were set up only to be knocked down. None of the deference Bradstreet shows in passages of the poem was meant for them. Her expressions of humility, presumably sincere acknowledgments of inferiority, were directed to recognized literary greats: Du Bartas, her poetic model; Demosthenes; perhaps Virgil; and all "ye high flown quills that soar the skies, / And ever with your prey still catch your praise." Long before Franklin, Bradstreet discovered that one could achieve the appearance of humility (and its rhetorical effect in placating a suspicious audience) by emulating the loftiest models and confessing failure.

Unlike Bradstreet's formal debate poems in which the contenders successively advance their individual cases, "The Prologue" maintains argumentative tension by its deft ordering of assertions and its ambiguous juxtapositions of ideas. Bradstreet develops both cases together, often seeming to capitulate to her opposition. But any male supremacist who read happily along, imagining no threat to his smugness, would eventually find his case pressed to the point of absurdity, while a more alert or ironic reader would be delighted throughout by the poet's cleverness in charming while outwitting her antagonist. If "The Prologue" was intended to win readers for the histories while building affection and respect for the poet, it served its purpose.

Beginning boldly with her echo of Virgil, Bradstreet immediately disclaims her obvious purpose. She had, indeed, written of wars, captains, kings, cities, and commonwealths, though not in the epic strains a reader might expect from one who thought of poesy as "Calliope's own child." Reference to her "obscure lines" could hardly disguise her purpose, at least for any reader with enough foresight to glance ahead into the book. Like

Chaucer's "I can namore," this statement deflects attention only slightly from the author's plan to develop the supposedly forsaken topic at great length.

Further developing the sense of authorial humility, Bradstreet moved into a sincere tribute to Du Bartas, still her poetic master. The admiration, however, was that which an aspiring writer of either sex might feel for an established poet. Such expressions of poetic inadequacy to a great theme and inferiority to a major writer were common among authors known to Bradstreet, and there is no reason to interpret her praise as specifically female submissiveness. In his dedicatory verse to *The Tenth Muse*, we should recall, John Woodbridge indited a parallel passage to acknowledge his inability to emulate Bradstreet herself.

> What I (poor silly I) prefix therefore,
> Can but do this, make yours admired the more;
> And if but only this I do attain,
> Content, that my disgrace may be your gain.

Praising Du Bartas's choice of subject matter, his "sugared lines," and even his "overfluent store" of verse, Bradstreet—"simple I"—called attention to qualities which she could reasonably hope to imitate according to her skill. And skill is a revealing word, placing emphasis on craftsmanship, which could be developed, rather than natural gifts, which might have been denied. "The Prologue" is itself a display of poetic skill, technically more artful than the histories or quaternions with their monotonous couplets. The stanzaic pattern, the sound effects, and the rhetorical devices of "The Prologue" consistently qualify its author's pretensions to simplicity.

The next stanza sounds more sincerely self-deprecating with its imagery of "broken strings" in a musical instrument and "a main defect" in an aesthetic structure. Bradstreet speaks of her "foolish, broken, blemished Muse" and acknowledges irreparable limitations. People have no right to expect music, she asserts, in cases where nature has denied some essential power.

Yet her next example, Demosthenes, reverses the conclusion drawn in stanza three. Surely a congenital speech impediment seems a natural defect precluding oratorical success. But art, in this case purposeful, concentrated, sustained self-discipline, led first to clarity and then to fluency and sweetness. With any natural endowment at all, then, Bradstreet shows that an ambitious artist can achieve excellence. Art corrects nature, except for the "weak or wounded brain" which "admits no cure." Readers who divide the poem structurally at this halfway point see the first four stanzas as submissive and self-abasing—especially the final line. Perhaps the statements are self-critical but only in the sense that she submits to the artistic claims of recognized literary masters and recognizes faults in herself which can be corrected through the stylistic apprenticeship on which she has already embarked, as anyone could discover by reading the poems introduced by "The Prologue." Only if she claims the weak and wounded brain as self-description need we interpret this part of the poem as an expression of defeat.

Note, however, that mention of weak and wounded brains leads Bradstreet directly to reflection on carping tongues, which may well articulate idiocy. At this point, she joins battle with her supposed critics and stops comparing herself with writers who deserve her respect. These scolds who would restrict a woman to domestic activities turn out to be contemptuous of thought and imagination in any form—not just when offered by a female wit. They refuse to look at evidence ("If what I do prove well . . ."), and they mistake skill for chance. Confronted with the analogy the Greeks drew between femininity and artistic inspiration as embodied in the Muses, they cut a Gordian knot with their brute disregard for cultural intricacies. Those who say that "The Greeks did nought, but play the fools and lie" demonstrate contempt for fiction and deadness to poetry. They can hardly be the readers she hoped to draw further into her manuscript, but in travestying their claims she might hope to entertain or even impress her proper audience.

In stanza seven Bradstreet spins out the clumsy assertions of her fancied enemies to the extreme limits of logical fallacy. "Let Greeks be Greeks, and women what they are," she begins as if to capitulate gracefully. But Greeks and women need not be regarded as mutually exclusive categories. Attentive readers, like John Woodbridge, could think of Sappho. The carpers, of course, could drift rapidly along, caught in a tidal wave of ironic concessions. Although it would be "but vain" for women "unjustly to wage war," it might at times be appropriate to rally female energies in justified aggression. The poet who seems to be calming tensions here and promising peace is the same author who later in *The Tenth Muse* let gracious young New England challenge her despondent mother with a decidedly militant call to arms:

> These are the days the Church's foes to crush,
> To root out Popelings head, tail, branch, and rush;
> Let's bring Baal's vestments forth to make a fire,
> Their miters, surplices, and all their tire,
> Copes, rochets, crosiers, and such empty trash,
> And let their names consume, but let the flash
> Light Christendom, and all the world to see
> We hate Rome's whore with all her trumpery.

Bradstreet completes the logical undoing of her opponents by wheeling in a veritable Trojan Horse to confirm the tentative peace. "Men can do best, and women know it well," she proclaims—right in the prologue to a series of history poems which will parade before her readers an astounding chronicle of disasters, defeats, and depravities involving both men and women rulers but featuring the generally more powerful males. Although Bradstreet gave greater attention to women rulers in her poems than she found in Raleigh's history, she never attempted to show one sex as morally or even politically superior in the use of power; certainly "The Four Monarchies" rebuts her generalization in "The Prologue," however, and indicates its irony. The crowning joke comes next, when she admits "Preeminence in all and each is yours." By extending claims of male supremacy to all areas of human experience, she seems to dismiss hopes for female excellence in government, oratory, and poetry while acknowledging male dominion in everything; presumably even needlework and childbearing.

This apparent capitulation to the irrational claims of her imagined critics violates common sense, of course, and conflicts as well with the argumentative pattern of the quaternions in which each element, humor, age, and season admits weaknesses as well as strengths. The resolution of these conflicts comes from a recognition of complementary functions, from awareness of multiple contributions to a final desired unity. The same reasoning characterizes Bradstreet's marriage poems, where husband and wife appear as mutually dependent and supportive partners. To restrict women from literature, then, or even from historical narration would be folly. The battle of the sexes, like the debates of the elements and humors, should never be won.

After this deft lobotomy of weak or wounded brains, Bradstreet concludes "The Prologue" with a modest but confident declaration of her literary hopes. In the final stanza she invokes the world's great writers in lines which themselves fly and flash with the eloquence of her praise. The masters soaring in the heavens may see her lines as "lowly," but she gives no indication that earthbound readers need concur. In comparison to a poet like Du Bartas or a rhetorician like Demosthenes, she is limited but hardly worthless. Her "mean and unrefined ore" highlights their "glist'ring gold" and may, with time, be enhanced by careful polishing.

The most striking image in this paean, however, is surely that of the "thyme or parsley wreath" Bradstreet requests in recognition of her poetry, discounting the traditional bay laurel. It seems a humble request: substitution of a kitchen herb for richer foliage. Bay leaves are also herbs, however, and there are cooks who plunge all three in the same aromatic pot. As far as honor goes, there may be less distinction here than the phrasing suggests. Elizabeth Wade White points out that thyme symbolized vitality and courage for the Greeks and that they sometimes honored athletes or dead heroes with the "fadeless foliage" of parsley wreaths. Even more familiar was the mythical background of the laurel as a symbol of poetry. In his verses "Upon Mrs. Anne Bradstreet Her Poems, Etc." prefaced to *The Tenth Muse*, John Rogers commended the Puritan poet for her avoidance of the wantonly lascivious topics provided by classical literature, specifically mentioning "How sage Apollo, Daphne hot pursues." C.B., in his introductory quatrain, wrote: "I cannot wonder at Apollo now, / That he with female laurel crowned his brow." The laurel crown commemorated Daphne, who was protectively transformed in her flight from lusty Apollo; so the bay leaves provided a female crown for male poets. The modesty that kept Anne Bradstreet from claiming such an honor, then, may have been more nearly allied to chastity than to humility. She may have felt sensitive to the mythic presentation of woman as simultaneously the object and victim of the god of poetry and the sign of glory for his disciples. It is clear, at any rate, that the concluding stanza expresses personal self-assurance as a poet, and the reader who has followed the stylistic, rhetorical, and logical devices by which she guides "The Prologue" from acknowledgment of her defects to assertion of her triumph is likely to accept the claim. Like Emily Dickinson, who contrasted "Carbon in the Coal" with "Carbon in the Gem" as queenly ornaments, Anne Bradstreet contrived to sound meek and vulnerable, even in the act of choosing among crowns.

Emily Dickinson: A Voice of War

Shira Wolosky

Emily Dickinson's poetry has rarely been approached in terms other than the private and personal. Even when wider contexts to her work have been admitted, they continue to be defined by her presumably self-enclosed and eccentric sensibility. That sensibility is further portrayed—by biographers, critics, and anthologists—as one of shy, frail timidity. Frightened by the world and disappointed in her hopes, Dickinson, it is said, retreated into a privacy that shielded her from exterior involvement. There, in accordance with the particular interpretation adopted, she is established as a martyr: to a lost love, to a neurotic state, to a religious ideal, or to her own literary pursuits. But Dickinson's verse, contrary to traditional conceptions of it, registers issues and events outside of her private sphere. Her poetry, when approached without the assumption of her complete isolation, can be seen as profoundly engaged in problems of the external world and aggressively so. It presents a point of intersection of literary, cultural, and metaphysical concerns, an arena in which conceptual structures and historical pressures implicate and generate linguistic configuration.

Privacy and fear are certainly present in Dickinson's work, as are anguish and morbid sensitivity. But their quality is different from that generally presumed. The overwhelming effect of Dickinson's verse is not delicacy. It is ferocity. Dickinson is an assertive and determined poet, as much fury as maiden, whose retirement is a stance of attack, whose timidity is aggressive. Her poetry leaves an impression of defiance rather than detachment, and her poetic is neither helpless nor quaking. It is, rather, one of ironic twists, sudden stabs, and poison:

> Go slow, my soul, to feed thyself
> Upon his rare approach—

> Go rapid, lest Competing Death
> Prevail upon the Coach—
> Go timid, should his final eye
> Determine thee amiss—
> Go boldly—for thou paid'st his price
> Redemption—for a Kiss-

This poem, never anthologized, is characteristic. In it, Dickinson presents her patience and timidity—and unmasks them. In appearance a litany of instruction to her modest soul, the poem ends as an attack upon her subject. The final stroke denounces God as a traitor who demands a Judas kiss for his mercy. In light of this end, the poet's fear of judgment is revealed as a false deference before one unworthy to judge. Her consciousness that "Competing Death" may prevail spurs her, but not to penitence. Instead, she is inspired with a sense of injustice that her time is so limited. And the initial hope of Christ's appearance becomes by the end an accusation that the divine approach is far too rare. This is God the betrayer; but it is finally the poet who betrays him, who exposes his nature as unjustly hidden, prevailing upon man with unjust weapons and reigning as an unjust judge. But the poet, too, has weapons and judgments, and in this poem, it is she who prevails.

Dickinson's slow timidity, then, is present here. But it is present in all its strenuous power. She shows herself rapid and bold even in her shyness. What the poem suggests is that Dickinson, while she may be agonized, is, even more, agonistic. She actively wrestles with the problems her poetry addresses and accuses the universe of evils and contradictions she finds all too real. It further suggests her characteristic religious stance. This is one of struggle against God, whom she defies, but also toward him and with herself. For although she writes to denounce him, she invokes liturgical modes in order to do so. And God remains her subject. God is not dismissed. He continues to stand in relation to the poet's soul in contradictory assertion.

Dickinson's religious position remains an embattled one. But its importance to her work extends beyond overtly religious concerns into the fundamental technical and conceptual aspects of her poetic. Dickinson's verse forms have long attracted attention for their technical irregularities and suggest a distinct self-consciousness regarding language as a medium. Her poems typically present temporal and causal discontinuities, ateleological organizations, and irregular prosody. Examination of these formal characteristics suggests that departures from linguistic convention are a function of a growing doubt concerning traditional metaphysical sanctions for causality, teleology, and axiology. Such categories are implicit in conventional structures of articulation, as Nietzsche, for instance, points out. The possible collapse of such categories is a theme in many Dickinson poems, which present the world as it would appear without them. And it is a force governing the language of her poems, which works against sequence in time and space, against harmonies between disparate entities, and against continuous logic and full designations.

The linguistic self-consciousness implicit in Dickinson's treatment of poetic forms thus emerges as an expression of her concern with the metaphysical assumptions that promised to govern her world, but that came to seem inadequate. Metaphysical structures had purported to define the direction, order, and goal of existence—categories that remained essential to Dickinson and in terms of which she persisted in conceiving her world. Her doubts regarding these structures finally raised the whole question of linguistic meaning and of meaning in general. Her language, which reflects dissatisfaction with metaphysical systems in its configuration, finally came to address those systems, to explore directly their suppositions—and in so doing, to reflect on itself. Consciousness of language as a medium becomes consciousness of language as such, representing an increased focus on the process of signification and its possible governing principles.

Such an interest in language is not accidental. In Dickinson's tradition, the principles governing meaning had been conceived as linguistic, in terms proposed by the Logos structure. In this structure, the Logos stands between the world of eternity and that of time. Truth is identified with the former and is only accessible to the latter through a Logos that remains most strongly identified with the eternal world. Meaning, and the possibility of discourse, must rely on a positive relation between the two realms, with the transcendent world as the source and locus of significance.

In Dickinson's work, however, the two realms come to conflict; and the sanctions and structures of linguistic signification threaten to collapse. Such collapse is never quite realized in Dickinson's work. But her confrontation with it profoundly informs her conceptions of language and her poetic expression—and not only hers. The mutual implication of metaphysics and language has a particular force and clarity in her poetry. In this she is singular, but not solitary. Melville's waved fists at an enigmatic Deity; Hawthorne's sense of a resistant and incremental evil far more certain than any possible grace; Whitman's assertion of the divine self; and Emerson's proscription that the poet take up the vestments fallen from the priesthood—all trace a growing instability in metaphysical structures once secure.

This instability becomes only more pronounced in later writers with linguistic consequences already suggested by Dickinson's verse. Literary movements such as symbolism, imagism, surrealism, dadaism, futurism, and concrete poetry render Dickinson's poetic less merely eccentric. What seemed personal symptom can instead be seen as symptomatic. And Dickinson's work particularly suggests such formal experiments to be a function of metaphysical crisis which is further expressed, both by her and by later poets, in meditations on language.

Recent criticism has come increasingly to consider this question of Dickinson in relation to other writers, both of her own and of subsequent periods. Her recognition by later poets, such as the American Imagistes, and the resemblance between her verse and verse written after her have begun to suggest affinities that qualify her hitherto unquestioned isolation. Thus Karl Keller, in *The Only Kangaroo among the Beauty*, examines Dickinson's work in the context of American traditions; David Porter, in *The Modern Idiom*, does so in the context of twentieth-century modernism. And feminist criticism particularly has progressed toward examining Dickinson in less constricting terms. Studies of the social realities of nineteenth-century America and of the actual pursuits of women within it, and the stratum of such concrete experience in Dickinson's poetry have broadened the perspectives of Dickinson criticism. Treatments of her as a woman writer have the added benefit of confronting her virginity and the sexuality of her poems as active powers within her identity and as more than signs of repression, aberration, and incompletion.

These studies, however, have continued to proceed, to a greater or lesser degree, from the premise of biographical reclusion. The contours of Dickinson's world are extended beyond her own psyche, but generally little further than her literary connections. Keller's book presents Dickinson exclusively in terms of American literary history, and Porter's, in terms of literary theory. Even the feminist approach in such a work as *The Madwoman in the Attic* tends to focus on Dickinson's literary affinities at the expense of any extraliterary contacts. But the context for Dickinson's work includes more than literary influences, just as it involves more than the sphere of her own home.

Because of her seclusion, it is assumed that whatever pain Dickinson felt, whatever questions disturbed her, must be defined by a privacy into which only literature could penetrate. The possibility that her uncertainties were not self-induced, and that her concerns were not entirely private, has never been explored. Yet poem after poem suggests that the self of the poet, however imperious, is not the sole boundary of her existence nor her sole concern:

> The Battle fought between the Soul
> And No Man—is the One
> Of all the Battles prevalent—
> By far the Greater One—
>
> No News of it is had abroad—
> Its Bodiless Campaign
> Establishes, and terminates—
> Invisible—Unknown—

(P 594)

Dickinson's inner world is the subject of this poem. Here she depicts her personal turmoil and even particularly insists on its private nature. The soul's inner strife remains unpublicized. Yet, she declares, it is the most terrible combat. Invisible and bodiless, it is still the most bloody.

In presenting this image of inner strife, however, Dickinson does so in terms provided by the world outside her. The poem was written in 1862: the very period when Antietam and Bull Run had begun to reveal fully the horrors of the Civil War. There are in Dickinson's opus many poems that register, directly or indirectly, the civil conflagration raging around her. The notion that Dickinson's morbid fear of death and preoccupation with suffering may not have been entirely the product of her own idiosyncratic and more or less pathological imagination has never been considered. But in this poem, although Dickinson centers attention on her private world, she does so in terms drawn from the public one. The initiative even seems to lie, startling as this may be, in the public realm. The invisible and unknown struggle within the self is given a form determined by visible and known violence. Her personal conflict takes on military proportions, and in this it reflects actual events in the world of history. That the personal is foremost does not obviate the fact that, in 1862, the bodiless campaign within the poet's soul had an objective counterpart in physical and palpable warfare.

In Dickinson's work, then, metaphysical conflict is accompanied by historical trauma, and the two spheres further conjoin in a poetic remarkable for disjunctions and discontinuities. Emily Dickinson was not a librarian, remaining indoors in order to sort her reading and sift her emotions into little packets reminiscent of a card catalog. Her language, instead, records the converging crises in metaphysics and culture that can be felt in the work of other American writers and that become a profound preoccupation in writers subsequent to her. Dickinson's work presents with striking force the metaphysical revisions that so characterize modernity, as this is implicated by cultural instability and as this implicates linguistic structures. For the critique of metaphysics announced by Nietzsche has broad implications for language, which itself has a primary function and importance in traditional systems. The Logos concept, in its Johannine formulation, presented the whole possibility of intercourse between transcendence and immanence in linguistic terms. The process of signification was defined as originating in the divine Logos, and through the incarnate Logos as the avenue of its truth, as finally emerging within the immanent world. Human language was meaningful and possible only as it participated, through the Logos, in the transcendent realm. But Dickinson's work testifies to an increasing hiatus between transcendence and immanence, Logos and language. Such hiatus precipitates a conflict between human language and the traditional sources of its significance, which has only increased in strength since the time of her writing and which challenges the once accepted patterns for interpreting reality and rendering it coherent.

In Dickinson, these issues ultimately conjoin in a confrontation between the language identified with an immutable world and the immanent words of human language. The characteristic result is, in Dickinson, blasphemy:

> Ended, ere it begun—
> The Title was scarcely told

> When the Preface perished from Consciousness
> The Story, unrevealed—
>
> Had it been mine, to print!
> Had it been yours, to read!
> That it was not Our privilege
> The interdict of God—
>
> (P 1088)

Dickinson's concern with language is evident in this poem. But the poem also places this concern in the metaphysical terms that consistently frame it for her. Here, a text has been interrupted. It is barely announced before its potential unfolding is engulfed: "Ended, ere it begun." Indeed, such interruption is the poem's first utterance, formally placing its own end before its beginning. The text's termination is so immediate as to seem to precede its commencement, in a profound temporal inversion.

This text takes place in the sphere of human language, which is itself identified as the poet's own world—for "Story" here figures not only as text but as universe and experience within it. This text-as-world could have been—and should have been—realized by the poet's human power, fulfilled within her human world. She would have it printed and read. But this has been willfully prevented by God's interdiction, which here has a particularly verbal resonance. God's decree forbids the completion of the human text. Divine language counters human language. What should support her utterance instead disrupts it. Nor does the poet gracefully bow to a higher, if mysterious, power. The poem is an assault. It does not declare the independence of immanent language from divine decree, but rather asserts divine decree only to attack, defame, and denounce it.

The poem thus stands poised between apostasy and affirmation—a poise that is, however, unstable and combative. There is no trace here of a timid Dickinson. The attack is frontal. And it is a linguistic attack, both as an assault through poetry and as a poem in which defiant human language strives against, but remains facing, the divine Word.

In this, Dickinson stands at the threshold of a modernity in which such struggle becomes typical. Later poets, however, could reach toward some resolution of the conflict between human and divine utterance by attempting either to reaffirm the traditional bond between them or to construct new frameworks based upon premises altogether different from the traditional ones. Dickinson, too, attempts such resolutions, but she does so without final success. She remains caught between the claims of each linguistic/metaphysical realm. The strife of this conflict, above all, informs her work. It does so not in a vacuum nor in a hermitage but in relation to the history that surrounds her. Nor does her strife render her helpless. She is furious with the God without whom she is unable to conceive her universe, but who, if responsible for a universe so incomprehensible, claims her enmity. Her poetry becomes the field of this combat with and against God. It registers, finally, the clash between his language and her own.

"Ransom in a Voice": Language as Defense in Dickinson's Poetry

Joanne Feit Diehl

I dwell in Possibility—
A fairer House than Prose—

"Let us sit at home with the cause," admonished Emerson in his seminal essay, "Self-Reliance." Of all the ambitious young Americans who took this essay to heart, none followed his advise so literally as Emily Dickinson or adhered to its demands more rigorously. She defined her version of the "cause" as a desire to reveal, through her poems, a responsive, wholly alive consciousness. No matter how frequently ignored or misunderstood, Dickinson continued speaking into the void. Whatever the particular origins of her sense of estrangement (and we need not look far to discover its most overt forms: absence from the ongoing cultural life of Boston and Concord, spiritual exclusion from the orthodoxy sweeping mid-century Amherst, misundertanding by those she hoped would recognize and nurture her genius), the austere originality of Dickinson's poetry develops from the tenor of her reaction to such exclusions, from her conversion of a potentially crippling alienation into a conception of language that serves as a defense against what she perceived not simply as an antipathetic society, but also as an adversarial nature and an inscrutable, if not fundamentally hostile, deity. From this estrangement, Dickinson develops a deeply skeptical, indeed, an antithetical approach toward the world beyond the self. Her pervasive skepticism toward both the world and language, moreover, foreshadows a distinctly modernist alienation. Although the reasons for Dickinson's and other nineteenth-century women poets' sense of exclusion from both nature and culture necessarily differ from the origins of rejection that fuel the modernist writers of our century, the character of their poetic responses presents a strong, albeit surprising resemblance. How Dickinson converts her estrangement into verbal power, just how her sense of alienation informs her vision of a defensive language that pushes the word ever closer to

From *Feminist Critics Read Emily Dickinson.* © 1983 by Indiana University Press.

indecipherability, are questions that lead back into her work and forward to a consideration of the possible ties between a feminist poetics and modernism.

The greatest danger facing a poet is, of course, the danger of silence. That Dickinson resists this temptation is proof of her energies; that she makes her alienation the subject of many of her most brilliant poems, thus transforming estrangement into a source of power, testifies to the strength of her imagination. No poet can accomplish this transformation in a single gesture, nor is the transformation of estrangement into power, once accomplished, permanently assured. Thus, Dickinson's poems, not unexpectedly, document a cyclical process in which the "I" initially experiences a rejection that provokes rage followed by resentment. This anger on the poet's part climaxes in the poems' assertion of a fiercely won independence from the very force or substance that she had originally been denied. Despite her disavowal of such appetite, "Art thou the thing I wanted? / Begone—my Tooth has grown—" (1282), no final resolution or poetic satiety can be achieved because of the very nature of the conflicts generated by repeated banishment and denial. In her attempts to marshal internal power against such continued threats to her autonomy, Dickinson makes language her strongest weapon. The Word becomes her defense as she assigns it sufficient force to devastate her adversaries and exercise her will even against Divine power. In response to the exclusionary silence of a hostile, or at best, incomprehensible world and a threatening poetic adversary, Dickinson invokes the powers of language, asserting that her word may vie with the Divine for authority over herself and her experience. If the word becomes a weapon, it also possesses, as Dickinson is well aware, the capacity to find its victim within the self. To assert that what determines survival or destruction resides within the self is simultaneously to acknowledge internal authority while denigrating the threat of any and all external forces.

Dickinson appropriates power for her own linguistic purposes by, among other ways, drawing upon the authority orthodox Christianity ascribes to Christ. Adopting qualities associated with the Christian deity, and transforming these into a linguistic process that she describes as both more humane and equable than the Christian, Dickinson creates an alternative power potentially subversive of any external authority based upon the sovereignty of a male-identified divinity or predicated upon the supremacy of those within the religious fold. In her boldest poetic statement of these alternative powers—the choosing of her words over against the force of God—Dickinson explores the possibilities for a poetics that yields nothing to forces beyond the self.

> A Word made Flesh is seldom
> And tremblingly partook
> Nor then perhaps reported
> But have I not mistook
> Each one of us has tasted
> With ecstasies of stealth

> The very food debated
> To our specific strength—
>
> A Word that breathes distinctly
> Has not the power to die
> Cohesive as the Spirit
> It may expire if He—
> "Made Flesh and dwelt among us
> Could condescension be
> Like this consent of Language
> This loved Philology.
>
> (1651)

One experiences a power commensurate with the Divine depending upon one's own capacity: the Word lives, the human word, as the Spirit. That Dickinson here chooses the power of the human word over the power of the Divine becomes apparent in the closing lines. The "condescension" of Christ, with that word's concealed arrogance of *descent* does not approach the mutuality of relationships expressed by "consent," the power of a human word to meet the reader on equal terms. As I have argued elsewhere, this poem can be viewed as Dickinson's central statement about language, her role as poet, and her relationship to the Divine. The process of transubstantiation here serves as a trope investing the poet's word with godlike authority. In a stunning inversion of orthodoxy, Dickinson takes the Word of God and makes it her own, which then serves as the criterion for measuring all power outside the self. Transubstantiation thus becomes a trope for poetic inspiration. Combined with this discourse of religion is the language of appetite, which Dickinson frequently identifies with the poetic enterprise. This transference of authority—"The Word made Flesh"—describes an alternative drama of mutuality between desire and fulfillment absent in the relations that exist within a hieratic Christianity. So sweeping is the usurpation of orthodox powers into the self that by the poem's final stanza, traditional incarnation can only hope to match the reciprocal relationship that informs "beloved philology." The closing words echo their own meaning in a circle of love *(philo-logos)*, the beloved love of the word.

Yet, if here the poetic word triumphs over LOGOS, elsewhere it assumes no such absolute or benign power, but is, instead, identified as functioning within an adversarial relationship, as a weapon used to defend the self against the self's own powers. Once such power resides solely within the single consciousness, once the poetic self attempts to replace external authority, the dangers for poetic identity grow more intimate and acute. As Dickinson remarks, "Jacob versus Esau, was a trifle in Litigation, compared to the Skirmish in my Mind—". Language, the usurping power of the imagination, becomes, then, both a weapon of salvation and the means for potential self-destruction. Dickinson underscores the lethal relationship between the potentially brilliant show of her Word (its destructive possibilities) in "She dealt her pretty words like blades," where language "glitters" and "shines" while it exposes, like a surgeon's knife, the nerves or "wantons with a Bone—". Such surgical "wanton"-ness may prove lethal to its victim. But this is a risk Dickinson must take if she is to direct her linguistic energies toward a confrontation with her personal and literary isolation, if she is to provide herself with a means for overcoming the strictures of circumstance.

The ground of poetry, alone, offers Dickinson the freedom to articulate her independence. Choosing to write from her perception of this alienated consciousness, she projects an inviolate territory where words, even if potentially self-destructive, are her weapons against limitation, orthodoxy, and a hostile world. Such an alternative territory emerges in the early poem, "There is a morn by men unseen—" (24). Here Dickinson describes a pastoral landscape but with a difference: process ceases, temporality fades, and, as in poem 1056, "Consciousness—is Noon." Characterizing this "mystic green" in terms of her own ambition, Dickinson seeks there a "morn by men unseen." Whether she is using "men" in the generic or the more specific, sex-related sense, she attests to an enchanted ground inhabited by "maids" who engage in their own "dance and game," those who participate in secret rituals of delight during their "holiday" (holy day).

> There is a morn by men unseen—
> Whose maids upon remoter green
> Keep their Seraphic May—
> And all day long, with dance and game,
> And gambol I may never name—
> Employ their holiday.

Whether the poet "may never name" these rituals because she does not know them or because she will not or cannot disclose them affects the interpretation of the remaining stanzas. However one decides to read the poem, and I will not attempt a full reading here, it is significant that Dickinson is invoking an alternative, sacred ground toward which she yearns to travel. Wishing to join that company of fairy maids who do not inhabit the earth, she finds in their magic "ring" a ground secure from the antipathetic forces that drove her from the daylight world of men and women. In a poem that itself describes a form of sacred play, one must take into account Dickinson's own play with words throughout the text. Puns and associative images create a complex web of meaning that reinforces the overall vision of the poem as a counter-revelation, another way for the poet to be, as opposed to the commonly received notion of poetic vocation and the daylight world of masculine orthodoxy. Not only is the holiday also a holy day, but the Chrysolite that shines in her alternative landscape is, perhaps, an alternative to Christ's light; the revels of the magic "maids" are a kind of play that replaces traditional "revelation."

> Like thee to dance—like thee to sing—
> People upon that mystic green—
> I ask, each new May Morn.

> I wait thy far, fantastic bells—
> Announcing me in other dells—
> Unto the different dawn!

Despite the jubilation of the closing stanza, this "different dawn" remains in the realm of ambition. The luminous powers of the "mystic green" are not yet experienced by the poet who *waits* for her call to election, to this counter-revelation of a natural, free-spirited, exuberant circle of other worldly "maids."

As this "different dawn" has yet to be attained, so Dickinson recognizes that she cannot stay in her self-made world of language forever. Her most impressive poems thus derive their energy from the conflict between the poetic self and a world she perceived as estranged, or "other." Yet, if nature is alien, society without comprehension of her poetic powers, the language Dickinson inherits is also, she recognizes, not fully her own. Language as she knows it is defined primarily by a long line of male poets—to rid her words of their literal meaning would be an act of liberation that would free her from a confining tradition, a gesture that would allow her access to a new mode of signification. Her quest for such a revision of language itself becomes a major subject for a number of her most remarkable poems and the beginning of a feminist poetics that treats the difficulties of a woman poet who struggles for the integrity of her own voice. By describing her experience of rejection in terms that only serve to deepen its ambiguities, Dickinson demonstrates the precariousness that governs her relationships to all outside the self, especially to nature and to God—the chief adversaries she must resist if she is to survive as woman and as poet. The terms of Dickinson's encounter with the world go beyond mere antagonism as God and nature turn against and actively pursue the inquisitive self.

> Nature and God—I neither knew
> Yet Both so well knew me
> They startled, like Executors
> Of My identity.
>
> Yet Neither told—that I could learn—
> My Secret as secure
> As Herschel's private interest
> Or Mercury's affair—

                                                    (835)

Here the ambiguities in Dickinson's relationships with external forces reveal themselves in a series of curiously inverted linguistic structures. First, note that the poem speaks of the I's relationship with nature and God in the past tense; whether this means that the relationship has subsequently altered or whether she is speaking of herself in the past in a eulogistic vein remains an open question. Although apparently a simple statement of her ignorance concerning God and nature, and their intimate knowledge of the "I," the poem is really more complex. For instance, after the opening lines assert that nature and God possess this knowledge, while she remains ignorant of them, she defines the character of this knowledge in terms of her response: "They startled, like Executors / Of My identity." In her choice of "executors," Dickinson begins the dichotomy that will set the poem against itself, for "executor" suggests both one who puts to death (perhaps explaining the posthumous tense of the poem), carrying out the verdict of society, and/or one who carries out the wishes of the deceased as expressed in her or his Will. Although the second alternative incorporates within its definition the sense of one who obeys, who thus subordinates himself to the wishes of an other, this acquiescence is precipitated by the death of the person who wrote the "will" and who now exercises that will through the very act of dying. "Executor" can, then, be either the agent of the victim's death or the one who protects her rights, sustains her will, after she has succumbed to other forces—most compellingly, the word may retain both these meanings and so operate dualistically, in an apparently antithetical relationship to itself. Thus, "executor" simultaneously contains both protective and potentially lethal meanings. The ambiguity associated with nature and God intensifies as Dickinson further complicates these relationships through additional syntactic complexities, the most obviously being her use of dashes and the pronoun "that," which discourages any single reading of the poem's final lines.

> Yet neither told—that I could learn—
> My Secret as secure
> As Herschel's private interest
> Or Mercury's affair—

The clause "that I could learn" again operates in two ways: first, as a parenthetical clarification—to the best of her knowledge, and second, nature and God did not tell their secret in ways *so* that she could learn. The reader cannot, moreover, be certain just what nature and God are refusing to disclose. The options might be these: either they will in good faith not reveal the "secret" information about the poet which would, she suggests, in some unnamed way, damage her were it told (thus she is protected by them as the deceased's wishes would be respected by her executors) and/or nature and God will not reveal *to her* what they know, preserving instead an inviolate secrecy. Within this second reading, "secure" functions as an ironic term, for the "I" cannot learn directly about either God or Nature, let alone about what they know of her; the secret is thus secured just because it is hidden from the self. What Herschel's private interest might be she cannot know, as Mercury's affair remains a mystery. These closing lines are themselves enigmatic in their brevity, but equally suggestive as well. The reader does not know, for example, to which Herschel the poem refers—to the distinguished astronomer, William, or to his remarkable sister and collaborator, Caroline, who discovered eight comets in her lifetime, or to William's son, John. Each of these names does, however, recall not simply an astronomer, but a scientist who discovered a celestial body hitherto unknown. A conjectural reading of "As Herschel's private interest" suggests that if Herschel's (any of the Herschels) public interests were so vast, how great might his/her secret interest have been; the speaker's secret is as secure as Herschel's because it also is cosmological in scope and as much a part of the hitherto unknown. The closing line with its reference to Mercury makes both the astronomical connection to Herschel and the link back to the Roman god, a pagan deity as opposed to the Judeo-Christian presence with whom the poem opens. But Mercury has other important connotations for this context as well: the planet is closest to the sun and extremely hard to view from the earth. (In what was most probably an apocryphal story, Copernicus on his deathbed reportedly stated that his one regret was never to have observed Mercury.) Moreover, because of its position in relation to the sun, one side of Mercury is constantly in light, the other in total darkness. Thus, Mercury could keep its secrets in two senses—as the planet so hard to see from the earth and as one that keeps half its form in constant night. The allusion to the pagan identity of Mercury functions ironically: as the messenger, the one who brings news, Mercury would disclose rather than withhold secret knowledge. In larger terms, two meanings operate antithetically here; the first more overt, perhaps, than the second, but both equally sustained through the poem's syntax and diction, creating an unresolvable tension rather than a resolution of interpretation. Such interpretative indeterminacy, moreover, places the reader in a position analogous to that of the "I" of the poem. Dickinson informs us of the terms in which she understands her predicament but gives no clear notion of exactly where her power or knowledge might reside.

Such interpretative ambiguities, brilliant as they may be, are a sign of a deeper ambivalence that manifests itself in the linguistic and syntactic complexities informing Dickinson's often richly multivalent texts. And yet, the extremely delicate process of articulating such indeterminacy is in itself the source of authority that surpasses nature's mystery by naming it. Whether such obscuring strategies have their origin in a deliberate desire to obscure or in an ironic evasiveness, or in both, no reader can ascertain; more alarming, such indeterminacy of language, despite the authoritative force of individual poems, may signal the potential breakdown of the word's capacity to bear the pressures of simultaneous, antithetical meanings that deconstruct each other.

Confronting her own awareness of the deconstructive possibilities in language, Dickinson finds that her weapons, her words, are double-edged. If language may serve as defense against an alien world and a rejecting father-God, it may, in the very act of its expression, further expose the sources of conflict that war within the self. Respect for the word and recognition of its power lead to a concomitant fear the language may turn precipitously, unannounced, against its author. If to "hurt" is "Not Steel's Affair" (479), when steel is the synecdochical knife of language, the word can be trusted neither to spare nor to protect; language may not only captivate—it may, alas, also condemn.

II

Such a vision of language leads Dickinson to an understanding of the world and her epistemological relation to it that is at once potentially dangerous and dangerously modern, for her poems speak repeatedly of a sense of a dislocation that neither depends upon nor assumes a ground of common or shared experience. The roots of such an alienated imagination draw their sustenance from isolation—both intellectual and physical. But the result of such depleting circumstances is, remarkably, a poetry that not only manifests a penchant for ambiguity (the double-edged ironic mode) but reveals as well experimentation with the possibilities of language to convey mutually conflicting meanings as the word pushes toward, and indeed at times *over*, the limits of communal understanding. Exclusion thus offers Dickinson the occasion to adopt a radical approach to experience that prompts her to invent a startlingly modernist poetics. In a world where nothing is certain, all relationships can be shifted, reversed, subverted, or kept indeterminate because they rely for their definition upon an isolate, rebellious consciousness, which itself is in a state of flux. Such radical solipsism often leads to a vertiginous freedom, what Dickinson herself names "that precarious Gait/ Some call experience." Dickinson's skeptical investigation of experience combined with her abiding sense of exclusion translates into poems that assert their defiance against the existing order and articulate a willful rejection of the very things she has most desired, what she has been denied. In this way, Dickinson's poems potentially free her to become "executor" of her own identity.

Although engendered by different anxieties, the skepticism often bordering on despair that precipitates so many of the major modernists' experiments finds a kindred manifestation in Dickinson's work. If the modernists turn to radical experimentation with language to reclaim poetry for contemporary experience (one thinks of Pound, of Eliot, of H. D.), to fashion a language adequate to a deeply altered, forever changed world, so, too, Dickinson, albeit in isolation and without the support gained from the knowledge of others striving toward a common goal, pits her language against the world in a gesture as defiant as that of any of those twentieth-century poets who were to follow. As a woman poet she experiences cultural rejection and isolation *earlier* than the male poets who will later feel themselves exiled by cataclysmic historical events beyond their control—the most fatefully being the turbulent changes wrought by the First World War and the cultural disruption that was its aftermath. These changes forced writers to confront an historical discontinuity between themselves and an irretrievable past. So, too, women poets had, generations earlier, felt themselves cut off from the post-Miltonic poetic tradition, which had never been theirs. Thus, one may begin to account for some of the indeterminate quality of Dickinson's poetics by viewing her as a proto-modernist whose radical ways were formed, in part, by a feminist impulse.

Dickinson's sense of dislocation emerges with an austere clarity in the following poem, with its strong Stevensian tone:

Four Trees—upon a solitary Acre—
Without Design
Or Order, or Apparent Action—
Maintain—

The Sun—upon a Morning meets them—
The Wind—
No nearer Neighbor—have they—
But God—

The Acre gives them—Place—
They—Him—Attention of Passer by—
Of Shadow, or of Squirrel, haply—
Or Boy—

What Deed is Their's unto the General Nature—
What Plan
They severally—retard—or further—
Unknown—

(742)

In this poem's strangely vacant opening, one hears the Stevensian "mind of winter," the listener who "nothing himself, beholds/Nothing that is not there and the nothing that is." This voice prophesies as well that quality of provisional apprehension that haunts Stevens's most austere poems. Dickinson presents a stark scene of four trees standing isolate in an otherwise bare acre, invoking this vision to suggest the absence of assured meaning either in the trees' relation to other natural facts or to an ordering principle beyond themselves—some unnamed teleological force. There remains, however, a slight demurral from this absence in the "apparent" of the poem's third line. Asking the question Robert Frost will pose in "Design" when he observes the minute death-drama taking place on the white "heal-all," Dickinson sustains the possibility that there may be a design that governs over against her provisional denial. The stanzas that follow elaborate this issue of motive or purpose beyond sheer physical presence. The sun "meets" (a word that suggests intent) the trees; yet, oddly, the effect of such a meeting is only to intensify the aura of isolation that demarcates the trees' existence. Distant light alone is this landscape's nearest neighbor—except God. Although the "but" that precedes "God" (stanza two, line four) would prepare the reader for a seemingly minor omission, an afterthought, it is here that the poem coyly confronts its central question, for the issue of the exclusion of God is an oversight of truly teleological significance. Despite this ironic maneuver, the poem resists any orthodox assertion of Divine omnipresence, proceeding instead to define other earthly relationships that are determined by chance and dependent upon the presence of an observer:

The Acre gives them—Place—
They—Him—Attention of Passer by—

> Of Shadow, or of Squirrel, haply—
> Or Boy—

"Shadow," "Squirrel," "Boy": the list moves from optical effect to sentient, hence potentially questioning, consciousness. In a movement that parallels the structure of the preceding stanza—in each case the final line introducing the crucial term with the offhandedness given an afterthought—the poem again evades as it draws attention to its own implications—this time, the impact of a human viewer's consciousness. Rather than resolve the underlying question of meaning, the problem of intelligence as well as the issue of belief, the closing stanza will not fully acknowledge the presence of a Divine or human observer who would imbue with meaning this bare landscape-vision, which thus remains equivocal and obscure.

Commenting more generally on the relationship between Dickinson and Stevens, Harold Bloom notes, "The connection with Stevens is that he and Dickinson, more than any other Americans, more than any other moderns, labor successfully to make the visible a little hard to see." Here Dickinson creates this obliqueness of vision by questioning the reality of the observing eye as well as the presence of an hierarchical power that would invest meaning, the clarity of intent, into the otherwise desolate landscape. This poem eschews any such recuperative possibility that would ascribe a specific significance to the scene, choosing instead to bear witness to a complete ignorance of the scene's function or its meaning. By rejecting the relationships asserted in the poem, the final stanza poses the essentially ontological question: for what purpose do these trees exist? "What Plan/ They severally—retard—or further—Unknown." The repeated "n" sounds separated by the long "o" of "unknown" re-sound the finality of the word's meaning and, simultaneously, the impossibility of ever achieving that meaning.

III

To live in such a world is to live, no matter how brilliantly, alone. Yet, if God will not reveal his meaning or the meaning of his world, there may yet be another faith to which Dickinson can turn, one based upon an alternative to the exclusive, rejecting patriarchal order she must herself renounce. This heterodox faith, or "other" way, may be founded upon the belief in the development of a tradition of women poets, distinct from that delineated by the male poetic tradition. In perhaps the most forthright and impassioned statement of this possible alternative faith, an order that would be founded upon the majesty of woman, Dickinson invokes the maternal forms of mountains as standard bearers of her especial truth. In contrast to those poems that sever the external manifestations of the world from an unknowable God's intent, here Dickinson maintains a connection between an alternative theodicy and the physical presence of natural forms. As one who felt herself inhabiting a world where order remains frustratingly provisional and God continuously hidden, how Dickinson must have yearned for the security of such imaginable, alternative relationships. In an imperative voice that, through its very assertiveness, conveys its desire to coerce geological forms into truth-telling mothers, Dickinson woos as she creates her distinct reality:

> Sweet Mountains—Ye tell Me no lie—
> Never deny Me—Never fly—
> Those same unvarying Eyes
> Turn on Me—When I fail—or feign,
> Or take the Royal names in vain—
> Their far—slow—Violet Gaze—
>
> My strong Madonnas—Cherish still—
> The Wayward Nun—beneath the Hill—
> Whose service—is to You—
> Her latest Worship—When the Day
> Fades from the Firmament away—
> To lift Her Brows on You—
>
> (722)

Constancy, fidelity, and unconditional acceptance—those qualities which Dickinson found missing in orthodox Christianity, she now seeks among the monumental "Strong Madonnas." For such heresy, the taking of the "Royal names in vain" and her assuming the role of the "Wayward Nun," the "I" anticipates a reciprocal allegiance. This very waywardness ironically legitimizes the self's demand for such unwavering constancy on the part of the "sweet mountains," as heterodoxy is converted into belief in the alternative power of the maternal. As Sandra M. Gilbert and Susan Gubar state, "Surely these 'Strong Madonnas' are sisters of the mother Awe to whom, Dickinson told Higginson, she ran home as a child, and surely it was such mothers who enabled (and empowered) this poet to escape her Nobodaddy's requirements, if only in secret." And yet, this alternative power receives only conditional allegiance; the imperative tone of the poem's opening: "Sweet Mountains—Ye tell Me no lie— / Never deny me—Never fly—" assumes the voice of a command. The poem asks for the belief of the mountains in the "I" who usurps Christ's role but adopts a diametrically opposite position, beneath the hill as Christ was at its summit. This "wayward nun" is, moreover, at once savior and worshipper. In the first stanza, the "I" undergoes trials of faith as she plays the part of defiant actor. (Note the negative terms in which these trials are described: "fail," "Feign," "or take the Royal names in vain.") She performs in these ways, the second stanza recounts, for the sake of the strong "Madonnas" whom she addresses as "My," thus making her the daughter of the savior's mother—Christ's sister forming an alternative religion of the mother: "Whose service—is to You—," rather than of the son. To see the mountains as madonnas is not simply to see religion in natural forms, but so to transform religion as to transplant it in nature. If the mountains in this poem appear as strong madonnas, they are elsewhere subsumed into the more general vision of a hostile natural world that can offer no solace. Even more disruptively, the mountains may turn volcanic, representing no outward hope but a power at once destructive and potent that smoulders within the self. It is to "Vesuvius at home" that Dickinson grants her primary allegiance. All gods or goddesses beyond this mouldering self may receive intermittent recognition, but none earns the devotion Dickinson bestows upon her own power.

Such allegiance to one's strength, however, is not free from danger; rather, the stakes for poetic survival increase as trust in all external forms fades before the self-inflicting powers of the imagination. The tenuousness of all reality beyond the self, the difficulty of ascertaining any ontological certainty whatsoever—a radically modernist dilemma—finally makes her immune to the solace of religious solutions, no matter how subversive. Instead, when Dickinson writes to her experience, she characteristically sees it as an adventure, a journey through rugged, hostile terrain toward an end both untested and potentially fatal. For companionship, she takes along only her consciousness. Dickinson elsewhere describes the climax of this travail; the terror she faces when confronting "The Forest of the Dead" renders her paralyzed before her goal, which is her end as well:

> Retreat—was out of Hope—
> Behind—a Sealed Route—
> Eternity's White Flag—Before—
> And God—at every Gate—
>
> (615)

The white flag of surrender and/or salvation may welcome the traveller or obscure the vision of God. But even prior to this moment of apocalyptic hesitation, the "routes" leading to it have been treacherous and fraught with danger. As a way of combatting the potential devastation of such risks, Dickinson vests her faith in the only internal power upon which she may rely, upon the power of the transformative Word. Renunciation becomes a viable strategy for poetic survival only to the extent that she can continue to articulate her rejection in the form of writing poems. If, in all other spheres, "Renunciation—is a piercing Virtue," language itself is not to be denied, but instead given renewed and redefined power through the force of her alienated imagination.

Once the poet grants that her word may supplant God's, however, she must be prepared to face the dangers of such redirected authority, hence those poems that witness the treacherous capacities of language, a language that may (with the very probity that lends the Word its force) cause it to shake the foundations of the self. How language can function in this way, as transcendent and transforming reality, is a difficult and problematic question. Dickinson both relies upon the process of articulation to serve for a weapon against her sense of isolation and exile and paradoxically dreads what this very act of verbalization may reveal concerning her hidden (what we would now call "unconscious") self. Such turning against the self, which produces a split identity, is a direct result of Dickinson's poetic ambitions. She fashions a poetics that functions as a counterlanguage eschewing communal identity, a poetics that depends upon, even as it attempts to transfigure the terms of, her exclusion.

IV

This concept of language as defense, as the only effective weapon in Dickinson's arsenal, develops into a strongly adversarial kind of poetics. A war rages in these poems, a war within the self for control over the potency of the word. Note the quasi-aggressive intimacy with which Dickinson describes such procedures:

> The Soul unto itself
> Is an imperial friend—
> Or the most agonizing Spy—
> An Enemy—could send—
>
> Secure against its own—
> No treason it can fear—
> Itself—it's Sovreign—of itself
> The Soul should stand in Awe—
>
> (683)

The repetition of "it's" serves to encode the doubling, the turning of self upon soul, the wrestling of intimate yet potentially antithetical identities. Out of such aggressive intimacy, there emerges awe, the same power Dickinson elsewhere identifies as the spur to her making poems. Even awe, however, contains within it its own paradoxical aspects: "I work to drive the awe away, Yet awe impels the work." What Dickinson asserts that she requires is the stimulus of defense, the sensation of warding off an external power that might destroy her. In response to such a threat, she reacts with a combination of fear and reverence that must be cast aside yet remains crucial to this process of composing poems. That awe is associated with the self's specific language-making function can be inferred from those poems that privilege the poetic act as they denigrate all authority that lies outside the single imagination.

In a hitherto largely neglected poem that directly addresses this conflict of world and word, a poem written during that great year of Dickinson's creative activity, 1862, she alludes to the process that will bestow joy upon the world; joy rising from the powers within the self. This regenerative process, however, leads inexorably to a chilling and personally devastating reversal. Particularly important is the role language assumes, functioning as the determinative power that creates a necessary distance between the self and the world as it staves off the world's destructive capacities. Dealing her "word of gold," Dickinson "dowers—all the World—." She transforms the world with her own resources. When she is robbed of her happiness, however, and finds in its stead only a barren existence, life becomes a "wilderness, which rolls back along (her) Golden lines," and, the poem implies, wipes them out. Language, with its transforming powers, extends over the landscape only to be vanquished by the emptiness of a world that reflects the poet's precipitating loss.

> It would never be Common—more—I said—
> Difference—had begun—
> Many a bitterness—had been—
> But that old sort—was done—
>
> Or—if it sometime—showed—as 'twill—
> Upon the Downiest—Morn—
> Such bliss—had I—for all the years—
> 'Twould give an Easier—pain—
>
> I'd so much joy—I told it—Red—
> Upon my simple Cheek—
> I felt it publish—in my Eye—
> 'Twas needless—any speak—
>
> I walked—as wings—my body bore—
> The feet—I former used—
> Unnecessary—now to me—
> As boots—would be—to Birds—
>
> I put my pleasure all abroad—
> I dealt a word of Gold
> To every Creature—that I met—
> And Dowered—all the World—
>
> When—suddenly—my Riches shrank—
> A Goblin—drank my Dew—
> My Palaces—dropped tenantless—
> Myself—was beggared—too—
>
> I clutched at sounds—
> I groped at shapes—
> I touched the tops of Films—
> I felt the Wilderness roll back
> Along my Golden lines—
>
> The Sackcloth—hangs upon the nail—
> The Frock I used to wear—
> But where my moment of Brocade—
> My—Drop—of India?

(430)

The miraculous change Dickinson describes in the poem's opening four stanzas, the change she felt "publish—in [her] eye," extends to her infusing the world with her joy through language. In a series of deliberate gestures, she "puts" her pleasure all abroad, "deals" a word of Gold, and "dowers" all the World. In these successive phrases, the poem creates an active, purposive self, who draws on internal powers to fill the world with her "word of Gold," thus simultaneously conveying beauty and value to all around her. Once "beggared," in an alarming and abrupt reversal that recalls a fairy-tale narrative with its charmed inevitability, the "I" is suddenly bereft of riches, of dew. Wealth, formerly hers, has vanished, as has the "dew" that nurtured her; her palaces, now without occupants, "tenantless," drop, and she finds herself destitute. Clutching and groping in her desperation, she feels the return of the wilderness as it rolls back along *her* golden lines. These "lines" may signify both the inroads her former bounteous self has made on the world and the poetic lines formed by her words spun of gold—thus, the association between the powers of language and the sources of her capacity to transform her universe. Ironically, at the poem's close, the very lines that had earlier marked her extensive reach into the world now serve as tracks or "guide-lines" for the inescapable encroachment of the formerly banished wilderness. The specific linguistic activity she had performed in her bounteous days was an Adamic one: naming, apportioning, assigning a word to every creature she encountered:

> I dealt a word of Gold
> To every Creature—that I met—
> And Dowered—all the world.

This Edenic condition, which derives its authority from the poet's own transformation, her excess of joy, recedes as suddenly as it came, erased by the nameless wilderness, a region devoid either of human control or of organizing principle. With its clearly delineated connection between linguistic power and continuous war waged between the competing forces of self and world, this poem serves as a paradigmatic expression of the conflict that marks Dickinson's understanding of her relationship to everything outside herself. To see only two—the word equal in power to its adversary, the world—is to envision a dangerously austere, dialogic cosmos where internal energies either overcome the world or are themselves devastated by it.

Even when Dickinson's poems attest to losing in such confrontations, however, they nevertheless reveal the high ambition of the individual consciousness to transcend the inhibitory powers of rejection. By asserting that one no longer wishes for or requires what one has been denied—by, in other words, willfully embracing renunciation, Dickinson attempts to conquer the forces that oppose the self. In the province of language, however, to do without another's voice, to deny all external sources of "inspiration," demands an intellectual self-sufficiency that may prove its own undoing, for the threat remains that devoid of others' language, the poetic voice will be stifled by such defensive isolation. Dickinson writes of this poetic double-bind, expressing a condition which may prove attainable in the realm of the ideal rather than in any recognizable reality:

To own the Art within the Soul
The Soul to entertain
With Silence as a Company
And Festival maintain

Is an unfurnished Circumstance
Possession is to One
As an Estate perpetual
Or a reduceless Mine.

(855)

The "Mine" that cannot be depleted would be the "mine" of the isolate self. Dickinson's possessive pronoun converts the terms of her deprivation into a potential resource whose hidden reserves will never fail because they lie buried deep within. To protect the imagination against the barrenness of circumstance, to guard herself against the deadening effects of a necessary isolation (the possibility that such an internal absence will produce linguistic autism), Dickinson draws upon the transformative capacities of the word. The word—her Word—thus may acquire the power to make things new as she seeks the possibility of redefining the terms of existence to coincide with the priorities of her individual consciousness. If language can achieve such authority, as it does only intermittently in Dickinson's poems, then it may indeed, as she asserts, challenge the preeminence of God's holy Word. To re-make the world according to her own image—this is the ambition of Dickinson's boldest poems. That she must renounce this attempt only to take it up once again, that she testifies to her own failures, does not diminish, but rather reaffirms the extent of her ambitions. For Dickinson imbues her poetic enterprise with a vision of language operating as defense against the pressures of rejection and exile that define her world. Here is a definition of poetry that possesses, like Blake's visionary language, the capacity to mold the terms of existence within the fires of her own imagination. Such a vision of language originates in the perceived absence of external allies and the poet's compensatory devotion not to the conditions of the world, but, instead, to what Dickinson called the "Art within the Soul." If there is "ransom in a voice," if the bounty that will restore the world to the Self resides within, then to speak in words that challenge the world is the only way a poet can endow and so change that world to make it yield to her authority. Recognizing that "all is the price of all," Dickinson creates in her self-imposed, domestic exile, a poetics of high ambition, a poetics that foreshadows the experimental, fiercely defiant voices of modernist literary experimentation. Dickinson explores the latent ambiguities of language to construct a deeply paradoxical, if, at times, bafflingly equivocal voice. By insisting upon the articulation of her own version of experience, she develops rhetorical strategies that break with tradition as they depend increasingly upon indeterminacies, upon the disruption of linguistic structures that would otherwise provide recognizable, coherent meanings.

Out of this alienation, Dickinson shapes a language that challenges the

Western literary tradition's shared assumptions about the very character of figurative language itself, for she disrupts the relationship between the signifier and the signified in two ways: first by trying to replace the signified with the signifier, to transcend the world through her word, and second by using signs so that their meaning itself is not simply ironic, but self-deconstructing. Words that can be read this way, however, do not reduce in meaning, but approach an indecipherability that seeks not merely to disrupt communal meaning but to move past language's image-making power to reach the word as insoluble, irreducible construct that defies any referent, or any combination of referents. To let the Word replace the World in both meaning and the irreducible "I am that I am" of immanence, this is Dickinson's double project and its tie to a modernist poetics that rejects normative definitions to strive for an alternative order privileged by art. If the pressures that led Dickinson to such experimentation were extreme, so the defensive poetics she employs threatens to slip at any moment into self-disintegration. Yet it is here, at the brink of poetic indecipherability, where the risks of language are greatest, that Dickinson achieves her full power. Finally, her feminist poetics emerges as an experimental project that approaches modernist theories of art, for Dickinson shapes a revisionary language that pursues the possibilities of internally generated meanings as it resists the confines of figuration, the potential clarities of signification. Thus, Dickinson pursues as well a sublime if potentially fatal course as she discovers within the very indeterminacy of language a radically modern linguistic home.

Et in Arcadia Ego: Representation, Death, and the Problem of Boundary in Emily Dickinson

Sharon Cameron

The events of the unconscious are timeless, that is, they are not ordered in time, are not changed by the passage of time, have no relation whatever to time.

—SIGMUND FREUD

The fact is that consciousness deteriorates as the result of any cerebral shock. Merely to faint is to annihilate it. How then is it possible to believe that the spirit survives the death of the body?

—MARCEL PROUST

The problem of boundaries is integral to some of our most profound concerns. What is the relationship between self and other, interior and exterior, literal and figural, past and present, time and timelessness? Were they not so crucial these questions would be pedestrian, and indeed how we answer them, whether we are able to answer them, is often an indication of the way in which we lead our lives. Jean Starobinski has recently pointed out that the connection we often make between history or past and interiority or depth is seductive precisely because it avoids the acknowledgment that some boundaries (in this case the one between past and present) render experience irrecoverable: "Making the most remote past coefficient to our most intimate depth is a way of refusing loss and separation, of preserving, in the crammed plenum we imagine history to be, every moment spent along the way. . . . To say that the individual constructed himself through his history is to say that the latter is cumulatively present in him and that even as it was elapsing, it was becoming internal structure." Such a conception may be regarded as a way of mediating between the absolute severance of past and present and their absolute fusion. For if the past is "inside us" rather than attending us, it is no longer necessarily subject to our conscious repossession. To be experienced again it must be re-presented. The past can be conceived, then, as having a diachronic progression that, once it comes into being, assumes synchronic structure. Such a conception both frees the self for future action by asserting that the past is safely contained behind or below the present, and simultaneously binds it by the selfsame fact of that containment. Like it or not, boundaries are not so easy to establish. While we

From *Lyric Time: Dickinson and the Limits of Genre.* © 1979 by The Johns Hopkins University Press.

frequently construe past and present by wedging a boundary between the parameters of each, as often in our conception of present and future, we hope to annihilate the severity of such boundaries, for could this be finessed, the present might be relieved of the indeterminacy that awaits it, and simultaneously gifted by the exhilarations of desired change.

I raise these issues in order to provide a context for, as well as to suggest the preliminary complexity of, characteristic problems of temporal boundary in Dickinson's poems. The most eschatological indication of boundary or division is, of course, death, and it is hence no accident that Dickinson's utterances hover around this subject with as much perseverance as the fly in one of her more noted poems. Indeed we might regard death as a special instance of the problem of boundary, representing the ultimate division, the extreme case, the infuriating challenge to a dream of synchrony. On the border of conception, the limits of experience, death both epitomizes the problem of boundary and offers itself as its severest manifestation. It is in this context that we shall examine Dickinson's death utterances, asking how the straying of a poem across impossible limits leads inevitably to the collapse of other boundaries, namely those that set themselves up as walls between figure and thing figured, between literal meanings and metaphoric ones. For if the problem Starobinski discusses may be construed as one of constructing boundaries, in Dickinson's death utterances, on which this chapter will focus, the problem is often one of destroying them. In the following pages, however, we shall see that the relationship between construction and destruction is a complex one—objects slip from one side of a line to another with the ease of a thought falling out of consciousness and rising back into it. And, as with consciousness, whose goal is to enlarge its own area of being, so with the life-space occupied by a poem that pushes with all its might against the line of death, in the hopes that it can, by however scant measure, enlarge its territory.

In part 2 of this [essay] I shall examine poems in which the question "Is death literal or figural?" does not admit of a simple or certain answer, in which death is neither a clearly phenomenological fact nor a clearly psychic phenomenon. In such instances we will see that it is difficult to distinguish between figure and thing figured because of their complex relationship to each other. In part 3 I shall turn briefly to poems that purport actually to mark the boundary between life and death and shall look, in conclusion, at those poems that trespass beyond it. I shall tentatively suppose that fusions between the literal and the figural (often represented in Dickinson's poems in terms of death and despair) are related to, and perhaps generative of, the temporal fusions that exist in larger scale in those poems where it is not clear on which side of the grave the speaker's utterance takes place. Finally, in examining these poems I shall want to ask how such fusions obscure the fact of death, blur its edges so that its future threat is undercut by the implicit assertion of its presence or prefigurement, and alternately to ask whether this prefigurement, ultimately subverted, throws death's outlines into sharper relief precisely by its distance from what, in the end, can only be intimated.

II

In many of Dickinson's poems, the relationship between death and despair is complex, not only because one may be the generative occasion for the other, but also and more significantly, because one is liable to be confused with the other. Thus in the following poem, while it is clear enough that the speaker has been reprieved from literal death, the psychic turmoil of its anticipation—or, in simple terms, the torture—so overwhelms the significance of what it anticipates that we are thrown off balance and can no longer specify the shape of the poem's predicament. Such a perplexity is acknowledged by the speaker herself, as the final question of the poem testifies:

> 'Twas like a Maelstrom, with a notch,
> That nearer, every Day,
> Kept narrowing its boiling Wheel
> Until the Agony
>
> Toyed coolly with the final inch
> Of your delirious Hem—
> And you dropt, lost,
> When something broke—
> And let you from a Dream—
>
> As if a Goblin with a Gauge—
> Kept measuring the Hours—
> Until you felt your Second
> Weigh, helpless, in his Paws—
>
> And not a Sinew—stirred—could help,
> And sense was setting numb—
> When God—remembered—and the Fiend
> Let go, then, Overcome—
>
> As if your Sentence stood—pronounced—
> And you were frozen led
> From Dungeon's luxury of Doubt
> To Gibbets, and the Dead—
>
> And when the Film had stitched your eyes
> A Creature gasped "Reprieve"!
> Which Anguish was the utterest—then—
> To perish, or to live?
>
> (P 414)

The anonymous creature who in the final analogy orders the halting of the death process seems, like the speaker, to be wrought to the breaking point; he is nothing akin to the demons who in calm "Toy coolly," practically, with the victim. Nor is he akin to the God whose calm borders on indifference. He seems rather to mediate between the two, as if only mediation could distinguish them. In fact it is not insignificant that the power which orders the reprieve should be of uncertain source, for the affliction is of uncertain source, and that uncertainty is reflected in the poem's diction, which rocks back and forth from one connotative sphere to another, as unsettled in its vocabulary for the experience as in the experience itself. This lack of clarity is illustrated in the initial image of the whirlpool. While it steers in the speaker's direction, we note that the "boiling Wheel" and the "notch" are both parts of the same cosmic machine whose complete shape is blanked out. As in a dream (and perhaps it is the dream feeling in the first stanza that prompts the explicit acknowledgment of dream in the next) the synecdochic distortion that isolates and magnifies is frightening precisely because it lacks a context. Disjoint, the only parts that can be seen are vengeful, annihilative. In stanza two the speaker is held upside down ("delirious") just perceptibly by the hem of her clothes, remaining only marginally in existence. What "breaks" in the stanza subsequently are the connections to that existence, and the speaker is delivered from the dream of this death, but delivered into what is unclear.

In the next four stanzas, the attempt to recapitulate a story whose meaning the speaker still does not know is laden with confusions of the earlier rendition. The impulse to tell and retell the same story has a quality of hysteria to it, for the implicit belief that to tell the story over will insure getting it straight is proved wrong. In the final lines the poem's focus shifts from the anticipation of death to a question about its status. If life is "like a Maelstrom, with a notch," and if what is being measured is human endurance, then "To perish" would at least end it. But the poem concludes, as it has been borne along, by the waves of its own exhaustion at the pervasiveness of psychic distress. The speaker may have been rescued from actual death but she seems as a consequence condemned to suffer the same torture to whose stages the poem's stanzas, we would have thought, promised her a terminal point.

While " 'Twas like a Maelstrom with a notch" explores the border between life and death—its most articulate denomination of that border contained in the harrowing image of the eyes almost "stitched" permanently—it also raises the question of whether death is a metaphor for the torture or whether the torture is only a prelude to death. Insofar as the poem's final question relocates its subject or, at any rate, calls it into question, we not only ask with the speaker which anguish is most extreme, we also question our prior understanding of the generative experience for the representation. The entire poem, beginning with the second word, understood as a series of analogies by necessity, casts its subject into doubt. The fact of death and the psychic anguish that anticipates it are really no longer separate. In effectively annihilating the boundary between the two, Dickinson forces us to transcend a line that we know, in reality, it is impossible to transcend. With this verbal fusion she perhaps harbors the illusion that she has gained knowledge of what lies over the border. For an implicit, if secondary, assumption of the poem is that the unsurpassable psychic anguish will guarantee her safe or, at any rate, unsurprised passage to death.

If actual death can best be conjured by descriptions of acute pain, Dickinson frequently reverses the representational fusion by summoning psychic anguish in the explicit terms of death and burial:

> I felt a Funeral, in my Brain,
> And Mourners to and fro
> Kept treading—treading—till it seemed
> That Sense was breaking through—
>
> And when they all were seated,
> A Service, like a Drum—
> Kept beating—beating—till I thought
> My Mind was going numb—
>
> And then I heard them lift a Box
> And creak across my Soul
> With those same Boots of Lead, again,
> Then Space—began to toll,
>
> As all the Heavens were a Bell,
> And Being, but an Ear,
> And I, and Silence, some strange Race
> Wrecked, solitary, here—
>
> And then a Plank in Reason, broke,
> And I dropped down, and down—
> And hit a World, at every plunge,
> And Finished knowing—then—
>
> (P 280)

We may speculate that the poem charts the stages in the speaker's loss of consciousness, and this loss of consciousness is a dramatization of the deadening forces that today would be known as repression. We may further suppose that the speaker is reconstructing—or currently knowing—an experience whose pain in the past rendered it impossible to know. We note that part of the strangeness of her speech lies in the fact that not only is the poem grammatically past tense, but it also seems emotionally past tense. It illustrates the way in which one can relate experience and, at the same time, suffer a disassociation from it. Of course in this case the experience itself is one of disassociation. Since the speaker adds no emotive comment to the recollection, it is as if even in the recounting the words did not penetrate the walls of her own understanding. That the poem is about knowledge and the consequence of its repression is clear enough from the poem's initial conceit, for people do not feel funerals and certainly not in the brain. In addition, as a consequence of the persistent downward motion of the poem, we see that the funeral is rendered in terms of a burial, and this fusion or confusion points to a parallel confusion between unconsciousness and death. The burial of something in the mind—of a thought or experience or wish—the rendering of it unconscious, lacks an etiology; its occasion and even content here remain unspecified. As a consequence our attention is fixed on the process itself.

Examining the conceit, we can speculate that the mourners represent that part of the self which fights to resurrect or keep alive the thought the speaker is trying to commit to burial. They stand for that part of the self which feels conflict about the repressive gesture. "Treading—treading—," the self in conflict goes over the same ground of its argument with itself, and sense threatens to dissolve, "break through—," because of the mind's inability to resolve its contradictory impulses. In the second stanza, on a literal level the participants of the funeral sit for the service and read words over the dead. On a figural level the confusion of the mind quiets to one unanimous voice issuing its consent to the burial of meaning. But the mind's unanimity, its single voice, is no less horrible. The speaker hears it as a drum: rhythmic, repetitious, numbing. In the fourth stanza, the repressive force lashes the speaker with retaliatory distortion: the "Heavens" and the cosmos they represent toll as one overwhelming "Bell"; "Being" is reduced to the "Ear" that must receive it. No longer fighting the repressive instinct (for the "Mourners" have disappeared, "Being" and "I" are united), the self is a victim passively awaiting its own annihilation. When the "Plank in Reason," the last stronghold to resist its own dissolution, gives, and the speaker plummets through successive levels of meaning (an acknowledgment that repression has degrees), the result is a death of consciousness. As J. V. Cunningham remarks, the poem is a representation of a "psychotic episode" at the end of which the speaker passes out.

But if we agree that the poem is not about actual death, why is the funeral rendered in such literal terms, terms that might well lead a careless reader to mistake its very subject? Paul de Man, distinguishing between irony and allegory, provides a suggestive answer. Allegory, he writes, involves "the tendency of the language toward narrative, the spreading out along the axis of an imaginary time in order to give duration to what is, in fact, simultaneous within the subject." The structure of irony is the reverse of this form—the reduction of time to one single moment in which the self appears double or disjoint. Irony, de Man writes, is "*staccato . . .* a synchronic structure, while allegory appears as a successive mode capable of engendering duration as the illusion of a continuity that it knows to be illusory." Irony and allegory, he concludes, are two faces of the same experience, opposite ways of rendering sequence and doubleness. De Man's distinctions are illuminating for our understanding of the fusions in "I felt a Funeral in my Brain," for the poem exhibits a double sense of its own experience and of the form in which that experience is to be rendered. With no terms of its own, it is through its very disembodiment, its self-reflexive disassociation, that the experience wields the power it does. If it could be made palpable and objectified, it might be known and hence mastered. Thus the allegory of the funeral attempts to exteriorize and give a temporal structure to what is in fact interior and simultaneous. Because we see the stages of the funeral (stages that correspond to steps that will complete the repressive instinct) we cannot help but view repression in terms of death. Thus the funeral imagery, replete with mourners, coffin, and service, seems both to distract from the poem's subject of repression and to insist on the severity of its consequences. But it is in the tension between the two modes of knowing and of representation, between an allegorical structure and an ironic one, that the poem's interest lies. For structure and sequence fall away in the ironic judgment of the poem's last line, which suggests, if implicitly, that action (exteriority) and knowledge (interiority) will always diverge. Even the attempt to reconstruct the experience and do it over with a different consequence leads, as it did the first time, to blankness. This divergence is further exemplified in the odd order of the poem's events: the funeral precedes death, at least the death of consciousness. Such inversion of normal sequence necessitates a figural reading of the poem and makes perfect sense within it, for Dickinson seems to be claiming we cannot "not know" in isolation and at will. What we choose not to know, what we submerge, like the buried root of a plant that sucks all water and life toward its source, pulls us down with a vengeance toward it.

If " 'Twas like a Maelstrom with a notch" suggests that agony may be a metaphor for death, and "I felt a Funeral in my Brain" that death is a metaphor for repressed agony, the problem of fusion becomes even more complex in the following poem, where it is truly impossible to tell whether death is a figure or the thing itself. In " 'Tis so appalling it exhilarates," as in other poems . . . in which naming is an indirect venture, this poem begins with an elusive "it":

> 'Tis so appalling—it exhilarates—
> So over Horror, it half Captivates—
> The Soul stares after it, secure—
> A Sepulchre, fears frost, no more—
>
> To scan a Ghost, is faint—
> But grappling, conquers it—
> How easy, Torment, now—
> Suspense kept sawing so—
>
> The Truth, is Bald, and Cold—
> But that will hold—
> If any are not sure—
> We show them—prayer—
> But we, who know,
> Stop hoping, now—
>
> Looking at Death, is Dying—
> Just let go the Breath—

And not the pillow at your Cheek
So Slumbereth—

Others, Can wrestle—
Your's, is done—
And so of Wo, bleak dreaded—come,
It sets the Fright at liberty—
And Terror's free—
Gay, Ghastly, Holiday!

(P 281)

While the subject remains unspecified, its identity seems almost not to matter, for that obscurity is overpowered in significance by the initial formulation which suggests a relationship between extremity and exhilaration, dread and release, excruciation and ease. The necessary arena for the free-play of terror is guaranteed by the absolute finality of the feared thing, and whether the finality is one of actual death or whether it is of a truth so "Bald" and "Cold—" as to precipitate the death of illusion is irrelevant. For to conceive of death seems to be to suffer its consequences, even if only in the imagination. "Looking at Death, is Dying—," or as Shakespeare wrote analogously in Sonnet 64 of the "ruin" implicit in the very "rumination" of loss: "This thought is as a death which cannot choose / But weep to have that which it fears to lose." In both instances the mind is liberated from hope and from the attendant anxiety about achieving its object. Since the task of Dickinson's poem is to distinguish between process and conclusion, intimation and knowledge, the dread of terror and its safe arrival, it rests its case on the implicit assertion that you cannot top or bottom a superlative. The content of the superlative thus matters very little; what must be appreciated is the consequence of mastering it.

In the poems discussed thus far in which Dickinson effects a fusion between death as figure and death as fact, the status of death—both called into question by the confusion between figure and fact and simultaneously dismissed by our inability to resolve it—is relegated to a secondary position, and what we are concerned with is a speaker's mastery of a condition that she understands no more than we do. In " 'Twas like a Maelstrom with a notch" the anticipatory state preceding death so partakes of death's characteristics that even on this side of death the speaker is not safe from them; in "I felt a Funeral in my Brain" the death of meaning blots consciousness out, brings a death to the mind so total that the body responds by losing cognizance of itself. In " 'Tis so appalling it exhilarates" any ultimate horror has the severity of death; that there is no distinction between the two seems to be precisely the lesson of the poem. In brief, all of these poems exemplify a duality that is both conscious of itself and dismissive of consciousness.

How such fusions of meaning occur is the explicit subject of the following poem in which Dickinson examines the very process whereby the synthesis we have been discussing comes into being:

There's a certain Slant of light,
Winter Afternoons—
That oppresses, like the Heft
Of Cathedral Tunes—

Heavenly Hurt, it gives us—
We can find no scar,
But internal difference,
Where the Meanings, are—

None may teach it—Any—
'Tis the Seal Despair—
An imperial affliction
Sent us of the Air—

When it comes, the Landscape listens—
Shadows—hold their breath—
When it goes, 'tis like the Distance
On the look of Death—

(P 258)

How does "light" come into relation with "Despair—" and "Despair—" into relation with "Death—"? What are the generative fusions of the poem and why is the grammar of its concluding lines itself so confusing? We note that light is a "Seal" or sign of despair and we remember that Dickinson was much too conscientious a reader of the Bible and particularly of the Book of Revelation not to have intended "the Seal Despair—" to point to an experience that was, if a secular experience can be so, both visionary and apocalyptic. In the Bible, however, while the self is "not worthy to open the scroll and break the seals" that will reveal divine agency, in the speaker's world meaning must be deduced within the privacy of a solitary consciousness. Thus "None may teach it [to] any [one else]"; "None may teach it any[thing]" (it is not subject to alteration); "None may teach it—[not] any[one]." But the "Meanings" of the event are not self-generated; if this is a poem about the solipsistic labor of experience, it is not about autism. To be credited as vision, despair must also seek its connection to the generative source outside itself. For light may seal despair in, make it internal and irrevocable, but the irrevocability, by a line of association that runs just under the poem's surface, prompts the larger thought of death.

In fact, the poem is about correlatives, about how interior transformations that are both invisible and immune to alteration from the outside world are at the same time generated by that world. The relationship between the "Slant of light" in the landscape and the "Seal Despair—" within may be clarified by an analogy to Erich Auerbach's distinction between figure and its fulfillment, for the "Slant of light" and the "Seal Despair—" are not in this poem merely premonitions of death, but are, in fact, kinds or *types* of death. Indeed it could be asserted that in the entire Dickinson canon, despair is often a *figura* for death, not as Auerbach uses the word to specify related historical events, but rather as he indicates the word to denote an event that prefigures an ultimate occurrence and at the same time is already imbued with its essence. Figural interpretation presupposes much greater equality between its terms than either allegory or symbol for, in the former, the sign is a mere form and, in the latter, the symbol is always fused with what it represents and can actually replace it. While it is true that figural interpretation ordinarily applies to historical events rather than to natural events, and while the "Slant of light" and the "Seal Despair—" are indeed natural and psychological events not separated by much time, they have a causal or prefigurative relationship to each other that is closer to the relationship implicit in the figural structure than to that in the symbolic one. Certainly it would be incorrect to say that they are symbols. "Light" and "Seal," however, are in relation to "Death—" as a premise is to a conclusion. Auerbach, speaking of the relationship between two historical events implicit in the figural structure, writes, "Both . . . have something provisional and incomplete about them; they point to one another and both point to something in the future, something still to come, which will be the actual, real, and definitive event." We may regard the "Slant of light" and the "Seal Despair—" as having just such a signatory relationship as that described above. For the light is indirect; it thus seeks a counterpart to help it deepen into meaning. The "definitive event" in the poem to which "light" and "Seal" point is, of course, "Death—." While we would expect the departure of the light to yield distance from the "look of Death—," instead the preposition "on" not only designates the space between the speaker and the light but also identifies that light as one cast by death, and in turn casting death on, or in the direction of, the speaker. The "Slant of light," recognized only at a distance—its meaning comprehended at the moment of its disappearance— is revelatory of "Death—", is "Death['s]—" prefiguration. Figure fuses with fact, interprets it, and what we initially called the confusion of the two now makes sense in the context of divination.

If the light is indeed one of death, then we have the answer to why and how it "oppresses" in the first stanza and to the earlier oblique comparison of it to "Cathedral Tunes—." What Dickinson achieves in the poem is truly remarkable, for she takes a traditional symbol and scours it so thoroughly of its traditional associations with life that before we get to the poem's conclusion the image leans in the direction of mystery, dread, and darkness. By the time we arrive at the final simile and at the direct association of light and death we are not so much surprised as relieved at the explicitness of the revelation. It is the indirect association of "light" and "Death—" (the "Slant" that pulls them together at first seemingly without purpose) that prompts "Despair—." We feel it indirectly, internally, obliquely. Were we to know it, it would be death. For Dickinson, death is the apocalyptic vision, the straightening of premonition into fact, figure into fulfillment.

The fusions I have been discussing either between literal reality and its metaphoric representation (where literal reality permanently assumes those metaphoric characteristics that seemed initially intended only to illuminate it) or between the more formal *figura* and its fulfillment (where events contain in a predictive relationship the essence as well as the form of each other) raise the question of whether we can ever know anything in its own terms, and suggest perhaps that knowledge is not, as we might have thought, absolute, but is rather always relational. If these fusions link the historical or natural world with the divine one, the analogue with the real thing, they are predicated on a structure of simultaneous correspondence rather than of linear progression. The truth that is "Bald, and Cold—" *is* death, it does not lead to it. The "certain Slant of light," although it prefigures death, also already contains its essence. The thing in other words is saturated in the terms of its own figuration. Given the synchrony of this relationship, we are not very far from those poems that strain to annihilate the boundaries of time itself and to treat death as if its very reality could be cast into the present tense, experienced, and somehow survived. The effort to know what cannot be known, to survive it, is thus carried one step further in those poems in which the speaker travels over the boundary from life to death to meet death on its own ground. Given the presumption of the quest, figural structure often gives way to allegory or at any rate to the acknowledgment of the inadequacy of simple analogue, for on the other side of death true knowledge can find no correspondences.

III

It was Heidegger who asserted that we perceive time only because we have to die. [Elsewhere, we have seen] how for Dickinson, too, despair or living death associates itself with timelessness, "When everything that ticked—has stopped—." In the following poem, actual death turns analogy into metaphor, the dead person imaged as a stopped clock:

> A Clock stopped—
> Not the Mantel's—
> Geneva's farthest skill
> Cant put the puppet bowing—
> That just now dangled still—
>
> An awe came on the Trinket!
> The Figures hunched, with pain—
> Then quivered out of Decimals—
> Into Degreeless Noon—
>
> It will not stir for Doctor's—
> This Pendulum of snow—
> This Shopman importunes it—
> While cool—concernless No—
>
> Nods from the Gilded pointers—
> Nods from the Seconds slim—

> Decades of Arrogance between
> The Dial life—
> And Him—
>
>   (P 287)

The dead person's "Arrogance" inheres in his silence, his stoic resistance to the "importun[ing]" of those who would set him going again. Given the enormousness of his refusal, the task of vitalizing him is regarded as a mechanical feat that meets overwhelming failure. If life is a "Dial" measured by the degrees to which it can undergo transformation, death is inert, a "Pendulum of snow—." This, of course, is one way of figuring it—the riddle of the human being no longer alive and therefore unrecognizable as human. For the dead person is a "Trinket" and a "puppet," and comes closest to becoming a "Figure" only in its earlier proximity to the pain of temporality. If part of Dickinson's intention in the poem is to make us "guess what" or "guess who" the subject is, it is largely a consequence of her insistence on our participation in the mystery of death's temporal transcendence.

But despite Dickinson's depiction of the clock-person, life is not synonymous with time. For life endures, or fails to, in the face of time that is continually passing away. It is to rectify this discrepancy, to cure the difference between time and the life that is at odds with it, that Dickinson suggests a temporal transcendence more daring than that of death's. Thus in her proleptic utterances, the dead person becomes one with time either dramatically, as in the preceding poem of the stopped clock, or more subtly, by collapsing the boundaries between past, present, and future. Moreover, the speakers' failure to distinguish temporal categories, the predicated fusion *between* them, suggests an analogous fusion *with* them. In this second fusion internal or subjective time (that clock by which a self measures what is of importance to it) becomes one with external or objective time (which encompasses, disregards, and most usually opposes such private meanings). That external events rarely coincide with internal ones, that our inner thoughts have their own tempo and hence their own significance—can, for example, race at breakneck speed while the clock on the wall goes steadily as usual— are facts so obvious they barely require elaboration. Of the difference between internal and external time, Friedrich Kümmel has written: "If only internal time had reality, death would have no meaning and, conversely, where only external time ruled, life would come to an end." But the fusion between the two in Dickinson's poems lies precisely in the fact that although the speaker *has* died, life has not come to an end. As a consequence, the dead person, having transcended time, can speak from beyond the grave. For the dead person who is like the Roman god Janus (the god of gates and transitions, who looks with one face into the past and the other into the future), speech seems to be a function of the expansion of the present to include past and future, as well as of the synthesis of subjective and objective time. Put succinctly, the speaker has passed the boundary of life while, at the same time, retaining all of the characteristic features of life: memory, feeling, expectation, and the ability to speak and tell stories of these.

Erwin Panofsky provides us with an interesting counterpart to this phenomenon in the visual arts. In his essay "Poussin and the Elegiac Tradition," Panofsky traces the transformation of the grammatically correct interpretation of the phrase *Et in Arcadia ego*, as it is represented in a painting by Guercino, to a misattribution of the phrase and a break in the medieval moralizing tradition, as it is represented in a painting by Poussin. Both paintings show human figures confronting death. But in Guercino's work the shepherds depicted are startled by their confrontation with death and the shock of their encounter seems naturally, as well as grammatically, to attribute the words "Even in Arcadia, there am I" to the death's-head, that is, to death itself. In Poussin's painting, we see four figures standing in front of a tomb, no longer in dramatic discovery of death, and attending tranquilly to speech that it therefore makes more sense to attribute not to the tomb but to the dead person who is buried within it. Thus it suddenly seems right to mistranslate the accompanying Latin phrase as "I, too, lived in Arcadia," that is to ascribe its words to a dead Arcadian shepherd or shepherdess. The misattribution of the Latin phrase prompted by Poussin's representation may do violence to Latin grammar but, Panofsky insists, it is in harmony with the new conception of the painting, which "projects the message of the Latin phrase from the present into the past—all the more forcibly as the behavior of the figures no longer expresses surprise and dismay but quiet, reminiscent meditation. . . . [With the] whole phrase projected into the past: what had been a menace has become a remembrance."

The transformation from terror to meditation, memento mori to elegy that Panofsky describes between Guercino's representation and Poussin's can be seen equally between those poems of Dickinson's that come upon and stop short of death's boundary and those poems that transcend it. In addition, the capacity to remember death rather than to anticipate it, to make past an experience of death that can really only be future, seems to have a similar consequence in Poussin's painting and in Dickinson's poems: in both cases it bequeathes speech to the dead person. We shall turn first to Dickinson's proleptic utterances (looking initially at three poems that stop short of the boundary line and, in so doing, mark it), then back to Panofsky's essay when, with more grounding in the questions it raises, we may explore its insights further. In scrutinizing Dickinson's proleptic poems, I shall be primarily interested in the two phenomena I have sketched above: the fusion of subjective and objective time, and the power of speech beyond the grave.

In the following poem in which the speaker documents the experience of near-death, the depiction is surrealistic, punctuated by the gaps in thought that attest to the terror of fragmentary comprehension:

That after Horror—that 'twas *us*—
That passed the mouldering Pier—
Just as the Granite Crumb let go—
Our Savior, by a Hair—

A second more, had dropped too deep
For Fisherman to plumb—
The very profile of the Thought
Puts Recollection numb—

The possibility—to pass
Without a Moment's Bell—
Into Conjecture's presence—
Is like a Face of Steel—
That suddenly looks into our's
With a metallic grin—
The Cordiality of Death—
Who drills his Welcome in—

(P 286)

Indeed one might speculate that it is the speaker's lost grip on the land that makes *it* appear to suffer dissolution. The dream-like image of a "mouldering Pier—," eaten away partly by water, partly by the spectre of death, belongs to and marks the end of the earthly terrain. Before that spectre the earth itself is reduced to a "Granite Crumb." Since the first stanza represents a state of rapid transition and passage, it is fitting that what the speaker comprehend be partial and partially rendered. Thus although the first stanza's last line implies a subjunctive ("If we had dropped a hair further, we would have met our savior"), the assertion is truncated and elliptical in the extreme, utterance representing the split-second of a miss and its retrospective appreciation. But, in fact, the speaker is not able to penetrate the instant of near-annihilation. Scrutiny does not expand the experiential instant, cannot pry it apart for more substantial examination. The recollection, like the reality, will not open itself up. A "profile of the Thought" is the most that can be tolerated without the speaker's blacking out. In stanza two, as in the first stanza, we are conscious of how thin and inhospitable to knowledge the moment of transition appears even in memory. The speaker gains entry to the experience only by distorting it, by re-presenting it in terms blunt and crude enough to provide room for her exploration.

Only the concluding stanza accomplishes what the first two cannot. It acknowledges the reserve of the boundary line, that fact that it provides no warning or "Bell—" of the enormity of transformation it is facilitating. The stanza then freezes its own conception so that "Conjecture's presence—" (that which can only be present to us by conjecture, specifically death) hardens into static knowledge. In the last five lines of the poem all the earlier characteristics of the experience suddenly reverse themselves and what was evasive is now inevitable; what vague, now harrowingly delimited. The

"Face of Steel—," the "metallic grin—," the "drill" of the "Welcome" close upon the speaker in the half-lewd gesture that, as we have seen, frequently connects death and sexuality in Dickinson's work, and nail her down. In the first two stanzas she had been suggesting that she could not know this experience if she tried; in the last stanza it is clear that she cannot help but know it. The passage completed, even if only conceptually, guarantees all the inevitability that attends any certain state. Only the shadow line separating life from death, which may be glimpsed and touched but not seen or inhabited, is a featureless no man's land free of specific characteristics. At the end of the poem the speaker is still tottering on the edge of the line dividing life from death, but the strength of the completed conception no longer admits of any resolve to turn back.

The attempt to glimpse death's visage while escaping its grip, to know its features from a distance, to straddle the line between ignorance and knowledge, is an abortive one in the preceding poem, and Dickinson acknowledges that fact. One cannot have knowledge and be protected from its consequences at the same time. The "possibility—to pass" over the line is "like a Face of Steel—" precisely because of how absolutely it seals off the route back.

If "That after Horror that 'twas *us*" represents an involuntary and sudden arrival at the line that separates life from death, the following two utterances suggest more considered attempts to anticipate such a juncture and, through anticipation, to forestall its consequences. In "I read my sentence steadily," the wit of the intellectual construction hastens to announce its nonchalance at the "sentence" of death, but the poem's cavalier railery and its matter-of-fact evenness of tone are belied by the profusion of pronouns and the schism within the self that they imply:

> I read my sentence—steadily—
> Reviewed it with my eyes,
> To see that I made no mistake
> In it's extremest clause—
> The Date, and manner, of the shame—
> And then the Pious Form
> That "God have mercy" on the Soul
> The Jury voted Him—
> I made my soul familiar—with her extremity—
> That at the last, it should not be a novel Agony—
> But she, and Death, acquainted—
> Meet tranquilly, as friends—
> Salute, and pass, without a Hint—
> And there, the Matter ends—

(P 412)

Charles Anderson's fine discussion of the poem as a dream-trial in which the mind discovers that the body has been condemned to death and, given no possibility of appeal, attempts to deal with the sentence by so

fragmenting the self that it escapes realistic association with the condemned
person renders further elaborate comment redundant. But in the context of
our discussion, we should note that the purpose of the "Review" is to
domesticate "extremity—," to make it "familiar—" so that the line separating life from death is apprehended prior to the speaker's encounter with it. In
fact, the nature of her acquaintance with death remains deliberately unspecified, and the result is an intimation of an unsettling partnership, more
strange for going unacknowledged ("without a Hint—"). We might simplify
the problem by saying that acquaintance without recognition is what the
speaker desires and hence depicts: to meet death without recognizing it, to
be spared recognition, to have the body dissolve (as the pun in the last line
smartly indicates) without the soul's witness to the dissolution, so neatly to
dispose of the "Matter" (the subject and the body) that pain is an extrava-
gance cleverly evaded. If the flippancy of the formulation and all the legal
wrangling deny that the "Agony" of ending cannot, by definition, but be
"novel," Dickinson faced it squarely in a more sober utterance:

> Our journey had advanced—
> Our feet were almost come
> To that odd Fork in Being's Road—
> Eternity—by Term—
>
> Our pace took sudden awe—
> Our feet—reluctant—led—
> Before—were Cities—but Between—
> The Forest of the Dead—
>
> Retreat—was out of Hope—
> Behind—a Sealed Route—
> Eternity's White Flag—Before—
> And God—at every Gate—
>
> (P 615)

In an earlier poem whose narration of a journey away from life recalls
"Our journey had advanced," Dickinson had written:

> 'Twas the old—road—through pain—
> That unfrequented—one—
> With many a turn—and thorn—
> That stops—at Heaven—
>
> (P 344)

But we note significant differences between the two narrations. For one
thing, the traveler in the first poem, as later stanzas indicate, is not the
speaker; for another, the journey's end is, finally, "too out of sight—" to
apprehend; but most important, since the terminal point in " 'Twas the old
road" is heaven, the brink of the speaker's vision, the boundary point that
prohibits further travel, remains just this side of death. Such a designation of
boundary is, as we have seen, characteristic of the poems we have been

examining. In "That after Horror that 'twas *us*," and even in poems whose subject is the relationship between figural and literal death ("I felt a Funeral in my Brain," and " 'Twas like a Maelstrom with a notch"), the placement of boundary occurs at that moment prior to death—or, in the case of the former poem, prior to unconsciousness—which mediates between life and death. In "Our journey had advanced," however, as Geoffrey Hartman, Robert Weisbuch, and Harold Bloom have suggested, an interesting displacement is effected: death, no longer the terminus of experience, becomes instead a mediating point, a middle ground from whose territory a speaker can gaze further, into the reaches of eternity. The poem's premise, in other words, might be explained as follows: if death is not conclusion, is in fact only a step, albeit a significant one, along the way then it can be depicted as known or, at any rate, subject to knowledge. For the psychological requirement of such poems seems to be not that death be depicted as unknowable, but rather that *some* terminal point be depicted as unknowable. Once one adds a new element to the customary sequence, a "beyond" to death, one extends and amplifies the phenomenologically inhabitable territory, and relocates the crucial boundary point not at the moment of death, but rather after it.

In "Our journey had advanced," which almost asks to be read as a diagram subject to its own revision, our picture of the poem's geography alters with the speaker's own more sophisticated appreciation of it. The first stanza seems to imply a conventional terminal point to experience: one branch of the fork is "Being" itself, the other branch is "Eternity—" or death; "Eternity—" is an implied consequence of death, with an effective fusion between the two. However, this way of depicting it is apprehended as mistaken close-up. "Sudden awe—" is a consequence of the speaker's recognition that death and "Eternity—" are not the same; the fork cannot be directly traversed, and the mediating point that separates "Being" from "Eternity—" has dimension and territory of its own. Indeed, as depicted, there is an implied vastness to "The Forest of the Dead—." What had seemed like a "Between—," a point that barely needed mention, has become a formidable space in its own right. Given such a recognition, the territory must now be mapped in new terms. The fork that, in stanza one, involved a simple and single split and that implicitly suggested options, in the concluding stanza straightens and narrows to preclude choice ("Retreat—was out of Hope—") and also to suggest that the road traversed is one-way ("Behind—a Sealed Route—"). What had been represented as a "Fork" is now more accurately depicted as a chronological progression: "Before—" (previous to this) "were Cities—," but they are past. "Between—" (the boundary point swelled to new dimension by the housing of its inhabitants) is "The Forest of the Dead—." Death, in other words, is present. And "Eternity's White Flag—Before—" (ahead) is future.

The two opposite connotations of "Before—" (meaning "prior to" and "in front of") within so brief a space afford a mimetic parody of the poem's pattern of intersecting "identities" that, upon scrutiny, turn out to be different, as "Eternity—" is, for example, different from death, although in stanza one they are perceived implicitly as the same. What appears single or unitary in meaning and identity ("Eternity—" and death) is double; what double (the two-pronged fork of "Being" and "Eternity—") is at least triple, as the designations of "Cities—," "Forest," and "White Flag—" illustrate. For "Eternity—" is not "Term[inus]—," or at least not as the speaker initially thought, but rather lies before her. If, as we saw in the previous chapter, in "Behind Me—dips Eternity—/Before Me—Immortality—," the speaker is, rather simply, the "Term between—" the two, in this more complicated geography, "at the boundary" or "Before—" designates "on both sides of." For in "Our journey had advanced," the boundary line can be re-placed or dis-placed in direct proportion to the speaker's recognition that ending itself, neither stable nor certain, remains subject to perpetual re-definition. In a letter to the Norcross sisters, Dickinson had confessed: "I cannot tell how Eternity seems." Then gesturing toward her own evasiveness: "It sweeps around me like a sea."

In "Our journey had advanced," the representations of boundary correct each other as vision sharpens into revelation and revelation, at the poem's conclusion, fades into blankness. The point at which the multiple conceptions of boundary intersect and the fact of the intersection is of significance, for the poem concludes by obliterating the very distinctions it has been at such pains to establish. White, that color enigmatic for interpretation in all of Dickinson's poems, is here a manifest emblem of inscrutability, a symbol purified of specific content. It signals the existence of eternity, marks it, and just as insistently seals it from view. If "Eternity's White Flag—" is the sign of meaning that cannot be divined at a distance, the poem's concluding line points to the agent of that meaning. But unlike the carefully charted areas of "Being," death and "Eternity—," "God—at every Gate—," or ubiquitous presence, obscures distinction and insists on showing up the intersection of meanings about which I spoke earlier. The poem concludes with a suffusion of whiteness and vigilance, both of which overpower and imply the merging of the separate states previously articulated. The speaker's apprehension of "Eternity—" and of God's presiding presence over everything has not so much its own meaning as an effect of obliterating discrete meanings. Swallowed up in the enormousness of colorlessness and divine presence, the terminus of meaning and distinction intersects with the end of their necessity.

"That after Horror that 'twas *us*," "I read my sentence steadily," and "Our journey had advanced" allow us to linger in death's presence without actually going beyond it. Unlike the poems that fuse the literal and the figural and unlike those that effect temporal fusions between life and death, these utterances are halted from fusion by the very prohibition to knowledge that experience implies. The following two poems defy such prohibitions. While the temporal fusion between life and death is more apparently dramatic than any we have encountered so far, its result seems to throw death into a form that shrugs off comprehension or correspondence. Death, in these poems, though assumed and, in one instance, personified, is not fused or confused with anything; it is most distinctly itself, and in both of the poems I shall examine its purpose seems to be the implicit chastisement of the speaker for the boldness of the poems' very premise. Make the future present though she will, death's meaning still lingers beyond it. A speaker may put herself in a carriage with death and hand him the reins, but for all the intimacy this implies, the journey's end remains a mystery.

The crossing point between life and death is seen from a new perspective when a dead person reflects on the past-tense occurrence of the moment of her dying and, in so doing, reconstructs it as if it were present. Dying here is not projected or imagined. It is rather recollected:

> I heard a Fly buzz—when I died—
> The Stillness in the Room
> Was like the Stillness in the Air—
> Between the Heaves of Storm—
>
> The Eyes around—had wrung them dry—
> And Breaths were gathering firm
> For that last Onset—when the King
> Be witnessed—in the Room—
>
> I willed my Keepsakes—Signed away
> What portion of me be
> Assignable—and then it was
> There interposed a Fly—
>
> With Blue—uncertain stumbling Buzz—
> Between the light—and me—
> And then the Windows failed—and then
> I could not see to see—
>
> (P 465)

We must imagine the speaker looking back on an experience in which her expectations of death were foiled by its reality. The poem begins with the speaker's perception of the fly, not yet a central awareness both because of the way in which the fly manifests itself (as sound) and because of the degree to which it manifests itself (as a triviality). As a consequence of the speaker's belief in the magnitude of the event and the propriety with which it should be enacted, the fly seems merely indecorous, as yet a marginal disturbance, attracting her attention the way in which something we have not yet invested with meaning does. In a poem very much concerned with the question of vision, it is perhaps strange that the dominant concern in stanza one should be auditory. But upon reflection it makes sense, for the speaker is hearing a droning in the background before the source of the noise comes into view. The poem describes the way in which things come into view, slowly.

What is striking in the second stanza is the speaker's lack of involvement in the little drama that is being played out. She is acutely conscious that there will be a struggle with death, but she imagines it is the people around her who will undergo it. Her detachment and tranquility seem appropriate if we imagine them to come in the aftermath of pain, a subject that is absent in the poem and whose absence helps to place the experience at the moment before death. At such a moment, the speaker's concern is focused on others, for being the center of attention with all eyes upon her, she is at leisure to return the stare. Her concern with her audience continues in the third stanza and prompts the tone of officiousness there. Wanting to set things straight, the speaker wishes to add the finishing touches to her life, to conclude it the way one would a business deal. The desire to structure and control experience is not, however, carried out in total blindness, for she is clearly cognizant of those "Keepsakes—" not hers to give. Even at this point her conception of dying may be a preconception but it is not one founded on total ignorance.

The speaker has been imagining herself as a queen about to leave her people, conscious of the majesty of the occasion, presiding over it. She expects to witness death as majestic, too, or so one infers from the way in which she speaks of him in stanza two. The staginess of the conception, however, has little to do with what Charles Anderson calls "an ironic reversal of the conventional attitudes of [Dickinson's] time and place toward the significance of the moment of death." If it did, the poem would arbitrate between the social meanings and personal ones. But the conflict between preconception and perception takes place inside. Or rather preconception gives way only to darkness. For at the conclusion of the third stanza the fly "interpose[s]," coming between the speaker and the onlookers, between her predictive fantasy of the event and its reality, between life and death. The fact that the fly obscures the former allows the speaker to see the latter. Perspective suddenly shifts to the right thing: from the ritual of dying to the fact of death. It is, of course, the fly who obliterates the speaker's false notions of death, for it is with his coming that she realizes that she is the witness and he the king, that the ceremony is a "stumbling" one. It is from a perspective schooled by the fly that she writes.

As several previous discussions of the poem have acknowledged, the final stanza begins with a complicated synesthesia: "With Blue—uncertain stumbling Buzz—." The adjective "stumbling" (used customarily to describe only an action) here also describes a sound, and the adverb "uncertain" the quality of that sound. The fusion would not be so interesting if its effect were not to evoke that moment in perception when it is about to fail. As in a high fever, noises are amplified, the light in the room takes on strange hues, one effect seems indistinguishable from another. Although there is a more naturalistic explanation for the word "stumbling" (to describe the way in which flies go in and out of our hearing), the poem is so predicated on the phenomenon of displacement and projection (of the speaker's feelings onto the onlookers, of the final blindness onto the "Windows," of the fact of perception onto the experience of death) that the image here suggests another dramatic displacement—the fusion of the fly's death with her own. Thus flies when they are about to die move as if poisoned, sometimes hurl themselves against a ceiling, pause, then rise to circle again, then drop. At this moment the changes the speaker is undergoing are fused with their agent: her experience becomes one with the fly's. It is her observance of that fly, being mesmerized by it (in a quite literal sense now, since death is quite literal), that causes her mind to fumble at the world and lose grip of it. The final two lines "And then the Windows failed—and then / I could not see to see—" are brilliant in their underlining of the poem's central premise; namely that death is survived by perception, for in these lines we are told that there are two senses of vision, one of which remains to see and document the speaker's own blindness ("and then / I could not see to see—"). The poem thus penetrates to the invisible imagination which strengthens in response to the loss of visible sight.

I mentioned earlier that the poem presumes a shift of perspective, an enlightened change from the preconception of death to its perception. In order to assume that the speaker is educated by her experience, we must assume the fact of it: we must credit the death as a real one. But the fiction required by the poem renders it logically baffling. For although the poem seems to proceed in a linear fashion toward an end, its entire premise is based on the lack of finality of that end, the speaker who survives death to tell her story of it. We are hence left wondering: How does the poem imagine an ending? If it does not, what replaces a sense of an ending? How does it conceive of the relationship between past, present, and future? To address these questions adequately, we need to look at some theories of time against which the poem's own singular conception may more sharply be visible.

In *Cosmos and History*, Mircea Eliade writes of the primitive desire to make past and present coexist. What supersedes time is a life structured by the repetition of archetypal acts, structured, that is, by "categories and not . . . events. . . . although [the life] takes place in time, [it] does not bear the burden of time, does not record time's irreversibility; in other words, completely ignores what is especially characteristic and decisive in a consciousness of time. Like the mystic, like the religious man in general, the primitive lives in a continual present." In the primitive world that Eliade describes historical acts still occur, but their meaning is metahistorical. Events bear an associative or analogical relationship to each other. The replacement of analogues by unique events, events that guarantee a new present at every moment and, in so doing, render the past irretrievably past, is contingent upon the acknowledgment that experience has a terminal point.

One might, in fact, say it is the garden of Eden that teaches us it is impossible to conceive of a past purified by the attendant conception of its loss. For to understand the meaning of permanence is already to have surrendered the fact of it. If we imagine the Fall to be that moment when man first perceives past and future as forever exiled from the present, lying always outside of it, the new conception destroys the illusion of events as repeating themselves, moving reversibly or in a cyclical direction. Indeed the very premise of Christianity and its providential history depends upon such an eschatology, for while the Old Testament promises a divine judgment that will take place within history, the New Testament promises a judgment that will end it.

The impulse to see patterns in history is very close to the interpretation of events as patterned by ritual repetition or analogue, and in this respect history is a comparable fiction, that which provides significance to what would otherwise be mere chronicity. But the difference between ritual event and historical event lies in the latter's consciousness of the conclusion to all events. In *Christ and Time*, Oscar Cullmann distinguishes between *chronos*, or passing time, and *kairos*, "a point of time that has a special place in the execution of God's plan of salvation," that is, a crucial moment in the drama of eschatology, one that gains significance by its relation to the end. If a shift from the ritual organization of experience to its temporal organization necessitates the acknowledgment of time, many of whose moments are empty of significance, the fiction of history is a means of preserving and systematizing *kairos*, of attending to critical events of the past by regarding them as events of crisis. Imaginative fictions, less constrained because they are not under compulsion to be even selectively true, similarly rescue the world from a random succession of moments; in the world of the imagination the subject matter is always the interruption of daily events by the extraordinary. But *kairos* must come to terms with the facts of chronicity, with the ordinary generation of moments, and this inevitably involves the compunction to understand the very relationship between past, present, and future that ritual repudiates. Augustine spoke of the three temporal senses as "the present of things past, the present of things present, and the present of things future." Attending to his mental synthesis of the three as he recited a psalm, he arrived at the following description:

> I am about to recite a psalm that I know. Before I begin, my expectation extends over the entire psalm. Once I have begun, my memory extends over as much of it as I shall separate off and assign to the past. The life of this action of mine is distended into memory by reason of the part I have spoken and into forethought by reason of the part I am about to speak. But attention is actually present and that which was to be is borne along by it so as to become past. The more this is done and done again, so much the more is memory lengthened by a shortening of expectation, until the entire expectation is exhausted. When this is done the whole action is completed and passes into memory. What takes place in the whole psalm takes place also in each of its parts and in each of its syllables. The same thing holds for a longer action, of which perhaps the psalm is a small part. The same thing holds for a man's entire life, the parts of which are all the man's actions. The same thing holds throughout the whole age of the sons of men, the parts of which are the lives of all men.

Contrary to Augustine's attempt to distinguish between the three temporal senses, the intention of much modern poetry and fiction lies precisely in the effort to fuse past and present, meaningful event and trivia. Thus the distinction between mere chronicity and crucial event, which the historical fiction tried so hard to establish, has been effectively annihilated. As Robbe-Grillet writes in *For a New Novel*, "In the modern narrative, time seems to be cut off from its temporality. It no longer passes. It no longer completes anything. . . . Here space destroys time, and time sabotages space. Description makes no headway, contradicts itself, turns in circles. Moment denies continuity." We may say that the representation has gone full circle: from the primitive denial of time and the "pastness" of experience, to the creation of a historical fiction in which experience is obsessed with the fact that it must end—and, in which, therefore, the present is in constant need of understanding its relationship to the past that generated it and to the future in which it will conclude—and, finally, as some critics would have it, the return in modern literature to the representation of experience as timeless and mythic. But what if these ostensibly alternate ways of representing experience are, in fact, not alternate at all, but must be seen as mutually exclusive possibilities that therefore . . . always appear in contradictory relationship to each other? For to stop the succession of moments is, nonetheless, to have their inevitable passing firmly, even desperately, in mind.

If we date our perception of radical boundaries that forever seal us from worlds we forever long to inhabit with the Fall, then we cannot see the denial of temporal and spatial features of experience as a return to mythic or ritual primitivism since that route is unalterably sealed, but must ask what in its own right does such denial mean? With this question we find ourselves back at the specific questions raised in connection with Dickinson's "I heard a Fly buzz when I died," but now with a context in which to consider them, for there the poem denies the very eschatological fact that its meaning depends upon.

I mentioned earlier that one consequence of the absence of a fixed boundary line between life and death is the fusion of subjective and objective time. In "I heard a Fly buzz," in other words, we have no sense of subjective or interior time as substantially different from objective to exterior time. Perhaps this is always the case in the lyric, for the lyric—unlike the novel, whose task it is to legislate the conflict between social and personal reality—presents interior reality as if there were no other with which it must regretfully contend. Hence the sense of leisure about speech (even passionate speech) in the lyric. Marvell's lover (protests to the contrary) can woo his lady for as long as he likes; the borders of the poem withstand any external interruption and, as long as the reader's eyes are on the page, effectively banish it. Sir Walter Raleigh "give[s] the world the lie" with more fervored documentation than we can sustain in comparable moods of skepticism. Dylan Thomas's recollection of childhood in "Fern Hill" walls out for the duration of the poem the very adult world he claims he cannot be free of. Even Milton's dream of his dead wife, "my late espoused saint," disappears only when he violates recollection by seeking to prove its existence in reality:

"But O as to embrace me she inclined / I waked, she fled, and day brought back my night." The poem, like Milton's vision, sustains its integrity for as long as one does not puncture it with the outside world. For the poem, like the vision, shrinks from mediation. Before the attempt at mediation with the social world, the poem ruptures, breaks off; it will not come into relation with, be on the same plane as, the social world. While this could, of course, be said of any imaginative fiction—talk to a character in a novel and he will not answer—no imaginative fiction is as resistant to the interruption of its interior speech as the lyric. For the lyric, unlike the drama or the novel, does not have to contend with authorial description, explanatory asides, or any other manipulative intrusion of its space. Nor need it weather the periodic interruptions guaranteed by act, scene, or chapter divisions. Most important, however, it must attend to no more than one (its own) speaking voice. This fact makes the self in the lyric unitary, and gives it the illusion of alone holding sway over the universe, there being, for all practical purposes, no one else, nothing else, to inhabit it.

As a consequence of the banishing of the social world, the network of lines that comprise the pressures of social or objective time are equally consigned to temporary obscurity. The consignment makes room for the poem by allowing it to hang, as it were, in front of social time much the way a painting hangs in front of a wall. While this covering procedure is, as I have been suggesting, a customary occurrence in all lyrics, it becomes noteworthy when a poem explicitly denies an aspect of social or objective fact that we know, on other terms, to be undeniable. The assertion that one can come back from the dead to tell one's story of it so clearly counters the possible that our attention is focused on the effective annihilation of reality; for in this case, the fiction not only "covers" reality, it also insists that reality does not exist. This may make "I heard a Fly buzz" appear to possess the characteristics Robbe-Grillet attributes to modern literature: the embrace of timeless, mythic reality, the externality and hence congruence of thought and event, all effective activity manifest on one plane. But appearance is, in this case, illusion. For the lyric which seems to evade social reality must at some point acknowledge its attachment to the social world which, however denied by the illusion of the lyric's freedom, must nonetheless be assured by its desire for intelligibility. At what point do illusion and reality intersect and how does illusion manage to camouflage the intersection with sufficient art to deny it? For since the relationship I have been describing is a covert one, it follows that in every fiction there will be a crucial tension between the fact of such a relationship and the lyric's efforts to deny, disguise, or transform it.

In order to maintain its status as fiction the lyric must assert its deviance from the strictures of reality and, at the same time, assert the unreliability of the adherence to the impossible. Thus not only tension but contradiction itself is at the heart of the lyric's power over us. . . .

The contradiction between social and private time is the lyric's generating impulse, for the self who would keep its own time, who would live in a world of perpetual *kairos* where events are significant because of the power one has to transform them, must acknowledge the less malleable dictates of the outside world, its scrupulous if simple-minded adherence to *chronos*. In "I heard a Fly buzz when I died," the collision between the two senses of time occurs at the poem's ending, and is just as resolutely uncommented upon by it. For the demands set by the fictional world of *kairos*, and by the equally clamoring world of *chronos*, make no concessions to each other. The most that can be hoped for is the discovery of the coincidence of the two, their temporary appearance at the same moment and along the same temporal plane. Hence in "I heard a Fly buzz," the moment of perception coincides with the moment of death at the poem's ending and, in so doing, effects a temporary rapprochement between the two. The conflict that it has been the poem's function to *manifest* here comes to an end. But we might more properly conclude not that the conflict has reached resolution, since by definition there is no resolution, but rather that it has momentarily played itself out. Indeed it is the genius of the poem to collapse the distinction between subjective and objective time, to assert that an eternity of consciousness and a finite consciousness painfully subject to instant termination at the mere caprice of an insensate world are time schemes compatible, even complementary. Thus two notions logically exclusive—that death is the end of life, specifically conceived of as loss of consciousness, and that perception is the end of life (consciousness continued, even heightened)—are in the poem stalwartly presented as if they were the same thing.

The relationship between perception (or consciousness) as terminus and death as terminus thus comes to be the implicit subject of the poem. The illusion that perception as finality replaces the finality of death so seems to prompt an exchange of the ordinary characteristics of each that perception assumes many of death's properties: secrecy, private apprehension, and closure. As a consequence of the intersection of perception and death, the boldness of the poem's flaunting of border is softened since its progression from the fact of death to the recollection of dying and back again to the moment of death leaves the reader at a conventional moment. It is as if the poem had moved along the same ground twice, but each time in an opposite direction: once from death back to life and, the second time, from life to death. Death, so often conceived by Dickinson as a journey, is here retraveled and hence presumed to be understood. In the previous chapter I suggested that the meaning of an experience could not be ascertained until its conclusion; hence the "Loaded Gun . . . /Without—the power to die—" (P 754) eludes interpretation. In these poems, too, completion is meaning now no longer from the point of view of the fragmentary life, but rather from the point of view of the life in touch with its own totality. If this is magical, Dickinson seems to assert that only from such magic can meaning be made. Like Eliade's description of the replacement of experience as event with experience as category, dying is here categorical rather than conclusive. That assumption is examined more explicitly in what is perhaps Dickinson's most complex utterance on the subject of death:

> Because I could not stop for Death—
> He kindly stopped for me—

The Carriage held but just Ourselves—
And Immortality.

We slowly drove—He knew no haste
And I had put away
My labor and my leisure too,
For His Civility—

We passed the School, where Children strove
At Recess—in the Ring—
We passed the Fields of Gazing Grain—
We passed the Setting Sun—

Or rather—He passed Us—
The Dews drew quivering and chill—
For only Gossamer, my Gown—
My Tippet—only Tulle—

We paused before a House that seemed
A Swelling of the Ground—
The Roof was scarcely visible—
The Cornice—in the Ground—

Since then—'tis Centuries—and yet
Feels shorter than the Day
I first surmised the Horses' Heads
Were toward Eternity—

(P 712)

Yvor Winters has spoken of the poem's subject as "the daily realization of the imminence of death—it is a poem of departure from life, an intensely conscious leave-taking." But in its final claim to actually experience death, Winters has found it fraudulent. There is, of course, a way out of or around the dilemma of posthumous speech and that is to suppose that the entire ride with death is, as the last stanza indicates, a "surmise," and " 'tis Centuries—," a colloquial hyperbole. But we ought not insist that the poem's interpretation pivot on the importance of this word. For we ignore its own struggle with extraordinary claims if we insist too quickly on its adherence to traditional limits.

In one respect, the speaker's assertions that she "could not stop for Death—" must be taken as the romantic protest of a self not yet disabused of the fantasy that her whims, however capricious, will withstand the larger temporal demands of the external world. Thus the first line, like any idiosyncratic representation of the world, must come to grips with the tyranny of more general meanings, not the least of which can be read in the inviolable stand of the universe, every bit as willful as the isolate self. But initially the world seems to cater to the self's needs; since the speaker does not have time (one implication of "could not stop") for death, she is deferred to by the world ("he kindly stopped for me—"). In another respect, we must see the first line not only as willful (had not time for) but also as the admission of a disabling fact (could not). The second line responds to the doubleness of conception. What, in other words, in one context is deference, in another is coercion, and since the poem balances tonally between these extremes it is important to note the dexterity with which they are compacted in the first two lines.

There is, of course, further sense in which death stops for the speaker, and that is in the fusion I alluded to earlier between interior and exterior senses of time, so that the consequence of the meeting in the carriage is the death of otherness. The poem presumes to rid death of its otherness, to familiarize it, literally to adopt its perspective and in so doing to effect a synthesis between self and other, internal time and the faster, more relentless beat of the world. Using more traditional terms to describe the union, Allen Tate speaks of the poem's "subtly interfused erotic motive, which the idea of death has presented to most romantic poets, love being a symbol interchangeable with death." It is true that the poem is charged with eroticism whose end or aim is union, perhaps as we conventionally know it, a synthesis of self and other for the explicit purpose of the transformation of other or, if that proves impossible, for the loss of self. Death's heralding phenomenon, the loss of self, would be almost welcomed if self at this point could be magically fused with other. . . .

Indeed the trinity of death, self, immortality, however ironic a parody of the holy paradigm, at least promises a conventional fulfillment of the idea that the body's end coincides with the soul's everlasting life. But, as in "Our journey had advanced," death so frequently conceptualized as identical with eternity here suffers a radical displacement from it. While both poems suggest a discrepancy between eternity and death, the former poem hedges on the question of where the speaker stands with respect to that discrepancy, at its conclusion seeming to locate her safely in front of or "before" death. "Because I could not stop for Death," on the other hand, pushes revision one step further, daring to leave the speaker stranded in the moment of death.

Along these revisionary lines, the ride to death that we might have supposed to take place through territory unknown, we discover in stanza three to reveal commonplace sights but now fused with spectacle. The path out of the world is also apparently the one through it and in the compression of the three images ("the School, where Children strove," "the Fields of Gazing Grain—," "the Setting Sun—") we are introduced to a new kind of visual shorthand. Perhaps what is extraordinary here is the elasticity of reference, how imposingly on the figural scale the images can weigh while, at the same time, never abandoning any of their quite literal specificity. Hence the sight of the children is a circumscribed one by virtue of the specificity of their placement "At Recess—in the Ring—" and, at the same time, the picture takes on the shadings of allegory. This referential flexibility or fusion of literal and figural meanings is potential in the suggestive connotations of the verb "strove," which is a metaphor in the context of the playground (that is, in its literal context) and a mere descriptive verb in the context of the implied larger world (that is, in its figural context). The "Fields of Gazing Grain—" also suggest a literal picture, but one that leans in the direction of emblem; thus the epithet "Gazing" has perhaps been anthropomorphized from the one-directional leaning of grain in the wind, the object of its gazing the speaker herself. The "Children" mark the presence of the world along one stage of the speaker's journey, the "Gazing Grain—" marks the passing of the world (its harkening after the speaker as she rides away from it), and the "Setting Sun—" marks its past. For at least as the third stanza conceives of it, the journey toward eternity is a series of successive and, in the case of the grain, displaced visions giving way finally to blankness.

But just as after the first two stanzas, we are again rescued in the fourth from any settled conception of this journey. As we were initially not to think of the journey taking place out of the world (and hence with the children we are brought back to it), the end of the third stanza having again moved us to the world's edge, we are redeemed from falling over it by the speaker's correction: "Or rather—He passed Us—." It is the defining movement of the poem to deliver us just over the boundary line between life and death and then to recall us. Thus while the poem gives the illusion of a one-directional movement, albeit a halting one, we discover upon closer scrutiny that the movements are multiple and, as in "I heard a Fly buzz when I died," constitutive of flux, back and forth over the boundary from life to death. Despite the correction, "Or rather—He passed Us—," the next lines register a response that would be entirely appropriate to the speaker's passing of the sun. "The Dews drew" round the speaker, her earthly clothes not only inadequate, but actually falling away in deference to the sensation of "chill—" that displaces them as she passes the boundary of the earth. Thus, on the one hand, "chill—" is a mere physiological response to the setting of the sun at night, on the other, it is a metaphor for the earlier assertion that the earth and earthly goods are being exchanged for something else. Implications in the poem, like the more explicit assertions, are contradictory and reflexive, circling back to underline the very premises they seem a moment ago to have denied. Given such ambiguity, we are constantly in a quandary about how to place the journey that, at any one point, undermines the very certainty of conception it has previously established. Something of the same ambiguity, and for similar reasons, is revealed in George Herbert's "Redemption":

> Having been tenant long to a rich Lord,
> Not thriving, I resolved to be bold,
> And make a suit unto him, to afford
>   A new small-rented lease, and cancell th' old.
>   In heaven at his manour I him sought:
> They told me there, that he was lately gone
> About some land, which he had dearly bought
>   Long since on earth, to take possession.

> I straight return'd, and knowing his great birth,
> Sought him accordingly in great resorts;
> In cities, theaters, gardens, parks and courts:
>   At length I heard a ragged noise and mirth
> Of theeves and murderers: there I him espied,
> Who straight, *Your suit is granted*, said and died.

More boldly perhaps and with an acutely dramatic sense of its own contradictions, "Redemption" fuses past and present; earth and heaven; the feudal lord with his earthly mansion and the heavenly Lord with His divine estate; the lease of a new house and the lease afforded by the new dispensation; the speaker as individual man making a petition to God and as all mankind for whose collective sake Christ sacrificed His life. These fusions are complemented by a series of effective displacements each of which depends upon the disregard of conventional boundary. Thus, for example, the speaker travels to heaven (without dying) where he expects to find Christ (whose existence he could not possibly know about prior to the occurrence in the last line) and finding Him absent (on earth for the explicit purpose of granting the petition the speaker has not yet made to Him) the speaker returns to earth (mistakenly imagining that wealth houses divinity) only to be distracted by the "ragged noise and mirth" of the crucifixion itself and the simultaneity of Christ's death and man's redemption. The intent of such fusions and boundary crossings or, at any rate, their *primary* effect, is two-fold: first, to cast the problem of man's salvation in inescapably personal terms that bring him into direct and literal relationship with Christ so that he finds himself both the explicit cause of the sacrifice and its only beneficiary; and second, to depict both the petition and its granting as unalterably present tense. No longer relegated to historical fact, in the timeless world of need and its fulfillment, the moment is charged with the history-making event of man's redemption, which converts past into an ineluctable present, and insists that meaning win its way free from generalization.

While Dickinson's representation of the ride with death is less histrionic, it is as insistent in our coming to terms with the personalization of the event and of its perpetual reenactment in the present. For the grave that is "paused before" in the fifth stanza, with the tombstone lying flat against the ground ("scarcely visible—"), is seen from the outside and then (by the transformation of spatial considerations into temporal ones) is passed by or through: "Since then—'tis Centuries—." The poem's concluding stanza both fulfills the traditional Christian notion that while the endurance of death is essential for the reaching of eternity, the two are not identical, and by splitting death and eternity with the space of "Centuries—," challenges that traditional notion. The poem that has thus far played havoc with our efforts to fix its journey in any conventional time or space, on this side of death or the other, concludes with an announcement about the origins of its speech, now explicitly equivocal: " 'tis Centuries—and yet/Feels shorter than the Day." What in "There's a certain Slant of light" had been a clear relationship between figure and its fulfillment (a sense of perceptive enlightenment accruing from the movement of one to the other) is in this poem manifestly baffling. For one might observe that for all the apparent movement here, there are no real progressions in the poem at all. If the correction "We passed the Setting Sun—/Or rather—He passed Us—" may be construed as a confirmation of the slowness of the drive alluded to earlier in the poem, the last stanza seems to insist that the carriage is standing still, moving if at all, as we say, in place. For the predominant sense of this journey is not simply its endlessness; it is also the curious back and forth sweep of its images conveying, as they do, the perpetual return to what has been perpetually taken leave of.

Angus Fletcher, speaking in terms applicable to "Because I could not stop for Death," documents the characteristics of allegorical journeys as surrealistic in imagery (as for example, the "Gazing Grain—"), paratactic in rhythm or structure (as indeed we can hear in the acknowledged form of movement: "We passed . . . We passed . . . We passed . . . Or rather—He passed Us . . . We Paused . . ."), and almost always incomplete: "It is logically quite natural for the extension to be infinite, since by definition there is no such thing as the whole of any analogy; all analogies are incomplete, and incompletable, and allegory simply records this analogical relation in a dramatic or narrative form."

But while the poem has some of the characteristics of allegory, it nonetheless seems to defy such easy classification. Thus the utterance is not quite allegory because it is not strongly iconographic (its figures do not have a one-to-one correspondence with a representational base), and at the same time, these figures are sufficiently rigid to preclude the freeing up of associations that is characteristic of the symbol. We recall Coleridge's distinction between a symbolic and an allegorical structure. A symbol presupposes a unity with its object. It denies the separateness between subject and object by creating a synecdochic relationship between itself and the totality of what it represents; like the relationship between figure and thing figured discussed in the first part of this chapter, it is always part of that totality. Allegory, on the other hand, is a sign that refers to a specific meaning from which it continually remains detached. Through its abstract embodiment, the allegorical form makes the distance between itself and its original meaning clearly manifest. It accentuates the absolute cleavage between subject and object. Since the speaker in "Because I could not stop for Death" balances between the boast of knowledge and the confession of ignorance, between a oneness with death and an inescapable difference from it, we may regard the poem as a partial allegory. The inability to know eternity, the failure to be at one with it, is, we might say, what the allegory of "Because I could not stop for Death" makes manifest. The ride with death, though it espouses to reveal a future that is past, in fact casts both past and future in the indeterminate present of the last stanza. Unable to arrive at a fixed conception, it must rest on the bravado (and it implicitly knows this) of its initial claim. Thus death is not really civilized; the boundary between otherness and self, life and death, is crossed, but only in presumption, and we might regard this fact as the real confession of disappointment in the poem's last stanza.

Ahab, in *Moby-Dick*, whom Daniel Hoffman has characterized as having "The most allegorical mind of any character in American fiction" because of his willful insistence on reducing protean experience to his monomaniacal meaning for it, wished to strike through the "pasteboard mask" of appearances to reality. Ishmael, no less mesmerized by the mask, albeit attributing a different name to it, spoke of that image which man is drawn to in rivers and fountains as "the ungraspable phantom of life." Treat that "phantom" as symbol, however, and the self, rapt in the contemplation of its own reflection, falls toward it in fusion and, like Narcissus, drowns. *Moby-Dick* may in fact be viewed as a struggle between allegorical modes of perceiving the world and symbolic ones. The extremity of either choice is black magic— the egotistical projection of the self, or the resolute withholding of it. In *American Renaissance*, F. O. Matthiessen's suggestive discussion of the symbolic and allegorical biases of Melville and Hawthorne seems, at times, to intend a definition of the pervasive dialectic of nineteenth-century America, for in the one case man attempts to transform the world by reshaping it, in the other, he "deals with fixities." Paul de Man, too, imagines the dialectical pull between symbolizing structures and allegorizing ones to define Romanticism and also to characterize its moral overtones, for the belief in organic totality is a delusive myth. Elaborating on the distinction between allegory and symbol in the specific terms of the temporal difference that separates the self from that with which it desires to fuse, de Man calls to mind the dilemma of Dickinson's speaker in "Because I could not stop for Death": "Whereas the symbol postulates the possibility of an identity of identification, allegory designates primarily a distance in relation to its own origin, and, renouncing the nostalgia and the desire to coincide, it establishes its language in the void of this temporal distance. In so doing, it prevents the self from an illusory identification with the non-self, which is now fully, though painfully, recognized as a non-self." The self is not the thing it aspires to know. Nor can its representation of reality dissolve the distinction between the two.

I dwell on such issues because they provide a context for that curious shift from the assertion of knowledge in "Because I could not stop for Death—" to the confession of its failure, from the intimation that the ride to death defies the phenomenal characteristics of the world, to the admission that it does not. This pendulum that swings back and forth across the boundary separating life from death, time from timelessness, becomes the dialectic in which the self comes to terms with its impulse for fusion and identic relationship, and with the loss attendant upon the realization that such fusion is truly illusory. The self coming to terms with the fact of its mortality from which no fusion with death can rescue it cannot complete or make good on the certain knowledge that the poem's first stanza implicitly promised. The effort to make all events associative ones, or "repetitive," in the sense of identic (to recall Eliade's description of the primitive organization of experience) is to deny the most painful boundary between self and other that the world makes manifest, to cheat the world of its otherness and hence, of necessity, the self of its defining integrity.

Yet art does attempt such a cheat: it will make its voice heard, will *have* a voice where no voice can really be, and this willful fact brings us back, as I promised, to Panofsky's essay on how the phrase *Et in Arcadia ego*, once attributed to a death's-head, grew with Poussin's painting of the scene to be attributed to a dead person himself; how, concomitantly, what was once a matter of terror became merely an occasion for meditative speculation on the fact of death. In Guercino's painting of the death's-head the fact of terror and the unknown quality of death are wedded to each other. For it is clear that the skull which represents death is a mere emblem of it, a sign that conceals its meaning. Similarly, in those poems discussed in the first half of this chapter, death's appearance is incomplete and unknown, a "boiling Wheel" or a "Maelstrom, with a notch," and hence prompts terror. The soul is "secure" only in the presence of "A Sepulchre" for, in the terms of "There's a certain Slant of light," figural reality loses its indirection or "Slant" only when it straightens into the fulfillment of death. In lieu of that fulfillment, these poems collapse the distinction between subject and object, figure and thing figured, as if collapse into, or fusion with, the object in question might substitute for knowledge. In the proleptic utterances, however ("I heard a Fly buzz when I died" and "Because I could not stop for Death"), which speak as if from beyond the grave, the turmoil of the earlier poems has been smoothed into tranquillity, for in the beginning of "Because I could not stop for Death," as in Poussin's painting, death is no otherness and it does not create otherness by its occurrence; the dead person still assumes mortal shape and still possesses voice sufficient to speak. That terror should disappear as a consequence of knowledge gained about the thing feared is not especially surprising. But what if the nostalgia implicit in both Poussin's painting and Dickinson's poem is occasioned not simply by the loss of life, but also by the loss of self, its translation into a mere emblem of survival, no longer recognizable in human terms?

Dickinson's intuition that she must preserve an otherness in order to preserve a self abruptly distorts the seeming unity of personae in the carriage. The acknowledgment of time (" 'tis Centuries—and yet/Feels shorter than the Day") is equally an acknowledgment that the desired and, for a time, achieved fusion between subjective and objective time will not hold. The speaker can finesse the illusion of such unity, but the last stanza points up all the problems with which it must come to terms. The experience of death still leaves eternity an unknown; the journey cannot be completed conceptually, is in need of an end that is not, and will never be, conceptually forthcoming. For allegory must come to terms with the conceptual inadequacy of its desire, with the real zero beyond which invention cannot go. Despite the fact that the allegoric impulse is contrary to the mimetic one— would rather perfect the world than represent it—it must nonetheless fall back on the same storehouse of images. Thus the transformation from the death's-head to the dead man who has words and, in Dickinson's poems, from the terror before death to the imaginative construction of speech after it, civilizes death in the only way we apparently know how. But such "civility" is an illusion. Death without the death of speech, death without the cessation of time—in a land of unlikeness, a true Arcadia, this is no place we know.

Where does the ride with Death and Immortality take place? And is it possible to say with any certainty how long—centuries or a day—it lasts? I suggested earlier that lyric time, although at some points coincidental with actual time, hangs in front of it observing only those properties of actuality that it chooses. Perhaps it would be more accurate to say not that the lyric defies the temporal-spatial axis but that it has its own referential axis, neither clearly future (though an utterance often implies its own continuous action) nor clearly past (though it often seems past because its own action is predicated on itself as on a history). " 'Tis so appalling—it exhilarates—/So over Horror, it half Captivates—/The Soul stares after it, secure—." "Stares," we might say, timelessly or for all time. Similarly, the "certain Slant of light,/ Winter Afternoons—/" "oppresses" with a present-tense verb of sufficient heft to secure both past and future under its aegis. "Slow tramp the Centuries,/And the Cycles wheel!" When and where are irrelevant questions. Even the past-tense "Because I could not stop for Death" brings us up short against the present of its disturbing conclusion. The speaker in the throes of the movement that pulls her forward seems to turn for a moment toward us and, in so doing, to stop the carriage's action allowing us to place it. And while "I heard a Fly buzz when I died" is narrated wholly in the past, it is no less adamant in its illusion that the incidents it relates are present. One might hazard the generalization that although Dickinson's poems on death assume the past tense with characteristic regularity precisely so that the death the speaker claims to have survived will be credited as a fait accompli, nonetheless, the very task of the entire poem is to re-present it.

George Wright, in "The Lyric Present: Simple Present Verbs in English Poems," offers conclusions to an important statistical study he has compiled on verb forms in the lyric. As the title of his essay implies, Wright documents the fact that the tense most characteristic of, and most frequently used in, the lyric is the simple present tense. But this present seems to contain a multiplicity of temporal features that we ordinarily think of as mutually exclusive. It is past-like as well as indicative of future. It locates action temporally, but not in time as we know it. Although timeless, this present tense implies duration. The distance cast by "the look of Death—" remains. Giving way to nothing else, it is what we return to every time we reread the poem. And, Wright suggests, the lyric not only implies temporal permanence and permanent temporal elusiveness, but a corresponding spatial dislocation as well, as its contradictions preserve the structure of the ambiguities that element it. A poem especially evasive about its spatial location is Yeats's "Among School Children," for if we ask where "Labour is blossoming or dancing," we are answered, but mysteriously:

> Labour is blossoming or dancing where
> The body is not bruised to pleasure soul,

Nor beauty born out of its own despair,
Nor blear-eyed wisdom out of midnight oil.

A present that houses the past as well as the future and that, moreover, evades spatial location and fixture is very close to the creation of a temporal myth built between past and future, real and imagined time, this world and some other. Keats's "Do I wake or sleep" poses a question about his state in the aftermath of the vision, but answer it either way and the vision still remains fixed, even in the permanence of its fleeting. The present tense is so characteristic of the lyric that Wright terms it "the lyric tense," and he adds that its assertion of presence may be the poem's dominant symbolic gesture—an idea we shall examine in the next chapter—as it transfixes reality so that reality remains caught precisely at the moment of its passing: "The lyric tense detail is almost always felt as symbolic, and as with Yeats's swans that drift or his birds that reel, the tense often appears at the most climactic moment, the moment at which some symbolic transformation, some metamorphosis takes place. . . . On such occasions the device of lyric tense seems not merely to frame but almost to *be* the metaphor."

Such metaphors inhere not simply in the slowing of action but also in the attribution of pivotal meaning to it, as if the poet assumed that, were action visible, the relational ties between subject and object might sharpen to clarity. These relations, the ones between subject and object, as well as between one temporal category and another, are, as I have been suggesting, compressed in the lyric or collapsed by it in what sometimes seems to be a mimetic gesture of the perceptual syntheses characteristic of thinking itself. Thus the poems are projective in nature, enacting the very displacements of experience. In them perception refuses to be riveted to one spot, shifts, as in "Our journey had advanced," to relocate itself in accordance with the progressive lessons of experience. The displacements we have seen (from the "Failed" windows in "I heard a Fly buzz when I died" to the "Gazing Grain—" in "Because I could not stop for Death") remind us how thoroughly the world remains saturated in our perceptual terms for it, how seductive syntheses and fusion are when we are overtaken by the starkness of the world's own terms. The color white, purged of meaning (which so haunts Dickinson's work, as we remember it haunts Melville's), is perhaps the way the world looks when we represent it accurately, but at such moments it is also bleached to nothing. The problem, of course, is how to give it coloration, to see it, as we say, in its own terms, for the very conception that something *has* its own terms is itself an anthropomorphic one. If the lyric shrinks from mediation with the outside world, it seeks no less to preserve the integrity of its own temporal fusions, for to mediate between them, to establish discrete barriers between past, present, and future is to distort the very synchrony of its knowledge. In Augustine's terms "the present of things past, the present of things present, and the present of things future" all have in common the shared moment of their acknowledgment.

Contradiction between social and personal time is, as I implied previously, the lyric's generating impulse, and Dickinson's proleptic utterances, by exaggerating these contradictions, draw our attention to them. The greatest contradiction lies in the lyric's fixity of its own present. This mythologizing of the lyric present, the insistence that present and, by implication, presence can achieve permanence is perhaps accounted for by the tenacious hold the past has on the present, by its dexterity in casting itself as if it still were. Hence the fusion between past and present is often so axiomatic as to escape attention, though in the next chapter we shall see that loss discovers its origin when space comes to intervene between the two. The present, here, then, seems permanent partly by virtue of how thoroughly it confuses itself with its own history, on the one hand, and its destiny, on the other. Unable to separate itself from what it has been and from what it desires to be, the present in Dickinson's poems (as if by association) projects even more daring fusions between the time before death and that after it. A passage from Beckett's *Malloy* which Wright calls our attention to indicates how natural such fusions are: "When I try and think riding I lose my balance and fall. I speak in the present tense, it is so easy to speak in the present tense, when speaking of the past. It is the mythological present, don't mind it." The present may be described as that moment in which all past moments (potentially) coincide with consciousness, just as the future only exists insofar as it can be conceived of or conjured by a consciousness that is present. The present is thus that fulcral moment that not only arbitrates between past and future but that also embodies them. For of themselves, both past and future may be conceived of as having subject without locution, spirit without body, the evasiveness of pure air. "Everything we say/of the past," wrote Wallace Stevens, "is description without place." Indeed, the same is true of our words for the future. Only the present has a sure space of its own.

In the poems discussed [elsewhere], death is eschewed, because it details the end of the self; here it is desired, but minus its consequences. Thus permanence (and hence an endless present) is attributed to death, and longed for in the form of fusion with it. Fusions are actively sought and achieved in the poems discussed in the first part of this chapter. In such poems, a state fuses with the terms of its own figuration, as death fuses with the image of light. In the proleptic utterances, however, where the fusion is sought perhaps even more strenuously because the stakes are higher, the gain of temporal fusion seems to necessitate the sacrifice of union between subject and object. The premise of these poems may be that temporal collapse will blur the distinction between subject and object, death and self, will make them one; the poems discover, however, that to preserve identity time and space must intervene. For the pain that binds the self to its own boundaries also defines it. What is restrictive in one context is definitional in another. Thus the poem may subject the world to reconstruction, but only one feature at a time. Temporal fusions *or* the fusion between subject and object—either may be ventured but not, apparently, at the same time. For knock down all the walls of the house at once and the structure crumbles to ruin.

Dickinson once wrote of "An Omen in the Bone/Of Death's tremendous nearness—" (P 532). Perhaps she took the omen for prophecy and with characteristic impatience pushed it toward a fulfillment she herself could appreciate. For her lyrics, as I have been suggesting, attempt to cross boundaries, to blur distinctions between life and death, time and timelessness, figure and its fulfillment, or, to put it more accurately, to wear a passage between them—which is the poem—and, in so doing, to seek refuge in a presence whose permanence will withstand temporal change. They thus go in search of the very mythical time that Wright tells us is characteristic of most lyric poems. For the idiosyncratic fusions Dickinson's lyrics make explicit, most lyrics imply. They record an event that, in Wright's words, "has happened—is happening—happens." In the mythological present the self goes forth bravely into places it does not and cannot know, dreaming the very landscapes to which it will forever be denied real access. It seeks symbolic correspondences and stumbles upon differences. It desires to break loose into timelessness and feels instead the weightless net of temporal ensnarement. It would give anything to become an otherness, but it must settle for itself. So it learns how to celebrate that self, even the confusions of its own contradictory impulses. In the process, and shaking itself free from all that would disembody it, the self finds a present, a being, and a voice. These the lyric memorializes.

Two Types of Obscurity
in the Writings of Gertrude Stein

Randa K. Dubnick

Many critics have tried to deal with the difficulties of Gertrude Stein's writing by labeling it "meaningless," "abstract," or "obscure." But such judgments often are inadequate and misleading in their failure to make some important distinctions. In the first place, not all of Stein's writing is obscure. And within that part of her work which is obscure, there are two distinct styles which might be characterized as "abstract," each of which represents a linguistically different kind of obscurity. The first of these two styles developed during the writing of *The Making of Americans* and reached maturity toward the end of that book (as well as in some of the literary "portraits" produced during that same time). The second style is best represented by Stein's *Tender Buttons*.

Stein called the first style *prose* and the second style *poetry*. As will be seen, her definition of each category, and her description of these two obscure styles seem to suggest some of the dualistic distinctions that structuralist thought (from Ferdinand de Saussure to Roman Jakobson and Roland Barthes) has made about language. What might be fruitful, then, and what the structuralist vocabulary seems to make possible, is an examination of the nature and stylistics of each of the two distinct ways in which Stein's writing moves towards the abstract and becomes obscure. All of Stein's writing can be viewed as made up of variations and combinations of the two stylistic preoccupations represented by the participial style of *The Making of Americans* and the associational style of *Tender Buttons*. To understand the stylistics of Gertrude Stein's two basic types of obscurity, one must begin with an examination of these two works. Structuralist theories can aid in this examination by supplying a vocabulary as well as a framework that may identify the basis of her obscurity as her concern with the nature of language

From *The Emporia State Research Studies* 24, no. 3 (Winter 1976). © 1976 by Emporia Kansas State College.

itself. This inquiry may lead to an understanding of the theoretical basis behind Stein's movement toward two kinds of abstraction. In this regard, a look at what was happening in painting, as Cubism also developed two obscure styles, may be helpful. The relationship between Stein's writing and Cubist painting, when seen from a structuralist perspective, seems to be based on common emphases on certain linguistic operations over others. What one discovers is that Stein's comparisons of her writing to the work of the Cubists do not belie a misguided attempt to apply to language artistic theories which are irrelevant and inappropriate to it, as some critics believe: rather, those comparisons represent concerns about the nature of language itself, concerns which are, therefore, appropriately explored within the realm of literature.

Gertrude Stein, in one of her famous lectures, explains the radical stylistic difference between *The Making of Americans* and *Tender Buttons* in terms of the distinction between prose (the main concern of which is the sentence) and poetry (the main concern of which is the noun):

> In *The Making of Americans* . . . a very long prose book made up of sentences and paragraphs . . . I had gotten rid of nouns and adjectives as much as possible by the method of living in adverbs, in pronouns, in adverbial clauses written or implied and in conjunctions. . . . really great written prose is bound to be made up more of verbs adverbs prepositional clauses and conjunctions than nouns. The vocabulary in prose of course is important if you like vocabulary is always important. . . .

However:

> the vocabulary in respect to prose is less important than the parts of speech, and the internal balance and the movement within a given space.

On the other hand,

> Poetry has to do with vocabulary just as prose has not. . . . Poetry is I say essentially a vocabulary just as prose is essentially not. . . .
> And what is the vocabulary of which poetry absolutely is. It is a vocabulary entirely based on the noun as prose is essentially and determinately and vigorously not based on the noun.

In asserting this different emphasis on, first, syntax and, then diction, Stein seems to be touching upon what structural linguists differentiate as the horizontal and vertical axes of language (as formulated by Saussure, Jakobson, and Barthes, with somewhat varying terminology). The horizontal axis links words contiguously. It is

> a combination of signs which has space as a support. In the articulated language, this space is linear and irreversible (it is the "spoken chain"): two elements cannot be pronounced at the same time

(enter, against all, human life): each term here derives it value from its opposition to what precedes and what follows; in the chain of speech, the terms are really united *in praesentia*.

When Stein says that the key element in prose is the sentence, and that verbs, prepositions, and conjunctions (which function to hold the syntax of the sentence together) are important in prose, she is implying an emphasis on the horizontal axis of language.

On the other hand, the vertical axis of language links words by associations based on similarity and/or opposition, and has to do with the selection of words.

"Beside the discourse (syntagmatic plane), the units which have something in common are associated in memory and thus form groups within which various relationships can be found": education can be associated, through its meaning, to *up-bringing* or *training*, and through its sound to *educate, education* or to *application, vindication*. . . . in each series unlike what happens at the syntagmatic level, the terms are united *in absentia*.

Stein characterizes poetry as concerned with vocabulary (and with the noun in particular). Hers is an oblique statement of the obvious observation that in poetry, word choice is of more concern than syntax, which is often suppressed, especially in modern poetry. The choice of a word from among a group of synonyms on the basis of qualities like rhythm and rhyme, or the choice of a poetic vocabulary from within an entire language, is an operation of selection. According to structural linguistic theories the operation of selection functions along the vertical axis of language.

As to Stein's remarks regarding the various parts of speech, Ronald Levinson points out in his article, "Gertrude Stein, William James, and Grammar," that Stein's theoretical formulation of the functions of the parts of speech was apparently greatly influenced by the theories of William James, who, in *Psychology*, compared the "stream of consciousness" to a series of "flights and perchings,"—the "perchings" being substantives ("occupied by sensorial imaginings"), and the "flights" being transitives, ("thoughts of relating, static and dynamic"), which depend on verbs, prepositions, and conjunctions. As Levinson points out, Stein in her philosophy of grammar set forth in "Poetry and Grammar" echoes some of James' theories, especially in the distinction she makes between static words (nouns) and dynamic words (verbs, prepositions). What is original is her use of James' theories as the basis of a distinction between poetry and prose. Here, prose is based on verbs, prepositions, and conjunctions (the "flights"): the words that support syntax. These words function along the horizontal axis and have to do with contiguity: they combine to hold the words of the sentence in relation to one another. Poetry, on the other hand, is based on the noun or the substantive; the "perchings." Roman Jakobson's linguistic analysis of aphasia indicates that these parts of speech have to do with the operation of selection (the vertical axis). Thus, Stein's distinction between prose and poetry is based not merely upon stylistic or formal considerations, but rather on a distinction in emphasis upon what structuralists have since identified as two linguistic, and even mental, operations: similarity (or selection or system) and contiguity (or combination or syntagm).

Though one can see the germs of some of these ideas in James' theories as set forth in *Psychology*, Stein extends and applies them in her creative writing. James describes consciousness as a continuous flow, distinguishes between static and dynamic parts of speech, and discerns two types of association. The first is based on contiguity, meaning habitual association of things existing together in time and space. (This kind of association James identifies as performed even by animals.) The second type is based on similarity of entities not linked in space or time. However, James does not extend this distinction from the realm of association and use it to bifurcate the whole of linguistic operations along these lines as do the theories of structuralism.

Stein's contribution is the creation of an aesthetic based on James's theories and on pragmatism in general, as Robert Haas points out. Through this effort, she arrives at two types of obscurity which function, perhaps coincidentally, as practical illustrations of linguistic theories that were yet to be published at the time she was creating those two styles. (Even the first and most limited formulation of these structural theories in Ferdinand de Saussure's *Course in General Linguistics* was not published until 1916, approximately four years after *Tender Buttons* was written, *circa* 1912.) Furthermore, her writing, which suppresses, first, the vertical axis at the expense of the horizontal axis, and, then, vice versa, foreshadows Jakobson's observations and, then, the other as it occurs in the speech of aphasic patients. Jakobson did not publish these observations until 1956 in "Two Aspects of Language and Two Types of Aphasic Disturbances." Of course, in aphasia, the suppression of either of the two linguistic operations of contiguity and similarity is entirely involuntary and pathological, while Stein's theoretical writings indicate that the creation of each of her two obscure styles was quite consciously undertaken for certain theoretical and aesthetic reasons—all arguments about "automatic writing" to the contrary!

The key stylistic interest in *The Making of Americans*, and in other works of Stein's participial style, is syntax. Grammatically correct but eccentric sentences spin themselves out and grow, clause linked to clause, until they are of paragraph length. She asserts that nothing "has ever been more exciting than diagramming sentences. . . . I like the feeling the everlasting feeling of sentences as they diagram themselves." Her long, repetitive sentences convey the feeling of process and duration, and of the time it gradually takes to get to know a person or to come to grips with an idea. She felt that sentences were not emotional (i.e., the syntax or "internal balance" of the sentence is a given) but that paragraphs were. She illustrates this principle by reference to her dog's drinking water from a dish. The paragraph is emotional in that it prolongs the duration of the idea or perception until the writer feels satisfied. This feeling of satisfaction is subjective and not arrived at by following rules of grammar By extending the sentence to the length approximately of a short paragraph, Stein was trying to achieve an emotional sentence. Many of the stylistic idiosyncrasies of her "participial" style function to extend the length of the sentence. What follows is a passage located near the end of *The Making of Americans*:

> Certainly he was one being living when he was being a being young one, he was often then quite certainly one being almost completely interested in being one being living, he was then quite often wanting to be one being completely interested in being one being living. He certainly then went on being living, he did this thing certainly all of his being living in being young living. He certainly when he was a young one was needing then sometimes to be sure that he was one being living, this is certainly what some being living are needing when they are ones being young ones in being living. David Hersland certainly was one almost completely one being one being living when he was being a young one. Some he was knowing then were certainly being completely living then and being then being young ones in being living then, some were quite a good deal not being one being completely living then when they were being young ones in being living. David Hersland did a good deal of living in being living then when he was a young one. He was knowing very many men and very many knew him then. He remembered some of them in his later living and he did not remember some of them. He certainly was one almost completely then interested in being one being living then.

In this characteristic paragraph (consisting of only nine sentences), Stein uses many grammatical and stylistic strategies to extend the syntax and physical duration of the utterance. For example, one way to extend the syntax is to create very complex sentences, such as "Some he was knowing then were not quite completely being ones being living then, some were a quite a good deal not being ones being completely living then when they were being young ones in being living" (*Making of Americans*). It is characteristic of her writing that, although she may link clause to clause, she often will suppress the use of relative pronouns such as "that" or "who." This method makes it more difficult to divide the sentences into individual clauses, forcing the reader to take a more active role in struggling to follow the sentence structure. Another simple, but less orthodox, means of extending the syntax is by fusing two or more sentences through the comma splice: "He certainly then went on being living, he did this thing certainly all of his being living in being young living" (*Making of Americans*). (One should note, here, that the sparse use of commas also functions to make the reader work harder to follow the sentence.) Another device for stretching the sentence almost to paragraph length is the mechanistic linking together of many independent clauses by a series of conjunctions:

Some are certainly needing to be ones doing something and they
are doing one thing and doing it again and again and again and
again and they are doing another thing and they are doing it again
and again and they are doing another thing and they are doing it
again and again and again and such a one might have been one
doing a very different thing then and doing that then each or any
one of them and doing it again and again and again.

(*Making of Americans*)

Stein's first style is full of participles that function as nouns or adjectives
and verb forms as well, a use which critics have termed a philosophical
choice. Participles prolong the time span to achieve a sense of duration and
process. Moreover, the participle, and particularly the gerund, also help
portray the pragmatic conception of the world as a constantly on-going
event. However, it should be noted that when Stein substitutes, "When he
was being a young one" for "When he was young," the sentence is lengthened by two syllables. Her substitution of the participle for a simpler form of
the verb has the cumulative effect of substantially lengthening the sentence,
especially in view of the fact that, as Hoffman points out, "Probably more
than half her verb forms use some form of the progressive ending." The Stein
sentence is also lengthened by the fact that she so often insists on the
"changing of an adjective into a substantive. Rather than saying 'Everybody
is real,' she changes 'real' into 'a real one.' " Again, this method has the
cumulative effect of lengthening the duration of the reading or the utterance.

In *The Making of Americans*, Stein stretches syntax almost to the breaking
point and simultaneously limits her vocabulary. She moves farther and
farther away from the concrete noun-centered vocabulary of the realistic
novel. In part, the movement is due to her subject matter. *The Making of
Americans* is a monumental attempt to create a chronicle of one family which
could serve as an eternally valid history of all people, past, present, and
future. Herein, she presents people as generalized types, and uses the
characters in the novel to represent all human possibilities. This method led
her from the essentially conventional narrative which dominates the beginning of the book to the generalized and theoretical kind of digression dispersed throughout the novel, but especially prominent towards the end of
the book.

Although the long passage cited earlier concerns David Hersland, Stein
has supplied very little concrete information about him because she was
trying to turn particular and perhaps personal facts (the Hersland family is
considered to be autobiographical by most critics) into universally valid
generalizations. This effort is reflected in the dearth of conventional nouns
and the wealth of pronouns. This is a move towards obscurity in that the
referent of a pronoun is more vague than that of a noun. Verbals are used
instead of conventional nouns and adjectives: "alive" becomes "being living." The same phrase is also used as a noun: David Hersland is interested in
"being living" rather than in life. Probably this construction reflects Stein's

desire to emphasize the transitive linguistic processes over the substantive ones in prose.

Conventional verbs are replaced by participles, which prolong and de-emphasize whatever action is being described. The participles contain very little concrete information. In the passage under discussion, there are only five participles, although each is repeated a number of times (*being, living, wanting, needing, knowing*). The least specific participles are those most often repeated. *Being* and *living* each occur nineteen times in the paragraph.

There are few conventional adjectives in the passage, aside from the participles. As for adverbs, *certainly* occurs a number of times, here, as it does throughout the book. Some critics think that Stein, in this case, is attempting to reassure herself and her reader of the universal validity of her typology. In addition, the fact that she must say *some, many*, and *a good deal* more and more often is seen as her growing recognition of the limitations of what she is doing. The adverb *then* is prevalent in the novel, perhaps related to her attempt to bring all knowledge gained over the passing of time into the present moment. It is also natural that a style which extends syntax will contain many relational words, like prepositions and conjunctions.

The stylistic concerns of Stein's early prose, in both *The Making of Americans* and the early (pre-1912) portraits, are the extension of syntax and the simultaneous circumscription of vocabulary, which is limited not merely in terms of the quantity of words, but also in the degree of specificity allowed to appear. The result is a very vague and generalized portrayal of the subject matter. Thus, *The Making of Americans* fits very neatly her requirements for prose. It is concerned with syntax, and contains many verbs, adverbs and conjunctions, while it reduces the vocabulary, and for the most part, eliminates conventional nouns in favor of pronouns and gerunds.

It is interesting to compare these observations about her prose style with Jakobson's observations about the two aspects of language as they relate to the speech of aphasics. Like Stein's writing, aphasia manifests two basic types of obscurity (although, of course, the obscurity in aphasia is pathological and involuntary, while that in Stein is a voluntary stylistic choice). Jakobson delineates two types of aphasia, each related to an inability to function in terms of one of the two linguistic axes which Roland Barthes has described as "system" (vertical axis) and "syntagm" (horizontal axis). Jakobson refers to these axes respectively as "selection" and "combination":

Any linguistic sign involves two modes of arrangement:

1) Combination. Any sign is made up of constituent signs and/ or occurs only in combination with other signs. This means that any linguistic unit at one and the same time serves as a context for simpler units and/or finds its own context in a more complex linguistic unit. Hence any actual grouping of linguistic units binds them into a superior unit: combination and contexture are two faces of the same operation.

2) Selection. A selection between alternatives implies the possi-

bility of substituting one for the other, equivalent to the former in one respect and different from it in another. Actually selection and substitution are two faces of the same operation.

He points out further that "speech disturbances may affect in varying degrees the individual's capacity for combination and selection of linguistic units, and, indeed, the question of which of these two operations is chiefly impaired proves to be of far-reaching significance in describing, analyzing, and classifying the diverse forms of aphasia." Some of Jakobson's observations regarding the language produced by patients suffering from an inability to perform the operation of selection are somewhat similar to what can be observed in the prose style of *The Making of Americans* and the early portraits. This similarity is not really surprising, since Stein is herein voluntarily suppressing the operation of selection by severely limiting her vocabulary and attempting to eliminate nouns. Jakobson describes some of the speech patterns of aphasics suffering from a similarity disorder as follows:

> the more a word is dependent on the other words of the same sentence and the more it refers to the syntactical context, the less it is affected by the speech disturbance. Therefore words syntactically subordinated by grammatical agreement or government are more tenacious, whereas the main subordinating agent of the sentence, namely the subject, tends to be omitted. . . . Key words may be dropped or superseded by abstract anaphoric substitutes. A specific noun, as Freud noticed, is replaced by a very general one, for instances *machin*, *chose* in the speech of French aphasics. In a dialectal German sample of "amnesiac aphasia" observed by Goldstein, . . . *Ding* "thing" or *Stuckle* "piece" were substituted for all inanimate nouns, and *uberfahren* "perform" for verbs which were identifiable from the context or situation and therefore appeared superfluous to the patient.
>
> Words with an inherent reference to the context, like pronouns and pronominal adverbs, and words serving merely to construct the context, such as connectives and auxiliaries, are particularly prone to survive.

As it will be seen, some of Jakobson's observations about the language of aphasics with a contiguity disorder seem to indicate that this particular form of pathological obscurity shares certain characteristics with Stein's second stylistic interest, which she identified as poetry. For example, *Tender Buttons* represents a radical change from the early prose style of *The Making of Americans* and of other works to that which she called poetry. From prose, with its emphasis on syntax and its suppression of vocabulary, she moved to a concern for poetry with its emphasis on vocabulary and its suppression of syntax. This change manifests itself in a shift of linguistic emphasis from the operation of combination (horizontal axis) to the operation of selection (vertical axis).

Tender Buttons attained "a certain notoriety" in the press and attracted polemical criticism, perhaps because it seemed to "veer off into meaninglessness," at least in conventional terms. But the work is more than a literary curiosity. Its marked stylistic change appears to have been a breakthrough that influenced the direction of much of Stein's future work. "*Tender Buttons* represented her full scale break out of the prison of conventional form into the colorful realm of the sensitized imagination."

In *The Making of Americans*, her concerns were those of imposing order upon the world by classifying its inhabitants into universal and eternally valid types, of creating a history of all human possibilities. This goal called for a language that expressed generalities in a very precise way. Her attempts to portray the "bottom nature" of a person, the essence which lay behind his superficial particularity, continued in her early portraits.

> Gertrude Stein had tried numerous techniques in her previous efforts to match her conception of a person with a style. She had generalized and reduced her vocabulary in order to make true statements, however simpleminded. She had constructed long, cumulative sentences on the model of This-is-the-house-that-Jack-built to convey the feeling of slowly becoming familiar with a person.

However, by the time Stein wrote *Tender Buttons*, her attention was no longer focused on the universals of experience, but now on the process of experiencing each moment in the present tense as it intersects with the consciousness. In *The Making of Americans*, she had subordinated particularity and individual differences to the type, an approach which she eventually abandoned. "But by rejecting her knowledge of types, she was faced with each experience as a unique thing, with even its importance unprejudiced, as simply different." She had simplified and generalized reality so as to impose an order upon it, but finally she "concluded that greater fidelity of representation might be achieved if she simply recorded the verbal responses her consciousness made to a particular subject, while minimizing her own manipulation of them."

In her lectures (written with the hindsight of many years, which perhaps lent her stylistic development more coherence than it had in actual fact), Stein discusses her new desire to see the world and return to the sensual particularity of experience as it was immediately available to her consciousness. After doing her portraits, she slowly became bothered by the fact that she was omitting a looking at the world. "So I began to do this thing, I tried to include color and movement, and what I do is . . . a volume called *Tender Buttons*."

The Making of Americans, with its historical orientation and its goal of classifying people according to type, necessitated remembering the past. Classification is based on resemblances, on similarities, which must be held over time in the mind. In her early portraits, Stein freed herself of the narrative and dealt with the presentation of perceptions one moment at a time, but these perceptions were not dealt with "in the raw." They had to be edited, selected, and generalized so that the person could be analyzed and presented in his essential reality. However, in *Tender Buttons*, she came to terms with the chaotic nature of real experience and "the existential swarm of her impressions." The physical world is experienced as unique and immediate in each present moment as the consciousness receives data.

In any attempt to deal with Stein's writing, the word "abstract" is bound to come up. This term has been a problem in Stein criticism because it is not usually defined clearly. Even Michael Hoffman's book, *The Development of Abstractionism in the Writing of Gertrude Stein*, fails to come to terms with "abstract." Hoffman's definition of abstractionism is essentially the dictionary definition, "the act or process of leaving out of consideration one or more qualities of a complex object so as to attend to others.'" That Stein follows this approach, as any artist must, is obvious. However, this definition does not seem adequate to deal with important questions like Stein's refusal of verisimilitude. Because of the vague definition, Hoffman, thus, uses *abstract* to describe all of Stein's work without clarifying the distinctions between *non-representational, plastic, arbitrary*, and *abstract*, although he seems aware of the development of diverse styles in her writing. Stein's relationship to the Cubists, to whose work she compared her own, is an important question that cannot be examined without these kinds of distinctions. When Hoffman compares her work to that of the Cubists, he shares the common failure to be consistent and rigorous in his distinctions between the stages of Cubism as it developed over time. John Malcolm Brinnin, in *The Third Rose*, alone saw that developments in the Cubist styles (analytic and synthetic) parallel stages in Stein's stylistic development as well. This observation is potentially useful in clarifying the distinction between the two kinds of obscure writing that Stein produces.

Too often, the term *abstract*, when used in regard to Stein's writing, is taken to mean non-representational, which her writing almost never is. She never really abandons subject matter. In her early work, the subject matter was the representation of types of people, which appears to have led to an interest in the process of perception itself. In the style which *Tender Buttons* exemplifies, the subject matter is the intersection of the object with consciousness. As attention is focused on the process of perception, that process becomes as much a part of the subject matter as the object perceived. "As I say a motor goes inside and the car goes on, but my business my ultimate business as an artist was not with where the car goes as it goes but with the movement inside that is of the essence of its going." In fact, Stein insisted on subject matter and disapproved of abstract art. That the Cubists' work was never abstract, i.e., never non-representational, is not always clearly understood, and confuses the comparison of Stein's writing to some of the work of those painters.

Subject matter is certainly not abandoned in *Tender Buttons*, nor does that book "signal an abandonment of control. Her practice was to concentrate upon an object as it existed in her mind. . . . Gertrude Stein perceived that the object was immersed in a continuum of sound, color, and association, which it was her business to reconstitute in writing." In *Tender Buttons*, the subject matter was not limited to a description of the objective world, but included mimesis of the intersection of the real world with the consciousness of the artist.

Nevertheless, it is possible to assert that the vocabulary of her early writing moves towards abstraction, if one means that it moves away from the concrete, that it is very general and contains few concrete nouns and verbs of action:

> He was one being living, then when he was quite a young one, and some knew him then and he knew some then. He was one being living then and he was being one and some knew he was that one the one he was then and some did not know then that he was that one the one he was then.
>
> (The Making of Americans)

Tender Buttons has a less abstract vocabulary in that it contains many more concrete nouns, sensual adjectives, and action verbs than does her earlier style:

> The stove is bigger. It was of a shape that made no audience bigger if the opening is assumed why should there not be kneeling. Any force which is bestowed on a floor shows rubbing. This is so nice and sweet and yet there comes the change, there comes the time to press more air. This does not mean the same as disappearance.

However, in a different sense, *Tender Buttons* taken as a whole is more abstract that *The Making of Americans* in that its words are used in a plastic, arbitrary way, and in that it is less concerned with traditional, discursive description.

> In the previous centuries writers had managed pretty well by assembling a number of adjectives and adjectival clauses side by side; the reader "obeyed" by furnishing images and concepts in his mind and the resultant "thing" in the reader's mind corresponded fairly well with that in the writer's. Miss Stein felt that process did not work any more. Her painter friends were showing clearly that the corresponding method of "description" had broken down in painting and she was sure that it had broken down in writing. . . .
>
> Miss Stein felt that writing must accomplish a revolution whereby it could report things as they were in themselves before our minds had appropriated them and robbed them of their objectivity "in pure existing." To this end she went about her house describing the objects she found there in the series of short "poems" which make up the volume called *Tender Buttons*.

As the concerns of Stein's writing gradually shift from an interest in orderly analysis of the world to an interest in the immediate perception of the world by the consciousness, her writing appears to deal more and more with the word itself: with the mental images called up by and associated with the word (signifieds), and with the qualities of words as things in themselves (signifiers). "Her imagination was stimulated then not by the object's particular qualities alone, but also by the associations it aroused . . . and by the words themselves as they took shape upon the page."

Perhaps coincidentally, a similar shift in emphasis was occurring in the painting of the Cubists around the time *Tender Buttons* was composed. Their earlier struggle, in Analytic Cubism, to see reality without the conventional and learned *trompe-l'oeil* of perspective focused their attention on the elements of composition and led them to the realization that the artist could use these elements arbitrarily rather than mimetically:

> in the winter of 1912–13 a fundamental change came about in the pictorial methods of the true Cubists. Whereas previously Braque and Picasso had analyzed and dissected the appearance of objects to discover a set of forms which would add up to their totality and provide the formal elements of a composition, now they found that they could begin by composing with purely pictorial elements (shaped forms, planes of color) and gradually endow them with an objective significance.

The Cubists had arrived at "the conclusion that they could create their own pictorial reality by building up towards it through a synthesis of different elements." That the elements of signification might have an importance in their own right and be used arbitrarily by the artist to create not a mirror of reality but an authentic new reality (the work of art as *tableau-objet*) was an important realization for this group and a conclusion that Stein seems to have arrived at, perhaps independently. Stein now realized that words need no longer be merely the means to the expression of another reality, but may become freed of their normal mimetic function (still retaining their meanings and associations) and be used plastically by the writer. In her lectures, she describes her growing concern with the quality of language as a thing in itself:

> I began to wonder at . . . just what one saw when one looked at anything . . . [Did] it make itself by description by a word that meant it or did it make itself by a word in itself. . . .
>
> I became more and more excited about how words which were the words which made whatever I looked at look like itself were not words that had in them any quality of description. . . .
>
> And the thing that excited me . . . is that the words that made what I looked at be itself were always words that to me very exactly related themselves to that thing . . . at which I was looking, but as often as not had as I say nothing whatever to do with what any words would do that described that thing.

Like the Cubists, Stein abandons conventional description of an object, although she is still concerned with the object as here "model," but she inverts the traditional descriptive relationship of word to object. Rather than the word evoking the mental image of the object, the object evokes words (associations, etc.) which the artist arbitrarily assembles into an independent linguistic object related to, but not descriptive of, the model or referent. In Analytic Cubism, the artist abstracts form from the given object and creates a representation of the object (however unconventional) on canvas. In Synthetic Cubism, forms have their genesis in the artist, although he uses them to create an object on the canvas. The function of the painting is no longer to describe or represent another reality, but to exist as a thing in itself. In Stein's early works (*The Making of Americans* and others, of her participial style), words are used to abstract generalities about the world to analyze or describe it on paper. However, in *Tender Buttons*, the words are not conventionally descriptive of the object, but have their genesis in the writer and in the associations which the object evokes in her. The function of the writing is not to describe the given object, but to become an entity in its own right.

In *Tender Buttons*, with the new attention to the immediately present moment and the abandoning of traditional description, Stein turned from her earlier "portraits" of people to the treatment of inanimate objects and seems to have felt some bond with the painters of still lives. Dealing with human beings "inevitably carried in its train realizing movements and expression and as such forced me into recognizing resemblances, and so forced remembering and in forcing remembering caused confusion of present with past and future time." Consequently, she turned from "portraits of men and women and children" to "portraits of food and rooms and everything because there I could avoid this difficulty of suggesting remembering more easily . . . than if I were to describe human beings." Stein also felt that this was a problem she shared with the painters:

> I began to make portraits of things and enclosures . . . because I needed to completely face the difficulty of how to include what is seen with hearing and listening and at first if I were to include a complicated listening and talking it would be too difficult to do. That is why painters paint still lives. You do see why they do.

Indeed, as the Cubists turned from an analysis of a given reality on canvas to a synthesis of a new reality from the pictorial elements, the Cubists, (Picasso especially), produced fewer portraits and more still lives. Perhaps the reason for this move is similar to the one that brought about the change in Stein's writing: dealing with inanimate objects allows the artist more freedom to treat the subject in an arbitrary manner. After all, the public expects a portrait to be a likeness of the model, who has the annoying habit of exhibiting his face in public, thus allowing it to be compared with the painting. But a still life is a small piece of reality that the artist arranges at will, and when he is finished, he can dismantle it, leaving the public nothing with which to compare the painting.

The new realization of Synthetic Cubism (that pictorial elements could be used arbitrarily) was marked by a return to color and texture in contrast to the predominantly grey paintings of Analytic Cubism. For Stein, the new interest in the sensory experiences of the present moment and the new-felt freedom in the use of words manifested itself in a richer, more sensual vocabulary, in contrast to the spare and spartan one of her earlier struggle to classify everyone into universal types. "The idea had entered her mind that lyricism contained a fuller measure of truth than could ever be encircled by making endless laboriously deliberate statements." The evocative power of the word called for more "decorative" approach. Freed from her concerns with remembering and classifying, she began to concentrate on the present moment and all of the phenomena therein, including the words called up by those phenomena and their effect upon her conscious mind. Thus, instead of the genderless pronouns, verbs of being, prepositions and conjunctions, and the virtual elimination of concrete words in her earlier style, there is a renaissance of the particular: concrete nouns, sensual adjectives, and specific verbs.

This new interest in the word itself, and especially in the noun and the associative powers of the word, was what Stein considered the essence of poetry. In *Tender Buttons* and other works that she held as poetry, the chief linguistic operation is association (given various labels by structuralists such as substitution, selection, system) and choice of words. The association of words and concepts by similarity or opposition, and the selection of a word from a group of synonyms, are operations that function along the vertical axis of language. Interestingly enough, the *Tender Buttons* style also suppresses syntax (the horizontal axis) while it is expanding vocabulary. Construction of syntax becomes increasingly fragmentary until syntax disappears altogether in some of the more extreme passages.

In *The Making of Americans*, the chief stylistic interest is syntax, but in *Tender Buttons*, the central concern seems to be diction, the selection of words based on association (in terms of both similarity and opposition). The long sentence-paragraph is abandoned as more attention is forced on the noun:

> after I had gone as far as I could in these long sentences and paragraphs . . . I then began very short thing . . . and I resolutely realized nouns and decided not to get around them but to meet them, to handle in short to refuse them by using them and in that way my real acquaintance with poetry was begun.

> I began to discover the names of things, that is . . . to discover the things . . . to see the things to look at and in so doing I had of course to name them not to give new names but to see that I could find out how to know that they were there by their names or by replacing their names. . . . They had their names and naturally I called them by the names they had and in doing so having begun looking at them I called them by their names with passion and that made poetry . . . it made the *Tender Buttons*.

However, as Stein begins to abandon her extension of the sentence and enriches her use of diction, the result is not more conventional writing but rather a new style, equally obscure, if not more so. It is even harder to read, in the traditional sense, than her first obscure style, because, in part, there is a disjunction between the two axes of language in this second style. One word often does not appear to have any relationship to other words in the sentence except in terms of their existence as pure words (in terms of grammatical structure, or rhyme, or word play).Of course, words cannot be divorced from their meanings; thus, each word (signifier) calls up a mental image or idea (signified), but *Tender Buttons* cannot be read with a conventional concern for subject matter because one cannot use the total configurations of these mental constructs to reconstruct the "subject matter." Sometimes a sentence in *Tender Buttons* may appear to have a normal syntax and to be orthodox grammatically, yet the words selected do not relate to each other in a traditional and discursive way. "The change of color is likely and a difference a very little difference is prepared. Sugar is not a vegetable" (*Tender Buttons*). These sentences are grammatically correct,though their punctuation is not conventional. One may achieve the feeling that the sentence would be perfectly comprehensible if the context were supplied. Stein is using both syntax and diction, but because of the disjunction between the two axes of language, the sentence does not "mean" in a conventional way.

Sometimes in *Tender Buttons* Stein explores the patterns of speech, repeating syntactical patterns, at the same time somewhat arbitrarily plugging in terms from the pool of associated words in her vocabulary:

> Almost very likely there is no seduction, almost very likely
> there is no stream, certainly very likely the height is penetrated,
> certainly certainly the target is cleaned, come to set, come to refuse,
> come to surround, come slowly and age is not lessening.

She explores the rhythm and patterns of speech that are present, even when discursive meaning is not. Like "Jabberwocky," this passage conveys a feeling of speech, even though its words do not relate to each other in a conventional way.

In *Tender Buttons*, Stein's sentences become shorter as her emphasis shifts to diction and association rather than syntax. She explains in a lecture that lines of poetry are shorter than prose because

> such a way to express oneself is the natural way when one expresses oneself in loving the name of anything. Think what you do . . . when you love the name of anything really love its name. Inevitably you express yourself . . . in the way poetry expresses itself that is in short lines in repeating what you began in order to do it again. Think of how you talk to anything whose name is new to you a lover a baby a dog or a new land. . . . Do you not inevitably repeat what you call out and is that calling out not of necessity in short lines.

Often in *Tender Buttons*, lines that appear to be sentences are not sentences at all: "Cutting shade, cool spades and little last beds, make violet violet when." Obviously, this fragment promises to be a sentence until it is truncated by the period after "when," a word normally expected to introduce a subordinate clause. The disjunction between diction and syntax manifests itself in false predication. For example, how can shade, spades, and beds make violet? Here, each word is quite independent from those which preceed and follow it in the speech chain, at least as far as the mental images or signifieds are concerned. (Obviously, however, there are relationships between some of the words in terms of sound.)

Stein uses punctuation in other ways to break up the continuity of the sentence: "This makes and eddy. Necessary" (*Tender Buttons*). Also: "Cream cut. Anywhere crumb. Left hop chambers" (*Tender Buttons*). She carries the disintegration of syntax even further, presenting a list within the horizontal structure of the sentence. (A list is usually a group of items associated with one another because they are similar in some way.) "Alas a doubt in case of more to go to say what is is cress. What it is. Mean. Potatoes. Loaves" (*Tender Buttons*). In some of her writing following *Tender Buttons*, Stein even entirely abandoned syntax and made lists of words or phrases in vertical columns on the page.

Again, one observes that some of the stylistic phenomena of Stein's second "obscure" style, emphasizing vocabulary and the noun while suppressing syntax, are strikingly close to Jakobson's observations about the language of aphasics suffering from a contiguity disorder, in which ability to use syntax becomes weakened or disappears, leaving the patient with *only* a vocabulary in extreme cases:

> The impairment of the ability to propositionalize, or, generally speaking, to combine simpler linguistic entities into more complex units, is actually confined to one type of aphasia. . . . There is no *wordlessness*, since the entity preserved in most of such cases is the *word*, which can be defined as the highest among the linguistic units compulsorily coded, i.e., we compose our own sentences and utterances out of the word stock supplied by the code.
>
> This contexture-deficient aphasia, which could be termed contiguity disorder, diminishes the extent and variety of sentences. The syntactical rules organizing words into a higher unit are lost; this loss, called agrammatism, causes the degeneration of the sentence into a mere "word heap. . . ." Word order becomes chaotic; the ties of grammatical coordination and subordination . . . are dissolved. As might be expected, words endowed with purely grammatical functions, like conjunctions, prepositions, pronouns, and articles, disappear first, giving rise to the so-called "telegraphic style," whereas in the case of similarity disorder they are the most resistant. The less a word depends grammatically on the context, the stronger is its tenacity in the speech of aphasics with a contigu-

ity disorder and the sooner it is dropped by patients with a similarity disorder. Thus the "kernel subject word" is the first to fall out of the sentence in cases of similarity disorder and conversely, it is the least destructible in the opposite type of aphasia.

In *Tender Buttons*, Stein's primary concern is words and their associations, and her selection of words often is imbued with a spirit of love and play:

> Poetry is concerned with using with abusing, with losing with wanting, with denying with avoiding with adoring with replacing the noun. . . . Poetry is doing nothing but losing refusing and pleasing and betraying and caressing nouns.

Sometimes the selection of words is obviously related to the subject:

A Petticoat

A light white, a disgrace, an ink spot, a rosy charm.

(Tender Buttons)

Without too much effort, one detects the associations between word and object. Petticoats are lightweight and often white; a petticoat that shows is a disgrace which might provoke a modest blush. (Stein has been greatly overread, but it seems safe to identify the obvious and public association.)

Even when the associations of word to object are chiefly based on associated meanings, similarities of spelling and sound may play a role:

A Method of a Cloak

A single climb to a line, a straight exchange to a cane, a desperate adventure and courage and a clock . . . all this makes an attractive black silver.

(Tender Buttons)

The "single climb to a line" might relate to the shape of the cloak, and the cane is related to the cloak as an object of apparel. (Both the cane and the cloak have a nostalgic, perhaps nineteenth-century flavor of elegance.) But the two phrases, "A single climb to a line" and "a straight exchange to a cane," have identical rhythmic patterns as well. The "desperate adventure" and "courage" might be related to the connotations of "cloak and dagger." Black may be the color of the clock which is "attractive;" perhaps silver was evoked by the sight of the lining of the cloak and the associated phrase, "silver lining." But clock seems to be associated with cloak because of the similarity in spelling and sound. In terms of association on the level of mental constructs (signifieds), Stein uses both association based on contiguity (defined by James as association of objects habitually found together in time and space, and identified by Jakobson as metonymy) and on similarity (which Jakobson identifies as metaphor.) Both kinds of association are operations of selection which function along the vertical axis of language. But the metaphorical type of association seems to predominate in *Tender Buttons*, as one might expect, given that "metaphor is alien to the similarity disorder and metonymy to the contiguity disorder." Moreover, the operation of association is stressed not only in terms of images and concepts (signifieds), but also in terms of the qualities of the words as words (signifiers).

Stein often plays with the qualities of words as *words* in *Tender Buttons* and chooses them on the basis of their associations with other words as signifiers. For instance, she oftens uses rhyme within the line: "all the joy in weak success, all the joyful tenderness, all the section and the tea, all the stouter symmetry. . . ." Similarly,

Chicken
    Alas a dirty word, alas a dirty third, alas a dirty third alas a dirty bird.

and: "The sister was not a mister."

She also associates words on the basis of alliteration: "The sight of a reason, the same sight slighter, the sight of a simpler negative answer, the same sore sounder, the intention to wishing, the same splendor, the same furniture." She even uses onomatopoeia:

Chicken
Stick stick call then, stick stick sticking, sticking with a chicken.

Playing with the sounds and meanings of words also leads to puns, as in the following, seemingly evoking the associations of Washington, Wellington, and veal Wellington:

Veal
Very well very well. Washing is old, washing is washing.

Additional punning occurs in the following:

Milk
    Climb up in sight climb in the whole utter needless and a guess a whole guess is hanging. Hanging, hanging.

She even plays with the spelling of words: "and easy express e. c."

The devices used here are certainly traditional, or at least they seem so now: indirect associations of imagery, obliqueness, fragmented syntax, rhyme, rhythm, alliteration, etc. What is it, then, that so many have found upsetting? Perhaps it is the lack of discursive meaning or the fact that the "subject matter" cannot be reconstructed from the images like a jigsaw puzzle, but these may be inappropriate expectations with which to approach Stein's writing.

It is ironic that, in spite of Stein's intention in writing *Tender Buttons* to capture immediate experience while consciousness grapples with it, there have been so many problems in the reading of that book. One problem inherent in the work itself is the disjunction of the two axes of language making it almost impossible to read the work for conventional discursive content. Moreover, this problem leads to another: the effort of trying to "figure it out," to reconstruct the content, not only exhausts the reader, but overdistances him from the work itself. Such an effort is futile anyway, for *Tender Buttons* demands to be dealt with in its own terms. The reader is given none of the literary allusions that the reader of Pound, Eliot, or Joyce can hold on to. As for inventing glosses for the little pieces in *Tender Buttons*, Sutherland points out that it is impossible and amusing to create them, but that "it is perfectly idle":

> Such a procedure puts the original in the position of being a riddle, a rhetorical complication of something rather unremarkable in itself. It would be rather like an exhibition of the original table tops, guitars, pipes, and people which were the subject matter of cubist paintings. The original subject matter is or was of importance to the painter as a source of sensations, relations, ideas, even, but it is not after all the beholder's business. The beholder's business is the picture in front of him, which is a new reality and something else, which does not add up to the nominal subject matter.

As Sutherland suggests, perhaps what the reader of Stein is required to do is to look *at* the work, rather than *through* it. One cannot look *through* it because it is an opaque, rather than transparent, style. If one does look *at* the work, what does one see in *Tender Buttons*? He sees the word presented as an entity in its own right. By forcing the reader to attend to the word, Stein makes the word seem new, again. In this effort, she does not ignore the meanings of words, as so may critics have claimed. However by presenting each word in an unusual context, she directs attention not only towards its sound but towards its sense as the reader is forced to grapple with each word, one at a time. One is forced to attend to the word, and to language, with a sense of bewilderment and perhaps with a sense of wonder and discovery:

> Nouns are the name of anything and anything is named, that is what Adam and Eve did and if you like it is what anybody does, but do they go on just using the name until perhaps they do not know what the name is or if they do know what the name is they do not care what the name is. . . . And what has that to do with poetry. A great deal I think. . . .

The role of poetry, then, is to give the word back its youth and vitality:

> you can love a name and if you love a name then saying that name any number of times only makes you love it more, more violently, more persistently, more tormentedly. Anybody knows how anybody calls out the name of anybody one loves. And so that is poetry really loving the name of anything. . . .

Stein's fascination with language, both its sound and its sense, and her interest in exploring the way it works are certainly evident in *Tender Buttons*.

Her intuitive grasp of the principles of its operation is manifested not only in her theories, but also in the very nature of the two so very different kinds of obscure styles that she created.

Richard Bridgman and Edmund Wilson are among those critics who attribute the relative unintelligibility of Stein's work to her need to write about her private passions and her simultaneous need to be discreet about the nature of those passions. As Stein herself might have said, "Interesting, if true." But the only relevance of this sexually motivated evasiveness is that it may have served as an impetus for her innovations with language. In *The Making of Americans* (as well as in other works of the same style), she stretches the contiguity of the sentence as far as it will go without snapping, at the same time reducing, to a minimum the vocabulary available for selection. In *Tender Buttons* and similar works, the available vocabulary becomes practically limitless while the syntax is shortened, destroyed, and even disintegrated into lists. As Jakobson's observations about aphasia indicate, conventionally intelligible language can only occur when both aspects of language are fully operative. Although one can only speculate that Stein's innovations grew out of a desire and a need to be unintelligible, one can say less uncertainly that her obscurity was a necessary consequence of the nature of her innovative experiments with language.

The Concept of Projection:
H. D.'s Visionary Powers

Adalaide Morris

In April 1920, while staying with her friend Bryher in a hotel on the island of Corfu, H. D. had a vision which marked and measured the rest of her life. It set the aims, announced the means, and disclosed the dimensions of her great work, the visionary epics *Trilogy* and *Helen in Egypt*, and it seemed to guarantee her gift as seer and prophet. It would be twenty years from the Corfu vision to the poems that first grasp its promise, however, years of drift and anxiety in which H. D. would write and rewrite the story of her vision. By the time the event achieves final formulation in the first part of *Tribute to Freud*, it is clear that, however charged the vision's imagery, the plot we are to follow, the *mythos* of the matter, is its method: the miraculous projection of the images.

As H. D. explains in *Tribute to Freud*, the images she witnessed had the clarity, intensity, and authenticity of dream symbols and yet took shape not inside her mind but on the wall between the foot of her bed and the washstand. Because it was late afternoon and their side of the hotel was already dim and because the images were outlined in light, the shapes that appeared could not have been cast shadows. Neither accidental nor random, they formed with a stately, steady purpose, one after another, and seemed inscribed by the same hand. Their abstract, impersonal, rather conventional notation—a head in profile, a chalice, a ladder, an angel named Victory or Niké—made them appear part of a picture-alphabet or heiroglyphic system, a supposition reinforced by their orderly succession, their syntax. For these reasons and because of the eerie, miraculous portentousness of the moment, H. D. calls this experience the "writing on the wall."

When Belshazzar witnessed the writing on his wall, he glimpsed along with the letters a part of the hand that wrote them. The origin of H. D.'s

From *Contemporary Literature* 25, no. 4 (Winter 1984). © 1984 by the Board of Regents of the University of Wisconsin System. University of Wisconsin Press, 1984.

writing is, if equally mysterious, less simply formulated. The agent is not a hand but a projective process: the casting of an image onto a screen. The vision's earlier images, which appear entire, are like magic lantern slides; the later ones, which draw themselves in dots of light elongating into lines, resemble primitive movies.

The path from mind to wall is direct. It at first seems to follow what H. D. calls her "sustained crystal-gazing stare" an aching concentration that propels the image outward on her eyebeam. Because the vision rides on will, she must not flag: "if I let go," she thinks, "lessen the intensity of my stare and shut my eyes or even blink my eyes, to rest them, the pictures will fade out." When, however, she drops her head in her hands, exhausted, the process continues and Bryher, who has until now seen nothing, witnesses the final image. What she sees—H. D.'s Niké elevated into the sun-disk—is so consistent with the preceding figures that H. D. compares it to "that 'determinative' that is used in the actual hieroglyph, the picture that contains the whole series of pictures in itself or helps clarify or explain them." With the power of the poet or prophet, H. D. has not only materialized the images of her psyche but cast them onto the consciousness of another and released her audience's own visionary capacities.

The images of the vision are described as flowing from, or at least through, H. D.'s psyche, yet their origin is obscured. What creates these slides or magic transparencies? Where do they come from? The answer given in *Tribute to Freud* is ambiguous. On the one hand, the images seem little different than the clips from memories or dream scenes that H. D. had earlier compared to "transparencies in a dark room, set before lighted candles." In this sense, however extraordinary, they would be "merely an extension of the artist's mind, a *picture* or an illustrated poem, taken out of the actual dream or daydream content and projected from within." On the other hand, in an interpretation H. D. clearly prefers, one sanctioned by the classical belief that gods speak through dreams and oracles, the images seem "projected from outside," messages from another world, another state of being.

Images as signs and warnings from her own subconscious, images as signs and wonders from another world; the artist as moving-picture machine, the artist as psychic, the artist as message-transmitter: what gives this odd combination of attributes unity and coherence, positions it within H. D.'s development, and makes it central to any interpretation of her work is the concept of projection. All the more apt for its abundant ambiguities, projection is the master metaphor of H. D.'s technique. Its operations connect the material, mental, and mystical realms and enact her belief that there is no physical reality that is not also psychic and spiritual. Without the energies of projection, H. D.'s work stalls and thins; with them, her writing has strength and brilliance. It is this excellence that the "projected pictures" at Corfu seem to promise.

The word *projection* appears throughout H. D.'s work. Though its meaning alters subtly and sometimes confusingly, it always marks an important moment in her creative process. From the verb meaning *to throw forward*, projection is the thrust that bridges two worlds. It is the movement across a borderline: between the mind and the wall, between the brain and the page, between inner and outer, between me and you, between states of being, across dimensions of time and space. The concept of projection informs H. D.'s transitions from Imagist to clairvoyant, to film theorist, analysand, and prophetic poet. What does it clarify at each stage? how does it change between stages? what light does it throw on the overall strategies and strengths of H. D.'s work? These will be the questions that guide our inquiry.

PROJECTION: THE ACT OF THROWING OR SHOOTING FORWARD

"Cut the cackle!" "Go in fear of abstractions!" "Don't be 'viewy'!" Most memorable Imagist statements are prescriptions against a poetic tradition condemned as rigid, overblown, and unoriginal. Cackle is the chatter of conventional verse. It fills long lines with flourishes Pound called "rhetorical bustuous rumpus": platitudes, circumlocutions, and rolling, ornamental din. To theorists like Pound and T. E. Hulme, these flourishes were self-generated and self-sustained, cut off from the world they purported to present. In its eagerness to pronounce upon the world and in the vaporous grandeur of its pronouncements, cackle went in fear neither of abstractions nor of viewiness.

The cure for cackle is contact. Imagist theory privileges sight as fresh, accurate access to the exterior world. Sight is the acid bath that dissolves the sticky sludge of rhetoric. It connects us directly, so the Imagists argue, with the things of this world. Bad art, for Hulme, is "words divorced from any real vision," strings of conventional locutions, abstractions, "counters" which, like "x" and "y" in an algebraic formula, replace six pounds of cashews and four Florida oranges. Formulaic words, like algebraic symbols, can be manipulated according to laws independent of their meaning. Hulme's test of good poetry is whether the words turn back into things that we can see.

The major Imagist theorists echo each other on this point. "Each *word* must be an image *seen*, not a counter," Hulme legislates. "Language in a healthy state," T. S. Eliot insists, "presents the object, is so close to the object that the two are identical." For Pound, "the very essence" of a writer's work is "the application of word to thing." It was Pound who discovered, through the work of Ernest Fenollosa, the ur-pattern of the word-thing: the Chinese ideogram which was assumed to be direct, visibly concrete, natural rather than conventional, a picture language within which, as Fenollosa put it, "Thinking is *thinging*."

The image of a thing, set into a poem, becomes for the Imagists the innocent word, the word that has somehow escaped the conventional, abstracting, mediating nature of language. The assumption of transparent expression is a correlate of the Bergsonian faith in the artist's direct intuition of the object. Where contemporary theorists hold that we see what we know, Imagists insist we know what we see. They find in vision the release from a shared system of signs into spontaneous, intuitive, unmediated apprehension of essences. Whatever her subsequent elaborations—and they are many and strange—this belief in the possibility of essential intuitions, so central to Imagism, remains at the core of H. D.'s projective practice.

Projection is the act of throwing or shooting forward. Though the Imagists don't use the term, they depend on the concept. In the genesis of the Imagist poem, a thing in the world projects its essence onto the poet's consciousness; the poet imprints the image, or record of the thing, in a poem; and the poem, in turn, projects the image onto the reader's consciousness. The model for this, the simplest form of projection, is the magic lantern show. It is Hulme's concrete display of images that "always endeavours to arrest you, and to make you continuously see a physical thing"; it is Pound's *phanopoeia*, the technique by which "you use a word to throw a visual concept on to the reader's imagination."

H. D.'s *Sea Garden* is full of *phanopoeia*. The reader's visual imagination is bombarded by sand, tree-bark, salt tracks, silver dust, wood violets, and thin, stinging twigs—objects in a world of clear, hard-edged, gritty particularity. The images have an almost hallucinatory specificity. The view is tight, close-up, almost too bright: on the beach, "hard sand breaks, / and the grains of it / are clear as wine"; in the late afternoon sun, "each leaf / cuts another leaf on the grass"; night, when it comes, curls "the petals / back from the stalk / . . . under till the rinds break, / back till each bent leaf / is parted from its stalk." Break, cut, curl: these moments are doubly projective. H. D.'s images, forcibly cast onto the reader's imagination, themselves record moments in which one thing, thrown onto another, opens, releases, or transforms it. In *Sea Garden*, objects are perpetually twisted, lifted, flung, split, scattered, slashed, and stripped clear by rushing energies that enact the impact the poet wishes to exert on the reader's imagination.

The rushing energies are the sea, the sun, and the night,but in H. D.'s world these are more than fierce weather: they testify to a sacred power and promise in the universe. Unlike other of the Imagists, H. D. conceived of essence as god-stuff. To her, each intense natural fact is the trace of a spiritual force; each charged landscape enshrines a deity. Thus, in *Sea Garden*, dryads haunt the groves, nereids the waves; Priapus transfuses the orchard, Artemis courses the woods; Hermes marks the crossroads, and the mysterious Wind Sleepers roam searching for their altar. The world glows with sacred energy.

This radiance, however, like a Derridean sigh, marks a presence that is vanished or just vanishing. Gods do not manifest directly to mortals, but they do, like Apollo at Delphi, leave us signs, the afterglow of sacred presence. The speaker in *Sea Garden* is a supplicant in search of deities that are everywhere immanent in the landscape: they beckon, stand tense, await us a moment, then surge away, leaving behind heel prints, snapped stalks, and a charged silence. The poet, like a skilled tracker, moves from sign to sign in rapt, sagacious pursuit.

As embodiments of essence, the deities might seem mere metaphors, relics of the kind of claptrap the Imagists despised. H. D.'s work, however, is spare, stripped, as Pound said, of slither. In it, the gods function not as the poems' ornament but as their absent center. The deities are both cause and condition of this poetry; the poems do not work if we don't posit the reality of the presence they yearn toward.

The poems in *Sea Garden* are thrown out as bridges to the sacred. They project themselves toward the gods with a plea that the gods will in return appear to us. Poems like "Sea Gods," "Hermes of the Ways," "The Helmsman," and "The Shrine" address the gods directly, compelling them from immanence to manifestation: "For you will come," H. D. presses, "you will come, / you will answer our taut hearts, / . . . and cherish and shelter us." Projection as *phanopoeia*, a poetic technique, here, in H. D.'s first important modification, broadens into a technique of meditation or prayer: an imaging used to summon a being from another world.

PROJECTION: A REPRESENTATION ON A PLANE SURFACE
OF ANY PART OF THE CELESTIAL SPHERE

Except for three brief reviews in *The Egoist*, H. D. took little part in the barrage of Imagist treatises and evaluations. Contrasting strongly with the polemics she later wrote for the cinema, this silence had several sources. She was a new poet, unused to literary disputations, and, until the arrival of Amy Lowell, she was the only woman in a contentious group of men. In addition, she held a constricted position in the movement: if Hulme was its principal theorist and Pound its chief publicist, H. D. was from the first the Imagiste extraordinaire, the movement's most effective practitioner. Her poems stimulated and exemplified positions held by others.

A third, more significant source of H. D.'s silence, however, lies in her hesitations about Imagist doctrine. Her *Egoist* review of John Gould Fletcher's *Goblins and Pagodas*, for example, makes an obligatory bow to Imagist principles but is compelled by something else. "He uses the direct image, it is true," H. D. writes, "but he seems to use it as a means of evoking other and vaguer images—a pebble, as it were, dropped into a quiet pool, in order to start across the silent water, wave on wave of light, of colour, of sound." Fletcher attempts "a more difficult and, when successfully handled, richer form of art: not that of direct presentation, but that of suggestion." The goblins and pagodas that title his volume testify to visionary capacities. His art pursues not the solidity of physical things so much as the spiritual enigmas that radiate from them.

The next stage of H. D.'s development furthers her own shift from pebbles to their radiating rings: from the objects of this world to the phantasms of light, color, and sound surrounding them; from our three dimensions to the largest ring of all, the fourth dimension or celestial sphere surrounding us. In 1919, after her bonds with Pound, Aldington, and the other Imagists had cracked, after her alliance with Bryher had begun and her daughter Perdita had been born, H. D. had a series of intense psychic experiences. The visions of 1919 and 1920 undid any remaining traces of

Imagist empiricism, affirmed a privileged role for the woman poet, and demonstrated H. D.'s clairvoyant powers. Applied to these experiences, the term *projection* registers not the poet's design on the reader or on the gods but rather the dynamics of clairvoyance. To this end H. D. extends the term by borrowing a metaphor from the art of cartography.

In the language of mapping, projection is the representation of a sphere on a flat surface. Like most figuration, projection simplifies, here reducing a curve to a plane. Two methods of charting the heavens clarify the distinction between general and cartographic projection. In the first sense, as Robert Duncan in *The H. D. Book* observes, we make the night "a projected screen" by casting our mythologies into the heavens and rendering "the sky-dome above . . . the image of another configuration in the skull-dome below." Cartographers reverse this movement and project intersecting coordinate lines from the sky down to our earthly charts. This entry of another dimension into our familiar figuration is the equivalent in H. D.'s work of the process by which material from the celestial or astral planes manifests on the earthly plane. It is this that haunts and compels her.

H. D. experienced what she felt was an inrush of material from other dimensions at least four times in 1919–20, all after surviving her near-fatal childbirth and all in the steadying company of Bryher. The first, in late spring 1919, involved "the transcendental feeling of the two globes or the two transparent half-globes enclosing me"; the second was the apparition of an ideal figure on the voyage to Greece in 1920; the third and fourth, in the hotel room at Corfu, were the projected pictures and a series of dance scenes conjured up for Bryher. Each of these seemed, as H. D. affirmed, "a godsend," an irradiation of the world of ordinary events and rules by an extraordinary grace.

The first of these experiences is described in *Notes on Thought and Vision*, a document composed for Havelock Ellis, whom H. D. and Bryher had been consulting and who subsequently accompanied them to Greece. Though rough and sometimes contradictory, these notes describe a matrix of creativity she calls the "jelly-fish" or "over-mind" state. The self is divided into body, mind, and over-mind. The artist-initiate begins, like the neophyte in the Eleusinian mysteries, with the body's desires and the brain's sensitivities, but the aim is to transcend these consciousnesses in the over-mind, the receptacle of mystical vision.

Like Ellis, H. D. begins her exposition with sexuality. All humans need physical relationships, she argues, but creative men and women crave them "to develop and draw forth their talents." The erotic personality, suffused with sympathetic, questing, and playful energies, is the artistic personality, par excellence, a hypothesis Ellis and H. D. both exemplify by evoking Leonardo da Vinci. Ellis, however, separates sexuality's primary reproductive function from a secondary spiritual function of "furthering the higher mental and emotional processes." H. D. counters this separation with a theory derived partly from the Eleusinian mysteries and partly from her own recent childbirth.

Complementing the "vision of the brain" is a force H. D. calls "vision of the womb." The term underscores the artist's receptive/procreative role. In the womb-brain, thoughts from another realm are received, nourished, brought to form, then projected out into the barrenness H. D. calls "the murky, dead, old, thousand-times explored old world." This model rewrites conventional phallic metaphors for creativity by depicting visionary consciousness as "a foetus in the body" which, after "grinding discomfort," is released in the miracle the mysteries celebrated as Kore's return. "Is it easier for a woman to attain this state of consciousness than for a man?" H. D. asks. Though both sexes possess this capacity, her formulation privileges her own particularly female experience of integration and regeneration.

Notes on Thought and Vision provide many explications of visionary consciousness, but the most pertinent to H. D.'s developing notion of projection are three ocular models. H. D.'s fascination with optics came from watching her father the astronomer and her grandfather the botanist gaze through lenses into a teeming world where before there had been only a blank. Each of her models postulates two kinds of vision, womb vision and brain vision, and each invents a way to adjust them so as to transform void to plenitude.

H. D.'s initial formulation describes the jellyfish state as enclosure in two caps of diving bells of consciousness, one over the forehead and one the the "love region." Each is a sort of amniotic sac, "like water, transparent, fluid yet with definite body, contained in a definite space . . . like a closed sea-plant, jelly-fish or anemone." This sack holds and nurtures the delicate, amorphous life of the over-mind, but it has a further function. Like a diver's mask or aquarium glass, the over-mind allows us to see the usually invisible inhabitants of the watery depths: here, H. D. explains, "thoughts pass and are visible like fish swimming under clear water."

The second formulation transforms these caps into dual lenses for a pair of psychic opera glasses. These, "properly adjusted, focused . . . bring the world of vision into consciousness. The two work separately, perceive separately, yet make one picture." What they see is the whole world of vision registered by the mystic, the philosopher, and the artist.

In the last and most evocative formulation, these lenses merge into a complexly constituted third eye. "The jelly-fish over my head," H. D. explains, "had become concentrated. . . . That is, all the spiritual energy seemed concentrated in the middle of my forehead, inside my skull, and it was small and giving out a very soft light, but not scattered light, light concentrated in itself as the light of a pearl would be." Like a crystal ball, this eye both receives and emits the force H. D. calls "over-world energy." It draws in, concentrates, then projects outward "pictures from the world of vision." This receptive/transmissive eye is the gift of vision, the pearl of great price.

The jellyfish eye opens the skull-dome. Into, out of, through this rupture pours all the prophetic soul-energy scientific materialism would deny and H. D.'s visions and visionary poetry affirm. Archetypal memories, dreams, the Corfu pictures all exemplify this projected vision, but a more excessive, startling instance is the sudden apparition of Peter Van Eck at the shiprail of the Borodino.

For more than twenty years, H. D. struggled to tell the story of Peter Van Eck, her code name for Peter Rodeck, architect, artist, spiritualist, and fellow passenger on the voyage to Greece. It formed the heart of a much rewritten novel entitled *Niké*, finally jettisoned in 1924. The most ample remaining accounts are in the pseudonymous short story "Mouse Island," published in 1932; in the analysis notebooks of 1933, published as part of *Tribute to Freud*; and in the unpublished autobiographical novel *The Majic Ring*, written in 1943–44.

It was sunset, neither day nor night, and the ocean was suffused with a soft violet-blue glow. The ship was approaching the Pillars of Hercules between the outer-waters of the Atlantic and the inner-sea of the Mediterranean. "We were crossing something," H. D. explains—a line, a boundary, perhaps a threshold. Alone at the rail of the Borodino, she stood "on the deck of a mythical ship as well, a ship that had no existence in the world of ordinary events and laws and rules." The sea was quiet, the boat moved smoothly, and the waves broke "in a thousand perfectly peaked wavelets like the waves in the background of a Botticelli." When she turned to search for Bryher, she saw a three-dimensional figure at the rail, a man who both was and was not Peter Van Eck. Taller, clearer, brighter than Van Eck, without his disfiguring scar and thick-rimmed glasses, this apparition summoned a band of leaping dolphins and disclosed, on the ship's seaward side, a chain of hilly islands. At the peak of the moment, H. D. reports, "his eyes, it seemed now, were my eyes. I was seeing his vision, what he (though I did not of course, realize it) was himself projecting. This was the promised land, the islands of the blest, the islands of Atlantis or of the Hesperides."

Was this a hallucination, a holographic illusion, an epiphany? If the latter, who was the being who directed or even impersonated Peter Van Eck? H. D. gives no consistent answer. *The Majic Ring* suggests it was "Anax Apollo, Helios, Lord of Magic and Prophecy and Music"; the letters to Silvia Dobson imply he was an astral double; the story "Mouse Island" compares him to Christ at Emmaus.

Whatever he was, all accounts agree he was a "projection" from another dimension into this one, a phenomenon for which "Mouse Island" gives the most extensive—and mechanical—explication. If each being is composed of two substances, "platinum sheet-metal over jellyfish" or body over soul, Van Eck's appearance was a "galvanized projection": soul-stuff shocked into form, transmitted through the third-eye opening in his skull, perceived through the opening in hers. "The inside could get out that way," the story tells us, "only when the top was broken. It was the transcendentalist inside that had met [Van Eck] in the storm on deck, when [Peter Van Eck] was downstairs in the smoking room."

The terminology is awkward, the physics creak, but the experience was real and haunted H. D. all her life. Van Eck's three-dimensionality was a kind of psychic *phanopoeia*—not all what Pound meant but very much H. D.'s technique in her later poetry. The visionary figures of *Trilogy*, the hordes of souls thronging *Helen in Egypt*, the angelic forces of *Hermetic Definition*, all are figures entering the imagination from another dimension and carrying with them the mysterious radiance by which H. D. gratefully remapped our "dead, old, thousand-times explored old world."

PROJECTION: THE DISPLAY OF MOTION PICTURES BY CASTING
AN IMAGE ON A SCREEN

When H. D. once again broached the Greek material in the 1940s, she reported that "the story, in its new form, began unwinding itself, like a roll of film that had been neatly stored in my brain, waiting for a propitious moment to be re-set in the projector and cast on a screen." This new twist to the term *projection* emerged from extensive experience. She had taken an exhilarating step into the technology of the cinema.

In spring 1929, when asked by *The Little Review* what she most liked to do, H. D. had no trouble answering. "I myself have learned to use the small projector," she replied, "and spend literally hundreds of hours alone in my apartment, making the mountains and village streets and my own acquaintances reel past me in the light and light and light." The projector belonged to POOL Productions, a company run by Bryher and Kenneth Macpherson, H. D.'s companions in film work in the late 1920s and early 1930s. H. D. wrote for their journal *Close Up*, acted in their films, did montage for one and publicity for two, and, finally, filled her contemporary poetry and fiction with images of light, focus, superimposition, and projection.

Most of H. D.'s film theory is in a series of essays composed for the first issues of *Close Up* and titled "The Cinema and the Classics." By "classics" H. D. meant, specifically, Greek culture and, more narrowly, the Greek amalgamation of the beautiful and the good. Despite Hollywood's fixation on "longdrawn out embraces and the artificially enhanced thud-offs of galloping bronchoes" and despite "the gigantic Cyclops, the American Censor" who prettifies beauty and homogenizes goodness, cinema offers our best opportunity to recapture Greek wisdom. In the hands of the avant-garde, film repossesses the visionary consciousness of Athens, Delphi, and Eleusis. Here, at last, "miracles and godhead are *not* out of place, are not awkward"; it is "a perfect medium . . . at last granted us."

The word *medium* resonates through H. D's meditations. Film is an artistic medium, one occupying a medial position between the filmmaker's visual imagination and our own, but for H. D. it also functions as a psychic medium externalizing and making perceptible invisible inward intentions and coherencies. The announcement of the POOL film *Wing Beat*, starring H. D. and Kenneth Macpherson, promises "Telepathy and attraction, the reaching out, the very edge of dimensions in dimensions." Film reads and reveals the far reaches of our minds, and this connects it for H. D. with the Delphian dictate "Know Thyself." The mediumship, however, is more than telepathic. Cinema discloses the thoughts of the gods, their power, knowledge, and beauty. It may even, finally, disclose their very being, for here "Hermes, indicated in faint light, may step forward, outlined in semi-obscurity, or simply dazzling the whole picture in a blaze of splendour. Helios may stand simply and restrained with uplifted arm."

Because film calls together in a dark room witnesses of charged hieratic images, images that make manifest what was mysterious, because it brings light to darkness and conveys the will of beauty and goodness, cinema is to us what the church was to H. D.'s ancestors and what the Delphic oracle was to the Greeks. The long two-part poem H. D. entitled "Projector" and published alongside her essays in *Close Up* names the Delphian Apollo as god of the cinema and envisions him reasserting his domain on a ray of image-bearing, world-creating light:

> This is his gift;
> light,
> light
> a wave
> that sweeps
> us
> from old fears
> and powers.

Just as Apollo claimed the power of prophecy at Delphi by slaying the monster Python, this projector-god destroys squalid commercialism and makes Hollywood into a "holy wood" where

> souls upon the screen
> live lives that might have been
> live lives that ever are.

H. D.'s ecstatic poem greets Apollo as he begins his miracles. The poem's clipped, incantatory lines and detailed invocation of the Delphic paradigm, however, suggest something more than simple salutation. H. D.'s advocacy asserts a place and function for herself. Apollo at Delphi works through his oracle, the Pythoness, who is a medium between the god and the seeker. She has what *Notes on Thought and Vision* calls "womb vision," for it is she who receives, rings to form, and throws forth his knowledge. As the transmitter of the prophetic message, her position precedes and predicts H. D.'s. Who, then, is the poem's "Projector"? It is Apollo, light-bearer; it is his Delphic oracle; it is H. D. herself, the projector-poet; and perhaps it is also the machine in her apartment which, in a coincidence that doubtless delighted H. D., rested, like the Pythoness herself, upon a tripod—symbol of prophecy, prophetic utterance, occult or hidden knowledge.

PROJECTION: A DEFENSE MECHANISM IN WHICH THE INDIVIDUAL
ATTRIBUTES AN IMPULSE OF HIS OWN TO SOME OTHER PERSON OR
OBJECT IN THE OUTSIDE WORLD

Close Up did not push a particular doctrine. It contained accounts of German and Russian cinema, translations of Eisenstein, reviews of film exhibitions and avant-garde screenings, vituperations against Hollywood's censor, advice on the newest cameras and projectors, and assorted editorial pronouncements. As Anne Friedberg notes, however, one consistent strain in its pages is psychoanalytic theory. Many of the writers cite Freud; Dr. Hanns Sachs, Bryher's analyst and a member of Freud's inner circle, and lay analysts Barbara Low and Mary Chadwick contribute essays; and editor Kenneth Macpherson frequently elaborates his positions with psychoanalytic concepts. This interest illuminates Macpherson's own most ambitious project, the full-length film *Borderline*, in which H. D., disguised in the credits as Helga Doorn, plays a character caught between conscious and unconscious pressures. Her work on *Borderline* provides a glimpse into H. D.'s preoccupations some three years prior to her analysis with Freud.

Macpherson intended to take the film "into the labyrinth of the human mind, with its queer impulses and tricks, its unreliability, its stresses and obsessions, its half-formed deductions, its glibness, its occasional amnesia, its fantasy, suppression, and desires." The plot is a tangle of desire, murder, and bigotry. Astrid, the sensitive and worldly neurotic played by H. D., comes with her alcoholic husband Thorne to a small Swiss border town; in this limbo, she becomes obsessed with Pete, a giant, half-vagrant black man played by Paul Robeson, and is stabbed to death by Thorne in a crime for which the town persecutes Pete. The frayed atmosphere is exacerbated by the movie's silence, by the camera's raking of symbolic landscapes and faces gouged with light, and finally, by Astrid's staring into the camera—as if she were emptying her mind out onto the screen, or, even more uncomfortably, as if she were attempting a direct transfer of her psychic content into the mind of the viewer.

The unsigned, thirty-nine page publicity pamphlet, almost certainly written by H. D., reminds us that "Astrid, the woman, terribly incarnated, is 'astral' in effect." The earthly/astral border is only one more in a film deliberately situated on every possible margin: physical, social, racial, sexual, mental, even, since Macpherson and his company were displaced and uncredentialed, professional. The film's terrain is the limbo that H. D.'s projection—Imagist, clairvoyant, cinematic, or prophetic—always traversed.

If the stark, otherwordly sequences that punctuate *Borderline* have a hieroglyphic portentousness, it is because they in fact originated in picture-writing. As the pamphlet explains, Macpherson drew 910 pen-and-ink sketches giving detailed directions for each shot. Each was a light sculpture, a dream scene, a hieroglyph designed for projection, a "welding of the psychic or super-normal to the things of precise everyday existence." For H. D. this places *Borderline* in the same psychic category as the Corfu pictures and the charged dreams of her accounts of analysis: "For myself," she writes in *Tribute to Freud*, "I consider this sort of dream or projected picture or vision as a sort of halfway state between ordinary dream and the vision of those who, for lack of a more definite term, we must call psychics or clairvoyants."

"Borderline" is, of course, a psychoanalytic term designating the halfway state between neurosis and psychosis. H. D. would know the term from Bryher, who in the late 1920s was both studying and undergoing analysis, from lectures she and Bryher attended in Berlin during these years, from the general theoretic climate of *Close Up*, and finally, from the fact that Macpherson in titling his film doubtless had the technical term in mind. While playing on all its other nuances, however, the pamphlet shuns the psychoanalytic meaning and resituates the borderline so that it lies not between the neurotic and the psychotic but between the neurotic and the psychic. This gesture typifies H. D.'s complex attitude toward psychoanalysis.

"*Borderline* is a dream," the pamphlet pronounces, entering its summation, "and perhaps when we say that we have said everything. The film is the art of dream portrayal and perhaps when we say that we have achieved the definition, the synthesis toward which we have been striving." For H. D., dream was always interior projection, a cinematic exhibition of the mind's submerged content. Like *Borderline* and the Corfu pictures, dreams display "the *hieroglyph of the unconscious.*" It is for "open[ing] the field to the study of this vast, unexplored region" that H. D. would be forever grateful to Freud.

Accounts of dreams are, as it were, projections of projections, and H. D. was justly proud of her command of the intricate transmutation. It was not simple. "The dream-picture focussed and projected by the mind, may perhaps achieve something of the character of a magic-lantern slide and may 'come true' in the projection," H. D. explains in *The Gift*, but to make it do so demands all the equipment developed by Freud: free association, command of the parallels between individual, biological, and racial development, and mastery of concepts like condensation, displacement, dramatization by visual imagery, superimposition, distortion, and screen memory. An admonitory passage from *The Gift* conveys H. D.'s delight in her descriptive skill:

> The dream, the memory, the unexpected related memories must be allowed to sway backward and forward, as if the sheet or screen upon which they are projected, blows and is rippled in the wind of whatever emotion or idea is entering a door, left open. The wind blows through the door, from outside, through long, long corridors of personal memory, of biological and of race-memory. Shut the door and you have a neat flat picture. Leave all the doors open and you are almost out-of-doors, almost within the un-walled province of the fourth-dimensional. This is creation in the truer sense, in *the wind bloweth where it listeth* way.

Her delight was matched—perhaps even sparked—by Freud's joy in the intense and haunting dreams of her two periods of analysis in 1933 and 1934.

"[Freud] has embarrassed me," H. D. writes Bryher in April 1933, "by telling me I have a rare type of mind he seldom meets with, in which thought crystalizes out in dream in a very special way." In their sessions they pour over dream after enigmatic dream, Freud complimenting her on their "very 'beautiful' construction," their invention of symbols, their "almost perfect mythological state." The fact that so much of H. D.'s post-analysis writing places her before a luminous dream that she both creates and analyzes, participates in and watches, surely repeats the exhilarations of her contact with Freud.

In the analysis of her dreams, H. D. and Freud are colleagues who heed, adjust, and validate each other's interpretations, but much of the analysis material indicates another kind of relationship. Here H. D. is a small, confused seeker and Freud is the wise Hermit on the edge of the Forest of the Unknown, Asklepios the blameless healer, Herakles struggling with Death, Jermiah discovering the well of living water, St. Michael who will slay the Dragon of her fears, even the infinitely old symbol weighing Psyche the soul in the Balance, even the Supreme Being. The formulations, as Freud taught us, call on another sort of projection: transference, or the process by which the patient directs toward the physician an intensity of feeling that is based on no real relation between them and can only be traced back to old fantasies rendered unconscious.

The first step in analysis, the establishment of transference, H. D. took easily, if somewhat ambiguously. To H. D., Freud became papa, the Professor, his study, like Professor Doolittle's, cluttered with erudite writings and "sacred objects"; to Freud, however, transference made him the gentle, intuitive mother. Both were right, for as Susan Friedman points out, "in an ultimate sense, he became both mother and father to her as he fused her mother's art and her father's science in the mysteries of psychoanalysis." Her transference love for Freud enabled H. D. to affirm herself as poet and visionary, release her blocked creativity, and write with passion and continuity throughout the rest of her life.

There was another, murkier transference in the analysis, however, one subject not to resolution but to repetition. This rendered every figure in her life a stand-in for someone else, every love a deflection, every trauma a replay of earlier disaster. The records of analysis swarm with formulae as Freud and H. D. decipher originary patterns beneath a palimpsest of repetition. Ellis as father, Freud as mother; Aldington as father, Bryher as mother; Rodeck as father, Bryher as mother; her "ideal" brothers Rodeck, Frances Gregg, and Bryher; her "real" brothers Pound, Aldington, and Macpherson—the list goes on and on. One fevered letter to Bryher in March 1933 indicates both the exuberance and the suspicion of futility beneath all this activity:

> My triangle is mother-brother-self. That is, early phallic-mother, baby brother or smaller brother and self. I have worked in and

around that, I have HAD the baby with my mother, and been the
phallic-baby, hence Moses in the bulrushes, I have HAD the baby
with the brother, hence Cuthbert [Adlington], Cecil Grey, Kenneth
etc. I have HAD the "illumination" or the back to the womb WITH
the brother, hence you and me in Corfu, island=mother. . . .
Well, well, well, I could go on and on and on, demonstrating but
once you get the first idea, all the other, later diverse-looking
manifestations fit in somehow. Savvy?????? It's all too queer and at
first, I felt life had been wasted in all this repetition etc. but somehow F. seems to find it amusing, sometimes.

Until the end of her life, H. D. deluged near strangers with intensities of
feeling belonging not to them but to their forerunners or even to the forerunners of their forerunners. Here transference was a condition not of cure but
of compulsion.

Dreams and transference are projective in a general sense, but psychoanalytic theory, of course, defines the term *projection* precisely: as a defense
mechanism that causes us to attribute an interior wish to a person or object in
the exterior world. This charged term formed an exemplary site for the
disagreement between Freud and H. D. about the nature of reality, and here
H. D. took Freud on, if not directly, nonetheless deftly.

The word *projection* occurs frequently in *Tribute to Freud*, but, like "borderline" in the movie pamphlet, not once with its Freudian denotation. The
"projected picture," images "projected" from the subconscious mind or
from outside, the strain of projection, the impact that "projected" a dream-
sequence: each use of the term points to the Corfu vision. Of all the events
that could have titled H. D.'s original account of analysis, her choice, "Writing on the Wall," privileges and gives biblical sanction to the vision at Corfu.
The phrase draws our attention from the analytic to the mystical and prepares our confrontation with the main question raised by the Corfu pictures.
Were they, as Freud maintained, a "dangerous 'symptom'," or were they
rather an upwelling of creativity, an inspiration, and a promise?

In Freud's use of the word, the "projected pictures" reduce to defensive
exteriorizations of unconscious material. In this sense they would be desperate strategies of containment. By H. D.'s definition, however, the projected
pictures are precisely the opposite: they open the boundaries of the self to
another, higher reality, not in order to deny its operations but in order to
claim and be claimed by them. The pictures predict—or project into the
future—not a repetition of palimpsestic transferences but a transcendence, a
breakthrough into a new dimension. In her final image, the angel Niké
moving through a field of tents, H. D. recognizes the aftermath of the next
world war: "When that war had completed itself," she writes, "rung by rung
or year by year, I, personally (I felt), would be free, I myself would go on in
another, a winged dimension." This vision of 1920, recalled and reaffirmed
through analysis with Freud, predicts the transmutations wrought two
decades later in the great poem H. D. would call her War Trilogy.

PROJECTION: THE CASTING OF SOME INGREDIENT INTO A CRUCIBLE; ESPECIALLY IN ALCHEMY, THE CASTING OF THE POWDER OF THE PHILOSOPHER'S STONE (POWDER OF PROJECTION) UPON A METAL IN FUSION TO EFFECT ITS TRANSMUTATION INTO GOLD OR SILVER

H. D.'s "Notes on Recent Writing," composed in 1949 for Norman Holmes Pearson, stresses the generation of *Trilogy* out of the ravages of World War Two. Throughout the Nazi air assault, H. D. had remained in London, close to the Hyde Park anti-aircraft batteries and in the thick of incendiary raids. Bombs—buzz bombs, fly bombs, oil bombs, doodle-bugs, and low, close V-1 rockets—in often nightly bombardments tore open apartments, leveled buildings, lodged unexploded shells in areaways and under pavements, and threw the survivors into unregistered dimensions of terror and powerlessness. "The fire has raged around the crystal," H. D. reported to Pearson. "The crystalline poetry to be projected, must of necessity, have that fire in it. You will find fire in *The Walls Do Not Fall, Tribute to the Angels* and *The Flowering of the Rod. Trilogy,* as we called the three volumes of poetry written during War II, seemed to project itself in time and out-of-time together. And with no effort."

After agonized blockage, H. D. was writing with assurance and speed, her typewriter clacking across the noise of the raids. In the last eight months of 1944 alone she composed three of her finest works: from May 17th to 31st, "Tribute to the Angels"; from September 19th to November 2nd, "Writing on the Wall"; from December 18th to 31st, "The Flowering of the Rod." The Freud memoir slid easily between the last two parts of *Trilogy,* for *Trilogy* performs, in its way, a kind of analysis. If, as Robert Duncan suggests, "in Freudian terms, the War is a manifestation of the latent content of the civilization and its discontents, a projection of the collective unconscious," *Trilogy* works to surface the terrors and redirect savage impulses to sublimer ends.

As in analysis, dream is the agent of transmutation. *Trilogy,* however, builds on a distinction made in "Writing on the Wall" between "trivial, confused dreams and . . . real dreams. The trivial dream bears the same relationship to the real as a column of gutter-press newsprint to a folio page of a play of Shakespeare." The enigmas of revelatory dreams emerge not from extravagantly repressed desire but from "the same source as the script or Scripture, the Holy Writ or Word." Dream is the active force of the sacred in human life. "Now it appears very clear," H. D. writes, "that the Holy Ghost, / childhood's mysterious enigma, / is the Dream":

> it merges the distant future
> with most distant antiquity,
>
> states economically
> in a simple dream-equation
>
> the most profound philosophy,
> discloses the alchemist's secret

and follows the Mage
in the desert.

Each of the three parts of *Trilogy* generates a real dream, a vision of eternal
beings who reappear with the recovery of "the alchemist's secret," the
process through which destruction precedes and permits new, more perfect
life.

War executes a horrifying reverse alchemy. Rails are melted down and
made into guns, books are pulped for cartridge cases, the Word is absorbed
in the Sword, and people become "wolves, jackals, / mongrel curs." Casting
back to "most distant antiquity" in order to project "the distant future,"
H. D. turns to the early alchemists. Though our culture cartoons them as
greedy bunglers struggling to turn dung into gold, alchemists were scholars
of spiritual transformation. Alchemical formulas and philosophy structure
Trilogy and give the metaphor of *projection* its final precise and complex
elaboration.

Until modern chemistry's mechanical and quantitative postulates re-
placed alchemy's organic, qualitative theory, four tenets seemed self-evident. The universe, alchemists believed, was everywhere alive, all matter
possessing body, passion, and soul. Because substances appear, grow,
decay, diminish, and disappear, secondly, transmutation is considered the
essence of life. Third, all transmutation moves toward perfection: the seed
becomes a tree, the worm turns into a butterfly, grains of sand round into
pearls. In this process, the seed splits, the worm bursts, the sand vanishes,
thus demonstrating the fourth alchemical tenet: the belief that all creation
requires an initial act of destruction.

Projection is the final stage of an alchemical transmutation, the act that
precipitates new, more perfect form. All *Trilogy* moves toward the moment
of projection, but to understand this moment we must look briefly at the
alchemists' explication of transformation. Like Aristotle, they believed that
each substance consists of indeterminate prime matter and specific form
impressed into it like a hot seal in wax. Changing a substance, therefore, was
simply a matter of altering its "form." Ingredients were cast into a crucible,
heated, and, in a process alchemists called "death" or "putrefaction," reduced to prime matter; then, after many intricate maneuvers—calcination,
distillation, sublimation, fermentation, separation, and more—the specific
form of a finer substance was projected into the crucible and new shape
sprang forth. However audacious or even preposterous this procedure might
now appear, to the alchemists it merely hastened a natural, universal
process.

The magical act—or, as H. D. would remind us, the act of the Mage—
was the making of the seed of perfection called the philosopher's stone or the
elixir of life. Formulas were inherited, debated, obfuscated, adulterated,
encoded, translated and mistranslated into and out of a dozen different
languages, but the basic schema remained the same. To effect what was
called "the alchemical marriage," sulphur, the male element, and mercury,

the female element, were fused in the crucible and this union generated the philosopher's stone, "the Royal Child" which, like Christ, redeemed all life to its highest form. H. D.'s spiritual challenge in *Trilogy* is no less than the reawakening of this transmuting, projecting power: "the alchemist's key . . . / the elixir of life, the philosopher's stone" which "is yours if you surrender // sterile logic, trivial reason."

Nearly every image in *Trilogy* enacts a transmutation meant to convince us of the universality of the process and to draw our perception along a continuous line from the poem's smallest event to its largest. These images are holograms or discrete cells of the poem containing in code the plan of the whole. The archetypal alchemical transformation, for example, the changing of lead to gold, reappears in a casually inserted icon as "corn . . . enclosed in black-lead, / ploughed land." Washed by earth's waters, heated by sun's fire, and strewn with seed, black-lead land becomes gold corn. "This is no rune nor riddle," H. D. reiterates; "it is happening everywhere." In alchemical crucibles, under pressure, again and again, metamorphosis occurs: the mollusc shell holds a sand-grain, the egg-shell an egg; the heart-shell lodges a seed dropped by the phoenix; the cocoon houses a caterpillar, the shroud a worm preparing resurrection. Even the brain in its skull-case ferments and distills, dissolving sterile logic, generating new vision.

These images prepare our understanding of the poem's larger sweep. With properly cryptic encoding, the sections together retell the story of the making of the philosopher's stone. Each section contains a crucible, a purifying fire, and a double movement of destruction and creation; each moves us backward through time and inward across logic and custom, closer and closer to the culminating miracle of projection.

In "The Walls Do Not Fall," part one of the *Trilogy*, the crucible is the city of London, flattened by ceaseless pounding, filled with the shards of civilization, flaming with "Apocryphal fire." London's ruin makes it "the tomb, the temple," a matrix of death and rebirth in which Old Testament wrath and vengeance yield to a higher form of being. In a dream-vision, H. D. witnesses the reborn god whom she calles "Ra, Osiris, *Amen*":

> he is the world-father,
> father of past aeons,
>
> present and future equally;
> beardless, not at all like Jehovah.

This slender figure is the anointed son, the Christos, whose luminous amber eyes shine like transforming fire. With his entry into the poem, H. D. has half the alchemical formula, traditionally represented as the sun, fire, sulphur, the fathering principle.

In "Tribute to the Angels," part two of *Trilogy*, the crucible becomes the poem-bowl and the shards the word-fragments that survive as traces of the great traditions of female divinity. After proper invocations, with reverence for her materials and awe at the powers they hold, H. D. the poet-alchemist begins:

Now polish the crucible
and in the bowl distill

a word most bitter, *marah*,
a word bitterer still, *mar*,

sea, brine, breaker, seducer,
giver of life, giver of tears;

Now polish the crucible
and set the jet of flame

under, till *marah-mar*
are melted, fuse and join

and change and alter,
mer, mere, mère, mater, Maia, Mary,

Star of the Sea,
Mother.

This alchemical transaction creates a pulsing green-white, opalescent jewel which lives, breathes, and gives off "a vibration that we can not name." After distilling, purifying, and refining this force, after witnessing intermediate manifestations and meditating on "the moon-cycle . . . the moon-shell," H. D. has a dream-vision that closes this stage of her alchemy. It is an epiphany of the Lady, stripped of her myriad old forms—Isis, Astarte, Aset, Aphrodite, the old Eve, the Virgin Mary, "Our Lady of the Goldfinch, / Our Lady of the Candelabra"—and released into new, as yet unnamed power. She is without the bridegroom, without the child; she is not hieratic; she is "no symbolic figure." The book she carries "is not / the tome of the ancient wisdom" but "the unwritten volume of the new." This as yet uninscribed essence is the renewed stuff of the other half of the alchemical formula, traditionally represented as the moon, mercury, the mothering principle.

In "The Flowering of the Rod," part three of *Trilogy*, the crucible is not a place or a poem but the legend of resurrection: "a tale of a Fisherman, / a tale of a jar or jars," an ancient story which in its Christian form is "the same— different—the same attributes, / different yet the same as before." What the poet-alchemist must break down here is the familiar racist and misogynist reading of the scriptures that dismisses Kaspar as a dark heathen and Mary Magdalene as a devil-ridden harlot, making both peripheral to the real story. In H. D.'s rewriting, they are central. The first two parts of *Trilogy* had precipitated a new male and female principle; now, in part three, they meet in alchemical marriage to effect the miraculous transformation. Kaspar, who might be Abraham or an Angel or even God, is here a somewhat forgetful and fallible philosopher, dream-interpreter, astrologer, and alchemist from a long line of Arabs who knew "the secret of the sacred process of distillation." He carries with him a sealed jar of myrrh exuding a fragrance that is the eternal essence "of all flowering things together": the elixir of life, the seed of resurrection.

Kaspar was traveling to "a coronation and a funeral," like all alchemical transmutations "a double affair," when found by Mary Magdalene, avatar of H. D.'s "mer, mere, mère, mater, Maia, Mary, // Star of the Sea, / Mother." When he momentarily abandons his patriarchal stiffness and, assuming a posture of reverence, stoops to pick up Mary's scarf, he is granted a vision that reaches back to "the islands of the Blest" and "the lost centre-island, Atlantis" and forward to "the whole scope and plan // of our and his civilization on this, / his and our earth." The spell he hears recovers the lost matriarchal genealogy, identifies Mary as heritor of *"Lilith born before Eve / and one born before Lilith, / and Eve"* (italics in original), and convinces Kaspar to yield her the precious myrrh. This act—in H. D.'s astonishing rewriting— seeds the resurrection. When Mary washes the feet of Christ, she anoints him with the elixir of life and insures that his crucifixion will be the first step in triumphant regeneration. Consecrated by Mary, Christ himself becomes the legendary philosopher's stone: the resurrection and the life.

Mary Magdalene's washing of the feet of Christ is the act of the alchemist: the projecting of the Mage's elixir onto substance prepared for transmutation. Behind the story of Kaspar and Mary is the old tale of sulphur and mercury; ahead of it is the work of the poet-alchemist who wanted to give us, through her combinations and recombinations of lost spells and legends, the power to transmute our own damaged civilization. The ultimate, audacious hope of *Trilogy* is that it might itself become an elixir of life, a resurrective power.

The mechanical philosophy that superseded alchemy posits a world of dead matter, matter without passion and without soul. This world of objects has often proved for its inhabitants a place of subjection, dejection, abjection, rejection—a place of energy twisted, repressed, or subverted. The nurturing universe H. D. glimpsed from the beginning of her career is profoundly different, a world of immanence and immediacy that could be called a projective universe. As the glow of radium with its puzzle of energy resident in matter led Marie Curie through her discoveries, the image of projection served as a conceptual and aesthetic focus for H. D.'s developing inquiries. An instrument of verbal organization and a source of intellectual and spiritual energies, projection was an act, an intuition, and an integration. It opened into, achieved, and helped to maintain the coherence and direction of her lifelong redemptive quest.

The "Feminine" Language
of Marianne Moore

Bonnie Costello

Several critics of Marianne Moore's poetry have remarked, directly or indirectly, on its "feminine" quality, although it is sometimes difficult to decide just what they mean by this. T. S. Eliot, for instance, concludes his 1923 essay on Moore with a statement he either seems to feel is self-explanatory or hasn't really examined: "And there is one final, and 'magnificent' compliment: Miss Moore's poetry is as 'feminine' as Christina Rossetti's, one never forgets that it is written by a woman; but with both one never thinks of this as anything but a positive virtue." What can he have in mind? Is it the "restraint" and "humility" that Randall Jarrell talks about in his essay on Moore, entitled "Her Shield"? Is it the ladylike quality, the "chastity" of taste (a term rarely applied to men) that R. P. Blackmur saw as both the virtue and defect of her work? Or perhaps Eliot was thinking of Moore's preoccupation with surfaces and objects of sense experience (especially trivial experience) which he and others have praised as her "genuineness" while they have distinguished genuineness from "greatness." Men write out of primitive or heroic occasions, women write out of everyday occasions. In his essay about Edna Saint Vincent Millay, "The Poet as Woman," John Crowe Ransom distinguishes Moore for having less "deficiency of masculinity," that is, (and he is explicit about this) "intellectual interest" than other women writers. Yet we feel a reserve of prejudice influencing his view of her, even when his purpose is to applaud, as in "On Being Modern with Distinction." Woman's love, he says in the Millay essay, is a fixation to natural sense objects (woman can't transcend mundane experience). Woman's love is devoted (she has no self). Man has lapsed, since childhood, from natural feelings, and his mind thus grows apart from woman's (woman remains childish). Woman does not go to the office (she has the leisure to be idle and cultivate her tenderness). Woman is set in her

From *Women and Language in Literature and Society*. © 1980 by Praeger Publishers.

"famous attitudes" (woman's mind is full of clichés and household truisms). These assumptions appear, under a gauze of affection, throughout criticism of Moore's poetry. Roy Harvey Pearce begins by praising Moore's modesty and ease, but his parenthetical criticisms make him sound a little insincere in wishing William Carlos Williams, Conrad Aiken, and E. E. Cummings had Moore's female virtue.

Surprisingly, in her staunchly feminist argument, Suzanne Juhasz agrees with the men, both in the way they read the poems and in how they evaluate them. Rather than reexamining the male standards she assumes them a priori. Rather than consider the possible complexity of Moore's predilections and the original strength of her verse, Juhasz accepts past interpretations and simply seeks to explain how Moore's social and historical situation might cause her to "retreat" into the "lesser" qualities of "spinsterly" writing for self-protection. Because she is looking for something else (confessional poetry), Juhasz completely misses the distinctiveness of Moore's inventions. To Juhasz, insofar as Moore's stylistic devices are "feminine" they are defenses.

Moore's art does display much of the taste and manners, the "vanity" as well as the "nobler virtue" our society ascribes to women. She is a lover of ornamental surfaces; she is fascinated with fashion and wrote several articles on the subject; she is "gossipy" and chatty, passing on bits of hearsay and borrowed phrases; she is a collector of knickknacks, her poems are like overstuffed cupboards, full of irrelevancies and distractions. Moore's life reflected the same tendencies and tastes. Her scrapbooks and library are full of literature on women's dress, interior design, jewelry, ornamental art. Her letters go on for paragraphs describing someone's living room, a new coat, a cat she is caring for. But somehow, when she is describing a friend's hat or a clay bird someone gave her, these particulars seem more important as *occasions* for imaginative response than for their conventional value.

Moore's critics have tended to identify her "feminine" qualities superficially, taking up her lexicon of virtues but applying their own definitions and prejudices to it. In context, I want to suggest, these qualities take on a special, powerful meaning, quite inverted in value. Moore purposely assumes the traditional "household" virtues and attributes in order to redefine them in the action of her poems. Moore's "feminine" virtues and manners do not glass-in or soften reality, do not trivialize experience or diminish the claims of the self, but on the contrary become in various ways the chief sources of energy in her work. Continually in her poetry and in her prose Moore shows a close relationship between moral and technical virtue. As Geoffrey Hartman has observed in a brief note on the poet, "her style does not embody a morality, it is one." The central morality of her style (and the chief source of its vitality) is a resistance to the complacencies of thought and language, to a tendency to accept given forms as descriptive of the world as it is. This is not a passive resistance, for it works in alliance with her mental voracity, continually readjusting the line and pushing against the limits of language. Moore's access to this central concern with the limits of language is through a conventional but redefined femininity. Or, conversely, the breaking up of our assumptions about certain types of virtue and manner is a natural instance of a larger concern for resisting complacencies of thought and language.

This is not, for Moore, an explicitly feminist issue. She nowhere indicates that she thinks of her poems or the values they advocate as particularly "feminine." In fact most of the animal figures that demonstrate these qualities are given male pronouns. But it seems only natural that Moore should select the attributes most readily applied to her as the focus of her efforts to rediscover language. Whether these qualities are a natural or inherited part of her femininity, however, one feels in reading her poems that a man could not have seen the potential in such qualities that Moore has seen and exploited.

One of Moore's favorite categories of virtue, observed throughout her poetry and criticism, is humility, with its analogues, restraint, and modesty. What a nineteenth-century reviewer said of the woman poet Felicia Hemans has been said in other ways (in the quotations above) of Moore: "she never forgets what is due feminine reserve." Indeed, Moore learned well the lesson of Bryn Mawr president Carey Thomas which she quotes in her essay on the "impassioned emancipator": she "behaved not with decorum but with marked decorum." This does not mean that Moore practiced humility without sincerity. Rather, she discovers in it a special value: "humility is a kind of armor." Critics usually take this to mean that by playing down the self, by making few overt claims to authority and power, we avoid subjecting ourselves to envy or attack. Moore's descriptiveness, her extensive use of quotation, her choice of peripheral subject matter, her circumlocution, are all pointed to as technical counterparts of her moral predilections. But what Moore, with Carey Thomas, understood is that strength and power are not necessarily stifled or even contained, but are on the contrary nurtured through acts of self-protection. Aggressive, indecorous, intolerant behavior wastes energy and creativity which can be better sustained and wielded with a certain guardedness. She quotes Thomas's remark: "Bryn Mawr must not be less guarded because it is good." Juhasz and others tend to see nothing but the armor, neglecting what is achieved by its use. Moore compromises nothing in her "self-protective" humility; she gains. Though the idea of "feminine reserve" may conventionally imply an attitude appropriate to inferiority, Moore does not even pretend to weakness. She shows humility to be a reserve, in the sense of a reservoir of power. At the end of "In This Age of Hard Trying," for instance, Moore shows how an apparent "inconsequence of manner" is more effective and durable than aggressive certitude. [All lines quoted from Marianne Moore's poetry are taken from *The Complete Poems of Marianne Moore* (New York: Viking, 1967).]

IN THIS AGE OF HARD TRYING,
NONCHALANCE IS GOOD AND

"really, it is not the
    business of the gods to bake clay pots." They did not

do it in this instance. A few
    revolved upon the axes of their worth
as if excessive popularity might be a pot;

they did not venture the
    profession of humility. The polished wedge
      that might have split the firmament
        was dumb. At last it threw itself away
and falling down, conferred on some poor fool, a privilege.

"Taller by the length of
    a conversation of five hundred years than all
      the others," there was one whose tales
        of what could never have been actual—
were better than the haggish, uncompanionable drawl

of certitude; his by—
    play was more terrible in its effectiveness
      than the fiercest frontal attack.
        The staff, the bag, the feigned inconsequence
of manner, best bespeak that weapon, self-protectiveness.

Humility, a guarded manner, has the advantage of taking the listener offguard. And Moore practices her point in a number of ways here. The prosaic, conversational tone, the long, meandering, run-on lines and shifts of figurative level, give the impression of nonchalance. She is not, she seems to suggest, writing anything so grand as a poem. But the design is present, though unobtrusive, acting on our imaginations almost without alerting us. We hardly notice, though we subliminally hear, the careful rhymes, the subtly extended metaphor, the logic of the tale, so that the final lines have a special bold effect in their paradoxical clarity.

Moore's feminine humility, then, is designing: she wants to create and sustain an interest which overt self-assertion or pronounced form would snuff out. Moore's humility and restraint are not passive defenses but ways of gathering force, as a bow is pulled back in order to carry the arrow farther when it is finally released. Such motives and strategies are at work in many of her best poems, especially "The Plumet Basilisk," "The Frigate Pelican," "To a Snail," and "The Pangolin," poems about animals she admires for elusive strengths similar to those she displays in her writing. The end of humility is not self-protection for its own sake so much as "gusto," the spark released in the discovery of and enthusiasm for what is out of our control. In language, "humility is an indispensable teacher, enabling concentration to heighten gusto." Whereas humility associated with women usually implies something negative, a withdrawal, a deference, Moore shows its positive outcome. She is one woman for whom humility is not an end but a means of inspiration and expression.

Humility is not armor against the aggressions of the world on the self so much as against those of the self on the world, against the "disease, My

Self," as she calls it. To impose the self and its accumulated structures on the world is to narrow the world and trap the self, a self-defeating gesture. "In Distrust of Merits" takes this theme up directly, but it is always present obliquely in Moore's verse. For her, humility "keeps the world large," preserves a place for something beyond the self that keeps us from complacency and satiation, consequently keeping us alive.

"His Shield" is the poem quoted most often in connection with Moore's idea of the armor of humility. She says it directly: "his shield was his humility." The poem warns against "greed and flattery," insisting that "freedom" is "the power of relinquishing what one would keep." Bravado does not please or improve anything, it simply attracts contenders, and wastes energy fighting them off. "Be dull, don't be envied or armed with a measuring rod." Don't attract envy by flaunting your achievement. This is a traditional code of femininity, but it usually implies that feminine achievement is incommensurate with envy or pride. Let us see how Moore understands her message.

The poem contrasts two kinds of armor, as several critics have pointed out. Moore finds that the spiny covering of the "edgehog miscalled hedgehog with all his edges out . . . won't do." Instead, "I'll wrap myself in salamander skin." The armor of "pig-fur" aggessing on the outside would scare things off. Its force is its inadequacy. But "asbestos" armor endures rather than extinguishes fire. It allows the outside world to enclose without annihilating the subject. Furthermore, it keeps the edges inside, keeps a fire alive internally rather than exhausting it in consuming ego. The ideal is "a lizard in the midst of flames, a firebrand that is life," who is, to use a phrase from Moore's critical essays, "galvanized against inertia." Where possession, and its verbal equivalent, singleminded assertion, imply stasis and complacency, survival and freedom require the constant readjustment of thought. At the level of the sentence, "humility" does not mean that one should be silent, but rather that language should continually be revised in the presence of what it cannot accommodate.

The utopia represented in the poem is an "unconquerable country of unpompous gusto." Power is not compromised, it is simply redistributed. Presbyter John, the hero of the poem, "styled himself but presbyter." Gusto is generated less out of self-aggrandizing conquest or consumption than out of awareness, out of a perpetually perceived difference between himself and the world, and the preservation of that difference and of desire. Resources are never used up in such a country.

Self-denial sounds like an odd basis for utopian experience, however. How can untapped wealth and power be considered as such? Moore manages to develop a sense of wealth without conquest through symbols of the potential effects of power. "Rubies large as tennis/balls conjoined in streams so/that the mountain seemed to bleed." The mountain only *seems* to bleed, but in doing so it marks a potential encounter. Emblematized strength is perpetual, exerted strength expires. Indeed, the emblem of external battle is only realized internally in the struggle for self-possession. The stream of blood, as the internalized warfare of humility, is only the blood stream, the "firebrand that is life."

If we think of the poet as presbyter, the vitality of Moore's lines comes from investing her thought in a presentation of the external world, hence so many poems in a descriptive mode which obliquely suggest a personal attitude. The oddity and apparent awkwardness of her lines comes from the sense of the inadequacy of the "measuring rod" to deal honestly with particulars. In language, "to relinquish what one would keep" is to continually resist available form. One way she does this is by having different forms displace each other to create a variegated surface. Images cut across each other to deny any rigid hierarchy. The "I" of the poem is swallowed up in description. Moral and discursive languages do not preside over the poem, but take their place in a range of languages: commercial, conversational, descriptive, metaphoric. While her lines expand and digress in pursuit of what is always posited as indefinable, they also create images of the self's internal activity, thereby steadying the flux of exploration. Thus, as Geoffrey Hartman has pointed out, "she achieves a dialogue of one, an ironic crossfire of statement that continually denies and reasserts the possibility of a selfless assertion of self . . . the armor she describes is the modesty whereby the self is made strong to resist itself, but also strong to assert its being against voracious dogmatism." The abnegation of self ultimately satisfies the self, for it widens the sphere of response, the self being continually discovered through response to the external world. It declares knowledge a matter of process rather than possession, and it ensures the continuance of that process. The aggressive self is identified in the conquest of one form over another, an impulse to narrow and exclude, which finally entraps the self in the form it has imposed. But the humble self flourishes in the multiplicity of form, identifying with none. It neither narrows its domain nor can be narrowed by the force of others, for it exists in resisting closure. Humility, restraint, paradoxically conduce to freedom.

The armor of humility appears as a recurrent theme and technique in the critical essays as well. "Humility, Concentration and Gusto" opens in the more than metaphorical context of war.

> In times like these we are tempted to disregard anything that has not a direct bearing on freedom; or should I say, an obvious bearing, for what is more persuasive than poetry, though as Robert Frost says, it works obliquely and delicately. Commander King-Hall, in his book *Total Victory*, is really saying that the pen is the sword when he says the object of war is to persuade the enemy to change his mind.

Such talk of persuasion would seem on the side of the porcupine's edgy, aggressive "battle dress." But what is persuasive, it turns out, what has bearing on freedom, is humility.

We don't want war, but it does conduce to humility, a someone said in the foreward to an exhibition catalogue of his work, "With what shall the artist arm himself save with his humility?" Humility, indeed, is armor, for it realizes that it is impossible to be original in the sense of doing something that has never been thought of before. Originality is in any case a byproduct of sincerity; that is to say, of feeling that is honest and accordingly rejects anything that might cloud the impression, such as unnecessary commas, modifying clauses, or delayed predicates.

One should not speak from ambition, then, but from honest feeling. The work, as one early critic of "female poetry" said, should "come from the heart, to be natural and true." Humility begins in this essay as a principle of simplicity and "quiet objectiveness," the reduction of self-assertion and the elevation of the external "impression." This is what Ransom "admired" in Millay, "a vein of poetry which is spontaneous, straightforward in diction, and excitingly womanlike; a distinguished objective record of a woman's mind." But humility becomes, as the essay goes on, a principle of difficulty standing for "the refusal to be false." When associated with "sincerity," the principle of humility and restraint becomes an agent of "gusto" by continually turning up a difference between the ways things are described and the way things are. "Gusto thrives on freedom," Moore explains, and freedom is preserved by failures of formal closure, by linguistic deviation. Daniel Berkeley Updike, Moore tells us, "has always seemed to me a phenomenon of eloquence because of the quiet objectiveness of his writing."

> And what he says of printing applies equally to poetry. It is true, is it not, that "style does not depend on decoration but on simplicity and proportion"? Nor can we dignify confusion by calling it baroque. Here, I may say, I am preaching to myself, since, when I am as complete as I like to be, I seem unable to get an effect plain enough.

But this is sophisticated humility on Moore's part. What is persuasive is her preaching to herself. Certainly we would not expect her to be less complete than she would like to be, so what might seem like ornament or excess in her verse is justified as honesty. Humility, which upholds an ideal of quiet objectiveness, of simplicity and proportion, also upholds sincerity, which will not force a perception into a dishonestly neat structure. What results from this ironic conflict is a lively play of impulses through a highly variegated, rebellious surface. Though she will not make public claims to "originality," her poems are certainly idiosyncratic and individual, and invite the interest of a public into the special world of a private enchantment.

Moore often speaks of her "natural reticence" in explaining the disobliging difficulty of some of her work. Conventionally, natural reticence belongs to woman's lesser capacity for logical assertion. As a supposedly intuitive rather than analytical creature, woman naturally has trouble being articulate: language is a system of codification and dissection. Moore herself says "feeling at its deepest tends to be inarticulate." But in her verse, once natural reticence gives way to speech it paradoxically causes an overflow of words.

The extreme digressiveness of surface in Moore's poetry has perplexed many critics. Juhasz sees it as deliberate evasiveness, her way "of not talking about what she is talking about and talking about what she is not talking about." Roy Harvey Pearce criticizes her "gossipy" quality and her "uncertainty as to direction." Though Pearce doesn't label these qualities "feminine" he implies as much, and Ransom is explicit. Woman's mind "has no direction or modulation except by its natural health." In other words, women live without purpose or focus beyond their immediate daily cares, to which they respond with inarticulate emotions. Their minds cannot sustain a logical argument or coherent structure because they have no powers of memory or projection, because they live in a continuous present.

Moore takes this digressive mode of thought and examines its special advantages. The mind that follows "its natural health" has a capacity for nuance which evades us where there is "too stern an intellectual emphasis." The "steam roller" mind crushes "all the particles down into close conformity." "As for butterflies, I can hardly conceive of one's attending upon you." The "aimless" mind, like "the magic flute" illogically weaves "what logic can't unweave." It is closer to the center of experience, alive to changes of an unconscious voice. It has a greater capacity for discovery, not blinded by its own hypotheses. It is more inclusive; it has more variety. Through her unwieldy, non-hierarchical structures, her elongated, loquacious sentences, Moore achieves a sense of "continuous present," a sense of the poem in process, the mind experiencing and discovering itself. Moore's prosody works to this same end, through inconspicuous syllabic measure, through dispersed rhyme and run-on lines. Ransom thinks women are always weak on form "because they are not strict enough and expert enough to manage forms, in their default of the discipline under which men are trained." Moore's form is indeed not uniform or abstractly applied; it depends upon movement and changes inflection, unleashing new impulses as they are called up.

Geoffrey Hartman has been unusually sensitive to the force of Moore's "gossipy" meanderings:

> one reads her poems less for their message (always suffused) than for the pleasure of seeing how style may become an act of the living—the infinitely inclusive and discriminating—mind.
>
> This mind, or rather Miss Moore's, is "an enchanting thing," it takes us by its very irrelevancies. Here too everything is surface; she talks, so to say, from the top of her mind and represents herself as a gossip on the baroque scale. But secretly she is a magician, and distracts on purpose. While her message eludes us through understatement, the poem itself remains teasingly alive through the

overstatement of its many tactics, till we accept the conventional rabbit, glorified by prestidigitation. Yet the magic of language becomes intensely moral on further acquaintance and her crazy-quilt of thoughts, quotations and sounds resolves into subtler units of meaning and rhythm. The free (but not formless) verse helps break up the automatic emphases of traditional syntax, and respects the more dynamic shifts of the inner, and not merely spoken voice.

Moore's elusive surfaces involve a moral prudence as well as an aesthetic one. She wants to dodge self-consciousness. What male critics have called a certain "fussiness" in Moore, she calls "unconscious fastidiousness" in which she finds "a great amount of poetry." What she seems to describe with the phrase is a kind of impulsive persistence in attempting to manage unmanageable material. Moore sees "unconscious fastidiousness" as an important part of the nurturing process, and imitates that process in her poems. Maternity is the subject of "The Paper Nautilus," and in comparing it to poetry she alters the conventional view of both. We conventionally think of maternal affection as a soft, graceful attitude, and similarly Moore's poetry has been prized, condescendingly, for its "relaxed ease." But the poem describes the process of nurture as a struggle beneath a surface of gentleness, a highly precarious restraint of power. Here unconscious fastidiousness means a high level of attentiveness without the imposition of rigid design which might impede natural development. The health of the eggs somehow depends upon maximum power and maximum restraint. The juxtaposition of "the ram's-horn cradled freight" and "a devilfish" and her eggs reinforces this tension. Later we are told of the shell's relative delicacy (like a wasp nest) and of its strength (like Ionic columns and the force of Parthenon sculpture). The tension described in holding back Hercules is clarified through a notion of a "fortress of love" but not relieved. We have metaphors of maximum impulse without the expiration of energy in action. The paper nautilus must "hide" her "freight" but not "crush" it. The same goes for poets. They too are "hindered to succeed."

> For authorities whose hopes
> are shaped by mercenaries?
>   Writers entrapped by
>   teatime fame and by
> commuters' comforts? Not for these
>   the paper nautilus
>   constructs her thin glass shell.

The poem starts by distinguishing two kinds of form, one which is complacent and commercial, generated by petty ambition, (and the association of mercenaries and commuters suggests a male domain) and another kind which will not "entrap" the writer or the audience. Appropriately, Moore will not "entrap" herself and her subject by restricting the tenor of this other kind. Rather, after an initial reference to writers, she shifts into a metaphor for metaphor itself: the shell in which our impression of the world can take shape without calcifying. But the shell is importantly the source and product of a maternal affection, a desire to nurture, in order finally to release the growing object. Her shell does not contain the eggs, or in terms of poetry, is not "the thing itself."

The feminine code of sacrifice says one must "relinquish what one would keep," and this is often applied to maternal relationships. But Moore changes this idea, in an artistic context, to a mode of freedom, not just a duty. Thus "the intensively watched eggs coming from/ the shell free it when they are freed." And the mother is free from her state of tension. Freedom, that is, requires differentiation.

We are curious when we sense something like ourselves yet different. Moore knows that observation is always in a way self-interested. Indeed, language is fundamentally of the self and not of the other, so self-expression is inevitable. Her mind follows likeness and finds difference, and again likeness, in the form of statements that are qualified, images which clash, rhymes that are interrupted, deviating detail, almost any form of verbal differentiation. In the process she does not accomplish "objectification" (curiosity is not satisfied) but something more interesting: a composition which metes out likeness and difference, visual and aural as well as seman-tic. The composition has the rhetorical power both to make associations and to suggest its own limits, since these verbal differences are made to seem like the difference between the world and what we say about it. Moore's compo-sitions are trails of associations which conduct the reader to their source. This identification occurs not only a our vicarious experience of her mental flux, but through her final, subtle self-portraiture. Moore begins by presenting an object apparently for its own sake, but in the process of describing it she borrows the object as a figure of her own activity. This self-portraiture is not the point of arrival of the poet's search for unity or for the thing itself, but a kind of parting embrace of words and things, a form of possession or appropriation that leaves the thing untouched while its ghost performs the function of analogy. Moore pursues the contours of objects for what she can discover of herself, but precisely because she learns about herself through observation of the external world, she can never declare her motive or speak of herself directly. "Imaginary possession" allows her to make associations without assumptions. She never gets to the point at which the idea subverts the observation.

The narcissists and sophisticates in the art world are the constant butt of Moore's satire, though they are "deaf to satire." In "Novices," for instance, she criticizes the "supertadpoles of expression" so attentive to their own egos

> so that they do not know "whether it is the buyer or the seller
> who gives the money"—
> an abstruse idea plain to none but the artist,
> the only seller who buys and holds on to the money.

> they write the sort of thing that would in their judgment
> > interest a lady;
> curious to know if we do not adore each letter of the alphabet
> > that goes to make a word of it—.

These "Will Honeycombs" who "anatomize their work," whose art is highly rational and symmetrical, are "bored by the detailless perspective of the sea," too absorbed in flattering themselves with their intellectual conquests to recognize the irrational power of nature. Moore contrasts their style with "the spontaneous unforced passion of the Hebrew language," which derives its "tempestuous energy" from a complete surrender to the sublimity of nature. In their example Moore shows that the self grows larger by imaginatively embracing something beyond its rational control.

But Moore is not simply advocating unconscious spontaneity or self-annihilation. Moore's is a highly conscious art, its objects derived primarily from books, not wild nature. It is the activity of tracing an "other," of knowing it in relation to oneself, as similar and different, that interests her, and she has called the "imaginary possession." With imaginary possession the mind is free to make associations, but at the same time knows them as such and does not identify them as exclusive truths. The task of "When I Buy Pictures," for instance, is to give both the illusion of a figure in the world who does not affect it, and to make a gesture of possession, to bring what is seen under the control of language.

> WHEN I BUY PICTURES
> or what is closer to the truth
> when I look at that of which I may regard myself as the
> > imaginary possessor,
> I fix upon what would give me pleasure in my average moments:
> the satire upon curiosity in which no more is discernible
> than the intensity of the mood;
> or quite the opposite—the old thing, the medieval decorated hat-
> > box,
> in which there are hounds with waists diminishing like the waist
> > of the hourglass,
> and deer and birds and seated people;

The game of imaginary possession involves discretion and humility, not prohibition:

> Too stern an intellectual emphasis upon this quality or that
> > detracts from one's enjoyment.
> It must not wish to disarm anything; nor may the approved
> > triumph easily be honored—
> that which is great because something else is small.

Of course these are not "average moments"; they are moments of luminosity, selected for their suggestiveness. The difference is that between selection which reveals a will and transformation which emblematizes a will. Moore does not simply direct her imagery toward a final or overarching intention. Her mind is attentive to the properties of each object and each word as it occurs. Age suggests images of age: hatboxes which bear images of old-fashioned hounds that are shaped like hourglasses whose waists remind her of time's waste and as these waists diminish the imagery narrows its reference to the matter of fact: deer, birds, and seated people. The coherence of a part takes her to the next, without rejecting the influence of the immediate details. But while avoiding "too stern an intellectual emphasis" a surprisingly complex range of associations, built upon the problems of time, distance and complexity, emerges in the movement from one image to the next, at no cost to the surface randomness of local association:

> It may be no more than a square of parquetry; the literal
> biography perhaps,
> in letters standing well apart upon a parchment-like expanse;
> an artichoke in six varieties of blue; the snipe-legged hieroglyphic
> in three parts;
> the silver fence protecting Adam's grave, or Michael taking
> Adam by the wrist.

Parquetry, artichoke, biography, hieroglyphic are all patterns of one kind or another. The range is inclusive and humorous. These orders are mocked, but shown to be natural. "Literal biography" is a contradiction reduced to its formal elements, letters standing well apart. We are directed through meaningless "orders" to consider our desire for possession, and the poem moves to emblems of our fall. These unite the previously separate and random problems of time, distance, and complexity raised in the imagery. Poems suppose a hierarchy of elements, but the rhetoric of the list resists our locating ourselves anywhere in particular in the poem. Moore quite consciously tempts our desire for architectonic, mythic structures, our need to privilege the "heroic" moment. She wants these associations while she restrains them from blocking their natural contexts. One does not forfeit the self, then, one does not resign all "views"; one simply explores them discreetly.

Of course the poem itself is a picture for sale. The satire on curiosity is a picture of ourselves since it is, finally, the intensity of the mood which is at issue. Its "opposite," the picture of receding things, draws the curious figure on until it becomes a mirror ("when I look at that of which I may regard myself"). The self does get expressed, through its own enchantment with something else, and this, I think, is what Virginia Woolf means in *A Room of One's Own* when she speaks of a woman's ability to get close to the fountain of creative energy.

While Moore's poetry is in a way "impersonal," in that the self is not the focus or dominant presence, we feel the movement of a distinct personality throughout. Indeed, Moore's very resistance to formal closure becomes for her a means of self-revelation. The "minor defects" of form, as she called unassimilated elements, are marks of style. And it is in style that we know this poet, not in subject or assertion. Though she never advocates "original-ity," the ambition to supersede the forms others have created, she is a great defender of "idiosyncrasy," an inevitable expression of "honest vision." Idiosyncrasy is connected with sincerity, a kind of non-competitive, oblique presentation of self; it does not require a personal subject or a show of power; it challenges no one.

Emily Watts, in *The Poetry of American Women*, identifies Moore's verse with a tradition of "feminine realism." What she and other critics are point-ing to in the use of this term is the combination of "mundane realities," "simple human and natural situations," and "natural sense objects," with ethical generalizations or "household morality." The feminine mind neatly integrates nature and morality. Randall Jarrell, for one, strongly objects to Moore's poetry on the basis of this integration. In clear sexual categories he challenges what he sees as Moore's domestic falsifications, upholding in-stead the male vision of amoral nature and its corresponding cosmic ambition.

But Moore has transformed the structure of feminine realism (which links observation to ethical generalization) in a number of ways. While she does detail nature, she celebrates her subjects for their recalcitrance. And the morality that accompanies these pictures is one of resisting the mind's impulse to circumscribe experience. In "Sea Unicorns and Land Unicorns," (about the Unicorn Tapestries) Moore points out that the unicorn remains "a puzzle to the hunters." Only the virgin knows him:

> Thus this strange animal with its miraculous elusiveness,
> has come to be unique,
> "impossible to take alive,"
> tamed only by a lady inoffensive like itself—
> as curiously wild and gentle;

All the poems follow a dictum of resistance even while they move through an apparent structure of observation-moral, for they continually propose defi-nitions only to unravel them. "Integration, too tough for infraction," integra-tion of the mind and the external world, of ethos and nature, is the goal of Moore's poetry, not its claim. And it is based on "efforts of affection" and not on aggression. It is achieved through process, through an open-ended dialectic of observing and making observations, in a continuous present.

While Moore follows the tendency in "feminine realism" to keep an eye on the external object, she is distinctly modern in her awareness of the limits of language to present that object. Moore's "descriptions" break up the conventions of composition, not to protect the self but to bring language into a more adequate relationship to experience, to discover a new realism which resists the habits of mind and eye. But what such resistance to referential conventions does, finally, is bring us into a closer awareness of the surface of language. By blocking the easy transfer from word to picture of meaning, by continually shifting the flow of counters and intruding on conventions which we too readily naturalize, Moore reminds us that we are not actually seeing, but only reading. This technique is especially effective in her poem "An Octopus," a long description of a glacier that concludes with a moral of "relentless accuracy." The extreme difficulty of accurately perceiving the object creates a corresponding difficulty in the words. Often the lengthy and cumbersome sentences lose their syntactic hold on us. We forget the subject or antecedent in the tow of subordinate clauses. Colons and semicolons are suspended between groups without an easy sense of their relation. Appositions become subjects with their own appositions in turn. Participial phrases go on for several lines until we cease even to anticipate their subjects. Where conventional "realism" trusts the parts of speech to represent reality, Moore's language continually demonstrates their failure. In its attempt to circumscribe the viscous presence, the language of "An Octopus," for instance, doubles back on itself with lines that refer outwardly to the objective experience, and inwardly to the experience of reading. "Completing the circle, you have been deceived into thinking that you have progressed." "Neatness of finish! Neatness of finish! Relentless accuracy is the nature of this octopus/ with its capacity for fact." Such self-reflective imagery admits that ultimately the "morals" we derive are not natural but represent our efforts to come to terms with nature. In that sense all of Moore's ethical generalizations have to do with her poetic activity.

"Neatness of finish" and "relentless accuracy" sound, in isolation, like mundane lessons. But in the context of this poem they present an enormous challenge to the eye and mind. And Moore proves the point she is making, for instead of rounding off the description with this abstract conclusion, she returns to the particular. She adopts, in the end, a policy of accuracy more relentless than before:

> Is "tree" the word for these things
> "flat on the ground like vines"?
> some "bent in half circle with branches on one side
> suggesting dust-brushes, not trees;
> some finding strength in union, forming little stunted groves
> their flattened mats of branches shrunk in trying to escape"
> from the hard mountain "planed by ice and polished by the
>   wind"—
> the white volcano with no weather side;
> the lightning flashing at its base,
> rain falling in the valleys, and snow falling on the peak—
> the glassy octopus symmetrically pointed,
> its claw cut by the avalanche
> "with a sound like the crack of a rifle
> in a curtain of powdered snow launched like a waterfall."

The breathlessness of the passage pulls us away from the organizing frame of grammar and syntax and hurls us into the midst of detail. Ethical generalization is returned to the level of perception. And yet even in the midst of detail, the mind makes associations. In this case the associations simply remind us of the controlling presence of language. At the end of the mountain is a curtain of snow; at the end of the poem—is a curtain of snow, the page. Her humility denies both the claims of an achieved realist and those of an achieved moralist; but her struggle for integration is vital and rewarding.

Moore transforms and toughens our understanding of familiar virtues when she uses them as stylistic devices. Humility, affection, reverse, are not passive but dynamic and vital modes of response. They do not protect but rather sustain the self in experience. In her redefinition and revaluation of what have been seen as "feminine" modes of identity, Moore displays a larger, encompassing concern to avoid all complacencies of mind. No container will hold her gusto.

> You have been compelled by hags to spin
>   gold thread from straw and have heard men say:
> "There is a feminine temperament in direct contrast to ours
>
> which makes her do these things. Circumscribed by a
>   heritage of blindness and native
>   incompetence, she will become wise and will be forced to
>   give in.
> Compelled by experience, she will turn back;
>
> water seeks its own level":
>   and you have smiled. "Water in motion is far
>   from level." You have seen it, when obstacles happen to bar
> the path, rise automatically.

In describing Ireland, Moore has obliquely celebrated the resilient power of the "feminine temperament." Ireland survives and deepens its identity by a combination of persistence and responsiveness. By rising to meet the shapes experience presents rather than either retreating or imposing artificial forms, Moore sustains a vital, creative contact between her self and her surroundings.

Emphatic Reticence
in Marianne Moore's Poems

David Bromwich

A fault of every good criticism of Moore I have ever read is the assumption of a generalized familiarity with the poetry, an atmosphere-of-Mooreishness, which allows the quotations to be copious and admiring and yet seldom anchored in a parent poem. And perhaps we know the poetry well enough; but do we know the poems? Many readers will want to reply: "Oh certainly, I know what they're *like*; whimsical, helter-skelter; odds and ends, all in sharp focus; alive with incidental humor—every word an incident." Because I was tired of giving this answer myself, I made a list of poems. The following groups are neither exhaustive nor mutually exclusive; but they do make room for a different sort of answer.

Riddles, anecdotes, squibs: "To Statecraft Embalmed," "To Military Progress," "To a Steam Roller," "Silence"; with innumerable unrhymed epigrams, and divagations of a too-charitable satirist.

Prayers; calls to fortitude: "What Are Years?", "In Distrust of Merits," "By Disposition of Angels," and the bulk of the later poems (epitomised by "Blessed Is the Man," with its echoes of Eisenhower and Omar Khayyam).

Trials of Ingenuity: "The Plumet Basilisk," "The Fish," "Peter," "England," "When I Buy Pictures," "The Labors of Hercules," "Snakes, Mongooses, Snake-Charmers, and the Like," "An Octopus," "Sojourn in the Whale," "The Student," "Spenser's Ireland," "Four Quartz Crystal Clocks," "Elephants," "His Shield."

Far-fetchers: "The Steeple-Jack," "The Hero," "The Jerboa," "The Frigate Pelican," "In the Days of Prismatic Color," "A Grave," "New York," "Marriage," "Virginia Britannia," "The Pangolin"; and, blameless outcast from the 1951 *Collected Poems*, "Melanchthon."

From *Poetry* 139, no. 6 (March 1982). © 1982 by the Modern Poetry Association.

The most searching of her inventions belong to the last two groups. Wit, as *ingenium,* or the reasoning intelligence—as finder of hidden analogies, or master of the sociable challenge and repartee—here delights in testing its object for all uncharted incongruities, and a map showing every turn would be no help. Who, coming to the end of "Four Quartz Crystal Clocks," will say where we forget the smart touch of the colloquist, and find that we have learned something about science and the morality of play?

> The lemur-student can see
>   that an aye-aye is not
>
> an angwan-tíbo, potto, or loris, The sea-
>   side burden should not embarrass
> the bell-boy with the buoy-ball
>   endeavoring to pass
> hotel patronesses; nor could a
>   practiced ear confuse the glass
>   eyes for taxidermists
>
> with eye-glasses from the optometrist. And as
>   MEridian-7 one-two
> one-two gives, each fifteenth second
>   in the same voice, the new
> data—"The time will be" so and so—
>   you realise that "when you
>   hear the signal," you'll be
>
> hearing Jupiter or jour pater, the day god—
>   the salvaged son of Father Time—
> telling the cannibal Chronos
>   (eater of his proxime
> newborn progeny) that punctuality
>   is not a crime.

After such beautiful display one may still prefer the extravagant persuasion of the far-fetchers; and to justify the preference there is a decisive aphorism in "Armor's Undermining Modesty": "What is more precise than precision? Illusion." That poem more than any other was Moore's apology for her work, and to her its credo had an obvious application.

She was most satisfied, and hoped we would be, with poems that argued the necessity of some single illusion—poems in which, after enough scruples to disarm the skeptic, she could welcome the believing mind for its strengths, especially strength of sight. Any illusion that assisted life to its ends was perhaps another name for single-mindedness. In "The Steeple-Jack" this quality is what favors the not-native observer of a native place: the citizen for whom the author cares most is the one who may set "part of a novel" in the town she describes. Since Moore dropped the full title, "Part of a Novel, Part of a Poem, Part of a Play"—which covered two further poems in sequence, "The Student" and "The Hero"—"The Steeple-Jack" may now seem a more complacent piece of naturalism than it really is. But her decision was correct for other reasons. The three did not answer each other deeply enough, and "The Hero" had more in common with "The Jerboa" than with its companions. Like "The Jerboa," it bears witness to a personal ideal of ascetic heroism, some of whose elements Moore named in an essay on "Humility, Concentration, and Gusto." As the "Too Much" section of "The Jerboa" concludes with the desert and its real animals, unenvyingly remote from civilization and its toy ones— "one would not be he/ who has nothing but plenty"—so "The Hero" moves from the tourist laden with his collected wits to the different figure, rich without plenty, who can follow a personal liking:

> He's not out
> seeing a sight but the rock
> crystal thing to see—the startling El Greco
> brimming with inner light—
> that covets nothing that it has let go.

These poems make as right a pair as "The Frigate Pelican" and "The Pangolin," in which an animal at once upsets and submits to be measured by the human scale of custom and value; or "New York" and "Virginia Britannia," one poem each for the North and South, in which the dream of paradise is close-woven with the dream of plunder. But the foregoing are all well-known or at least much-recognized poems, and this late in the history of Moore's reputation I would rather concentrate on three that seem to me too little read: "A Grave," "Marriage," and "In the Days of Prismatic Color."

"A Grave" is propositional in structure, categorical in mood, shorn of even such heterodox exuberances as Moore sometimes allows to flourish within the parallel rows of a catalogue. It is a poem about death, as dry as life can make it.

> Man looking into the sea,
> taking the view from those who have as much right to it as
> you have to it yourself,
> it is human nature to stand in the middle of a thing,
> but you cannot stand in the middle of this;
> the sea has nothing to give but a well excavated grave.
> The firs stand in a procession, each with an emerald turkey-
> foot at the top,
> reserved as their contours, saying nothing;
> repression, however, is not the most obvious characteristic of
> the sea;
> the sea is a collector, quick to return a rapacious look.
> There are others besides you who have worn that look—

whose expression is no longer a protest; the fish no longer
                                     investigate them
for their bones have not lasted:
men lower nets, unconscious of the fact that they are
                                   desecrating a grave,
and row quickly away—the blades of the oars
moving together like the feet of water-spiders as if there were
                                   no such thing as death.
The wrinkles progress among themselves in a phalanx—
                         beautiful under networks of foam,
and fade breathlessly while the sea rustles in and out of the
                                      seaweed:
the birds swim through the air at top speed, emitting cat-calls
                                 as heretofore—
the tortoise-shell scourges about the feet of the cliffs, in motion
                                beneath them;
and the ocean, under the pulsation of lighthouses and noise of
                                  bell-buoys,
advances as usual, looking as if it were not that ocean in which
                         dropped things are bound to sink—
in which if they turn or twist, it is neither with volition nor
                                  consciousness.

One sees the poem just as one hears it—a respectful monochrome, unflattering to man, of something larger than man: but how does it get this consistency of effect? One notes first the use of words at several removes from any lively particular, words like "unconscious," "volition," "characteristic," "contours," "repression," along with the careless drab music of the vernacular, "at top speed," "no such thing," "as much right to it," "the fact that," "as usual." T. S. Eliot would have had in mind words and phrases like these, when he praised Moore for having heard, in "the curious jargon produced in America by universal university education," one of the possible languages of men in a state of vivid sensation. And yet there seems, at a glance, hardly one vivid feature in this poem; it seems almost wrong to call it a poem. Only on the return visit that it somehow compels, and a step or so back from its subject, do certain details emerge from the flat continuous statement; and then it takes on quite suddenly the answering bluntness and unanswerable severity of an Aeschylean chorus: nothing could be more direct, more like words mean to surprise and unenchant, than "it is human nature to stand in the middle of a thing, / but you cannot stand in the middle of this"; and, "the sea is a collector, quick to return a rapacious look. / There are others besides you who have worn that look"; down to the theorem-like and almost affectless "dropped things are bound to sink." It would be hard to imagine any poem that sustained a more uncanny gravity. Under its law we naturally reserve for ourselves the few stage-properties of the sea, to make an interval of elation and release before the end: the sound of the bell-buoys and sight of the lighthouse, the "phalanx" of wrinkles beneath the foam, and birds swimming in the air, "emitting cat-calls as heretofore," with the ghostly tortoise-shell (no tortoise) moving among the cliffs below. Yet, much as these things may please us, the poem absorbs them without pleasure; and the detail we remember most irresistibly, a metaphor powerful enough to survive paraphrase, is also the most disquieting of all: the men, ignorant of death and of the figure they cut beside it, rowing quickly away from the thing they do not know is a grave, their oars "moving together like the feet of water-spiders as if there were no such thing as death." It is a long line without pause in which surely no reader has ever skipped one word. The entire poem must have been a favorite of Elizabeth Bishop's: some of it is still going in the background of "At the Fishhouses"; a smaller borrowing, but as gifted with appreciation and command as Bishop's use of a familiar Moore-genre in "The Man-Moth."

By an impartial observer, "Marriage" might be described as a duel of quotations. But we are none of us impartial; so let it be a male critic who says, In this poem man holds the chains and one woman, the words; yet she is cunning as a whisper and makes it seem, almost to the end, a remarkably equal match. The contestants are Adam and Eve, or the virtues of Adam and Eve. And Moore's Adam is the same as Milton's, though she does not tell us so; he whose first recorded words, to the first of women, are "Sole partner and sole part of all these joys," dull, sententious, and good, the temple of a selfless mastery. Who else could be let down so gently but so finally by Moore's reference to "the ease of the philosopher/ unfathered by a woman"? Many unkindnesses as well as (one feels) many liberties and general vexings, were required to move her to this. But steel against satire, Adam—the old and ever-renewed, in marriage—will be heard out; while Eve calmly wonders at

> the spiked hand
> that has an affection for one
> and proves it to the bone,
> impatient to assure you
> that impatience is a mark of independence
> not of bondage.

For, marrying, she has joined that locus

> 'of circular traditions and impostures,
> committing many spoils,'
> requiring all one's criminal ingenuity
> to avoid

—and, crushed by his single stroke of wit, his "Why not be alone together," she now dwells in those circles, a listener. The poet comes confusingly near a gesture of sentimental homage, when she speaks of

> This institution,
> perhaps one should say enterprise
> out of respect for which
> one says one need not change one's mind
> about a thing one has believed in,

but she recoils by the end, and transposes even this tentative melody into a more dubious key, with a minefield of sharps and flats:

> What can one do for them—
> these savages
> condemned to disaffect
> all those who are not visionaries
> alert to the silly task
> of making people noble?

But this is not quite the end; we see the wife a last time, still listening to her husband, whose eloquence now has something of "the statesmanship / of an archaic Daniel Webster," proclaiming "Liberty and Union / now and forever"; yet another man, husband, orator, in a poem that has featured everyone from Adam to Edmund Burke. There is more bitterness than affection in this wind-up; it is an unexpected tone, for which we are glad: suitable, after all, to a poet whose refusal to be assured about her impatience was the making of her. Besides, in the masterly orchestration of the thing, a great many other voices have been heard—Bacon, Shakespeare, Pound, Richard Baxter, Charles Reade, and at last a voice close to Moore's own, which turns out to be La Fontaine:

> Everything to do with love is mystery;
> it is more than a day's work
> to investigate this science.

There is in this more wonder than bitterness; and the quotations generally help Moore to keep her balance.

> Psychology which explains everything
> explains nothing
> and we are still in doubt.

For every Adam there must be an Eve, who listens and smiles, and does not show her smile. The hurtful acuteness of some passages comes, notwithstanding the disclaimer, from the habitual care of a good and disturbing psychologist; and any writer who can describe Satan's investment in the serpent as "that invaluable accident / exonerating Adam," is none the worse for having a *parti pris*.

To square the account, she included in her *Selected Poems*, and reprinted ever after, a poem about Adam before Eve.

when there was no smoke and color was
fine, not with the refinement of early civilization art, but because
of its originality.

The poem, "In the Days of Prismatic Color," is alert to the snares of its myth; it knows that this sort of aboriginal earliness can never exist as its own contemporary; it is not born but comes to be original, when later eyes have seen it so. History alone, with memory, can make those days, and Moore writes out the history that her poem seems to deny, by adopting an idiom she has employed at other times—refined, self-conscious, derivative, *and fine*—and pressing it beyond any known reach of the abstract. We arrive at originality by this curious route; so that she can say, of Adam's solitude and perfect vision,

> obliqueness was a variation
> of the perpendicular, plain to see and
> to account for: it is no
> longer that; nor did the blue-red-yellow band
> of incandescence that was color keep its stripe.

That is science not poetry, we may say, too stupid to read our myths deviously; but the image stops us short: it is the first poetic rainbow in half a century that one can admire without embarrassment. This poem is no friend of complexity, which it admits may not be "a crime, but carry / it to the point of murkiness / and nothing is plain"; nor of sophistication, which it suspects of being "Principally throat," and "at the antipodes from the init / ial great truths." Yet it is wonderfully aware throughout that our originals though great can never be simple, except in their power to survive. We reduce them only from our need for something uncompounded to serve as the givens of thought and reliables of metaphor. But when they first appeared, before they could be remembered, there was always the stumbling, the obliqueness of the rude assault:

> "Part of it was crawling, part of it
> was about to crawl, the rest
>   was torpid in its lair." In the short-legged, fit-
> ful advance, the gurgling and all the minutiae—we have the
>   classic
> multitude of feet. To what purpose! Truth is no Apollo
>   Belvedere, no formal thing. The wave may go over it if it likes.
> Know that it will be there when it says,
>   "I shall be there when the wave has gone by."

In those lines originality becomes one with the self-confidence of genius anywhere. Seeing the naturalness of the transition, from "the gurgling and all the minutiae" to "the classic / multitude of feet," we are educated in how originals make their way, and incidentally shown a distinction Moore keeps

in view all the time, between the precisionist's dreaming with one eye open
and the formalist's interrogation with both eyes closed.

So far I have said nothing about Moore's verse forms—and after all, too
much has been said by others. To most readers they probably still convey, for
a little while, the sense of an absorbing peculiarity, like a friend's matinal
fondness for mango juice. But one soon accepts them like any other convention, and once accepted they join the form of life with which the author has
linked them permanently in our minds. Beyond that, what does anyone care
about their appropriateness? They are uniquely suited, or unsuited, to the
person who chose them, just as all poetry is; one can learn nothing more
essential about Moore from her syllabic lay-outs than one can about Collins
from the English-cucumber-shape of an irregular ode: the important thing
about both is that they are products of a given age and climate, streaked by
the weather that followed, but undesirable or obsolete only in the dimmest of
short runs. Moore herself, in "The Past Is The Present," says this best:
"Ecstasy affords / the occasion and expediency determines the form." Yet an
audience for whom modernism was never new may pass by her innovations
unnoticing and therefore unalarmed; what they will want to have explained
is her didactic freedom with aphorisms; for it is this that makes her remote
not only from modernist practice but from all that has succeeded it. The
causes of her uniqueness are rooted in what can sometimes feel like the land
poetry forgot. I mean the Eighteenth Century—one of Moore's cherished
haunts, and *not* her idea of the second fall of man, as it was to Pound and
Eliot—when critics rashly spoke of "casting one's eye over mankind."
Poems could then be praised for their sentiment. By this was generally meant
the perfect utterance of a common feeling which no one could know was
common until the poet made it so. Apart from poetry governed by the most
relentless logical structure, sentiments might easily serve the purpose of
classical *sententiae*: they were simply the best means by which the
performer-with-words could recommend himself to the trust of his listeners.
Moore's poems abound in wise feelings, which she often appears to set in
place with an air of having left room for something of that sort, in case it
should ask for admission. The reader who wonders at her daring must
remember that among the writers she most admired were Pope, Johnson,
Blake—and Shaw, a latecomer not at all strange to this company. She would
have agreed with everyone who pointed out that a poem cannot be all
poetry: only, she would have added, we ought in that case to change our
definition of poetry. She did it more by example than precept, with "the
physiognomy of conduct must not reveal the skeleton," and "Denunciations
do not affect / the culprit; nor blows, but it / is torture to him not to be spoken
to"; with "why dissect destiny with instruments / more highly specialized
than components of destiny itself?" and "He can talk but insolently says
nothing. What of it? / When one is frank, one's very presence is a compliment" and "The passion for setting people right is in itself an afflictive
disease. / Distaste which takes no credit to itself is best."

Statements like these may look planted. But how different are they from those others, obviously at home in one place, which have a hardy existence on almost any soil? One does not need to know the title of the poem, "People's Surroundings," or the topic for discussion, the flats of Utah and Texas, to appreciate Moore's qualified love of "those cool sirs with the explicit sensory apparatus of common sense, / who know the exact distance between two points as the crow flies." In "Elephants," the relevant context can seem almost a pettiness to recall, after she speaks of one creature in particular as "too wise / to mourn—a life prisoner but reconciled." Again, how different are these in turn from the many celebrated passages of "straight" description, in which animal traits, refigured as man-mores, are esteemed as tokens of character and then of virtue?

> Make hay; keep
> the shop; I have one sheep; were a less
> limber animal's mottoes. This one
> finds sticks for the swan's-down-dress
> of his child to rest upon and would
> not know Gretel from Hänsel.
> As impassioned Handel—
>
> meant for a lawyer and a masculine German domestic
> career—clandestinely studied the harpsichord
> and never was known to have fallen in love,
> the unconfiding frigate-bird hides
> in the height and in the majestic
> display of his art. He glides
> a hundred feet or quivers about
> as charred paper behaves—full
> of feints; and an eagle
>
> of vigilance.

The final phrase, tucked into a new stanza, nicely conceals its satisfaction at having found a witty way of obliging man to serve as a middle man—nothing but a German domestic could translate the eagle into a language the pelican understands: this done, the poem is done with Germany, Handel, and harpsichords. The perception starts from and returns to its formative sayings. In the meantime it has made havoc of our pedagogic aids, which read, in a march of progress, "From Abstract to Concrete" or "From General to Particular."

As a composer of words Moore's greatest affinities are with Francis Bacon, and the Baconian essay or prose-amble may be the least misleading analogy for one of her poems. To be curt, undeviating, end-stopped wherever a thought might enter, but at the same time vivid, striking, inventive in the highest degree conscionable, is the ideal of both writers. Like Bacon a despiser of ornament, Moore rejects with equal vehemence the aims of bringing conceit for a matter or matter for a conceit. She will frame no description that has any hint of the superlative, unless she can first set in the middle of it a skeptical gargoyle at least six syllables long:

> Rare unscent-
> ed, provident-
> ly hot, too sweet, inconsistent flower bed!

She refuses to claim the literary exemption from syllogisms, dependent clauses, subordinate conjunctions, and everything that smacks of the uncraftily sheltered: she will submit with the worst of us, and find her poetry there besides. Bacon's untheatrical rigor would have found nothing wanting in her resolve to be literal, and for range of style he leaves her plenty. "Nature is often hidden; sometimes overcome; seldom extinguished," is a sentence one can imagine her writing, or quoting, as easily as "It is good to commit the beginnings of all great actions to Argos with his hundred eyes, and the ends to Briareus with his hundred hands; first to watch, and then to speed."

But Bacon's essays sometimes trail off in QEDs, whereas Moore was born to the stroke they call in tennis *a concluder*. An extraordinary number of her endings are extraordinarily beautiful. In "The Student," "Sojourn in the Whale," "The Hero," the first section of "The Jerboa," she lifts the errant thing to its resting seat, with a parental touch so quick and encircling that we come to rely on her in every playground, including Eden. Nor does she ring a particle of pomp to occasions that need a different sort of authority: "Spenser's Ireland" and "To a Steam Roller" are famous because they close with famous jokes. Yet above all these are the endings carried out in perfect earnest. First, "Elephants," which has warned us hardship makes the soldier, teachableness the philosopher, and then turns to Socrates, who

> prudently testing the suspicious thing, knew
> the wisest is he who's not sure that he knows.
> Who rides on a tiger can never dismount;
> asleep on an elephant, that is repose.

These lines once had and still deserve for company, the last of another elephant-poem, "Melanchthon," with their less reconciled note: "Will / depth be depth, thick skin be thick, to one who can see no / beautiful element of unreason under it?" However, Moore never outdid the description of man in "The Pangolin"—bringing him by chance to the fore ("To explain grace requires a curious hand"), keeping him there till he changed everything— and this she left standing.

> Consistent with the
> formula—warm blood, no gills, two pairs of hands and a few
>   hairs—that
> is a mammal; there he sits in his own habitat,
>   serge-clad, strong-shod. The prey of fear, he, always
>   curtailed, extinguished, thwarted by the dusk, work
>   partly done,

> says to the alternating blaze,
>   "Again the sun!
>   anew each day; and new and new and new,
>   that comes into and steadies my soul."

Felicities which here sound accidental the whole poem makes essential: man "curtailed," for instance, which takes us back to the pangolin "strongly intailed," a pun encouraging to all who if they pursue symbolic logic feel that they must do it on four legs.

In a memorable criticism Kenneth Burke conceived of Moore's "objectivist idiom" as fostering "an appraisal or judgment of many things in and for themselves. They would be encouraged to disclose their traits, not simply that they might exist through the vicarage of words, but that they might reveal their properties as workmanship (workmanship being a trait in which the ethical and the esthetic are one)." Only the first part of this seems to me false. It brings her too much into line with Williams, whose work vaguely resembles hers in matters of the surface, but whose brittler temperament had much to do with his interest in programs like objectivism. Pound, who usually comes next in the effort to triangulate her, is just as wrong for comparison, in spite of their mutual loyalty. Irony like Pound's, of the nervous modern sort, which regards its object from an unsteady point of view but with an advanced degree of scorn, was never part of her armor or weaponry, and she could have written "Mauberley" without the quotation marks. Her intellectual virtues came from the enlightenment and protestantism; from the start, she had the concerns of a genuine moralist, as well as the ambition to be one; and she knew that the gesture of humility was to ask forgiveness from enemies rather than friends. These things helped to make "In Distrust of Merits" a better poem than "Pull Down Thy Vanity."

Of all her contemporaries, the Stevens of *Harmonium* and the early Eliot, who also called his work "observations," seem closest to the spirit of her poetry. In one appreciation of Eliot she mentions "certain qualities" that he shares with Stevens—qualities she supposed would be sufficiently plain to her readers, though they were not so to the authors themselves—"reticent candor and emphasis by understatement" being the two she cares for most. Some lines from "La Figlia che Piange" and "Peter Quince at the Clavier" are quoted as proof: a juxtaposition both strange and right, which it took Moore to imagine. And with those poems in view, one can understand how far she does belong to her generation after all, the generation of "Prufrock," "Le Monocle de Mon Oncle," and "Marriage." Eliot was alluding to their shared enterprise when in a letter to Moore he thanked her for writing poems that forced him to consider each word. Revolutions in taste cannot give us better monuments; but they may force us to work at the new ones slowly. Moore knew what she had done and what she had made possible, and nothing could be more emphatic than the reticence with which she told us so: "Know that it will be there when it says, / 'I shall be there when the wave has gone by.' "

The Problem of the Woman Artist:
Louise Bogan, "The Alchemist"

Diane Wood Middlebrook

To tell the truth, there is very little that one can say about women poets, past, present, and (presumably) to come. One truth about them is an open secret: when they are bad they are very very bad, and when they are good, they are magnificent. . . . The problem of the woman artist remains unchanged. Henry James, in *The Tragic Muse*, spoke of "that oddest of animals, the artist who happens to be born a woman." (Louise Bogan, "What the Women Said," lecture at Bennington College, 1962)

Louise Bogan is one of a generation of distinguished American woman poets born between 1885–1900 whose art expresses a felt contradiction between writing and living a woman's life. The milieu of the early twentieth century—thanks to the recognized genius of Bogan's contemporaries Yeats, Eliot, Pound, Stevens, and Williams—saw a genuine cultural renaissance of poetry. But women writers remained marginal to this renaissance. The list of Bogan's female peers would include Elizabeth Madox Roberts, Elinor Wylie, H. D., Edna St. Vincent Millay, Genevieve Taggard, Babette Deutsch, Léonie Adams, and Marya Zaturenska, and among fiction writers, Katherine Anne Porter and Janet Lewis. Each is an impeccable stylist highly respected by fellow artists. Yet all worked in a climate of awareness that a woman must, as Léonie Adams said of Louise Bogan, "function not only as a poet of her own time but within the limits accorded a woman poet. . . . There could never be any confusion of the role of woman and the role of poet, or any exploitation of the role of woman. She knew, moreover, that she should not model herself upon the women she admired or who were closest to her in time."

Bogan rarely wrote directly about her mistrust of the origins of her poetry in a specifically female experience of the world: But her collected poems, *The Blue Estuaries: Poems, 1923–1968*, contains a handful of poems on this theme which gives us what might be described as a private mythology

From *Critical Essays on Louise Bogan.* © 1984 by Martha Collins. G. K. Hall & Co., 1984.

constructed to account for her creativity. Bogan did not, in these poems, analyze her cultural situation; rather, she reflected its influence in a body of symbols that express the contradiction woman/artist in other bipolar metaphors: flesh/breath, low/high, earth/heaven, silence/voice. Central to the symbolisms of this mythology are, on the one hand, anxiety about aspects of the self which cannot be controlled; on the other hand, reverence for the mind and its powers. "The Alchemist," "Cassandra," and "Fifteenth Farewell" are among the poems which elaborate this myth. In them art is viewed as the product of both a freedom and a control hard to attain within the limits of a woman's mind, which Bogan viewed as sometimes helpless, often under domination by unconscious forces. Woman, in this mythology, is carefully distinguished from artist.

"The Alchemist"—written by the time Louise Bogan was twenty-five— displays her characteristic strength: a skilled formalism in which the syntax is simple and straightforward ("I broke my life, to seek relief"; "I had found unmysterious flesh"). And in it she addresses symbolically the problem of "that oddest of animals, the artist who happens to be born a woman."

In "The Alchemist" the contradiction between woman and artist is an implication latent within the explicit subject of the poem: the desire to attain self-transcendence through brutal self-control.

> I burned my life, that I might find
> A passion wholly of the mind,
> Thought divorced from eye and bone,
> Ecstasy come to breath alone.
> I broke my life, to seek relief
> From the flawed light of love and grief.
>
> With mounting beat the utter fire
> Charred existence and desire.
> It died low, ceased its sudden thresh.
> I had found unmysterious flesh—
> Not the mind's avid substance—still
> Passionate beyond the will.

Alchemy—one of the earliest efforts to develop an exact science that would combine philosophy and technology—regarded gold as the most spiritual metal. Bogan's poem is about an analogous quasi-scientific quest for purity. Her alchemist is a metaphor for the human type, frequently regarded as heroic, who seeks spiritual transcendence through esoteric study requiring rejection of the common life. Poetry is full of esoteric study requiring rejection of the common life. Poetry is full of such heroes: Shelley's Alastor, Byron's Manfred, Arnold's Scholar Gypsy. The narrator in Yeats's "Sailing to Byzantium" offers a close analogy to the speaker in "The Alchemist," for he too is a being "sick with desire" seeking the relief of a wisdom that can only be secure when he has attained a condition wholly of the mind. "Consume my heart away," he appeals, embracing like Bogan's alchemist a refining, intellectual fire. He too desires a form of existence divorced from eye and bone: "Once out of nature I shall never take / My bodily form in any natural thing." Bogan's poem, however, rejects the idea affirmed in "Sailing to Byzantium" that a world of pure spirit exists beyond the sphere of physical existence, to be attained by deserting or destroying the physical. The alchemist does indeed find in the crucible something in a pure form, but it is not "the mind's avid substance." It is "unmysterious flesh—still / Passionate." The creative mind may only deny, it may never escape, its dependence on tormented sensuous existence.

"The Alchemist," then, can be interpreted as a critique of a romantic theory of art. The meaning of the poem changes, however, if we view the alchemist not as a symbol for the romantic poet heroically bent on defying nature—Shelley, Bryon, Yeats—but as a *woman* poet hoplessly defying the social significance of her femininity.

From this perspective, the will to deny the body expressed in "The Alchemist" grows poignantly comprehensible. For the metaphorical gold she seeks—"passion wholly of the mind," "Thought," "Ecstasy come to breath"—are attainments essential to creativity: but in Western culture they have always been regarded as "masculine" attainments. Throughout her long career, Bogan's poetry reflects ambivalent acquiescence to the stereotype that makes aspiration to intellectual power a contradiction of the "feminine." This contradiction is rarely expressed in direct statement; rather, it infuses most of the poems that, like "The Alchemist," deal with a conflict between mental power and sexual passion. It is expressed in metaphors where "flesh" and "breath" form fateful polarities. "Flesh" is mortal, dumb, blind, hopelessly instinctual; it is low, associated with darkness and the earth, and it is feminine. "Breath," by contrast, is the medium of inspiration, speech, music—high achievements, not associated with the feminine sphere. This polarity is the explicit theme of a powerful poem, "Cassandra," in which Bogan imagines Cassandra's clairvoyance as a consequence of liberation from feminine roles:

> To me, one silly task is like another.
> I bare the shambling tricks of lust and pride.
> This flesh will never give a child its mother,—
> Song, like a wing, tears through my breast, my side,
>
> And madness chooses out my voice again,
> Again. I am the chosen no hand saves:
> The shrieking heaven lifted over men,
> Not the dumb earth, wherein they set their graves.

Cassandra's fate as seer tragically ignored by the princes of Troy was the punishment Apollo ordained when she withheld promised sexual favors. She paid a high price for her ascent from femininity. In this respect, "Cassandra" is typical, for in Bogan's vision woman is frighteningly bound to and by her sexuality. It brings her low. In "The Crows," for example, Bogan likens an old woman who is still full of sexual passion to a harvested field, in which "there is only bitter / Winter-burning." The girl in "Chanson un Peu Naïve" is a "body . . . ploughed, / Sown, and broken yearly". Another, in "Girl's Song," lies with her lover in a field as on a grave: "And, since she loves [him], and she must, / Puts her young cheek against the dust."

Identification of the feminine with fields, seasonal cycles, and mortality has other implications in Bogan's poetry. The field is not only a fertile space, it is space enclosed for others' use. The gate to its enclosures is the awakening of sexuality. Before love, the girl in "Betrothed" has roamed freely with other maidens "In air traversed of birds"—"But there is only evening here, / And the sound of willows / Now and again dipping their long oval leaves in the water." The feminine personae in Bogan's early poems are as fatally determined as heroines in Hardy—and by the same rural and sexual cultural conventions. As Bogan writes in "Women":

> They cannot think of so many crops to a field
> Or of clean wood cleft by an axe.
> Their love is an eager meaninglessness
> Too tense, or too lax.
>
> They hear in every whisper that speaks to them
> A shout and a cry.
> As like as not, when they take life over their door-sills
> They should let it go by.

In these lyrics, Bogan is working with stereotypes of the feminine from which she, as author, maintains a knowing distance. These are *some* women, *other* women. Yet the same conflicting opposites—low/high, flesh/breath, feminine/masculine—furnish the imagery in which Bogan speaks as "I" describing her own creative powers. In these poems, as in "The Alchemist," the speaker seeks to purify herself of personal history, to become "thought divorced from eye and bone."

"Fifteenth Farewell" is a pair of sonnets in which the speaker wills a commitment to "breath"—identified with both life and art—as an escape from an unmanageable and painful sexual passion:

I

> You may have all things from me, save my breath,
> The slight life in my throat will not give pause
> For your love, nor your loss, nor any cause.
> Shall I be made a panderer to death,
> Dig the green ground for darkness underneath,
> Let the dust serve me, covering all that was
> With all that will be? Better, from time's claws,
> The hardened face under the subtle wreath.
>
> Cooler than stones in wells, sweeter, more kind
> Than hot, perfidious words, my breathing moves

Close to my plunging blood. Be strong, and hang
Unriven mist over my breast and mind,
My breath! we shall forget the heart that loves,
Though in my body beat its blade, and its fang.

II

I erred, when I thought loneliness the wide
Scent of mown grass over forsaken fields,
Or any shadow isolation yields.
Loneliness was the heart within your side.
Your thought, beyond my touch, was tilted air
Ringed with as many borders as the wind.
How could I judge you gentle or unkind
When all bright flying space was in your care?

Now that I leave you, I shall be made lonely
By simple empty days,—never that chill
Resonant heart to strike between my arms
Again, as though distraught for distance,—only
Levels of evening, now, behind a hill,
Or a late cock-crow from the darkening farms.

In the first sonnet, "You" is unmistakably a lover. But "you" also denotes in both sonnets the power of the masculine over the feminine as these two abstractions are consistently rendered in Bogan's poems, where "he" is nearly always either a voice or a pair of censorious and faithless eyes. This man, Bogan says, has always been in some sense beyond her, or at least beyond what she could gain by touching him physically. She could not apply ordinary value judgments ("gentle," "unkind") to one whose thought and ambition appeared boundless. Nor could she approach his mind by holding the man in her arms. Rather, his heart delivered blows and taught her by example to be definitively alone. "Fifteenth Farewell," part II, also makes use of the polarities described above, which place the feminine in the context of "forsaken fields" rather than "bright flying space," of "levels" rather than "tilted air," of a loneliness which is willed rather than sought. The masculine is above and beyond the imperiousness of flesh and seeks a noble though desperate distance from it.

Yet, if the masculine is identified with "air" in this elevated, authoritative sense, air is not exclusively the domain of men. This is the theme of "Fifteenth Farewell," part I, explicitly a rejection of suicide. The tone of triumph is almost militant and comes, significantly, from the speaker's recognition that she possesses "breath." Not merely ongoing life, "breath" is a creative power, like the "air" of thought in the second sonnet. It flows coolly in the throat, above as well as "close to" that source of "hot, perfidious words," the plunging blood; it appears to be the breath which shapes from active pain a formal art, "The hardened face under the subtle wreath." This is the kind of transformation which may be won by denial of the feminine, the body in which beat "love's blade and its fang."

All these poems may be seen to bear upon the project undertaken in "The Alchemist" to separate flesh from breath, to break one's life in order to attain a mental ecstasy, to transmute base metal into gold. At the opening of the poem the alchemist seems to think that if she could purge her passionate thought of any trace of its origins in a (female) body, she might ascend to that high plane occupied by the greatest spirits. But at the end of the poem, the "utter fire" of acute intelligence illuminates the absurdity, even the unworthiness, of such a goal. Hence, failure of the alchemist may be interpreted as a liberation of the woman as artist. The poem ends on a note of self-mocking relief, wry rather than bitter: "I had found unmysterious flesh." Explicitly, she denies a distinction between matter and spirit. Implicitly, she accepts her sex as a fundamental basis of her art. Implicitly, too, she challenges the long tradition in which the woman artist seems, in James's phrase, "that oddest of animals." While in her life Bogan never conquered the ambivalence toward the woman artist that colored her cultural milieu, "The Alchemist" in its technical and spiritual confidence testifies eloquently to the power of the female imagination. Further, it foreshadows the project of contemporary literary criticism to expose the cultural biases of the ahistorical ideologies of the early modern poets, as well as the project of contemporary women poets to transform art by asserting the validity of their subjectivity. In retrospect, Louise Bogan emerges as an unknowing precursor of those women poets who write today liberated from many constraints of that old contradiction— liberated, that is, from all but the inescapable constraints of poetry itself.

"The Repressed Becomes the Poem": Landscape and Quest in Two Poems by Louise Bogan

Sandra Cookson

Louise Bogan was an intensely personal poet whose poems were made from the most intimate material of her life: love, death, the mysteries of the unconscious, the terrors of mental illness, the ponderings of a subtle and analytical mind on the nature of life and art. But she was a personal poet who rejected direct autobiographical statement in her poems, except rarely and in the earlier work, and employed instead the obliquity of image used as symbol; who relied upon a symbolic language and the combined power of sound and rhythm and rhyme—form, in short—to convey meaning and emotion.

Although her poems are formal and symbolic structures, they cannot be separated from the most intimate psychological events of her life. For instance, in her poems that explore the unconscious in dream or vision and in her poems about sexual passion, images of a ravaged or hellish landscape symbolize the devastation of the psyche from assaults upon it by violently disruptive feelings which Bogan identifies as rooted deeply in her childhood. Archetypal images of the Medusa and the Furies, as well as a small gallery of more private myth figures, personify the poet's deepest fears and impulses. Thus, contrary to what one might expect from a poet who relies upon generalizing images such as these archetypal ones, and upon formal and traditional poetic structures, the urge toward the personal is always powerfully felt in Bogan's work. Her own brief remarks from a journal entry written late in life are of interest as the poet's view of the uses she made of her experience: "The poet represses the outright narrative of his life. He absorbs it, along with life itself. The repressed becomes the poem. Actually, I have written down my experience in the closest detail. But the rough and vulgar facts of it are not there." The poet's conviction of absolute fidelity to her

From *Critical Essays on Louise Bogan*. © 1984 by Martha Collins. G. K. Hall & Co., 1984.

experience, although she has transformed "the rough and vulgar facts" of it, is a traditional aesthetic position, with moral overtones, of formalist lyric poets. Bogan's notion that "the repressed becomes the poem" is a kind of twentieth-century commentary on Wordsworth's idea of the poem as experience "recollected in tranquillity."

The remark further illuminates the unique power of Bogan's poetry by providing an insight into her belief that the repressed material of her life was her true poetic raw material, that therefore true poetry comes from the unconscious, a belief she stated many times in reference to her poems. Bogan spent many years of her life in psychotherapy, but her greatest poems bear out the implication that her true access to "repressed" material remained largely a mystery of the poetic process.

Bogan's life and her poems are marked by two obsessions. The first is her preoccupation with a childhood full of half-remembered scenes of violence between her parents, which she focuses upon her mother. The second is her marriage to the poet and novelist Raymond Holden. Bogan left Holden in 1934 and divorced him in 1937, but his presence persisted in her poems. Both the poems and journal entries written late in life suggest that while Bogan probably succeeded in freeing herself from the Holden obsession, the terrors of her childhood remained with her to her death.

From her earliest poems to her latest, Bogan's landscapes and seascapes represent the poet's mental universe. Often they are the settings for journeys into the darkest regions of the self, undertaken in order to achieve peace through understanding. Understanding, Bogan hoped, would allow her to exorcise her personal demons, which she identified as hatred and sexual jealousy. Two of Bogan's most distinguished poems, "Putting to Sea" (1936) and "Psychiatrist's Song" (1967), complement each other as poems of quest and reconciliation. "Putting to Sea" concerns liberation from the violence of sexual jealousy and the rage which were exacerbated by the last years of the Holden relationship. "Psychiatrist's Song," looking back on that struggle from a distance of thirty years, celebrates the achievement of psychic equilibrium. Yet it still contains the haunting image of the damaged child, the victim of experiences too painful ever to fully come to light.

The sea voyage is the mode of these psychological and spiritual journeys, and Bogan signaled its importance in her work when she chose "A Tale" (1921) as the opening poem in her collected poems, *The Blue Estuaries* (1968). "A Tale," though it is not chronologically the book's earliest, is Bogan's prototypical voyage poem. In it, a "youth" prepares to relinquish the everyday world of time and flux ("the break / Of waters in a land of change") in search of something enduring, "a light that waits / Still as a lamp upon a shelf." The ideal country which he seeks will be an austere place "where no sea leaps upon itself."

The poet, however, tells us that the youth's journey will not bring him wisdom attended by peace and steadiness of spirit. If, indeed, he does journey far enough to find the truth, it will be just the opposite of what he has hoped for:

> But he will find that nothing dares
> To be enduring, save where, south
> Of hidden deserts, torn fire glares
> On beauty with a rusted mouth,—
>
> Where something dreadful and another
> Look quietly upon each other.

At the center of his universe, the youthful voyager will find nameless terror, corrupted love, and presences monstrous beyond his comprehension. This hellish landscape, populated by demons, will recur throughout Bogan's poetry as the terrain of the unconscious.

In "Medusa," written at about the same time as a "A Tale," the speaker, paralyzed by the monster's gaze, finds herself suspended in a vast surreal landscape where she is condemned for eternity to watch "the yellow dust" rising in the wind. Another version of this hell is depicted in "M., Singing," written about fifteen years later, in which the song of a young girl releases the demons of the unconscious, "Those beings without heart or name," permitting them to "Leave the long harvest which they reap / In the sunk land of dust and flame."

Bogan was remarkably consistent in her use of a particular landscape with its cluster of images to signify an emotion or state of feeling. In the poems of her first book, *Body of This Death* (1923), passion is the "breeze of flame" ("Ad Castitatem") that consumes the field set afire and burned back to stubble after harvest. The image may originate in the agricultural practice of slash-and-burn, common in some tropical countries. The youthful Bogan lived in Panama for about a year with her first husband, and must have seen on many occasions whole fields set alight, the flames racing over the dry stalks. "Feuernacht" (1927) is a remarkably faithful depiction of such an event, while at the same time it clearly suggests the all-consuming power of sexual passion.

The blackened stubble which remains after the fire has burned itself out is a recurring image in these early poems, and signifies the woman's sexuality depleted by the fires of passion. The image belongs to Bogan's youth, and it disappears from her poems after the beautiful lyric of 1930, entitled "Song," in which the speaker attempts to renounce an impulse to sexual passion, claiming that she has long since paid her dues to it.

> Years back I paid my tithe
> And earned my salt in kind,
> And watched the long slow scythe
> Move where the grain is lined,
> And saw the stubble burn
> Under the darker sheaves.

Though it appears to have been Bogan's unhappy first marriage that gave expression to the pain of passion, the image of the young woman's sexuality as a "ravaged country" ("Ad Castitatem") carries over into the

Holden years, where it is transformed into another tortured sexual landscape, the obscene and sterile tropical country of "Putting to Sea." Thirty years later in "Psychiatrist's Song," the same landscape recurs, but it is merely a dim shape on the horizon to the voyager now freed of the torments which it represents in the earlier poem.

In "Putting to Sea," the sea-voyage metaphor symbolizes the undertaking of a journey into the deepest self ("the gulf, the vast, the deep"), with the specific purpose of freeing the voyager from the obscenity of hatred. To accomplish this, she must confront it, and rejects its temptations, which take shape in the poem's unnatural tropical landscape. "With so much hated still so close behind / The sterile shores before us must be faced. . . ."

The voyager, first of the poem's two speakers, is the conscious self and controls the narrative. "Who, in the dark, has cast the harbor chain?" she asks, as if the journey were compelled by a force beyond her will. The land she is leaving is the everyday world described in natural, cyclical images, which connect it to sensual experience, as these lines suggest: "Sodden with summer, stupid with its loves, / The country which we leave . . . ." Its counterpart in the unconscious is the tropical land, described by the poem's second speaker, the voice of the treacherous unconscious. The voyager, shunning all inducements toward the tropical shore, must journey into an awesome moral proving ground, the "bare circle of ocean," which is deep as heaven's height and "barren with despair." Later in the poem, the landscape of the quotidian, the sea, and the tropical shore will be joined by a fourth psychological country, which suggests the tender promise of childhood left unfulfilled.

The voyager understands that the second speaker's tantalizing descriptions of a gaudy and exotically flamboyant artificial land where "love fountains from its deeps" are meant to seduce her with false promises of love and fulfillment. The sly tone of this voice is supposed to conceal from her the true hideousness of the landscape:

> "O, but you should rejoice! The course we steer
> Points to a beach bright to the rocks with love,
> Where, in hot calms, blades clatter on the ear;
>
> And spiny fruits up through the earth are fed
> With fire; the palm trees clatter; the wave leaps.
>
> Fleeing a shore where heart-loathed love lies dead
> We point lands where love fountains from its deeps.
>
> Through every season the coarse fruits are set
> In earth not fed by streams."

The voyager is not taken in. She knows that this is really the landscape of madness. It is fiend's country, far more dangerous than the everyday world she has fled "where heart-loathed love lies dead." Bogan's specific reference is to the failure of her second marriage, to Raymond Holden, for which she was later to blame herself as a "demon of jealousy." In 1936, she wrote her friend and editor at Scribner's, John Hall Wheelock, that this poem would "sum up the Holden suffering, endured so long, but now, at last, completely over."

With the resumption of the narrative by the first speaker, following the passage just quoted, a new landscape enters the poem.

> Soft into time
> Once broke the flower: pear and violet,
> The cinquefoil. The tall elm tree and the lime
>
> Once held out fruitless boughs, and fluid green
> Once rained about us, pulse of earth indeed.

The "birth" of flowers, emblematic for Bogan of New England where she was born and raised, suggests her own "early time." These limpid and tender lines also contrast with the harshness of the preceding images. Moreover, "fluid green" and "pulse of earth" suggest a primordial condition that is full of promise, teeming with life, but unformed.

The potential of this tender land is not to be realized, however. With the contrasting landscapes as her psychological terrain, the first speaker traces the seeds of her destructive impulses back to her childhood: "There, out of metal, and to light obscene, / The flamy blooms burn backward to their seed." Childhood is a land of promise, but within its tender depths anything can take root. In her view, the compulsion from which the voyager now seeks catharsis stems from this time of unformed life, from her childhood.

The poet-voyager has set herself a hard task. Lacking even the celestial guides of the mariner, she wonders at the necessity of this dark and perilous journey:

> The Way should mark our course within the night,
> The streaming System, turned without a sound.
> What choice is this—profundity and flight—
> Great sea? Our lives through we have trod the ground.
>
> Motion beneath us, fixity above.

"Putting to Sea" derives its power from the depiction of this moral/psychological deep. The descriptions of the great mythic sea and the stars have a silent and formidable grandeur, evoked equally by the bare, grand simplicity of the adjectives and the vibrations of a long tradition they set in motion. A line like "The streaming System, turned without a sound" is so suggestive that, while it is describing the absence of stars in the heavens, it evokes their presence by the infusion of light "streaming" produces. At the same time, the void and utter silence of these disturbed heavens must recall, in "turned without a sound," the ancient music of the spheres, so out of place in this poem where the heavens themselves conspire in the voyager's bafflement.

In the same letter to Wheelock, Bogan remarks on the poem's provenance. "I know what it's about, with my upper reason, just a little; it came from pretty far down, thank God." Bogan's comment states her conviction of the poem's origin in her subconscious, but it also suggests why "Putting to Sea" has such power; for in it resound echoes of the great mythic voyages which preceded it. The most reverberant of all is the quest of Odysseus. Dante provided Tennyson with the model for his Ulysses, and the opening lines of Bogan's last stanza suggest the spirit and tone of Tennyson's version of Ulysses' speech to his mariners:

> There lies the port; the vessel puffs her sail:
> There gloom the dark broad seas. My mariners,
> Souls that have toil'd, and wrought, and thought with me—

Bogan addresses her "mariners" with similar gravity: "Bend to the chart, in the extinguished night / Mariners! Make way slowly; stay from sleep."

Bogan may also be indebted to Baudelaire, if not for the actual sea-voyage metaphor, at least for certain aspects of its treatment in "Putting to Sea." Bogan's voyager has a specific moral purpose for her journey into the unknown, while Baudelaire's persona is a restless seeker after experience. Yet both poets share the belief that truth may be found in the search for the self. Bogan's final line, "And learn, with joy, the gulf, the vast, the deep," is almost an imitation of the last two lines of Baudeliare's "Le voyage": "Plonger au fond du gouffre, Enfer ou Ciel, qu'importe? / Au fond de l'Inconnu pour trouver du *nouveau!*" While Baudelaire exhorts his voyager to experience for its own sake, Bogan urges the striving for understanding. Her final line reaffirms her conviction that suffering can be surmounted as well as endured.

The most contemporary voyage which "Putting to Sea" recalls is the brief echo of "Sailing to Byzantium" heard in the second line. The voyager wonders at the extraordinary journey she is about to undertake. "This is no journey to a land we know," she says, echoing Yeats, who also rejects the everyday world, remarking of it, "That is no country for old men." Each of these poems partakes of the common impulse to represent the human journey as a sea voyage. In "Putting to Sea," Bogan both epitomizes that tradition and creates a poem uniquely her own.

Early in 1967, thirty years after the publication of "Putting to Sea" and just three years before her death, Bogan sent three "songs" to *New Yorker* poetry editor Howard Moss, with the note that they "seem to go together . . . [as poems] of dream and aberration." A way to read the shifting and merging voices in "Psychiatrist's Song" is in the light of dream logic, in which identities are often fluid and interchangeable. Moreover, in the course of the long journey which psychotherapy was for Bogan, perhaps psychiatrist and patient each take on attributes of the other.

In a typescript of the poem, the only draft extant, the title reads "Psychiatrist's Recitative and Aria." The published version retains the same stanzaic divisions. In the poem's opening section, which would be the recitative, the psychiatrist begins his monologue, musing in a general way upon the persons who have played crucial roles in the lives of his patients, but of whom "they" (the patients) cannot speak directly: "Those / Concerning whom they have never spoken and thought never to speak . . . ." In spite of the psychiatrist's hint that patients deliberately conceal things, we may infer that the reason they do not have access to the whole narrative of their lives is that much of what is crucial has been repressed, and remains hidden in the unconscious:

> That place
> Hidden, preserved,
> That even the exquisite eye of the soul
> Cannot completely see.

From that generalized and somewhat rambling diagnostic beginning, the psychiatrist's attention soon settles upon particulars, and we realize that he must now be thinking of one patient:

> But they are there:
> Those people, and that house, and that evening, seen
> Newly above the dividing window sash—

At this point the narrative intensifies. Another voice enters, and from this moment to the end of the poem, the voice of the psychiatrist contains the voice of the patient. The sudden shift from generalities to particular details— "that house . . . that evening . . . the dividing window sash"—and the personal cry of anguish in the lines that follow, indicate that the point of view has shifted to that of the patient; yet there is no break in the narrative:

> The young will broken
> And all time to endure.
>
> Those hours when murderous wounds are made,
> Often in joy.

The images of the damaged child and the treacheries of passion recall major themes in Bogan's poems. As the recitative, providing exposition or background for the rest of the poem, this opening section, with its merging voices of psychiatrist and patient, is a poetic statement of the psychological traumas for which the journey of the next section was undertaken.

The second section, the aria of the typescript, begins with the line "I hear." The merging voices of psychiatrist and patient acknowledge the warning contained in the last line of the preceding section about the treachery of passion. The narration of the journey is taken over by the patient, whose voice dominates from now on, though the guiding presence of the psychiatrist is felt in the poem until the final stanzas. Since the patient is also the poet-voyager of "Putting to Sea," thirty years after, this "I" stands for the several selves of the poet. That she has absorbed the psychiatrist persona completely by the end of the poem suggests, perhaps, the health of the psyche achieved.

Although the old temptations to the evils of fiend's country are recalled in the opening lines, this tropical landscape is "far away" and no longer threatens the voyager. The old motif of sexual jealousy echoes mockingly in the three repetitions of "man"-words, probably a play on the free-associative technique often used in psychotherapy: "the *man*go trees (the *man*grove swamps, the *man*drake root . . .)." The reminder of the "clattering" palms from "Putting to Sea" fixes the identity of this receding landscape, hazy now, having lost its clear sense of evil. The voyager "watches" the thicket of palms—not even sure anymore that they are palm trees, "as though at the edge of sleep." Indeed, the narration of this section has the dream character of a perfectly sequential and straightforward presentation of fantastic events.

The voyager has now achieved such control and certainty that she can journey toward the once disastrous landscape represented by the palms "in a boat without oars, / Trusting to rudder and sail." The idea that the voyager is in control of the journey contrasts with the formidable voyage of "Putting to Sea." Moreover, the whole landscape has been scaled down from the enormous and overpowering sea and sky of the earlier poem to a size more manageably human. She now leaves the boat and walks "fearlessly" to shore. Previously, even the ripples of the shallows might have been full of peril, for the sea has, until now, been an awesome and uncharted place. The lines that suggest control over a sea which will bring the speaker to a place of repose are reminiscent of Eliot's "*Damyata:* The Boat responded / Gaily, to the hand expert with sail and oar," from part 5 of *The Waste Land*, in which the rain brings with it the possibility of the renewal of life and hope.

The dangerous landscapes of ocean and palm trees recede, and the voyager finds herself "on firm dry land," with the solidity of earth all around her. The last stanza banishes the old terrors of "flesh and of ocean" that were given full expression in "Putting to Sea." If the last stanzas also evoke death in images of imminence, darkening, and silence, it is death welcomed, celebrated even, as the final healing. We need not be troubled by the implication that the cure for human suffering is death. Bogan was sixty-nine years old and in failing health when she wrote "Psychiatrist's Song." It is nearly her last poem, and marks the very last time she would use the voyage metaphor to set down in a poem the long struggle with her private demons. The truce between them was always, at best, a "troubled peace."

Bogan places a great deal of the burden for making the poem intelligible upon the reader. In "Putting to Sea" the poem's two voices were clearly separated. The voice out of fiend's country spoke a different language from that of the voyager or conscious self in the poem, and her speeches were set off from the voyager's narration by quotation marks. Bogan's decision to remove the recitative and aria directions from "Psychiatrist's Song" suggests a lightening of the poet's hand, a willingness to let the narrative take its own way.

Bogan takes more chances with language and form than she has done previously, and can risk beginning the poem with the halting awkwardness of a slightly pedantic and visually ungainly line. The play on "man" in "mango," "mangrove," and "mandrake," and the many irregularities in the free-verse line indicate greater flexibility and the freedom to experiment with the line and with the rhythms of common speech. The third line of the second section, with its truncated thought, "And the thickets of—are they palms?" is an illustration. And in the simple but strung-together statements of the line, "Coming to the shore, I step out of the boat; I leave it to its anchor," Bogan risks a kind of austere prosiness. In addition to its echoes of *The Waste Land*, "Psychiatrist's Song," is reminiscent throughout of Eliot's later poems of the 1930s, in particular "Marina" and "Coriolan."

The classical and formal Bogan still dominates in "Psychiatrist's Song," but her willingness to chance being prosaic places in relief the more poetically gorgeous phrases, such as "the exquisite eye of the soul," and the line with which she bridges the poem's two major sections, "Those hours when murderous wounds are made, / Often in joy." The elevated simplicity of the penultimate stanza is due in part to the extreme economy of the spare, predominantly one-syllable words. The luminosity of another late major poem, "After the Persian" (1951–53), glows for a moment in the final stanza. In the hortatory tone that is reminiscent of part 5, the "farewell" section of that poem, Bogan sounds again the note of sage or prophet, which is the final expression of her lifelong consciousness of herself as poet. Like "Putting to Sea," "Psychiatrist's Song" closes with an exhortation. But Bogan lowers the tone, and the moving prayer to earth, "Heal and receive me," ends the poem in an affecting combination of dignity and vulnerability.

Elizabeth Bishop: Domestication, Domesticity, and the Otherworldly

Helen Vendler

Elizabeth Bishop's poems in *Geography III* put into relief the continuing vibration of her work between two frequencies—the domestic and the strange. In another poet the alternation might seem a debate, but Bishop drifts rather than divides, gazes rather than chooses. Though the exotic is frequent in her poems of travel, it is not only the exotic that is strange and not only the local that is domestic. (It is more exact to speak, with regard to Bishop, of the domestic rather than the familiar, because what is familiar is always named, in her poetry, in terms of a house, a family, someone beloved, home. And it is truer to speak of the strange rather than of the exotic, because the strange can occur even in the bosom of the familiar, even, most unnervingly, at the domestic hearth.)

To show the interpenetration of the domestic and the strange at their most inseparable, it is necessary to glance back at some poems printed in *Questions of Travel*. In one, "Sestina," the components are almost entirely innocent —a house, a grandmother, a child, a Little Marvel Stove, and an almanac. The strange component, which finally renders the whole house unnatural, is tears. Although the grandmother hides her tears and says only "It's time for tea now," the child senses the tears unshed and displaces them everywhere—into the dancing waterdrops from the teakettle, into the rain on the roof, into the tea in the grandmother's cup.

> the child
> is watching the teakettle's small hard tears
> dance like mad on the hot black stove
> the way the rain must dance on the house . . .

From *World Literature Today* 51, no. 1 (Winter 1977). © 1977 by the University of Oklahoma Press.

> the almanac
> hovers half open above the child,
> hovers above the old grandmother
> and her teacup full of dark brown tears.

The child's sense of the world is expressed only in the rigid house she draws (I say "she," but the child, in the folk-order of the poem, is of indeterminate sex). The child must translate the tears she has felt, and so she "puts . . . a man with buttons like tears" into her drawing, while

> the little moons fall down like tears
> from between the pages of the almanac
> into the flower bed the child
> has carefully placed in the front of the house.

The tercet ending the sestina draws together all the elements of the collage:

> *Time to plant tears*, says the almanac.
> The grandmother sings to the marvellous stove
> and the child draws another inscrutable house.

The absence of the child's parents is the unspoken cause of those tears, so unconcealable though so concealed. For all the efforts of the grandmother, for all the silence of the child, for all the brave cheer of the Little Marvel Stove, the house remains frozen, and the blank center stands for the definitive presence of the unnatural in the child's domestic experience—*especially* in the child's domestic experience. Of all the things that should not be inscrutable, one's house comes first. The fact that one's house always *is* inscrutable, that nothing is more enigmatic than the heart of the domestic scene, offers Bishop one of her recurrent subjects.

The centrality of the domestic provokes as well one of Bishop's most characteristic forms of expression. When she is not actually representing herself as a child, she is, often, sounding like one. The sestina, which borrows from the eternally childlike diction of the folktale, is a case in point. Not only the diction of the folktale, but also its fixity of relation appears in the poem, especially in its processional close, which places the almanac, the grandmother, and the child in an arrangement as unmoving as those found in medieval painting, with the almanac representing the overarching Divine Necessity, the grandmother as the elder principle, and the child as the principle of youth. The voice speaking the last three lines dispassionately records the coincident presence of grief, song, necessity, and the marvelous; but in spite of the "equal" placing of the last three lines, the ultimate weight on inscrutability, even in the heart of the domestic, draws this poem into the orbit of the strange.

A poem close by in *Questions of Travel* tips the balance in the other direction, toward the domestic. The filling station which gives its name to the poem seems at first the antithesis of beauty, at least in the eye of the beholder who speaks the poem. The station is dirty, oil-soaked, oil-permeated; the father's suit is dirty; his sons are greasy; all is "quite thoroughly dirty"; there is even "a dirty dog." The speaker, though filled with "a horror so refined," is unable to look away from the proliferating detail which, though this is a filling station, becomes ever more relentlessly domestic. "Do they live in the station?" wonders the speaker, and notes incredulously a porch, "a set of crushed and grease-/ impregnated wickerwork," the dog "quite comfy" on the wicker sofa, comics, a taboret covered by a doily, and "a big hirsute begonia." The domestic, we perceive, becomes a compulsion that we take with us even to the most unpromising locations, where we busy ourselves establishing domestic tranquillity as a demonstration of meaningfulness, as a proof of "love." Is our theology only a reflection of our nesting habits?

> Why the extraneous plant?
> Why the taboret?
> Why, oh why, the doily? . . .
>
> Somebody embroidered the doily.
> Somebody waters the plant,
> or oils it, maybe. Somebody
> arranges the rows of cans
> so that they softly say:
> ESSO-SO-SO-SO
> to high-strung automobiles.
> Somebody loves us all.

In this parody of metaphysical questioning and the theological argument from design, the "awful but cheerful" activities of the world include the acts by which man domesticates his surroundings, even if those surroundings are purely mechanical, like the filling station or the truck in Brazil painted with "throbbing rosebuds."

The existence of the domestic is most imperiled by death. By definition, the domestic is the conjoined intimate: in American literature the quintessential poem of domesticity is "Snowbound." When death intrudes on the domestic circle, the laying-out of the corpse at home, in the old fashion, forces domesticity to its ultimate powers of accomodation. Stevens's "Emperor of Ice-Cream" places the cold and dumb corpse at the home wake in grotesque conjunction with the funeral baked meats, so to speak, which are being confected in the kitchen, as the primitive impulse to feast over the dead is seen surviving, instinctive and barbaric, even in our "civilized" society. Bishop's "First Death in Nova Scotia" places the poet as a child in a familiar parlor transfixed in perception by the presence of a coffin containing "little cousin Arthur":

> In the cold, cold parlor
> my mother laid out Arthur
> beneath the chromographs:
> Edward, Prince of Wales,

> with Princess Alexandra,
> and King George with Queen Mary.
> Below them on the table
> stood a stuffed loon
> shot and stuffed by Uncle
> Arthur, Arthur's father.

All of these details are immemorially known to the child. But focused by the coffin, the familiar becomes unreal: the stuffed loon becomes alive, his taciturnity seems voluntary, his red glass eyes can see.

> Since Uncle Arthur fired
> a bullet into him,
> he hadn't said a word.
> He kept his own counsel . . .
>
> Arthur's coffin was
> a little frosted cake,
> and the red-eyed loon eyed it
> from his white, frozen lake.

The adults conspire in a fantasy of communication still possible, as the child is told, "say good-bye / to your little cousin Arthur" and given a lily of the valley to put in the hand of the corpse. The child joins in the fantasy, first by imagining that the chill in the parlor makes it the domain of Jack Frost, who has painted Arthur's red hair as he paints the Maple Leaf of Canada, and next by imagining that "the gracious royal couples" in the chromographs have "invited Arthur to be / the smallest page at court." The constrained effort by all in the parlor to encompass Arthur's death in the domestic scene culminates in the child's effort to make a gestalt of parlor, coffin, corpse, chromographs, loon, Jack Frost, the Maple Leaf Forever, and the lily. But the strain is too great for the child, who allows doubt and dismay to creep in—not as to ultimate destiny, oh no, for Arthur is sure to become "the smallest page" at court, that confusing place of grander domesticity, half-palace, half-heaven; but rather displaced onto means.

> But how could Arthur go,
> clutching his tiny lily,
> with his eyes shut up so tight
> and the roads deep in snow?

Domesticity is frail, and it is shaken by the final strangeness of death. Until death, and even after it, the work of domestication of the unfamiliar goes on, all of it a substitute for some assurance of transcendent domesticity, some belief that we are truly, in this world, in our mother's house, that "somebody loves us all." After a loss that destroys one form of domesticity, the effort to reconstitute it in another form begins. The definition of death in certain of Bishop's poems is to have given up on domesticating the world and reestablishing yet once more some form of intimacy. Conversely, the definition of life in the conversion of the strange to the familial, of the unexplored to the knowable, of the alien to the beloved.

No domesticity is entirely safe. As in the midst of life we are in death, so, in Bishop's poetry, in the midst of the familiar, and most especially there, we feel the familiar as the unknowable. This guerrilla attack of the alien, springing from the very bulwarks of the familiar, is the subject of "In the Waiting Room." It is 1918, and a child, almost seven, waits, reading the *National Geographic,* while her aunt is being treated in the dentist's office. The scene is unremarkable: "grown-up people, / arctics and overcoats, / lamps and magazines," but two things unnerve the child. The first is a picture in the magazine: "black, naked women with necks / wound round and round with wire / like the necks of light bulbs. / Their breasts were horrifying"; and the second is "an *oh!* of pain /—Aunt Consuelo's voice" from inside. The child is attacked by vertigo, feels the cry to be her own uttered in "the family voice" and knows at once her separateness and her identity as one of the human group.

> But I felt: you are an *I*,
> you are an *Elizabeth*,
> you are one of *them*.
> *Why* should you be one too?
>
> . . . .
>
> What similarities—
> boots, hands, the family voice
> I felt in my throat, or even
> the *National Geographic*
> and those awful hanging breasts—
> held us all together
> or made us all just one?

In "There Was a Child Went Forth" Whitman speaks of a comparable first moment of metaphysical doubt:

> the sense of what is real, the thought if after all it should
>   prove unreal,
> The doubts of day-time and the doubts of night-time, the curious
>   whether and how,
> Whether that which appears so is so, or is it all flashes and specks?
> Men and women crowding fast in the streets, if they are not flashes
>   and specks what are they?

It is typical of Whitman that after his momentary vertigo he should tether himself to the natural world of sea and sky. It is equally typical of Bishop, after the waiting room slides "beneath a big black wave, / another, and another," to return to the sober certainty of waking fact, though with a selection of fact dictated by feeling.

> The War was on. Outside,
> in Worcester, Massachusetts,
> were night and slush and cold,
> and it was still the fifth
> of February, 1918.

The child's compulsion to include in her world even the most unfamiliar data, to couple the exotica of the *National Geographic* with the knees and trousers and skirts of her neighbors in the waiting room, brings together the strange at its most horrifying with the quintessence of the familiar—oneself, one's aunt, the "family voice." In the end, will the savage be domesticated or oneself rendered unknowable? The child cannot bear the conjunction and faints. Language fails the six-year-old. "How—I didn't know any / word for it—how 'unlikely.' "

That understatement, so common in Bishop, gives words their full weight. As the fact of her own contingency strikes the child, "familiar" and "strange" become concepts which have lost all meaning. "Mrs. Anderson's Swedish baby," says Stevens, "might well have been German or Spanish." Carlos Drummond de Andrade (whose rhythms perhaps suggested the trimeters of "In the Waiting Room") says in a poem translated by Bishop:

> Mundo mundo vasto mundo,
> se eu me chamasse Raimundo
> seria uma rima, não seria uma solução.

If one's name rhymed with the name of the cosmos, as "Raimundo" rhymes with "mundo," there would appear to be a congruence between self and world, and domestication of the world to man's dimensions would seem possible. But, says Drummond, that would be a rhyme, not a solution. The child of "In the Waiting Room" discovers that she is in no intelligible relation to her world, and, too young yet to conceive of domination of the world by will or domestication of the world by love, she slides into an abyss of darkness.

In "Poem" ("About the size of an old-style dollar bill") the poet gazes idly at a small painting done by her great-uncle and begins yet another meditation on the domestication of the world. She gazes idly—that is, until she realizes that the painting is of a place she has lived: "Heavens, I recognize the place, I know it!" In a beautiful tour de force "the place" is described three times. The first time it is rendered visually, exactly, interestedly, appreciatively, and so on: such, we realize, is pure visual pleasure touched with relatively impersonal recognition ("It must be Nova Scotia; only there / does one see gabled wooden houses / painted that awful shade of brown"). Here is the painting as first seen:

> Elm trees, low hills, a thin church steeple
> —that gray-blue wisp—or is it? In the foreground
> a water meadow with some tiny cows,
> two brushstrokes each, but confidently cows;

> two minuscule white geese in the blue water,
> back-to-back, feeding, and a slanting stick.
> Up closer, a wild iris, white and yellow,
> fresh-squiggled from the tube.
> The air is fresh and cold; cold early spring
> clear as gray glass; a half inch of blue sky
> below the steel-gray storm clouds.

Then the recognition—"Heavens, I know it!"—intervenes, and with it a double transfiguration occurs: the mind enlarges the picture beyond the limits of the frame, placing the painted scene in a larger, remembered landscape, and the items in the picture are given a local habitation and a name.

> Heavens, I recognize the place, I know it!
> It's behind—I can almost remember the farmer's name.
> His barn backed on that meadow. There it is,
> titanium white, one dab. The hint of steeple,
> filaments of brush-hairs, barely there,
> must be the Presbyterian church.
> Would that be Miss Gillespie's house?
> Those particular geese and cows
> are naturally before my time.

In spite of the connection between self and picture, the painting remains a painting, described by someone recognizing its means—a dab of titanium white here, some fine brushwork there. And the scene is set back in time— those geese and cows belong to another era. But by the end of the poem the poet has united herself with the artist. They have both loved this unimportant corner of the earth; it has existed in their lives, in their memories and in their art.

> Art "copying from life" and life itself,
> life and the memory of it so compressed
> they're turned into each other. Which is which?
> Life and the memory of it cramped,
> dim, on a piece of Bristol board,
> dim, but how live, how touching in detail
> —the little that we get for free,
> the little of our earthly trust. Not much.

Out of the world a small piece is lived in, domesticated, remembered, memorialized, even immortalized. Immortalized because the third time that the painting is described, it is seen not by the eye—whether the eye of the connoisseur or the eye of the local inhabitant contemplating a past era—but by the heart, touched into participation. There is no longer any mention of tube or brushstrokes or paint colors or Bristol board; we are in the scene itself.

> Not much.
> About the size of our abidance
> along with theirs: the munching cows,
> the iris, crisp and shivering, the water
> still standing from spring freshets,
> the yet-to-be dismantled elms, the geese.

Though the effect of being in the landscape arises in part from the present participles (the munching cows, the shivering iris, the standing water), it comes as well from the repetition of nouns from earlier passages (cows, iris), now denuded of their "paint" modifiers ("two brushstrokes each," "squiggled from the tube"), from the replication of the twice-repeated early "fresh" in "freshets" and most of all from the prophecy of the "yet-to-be-dismantled" elms. As lightly as possible, the word "dismantled" then refutes the whole illusion of entire absorption in the memorial scene; the world of the child who was once the poet now seems the scenery arranged for a drama with only too brief a tenure on the stage—the play once over, the set is dismantled, the illusion gone. The poem, having taken the reader through the process that we name domestication and by which a strange terrain becomes first recognizable, then familiar, and then beloved, releases the reader at last from the intimacy it has induced. Domestication is followed, almost inevitably, by that dismantling which is, in its acute form, disaster, the "One Art" of another poem:

> I lost my mother's watch. And look! my last, or
> next-to-last of three loved houses went . . .
>
> I lost two cities, lovely ones. And, vaster,
> some realms I owned, two rivers, a continent . . .
>
> the art of losing's not too hard to master
> though it may look like (*Write* it!) like disaster.

That is the tone of disaster confronted, with whatever irony.

A more straightforward account of the whole cycle of domestication and loss can be seen in the long monologue, "Crusoe in England." Crusoe is safely back in England, and his long autobiographical retrospect exposes in full clarity the imperfection of the domestication of nature so long as love is missing, the exhaustion of solitary colonization.

> I'd have
> nightmares of other islands
> stretching away from mine, infinities
> of islands, islands spawning islands,
> like frogs' eggs turning into polliwogs
> of islands, knowing that I had to live
> on each and every one, eventually
> for ages, registering their flora,
> their fauna, their geography.

Crusoe's efforts at the domestication of nature (making a flute, distilling home brew, even devising a dye out of red berries) create a certain degree of pleasure ("I felt a deep affection for / the smallest of my island industries"), and yet the lack of any society except that of turtles and goats and water-spouts ("sacerdotal beings of glass . . . / Beautiful, yes, but not much company")causes both self-pity and a barely admitted hope. Crusoe, in a metaphysical moment, christens one volcano *"Mont d'Espoir or Mount Despair,"* mirroring both his desolation and his expectancy. The island land-scape has been domesticated, "home-made," and yet domestication can turn to domesticity only with the arrival of Friday: "Just when I thought I couldn't stand it / another minute longer, Friday came." Speechless with joy, Crusoe can speak only in the most vacant and consequently the most com-prehensive of words.

> Friday was nice.
> Friday was nice, and we were friends.
> . . . he had a pretty body.

Love escapes language. Crusoe could describe with the precision of a geogra-pher the exact appearances of volcanoes, turtles, clouds, lava, goats, and waterspouts and waves, but he is reduced to gesture and sketch before the reality of domesticity.

In the final, recapitulatory movement of the poem Bishop first reiterates the conferral of meaning implicit in the domestication of the universe and then contemplates the loss of meaning once the arena of domestication is abandoned.

> The knife there on the shelf—
> it reeked of meaning, like a crucifix.
> It lived . . .
> I knew each nick and scratch by heart . . .
> Now it won't look at me at all.
> The living soul has dribbled away.
> My eyes rest on it and pass on.

Unlike the meanings of domestication, which repose in presence and use, the meaning of domesticity is mysterious and permanent. The monologue ends:

> The local museum's asked me to
> leave everything to them:
> the flute, the knife, the shrivelled shoes . . .
> How can anyone want such things?
> —And Friday, my dear Friday, died of measles
> seventeen years ago come March.

The ultimate locus of domestication is the heart, which, once cultivated, retains its "living soul" forever.

This dream of eternal and undismantled fidelity in domesticity, unaffected even by death, is one extreme reached by Bishop's imagination as it turns round its theme. But more profound, I think, is the version of life's experience recounted in "The Moose," a poem in which no lasting exclusive companionship between human beings is envisaged, but in which a series of deep and inexplicable satisfactions unroll in sequence, each of them precious. Domestication of the land is one, domesticity of the affections is another, and the contemplation of the sublimity of the nonhuman world is the third.

In the first half of the poem one of the geographies of the world is given an ineffable beauty, both plain and luxurious. Nova Scotia's tides, sunsets, villages, fog, flora, fauna, and people are all summoned quietly into the verse, as if for a last farewell, as the speaker journeys away to Boston. The verse, like the landscape, is "old-fashioned."

> The bus starts. The light
> is deepening; the fog
> shifting, salty, thin,
> comes closing in.
>
> Its cold, round crystals
> form and slide and settle
> in the white hens' feathers,
> in gray glazed cabbages,
> on the cabbage roses
> and lupins like apostles;
>
> the sweet peas cling
> to wet white string
> on the whitewashed fences;
> bumblebees creep
> inside the foxgloves,
> and evening commences.

The exquisitely noticed modulations of whiteness, the evening harmony of settling and clinging and closing and creeping, the delicate touch of each clause, the valedictory air of the whole, the momentary identification with hens, sweet peas, and bumblebees all speak of the attentive and yielding soul through which the landscape is being articulated.

As darkness settles, the awakened soul is slowly lulled into "a dreamy divagation / . . . / a gentle, auditory, slow hallucination." This central passage embodies a regression into childhood, as the speaker imagines that the muffled noises in the bus are the tones of "an old conversation":

> Grandparents' voices
>
> uninterruptedly
> talking, in Eternity:
> names being mentioned,
> things cleared up finally . . .

> Talking the way they talked
> in the old featherbed,
> peacefully, on and on . . .
>
> Now, it's all right now
> even to fall asleep
> just as on all those nights.

Life, in the world of this poem, has so far only two components: a beloved landscape and beloved people, that which can be domesticated and those who have joined in domesticity. The grandparents' voices have mulled over all the human concerns of the village:

> what he said, what she said,
> who got pensioned;
>
> deaths, deaths and sicknesses;
> the year he re-married;
> the year (something) happened.
> She died in childbirth.
> That was the son lost
> when the schooner foundered.
>
> He took to drink. Yes.
> She went to the bad.
> When Amos began to pray
> even in the store and
> finally the family had
> to put him away.
>
> "Yes . . ." that peculiar
> affirmative. "Yes . . ."
> A sharp, indrawn breath,
> half-groan, half-acceptance.

In this passage, so plainly different in its rural talk and sorrow from the ravishing aestheticism of the earlier descriptive passage, Bishop joins herself to the Wordsworth of the *Lyrical Ballads*. The domestic affections become, for a moment, all there is. Amos who went mad, the son lost at sea, the mother who died, the girl gone to the bad—these could all have figured in poems like "Michael" or "The Thorn." The litany of names evoking the bonds of domestic sympathy becomes one form of poetry, and the views of the "meadows, hills, and groves" of Nova Scotia is another. What this surrounding world looks like, we know; that "Life's like that" (as the sighed "Yes" implies), we also know. The poem might seem complete. But just as the speaker is about to drowse almost beyond consciousness, there is a jolt, and the bus stops in the moonlight, because "A moose has come out of / the impenetrable wood." This moose, looming "high as a church, / homely as a house," strikes wonder in the passengers, who "exclaim in whispers, / childishly, softly." The moose remains.

> Taking her time,
> she looks the bus over,
> grand, other-worldly.
> Why, why do we feel
> (we all feel) this sweet
> sensation of joy?

What is this joy?

In "The Most of It" Frost uses a variant of this fable. There, as in Bishop's poem, a creature emerges from "the impenetrable wood" and is beheld. But Frost's beast disappoints expectation. The poet had wanted "counter-love, original response," but the "embodiment that crashed" proves to be not "human," not "someone else additional to him," but rather a large buck, which disappears as it came. Frost's beast is male, Bishop's female; Frost's a symbol of brute force, Bishop's a creature "safe as houses"; Frost's a challenge, Bishop's a reassurance. The presence approaching from the wood plays, in both these poems, the role that a god would play in a pre-Wordsworthian poem and the role that a human being—a leech-gatherer, an ancient soldier, a beggar—would play in Wordsworth. These human beings, when they appear in Wordsworth's poetry, are partly iconic, partly subhuman, as the Leech-Gatherer is part statue, part sea-beast, and as the old man in "Animal Tranquillity and Decay" is "insensibly subdued" to a state of peace more animal than human. "I think I could turn and live with animals," says Whitman, foreshadowing a modernity that finds the alternative to the human not in the divine but in the animal. Animal life is pure presence, with its own grandeur. It assures the poet of the inexhaustibility of being. Bishop's moose is at once maternal, inscrutable, and mild. If the occupants of the bus are bound, in their human vehicle, to the world of village catastrophe and pained acknowledgment, they feel a releasing joy in glimpsing some large, grand solidity, even a vaguely grotesque one, which exists outside their tales and sighs, which is entirely "otherworldly." "The darkness drops again," as the bus moves on; the "dim smell of moose" fades in comparison to "the acrid smell of gasoline."

"The Moose" is such a purely linear poem, following as it does the journey of the bus, that an effort of will is required to gaze at it whole. The immediacy of each separate section—as we see the landscape, then the people, then the moose—blots out what has gone before. But the temptation—felt when the poem is contemplated entire—to say something global, something almost allegorical, suggests that something in the sequence is more than purely arbitrary. The poem passes from adult observation of a familiar landscape to the unending ritual, first glimpsed in childhood, of human sorrow and narration, to a final joy in the otherworldly, in whatever lies within the impenetrable wood and from time to time allows itself to be beheld. Beyond or behind the familiar, whether the visual or the human familiar, lies the perpetually strange and mysterious. It is that mystery which causes those whispered exclamations alternating with the pained "Yes" provoked by human vicissitude. It guarantees the poet more to do. On it depends all the impulse to domestication. Though the human effort is bent to the elimination of the wild, nothing is more restorative than to know that earth's being is larger than our human enclosures. Elizabeth Bishop's poetry of domestication and domesticity depends, in the last analysis, on her equal apprehension of the reserves of mystery which give, in their own way, a joy more strange than the familiar blessings of the world made human.

The Geography of Gender: Elizabeth Bishop's "In the Waiting Room"

Lee Edelman

> *I always tell the truth in my poems. With* The Fish, *that's exactly how it happened. It was in Key West, and I did catch it just as the poem says. That was in 1938. Oh, but I did change one thing . . .*
>
> —ELIZABETH BISHOP

Time and again in discussing her poetry Elizabeth Bishop insists on its fidelity to literal reality. "It was all true," she affirms of "The Moose," "it was all exactly the way I described it except that I say 'seven relatives.' Well, they weren't really relatives, they were various stepsons and so on, but that's the only thing that isn't quite true." In her attempts to "place" her poetry by means of such comments, Bishop reproduces a central gesture of the poetry itself. For that poetry, in Bishop's master-trope, takes place beneath the aegis of "geography," a study of places that leads her, invariably, to the question of poetic positioning—a question that converges, in turn, with the quest for, and the questioning of, poetic authority. Even in the casual remarks cited above, Bishop undertakes to authenticate her work, and she does so, tellingly, by fixing its origin on the solid ground of literality—a literality that Bishop repeatedly identifies as "truth."

But what does it mean to assert that a poem is "true," is somehow literal? Is it, in fact, ever possible to read such an assertion literally? Or, to put it another way, for what is such an appeal to literality a figure? Against what does it defend? These questions must color any reading of Bishop's poetry precisely because that poetry insists on the figural subtlety with which it represents the world. "More delicate than the historians' are the mapmakers' colors," Bishop writes in "The Map," the poem she placed first in her first book of poems. And that poem provides a key to the landscape of her poetry by directing attention to issues of textuality and trope. The truth that interests Bishop from the outset is not the truth of history or fact *per se*, but the more "delicate" matter of representation, the finely discriminated "colors" that lead back to the functioning of poetic coloration, or trope. If Bishop, as map-maker, "colors" her world, she has less in common with the

From *Contemporary Literature* 26, no. 2 (Summer 1985). © 1985 by the Board of Regents of the University of Wisconsin System. University of Wisconsin Press, 1984.

sort of Stevensian literalist of the first idea as she presents herself at times, than she does with Stevens's sublimely solipsistic Hoon, who calls forth a world from within himself to find himself "more truly and more strange."

To make such a claim about Bishop's work, however, is to displace truth from its relation to literality. To link the ability to see "truly" to the ability to make reality "more strange" is to make truth itself a stranger term—and one more problematic. For truth now comes into alignment with trope, literal and figurative effectively change places. Bishop's remarks about the literal origins of her poetry become significant, in this light, less for their assertions than for their qualifications: "that's *exactly* how it happened . . . Oh, but I did change *one* thing"; "it was all exactly the way I described it . . . Well, they weren't really relatives." Like the poetry itself, Bishop's characterizations of that poetry question the relationship between literal and figurative, observation and invention, perception and vision. All of which is to say that Bishop's is a poetry conscious of the difficulty and the necessity of reading, conscious of the inevitable mediations of selfhood, the intrusions of the "I," that make direct contact with any literality—with any "truth"—an impossibility.

But critics, for the most part, have refrained from seriously reading Bishop's readings of reading. They have cited her work, instead, as exemplary of precise observation and accurate detail, presenting us with an Elizabeth Bishop who seems startlingly like some latterday "gentle Jane." David Kalstone suggests something of the problem when he notes that "critics have praised her descriptive powers and treated her as something of a miniaturist. As mistakenly as with the work of Marianne Moore, they have sometimes asked if Bishop's is poetry at all." It is indeed significant that Moore and Bishop, two of the most widely praised female American poets of the century, have been championed for their careful observation, their scrupulous particularity, their characteristic restraint. As Sandra Gilbert and Susan Gubar point out in *The Madwoman in the Attic,* these are qualities less often associated with lyric poetry than with prose fiction. They define the skills necessary for success in a genre that historically has been more hospitable to women, perhaps because its conventions, themselves more social and domestic, rely upon powers of perception and narration that coincide with traditional perspectives on women as analysts of emotion, on the one hand, and as busybodies or gossips, on the other. If few would reduce Bishop to the status of a gossip, many have noted the distinct and engaging quality of the voice that seems to emanate from her work—a voice described by John Ashbery as speaking in "a pleasant, chatty vernacular tone . . . calmly and unpoetically." It is this "unpoetic" voice—Robert Lowell called it "unrhetorical"—in combination with her alert and disciplined eye, that has led critics to read Bishop's poetry, in John Hollander's words, "almost as if she were a novelist." Viewing it as a species of moral anecdote, even admirers of Bishop's work have tended to ignore the rigor of her intellect, the range of her allusiveness, the complexity of her tropes. Instead, they imply what Anne Stevenson, in her book on Bishop's life and work, asserts:

"Whatever ideas emerge have not been arrived at over a period of time but perceived, it would seem, in passing. They are the by-products of her meticulous observations."

Bishop, of course, has encouraged such misreadings by characterizing her poetry as "just description" and by emphasizing its grounding in the literal. I have suggested that this assertion of literality must itself be interpreted as a figure, that it defines for Bishop a strategy of evasion the sources of which this paper will attempt, in part, to trace. But the critical reception of Bishop, with its complicity in her reductive self-definition, with its acceptance of her willful evasions and its misprisions of her irony, exemplifies an interpretive blindness, which is to say, an ideological blindness, that enacts the very problems of reading on which Bishop's poetry frequently dwells. Readings that appropriate Bishop either to the company of poetic observers and reporters or to the ranks of moral fabulists, readings that place her in a clear relation to the literal reality her work is said to register, have the odd effect of seeming, instead, to be already placed or inscribed within that work, within her meditations on the way in which questions of placement and appropriation necessarily inform the very act of reading. No text better demonstrates the intricate connections among these concerns, or better locates the uncanny nature of her poetry's anticipation of its own misreadings, than does "In the Waiting Room," the poem with which Bishop introduced her last published volume, *Geography III*. A reading of that poem, which is a poem about reading, and a reading that interrogates the various readings of the poem, may suggest something of what is at stake in Bishop's reading of reading and show how "In the Waiting Room" effectively positions itself to read its readers.

> First, however, . . . I shall read very carefully (or try to read, since they may be partly obliterated, or in a foreign language) the inscriptions already there. Then I shall adapt my own compositions, in order that they may not conflict with those written by the prisoner before me. The voice of a new inmate will be noticeable, but there will be no contradictions or criticisms of what has already been laid down, rather a "commentary."
>
> (Elizabeth Bishop)

Commentaries on "In the Waiting Room" tend to agree that the poem presents a young girl's moment of awakening to the separations and the bonds among human beings, to the forces that shape individual identity through the interrelated recognitions of community and isolation. More remarkable than this unaccustomed critical consensus, however, is the degree to which its readers concur in identifying the poem's narrative or "plot" as the locus of the interpretive issues raised by the text. It is significant, in consequence, that critics have felt themselves both able and obliged to summarize the "story," to rehearse the events on which the poem's act of recognition hinges. Helen Vendler, for example, recapitulates the plot as follows: "waiting in a dentist's office, reading the *National Geographic*, feeling horrified at pictures of savages, hearing her aunt cry out in pain from inside the dentist's room, the child feels vertigo." Michael Wood directs attention to this same central episode when he describes "In the Waiting Room" as a poem in which "an almost-seven-year-old Elizabeth Bishop is horrified by the hanging breasts of African women seen in a copy of the *National Geographic*, and hears her own voice when her aunt cries out in pain." Similarly, Sybil Estess focuses on this narrative relationship when she writes that the child's "encounter with the strange pictures in the *National Geographic* is simultaneous with hearing her aunt's muffled cry of suffering."

These redactions would seem to rule out the possibility of hidden textual complications by the uniformity with which they define the poem's critical events. Yet when I suggest that there is something unusual and telling about the uniformity of these summaries, I anticipate that some will wonder why it should be considered odd that accounts of the same text should focus on the same significant episodes. What, one might ask, is so strange about critical agreement on the literal events that take place within the poem?

One response to such a question might begin by observing that the text itself seems to undermine the stability of the literal. Certainly the poem appears to appropriate—and to ground itself in—the particulars of a literal reality or truth. Bishop takes pains, for instance, to describe the contents of the magazine read by the young girl in the waiting room. Not only does she evoke in detail its pictures of volcanoes and of "black, naked women," but she specifies the particular issue of the magazine, identifying it as the *National Geographic* of February, 1918. But Bishop, as Jerome Mazzaro puts it, "tampers with the actual contents." While that issue of the magazine does indeed contain an article on volcanoes—lavishly titled "The Valley of Ten Thousand Smokes: An Account of the Discovery and Exploration of the Most Wonderful Volcanic Region in the World"—it offers no images of "Babies with pointed heads," no pictures of "black, naked women with necks/ wound round and round with wire." In an interview with George Starbuck, Bishop, responding to the critics who noticed the factual "error" in her text, declared: "My memory had confused two 1918 issues of the *Geographic*. Not having seen them since then, I checked it out in the New York Public Library. In the February issue there was an article, 'The Valley of 10,000 Smokes,' about Alaska that I'd remembered, too. But the African things, it turned out, were in the *next* issue, in March." Bishop's clarification only underscores her insistence on literal origins—and her wariness of her own imaginative powers. For the curious reader will discover what might have been suspected all along: the "African things" are not to be found in the March issue of the *National Geographic*, either. In fact, that issue has no essay about Africa at all.

With this in mind we are prepared for the warning that Alfred Corn offers the unsuspecting reader. He notes that, just as the picture essay Bishop describes "is not to be found in the February 1918 *National Geographic*," so "Anyone checking to see whether Miss Bishop's aunt was named Consuelo probably ought to be prepared for a similar thwarting of curiosity." In the face of this, one might well pose the question that Corn then frames: "If the facts are 'wrong,' why did Bishop make such a point of then frames: "If the facts are 'wrong,' why did Bishop make such a point of them in the poem?" Or, to put the question another way, toward what end does Bishop attempt to appropriate a literal grounding for her poem if that poem insists on fracturing the literality on which it positions itself? Whatever answer one might posit in response to such a question, the very fact that the poem invites us to ask it, the very fact that the poem revises simplistic conceptions of "fact" or literality may answer objections to my remark that there is something strange about the critics' agreement on the literal events that take place within the text.

But a new objection will surely be raised, accusing me of conflating two different senses of the "literal," or even of using "literal" in a way that is itself not strictly literal. While there may be questions, the objectors will insist, about the text's fidelity to the facts outside of it—questions, that is, about the literal truth of the text—those questions do not prevent us from articulating literally what happens within that text. Whether or not Bishop had a real Aunt Consuelo, there can be no doubt, they will argue, that Vendler and Estess and Wood are correct in asserting that, literally, within the poem, and as one of its crucial events, Aunt Consuelo cries out in pain from inside the dentist's office. And yet I intend not only to cast doubt upon that central event, but to suggest that the poem itself is less interested in the event than in the doubts about it, and that the critics' certainties distort the poem's insistence on confusion.

My own comments, of course, must repeat the error of attempted clarification. So I will approach this episode at the center of the text by way of my own brief summary of what occurs before it. The young girl, sitting outside in the waiting room while her aunt is in the dentist's office, reads the *National Geographic* "straight through," from cover to cover, and then, having closed the magazine, she begins to inspect the cover itself.

> Suddenly, from inside,
> came an *oh!* of pain
> —Aunt Consuelo's voice—
> not very loud or long.
> I wasn't at all surprised;
> even then I knew she was
> a foolish, timid woman.
> I might have been embarrassed,
> but wasn't. What took me
> completely by surprise
> was that it was *me:*
> my voice, in my mouth.
> Without thinking at all
> I was my foolish aunt,
> I—we—were falling, falling,
> our eyes glued to the cover
> of the *National Geographic,*
> February, 1918.

To gloss this passage as the young girl hearing "her aunt cry out in pain" is surely to ignore the real problem that both the girl and the text experience here: the problem of determining the place from which this voice originates. Since the poem asserts that it comes from "inside," the meanings of "inside" and "outside" must be determined, their geographical relation, as it were, must be mapped. The difficulty of making such determinations, however, springs from the overdetermination of meaning in this passage. The voice that cries out and, in so doing, sends the young girl—later identified as "Elizabeth"—plunging into the abyss that constitutes identity, disorients not by any lack of specification, but by the undecidable doubleness with which it is specified. The child recognizes the voice at once as Aunt Consuelo's and as her own. Any attempt to fix a clear relationship between these two alternatives, to label one as the ground upon which the other appears as figure, must presuppose an ability to penetrate the text, to get inside of it and thereby determine what it signifies by "inside." The critical consensus that attributes the cry of pain to Aunt Consuelo does, of course, precisely that. It refers the literal sense of "inside" to Aunt Consuelo's situation inside the dentist's office and thereby implies an interpretive model that rests upon an ability to distinguish the inside from the outside, the literal from the figurative. It suggests, moreover, that the literal is the textual "inside" on which the figural "outside" depends, and, therefore, that critical understanding must proceed by piercing or reading through the confusions of figuration in order to recover the literal ground that not only enables us to "place" the figural, but also allows us, by so doing, to keep the figural in its place.

Bishop's geography, however, persistently refuses the consolations of hierarchy or placement; instead, it defines itself as the questioning of places—a project emblematized by the way in which Bishop tropes upon the volume's epigraph from a geography textbook of 1884. She appends to its confident litany of answers to questions about the world ("*What is the Earth? / The planet or body on which we live. / What is the shape of the Earth? / Round, like a ball*") a series of inquiries that seek to evade the reductive literalism of such an Idiot Questioner:

> *In what direction is the Volcano? The*
> *Cape? The Bay? The Lake? The Strait?*
> *The Mountains? The Isthmus?*
> *What is in the East? In the West? In the*
> *South? In the North? In the Northwest?*
> *In the Southeast? In the Northeast?*
> *In the Southwest?*

Given Bishop's insistent questioning of places, we can say that in a very real sense those commentators who put themselves in a position to identify Aunt Consuelo as the source of the cry of pain in "In the Waiting Room" take the words out of Bishop's mouth in taking the cry out of "Elizabeth" 's. Their need to locate the place from which the cry or voice originates places the question of the voice's origination at the origin of the textual problem in the poem. That is to say, it locates the poem as an effect of the voice's origination, enabling them to read it as a fable of humanization through identification, a lesson in the sort of Wordsworthian "primal sympathy" that shapes "the human heart by which we live."

But within the poem itself the voice is contextually located, and since the logic of poetry allows some truth to *post hoc ergo propter hoc*, this location determines the voice itself as an effect—as, specifically, a reading-effect. The cry that the text tells us comes "Suddenly, from inside," comes, within the text, after "Elizabeth" has finished reading the *National Geographic* and is scrutinizing its cover. To understand that cry, then, and the meaning of its place—or, more precisely of its displacement—requires a more careful study of the scene of reading that comes before it and, in some sense, calls it forth.

Evoking herself as an almost-seven-year-old child sitting in the dentist's waiting room, the "Elizabeth" whose memory constitutes the poem offers off-handedly, in a parenthetical aside, the assertion that governs the whole of the passage preceding the cry: "(I could read)." However casually the parentheses introduce this simple statement, both the statement itself and the simplicity with which it is presented identify a claim to authority. For the child, that authority derives from her mastery of the mystery of written language and from her concomitant access to the documents of culture, the inscriptions of society. Just as she has mastered reading, and as reading allows for a mastery of culture, so reading itself, for the young "Elizabeth," is understood as an exercise of mastery. The child of whose ability to read we are assured implicitly assumes the readability of texts, since reading for her is a process of perceiving the real and stable relationships that exist between word and image, past and present, cause and effect. The juxtaposition of photographs and captions, therefore, is transparently meaningful for "Elizabeth." From her position as a reader, outside of the text, she can readily decipher the fixed relationships that are delineated within it.

But the critical moment in the poem is precipitated at just the point when this model of reading as mastery comes undone, when the division between inside and outside breaks down and, as a result, the determinacy of textual relationships is called into question. Though only in the course of reading the magazine does "Elizabeth" perceive the inadequacy of her positioning as a reader, Bishop's text implies from the outset the insufficiency of any mode of interpretation that claims to release the meaning it locates "inside" a text by asserting its own ability to speak from a position of mastery "outside" of it. For this reason everything that "Elizabeth" encounters in the pages of the *National Geographic* serves to disturb the stability of a binary opposition. The first photographs that she recalls looking at, for instance, strategically define a sequential process:

> the inside of a volcano,
> black, and full of ashes;
> then it was spilling over
> in rivulets of fire.

Not only do these images undo the central distinction between inside and outside, but they do so by positing an excess of interiority that displaces itself onto the exterior. In other words, the inside here obtrudes upon the outside and thereby asserts its claim to mastery by transforming the landscape and showing how the exterior, how the landscape itself, is composed of interior matter.

The inside/outside dichotomy is reversed and discredited at once, and the effect of this maneuver on the theory of reading is to imply that the textual inside masters the reader outside of it far more than the reader can ever master the text. Or, more precisely, the very distinction between reader and text is untenable: the reader finds herself read by the text in which she is already inscribed and in which she reinscribes herself in the process of performing her reading. Since "Elizabeth" asserts that she "carefully studied" these photographs, it is worth noting, too, that not only do they disrupt the opposition between inside and outside, but also, insofar as the "ashes" in the first picture produce the "rivulets of fire" in the second, they disrupt the natural or logical relationship ascribed to cause and effect.

Inasmuch as Bishop's version of the *National Geographic* for February, 1918 corresponds to the actual issue of that magazine only in that both include images of volcanoes, her imagined periodical must function as a sort of exemplary text contrived to instruct young "Elizabeth," and us, in the difficulty of reading. Toward this end the photograph of Osa and Martin Johnson, though it seems less violently subversive than Bishop's Dickinsonian volcanoes, plays a significant part. The Johnsons, in the first decades of this century, achieved fame as a husband and wife team of explorers and naturalists, and in her autobiography, *I Married Adventure,* Osa Johnson provides information that may have inspired, and certainly sheds light on, the rest of the items that Bishop chooses to include in her magazine. But the photograph of the Johnsons themselves does more than allude to one of Bishop's likely sources. Her portrait of husband and wife focuses attention on the particulars of their clothing, and the most significant aspect of their clothing is the fact that it is identical. Both appear "dressed in riding breeches, / laced boots, and pith helmets." (I might add that there is a picture of Osa and Martin Johnson in which she appears in such a costume, but her husband, interestingly enough, does not wear an identical outfit.) In terms of Osa's autobiography, this image metonymically represents her transformation from a typical Kansas girl of sixteen, dreaming of weddings and weeping "with all the persecuted little picture heroines of the day," into an adventurer able to hold her own in a world of cannibals and headhunters. Osa underscores this transformation precisely in terms of clothing in two passages from *I Married Adventure*. The first time that her future husband calls on her at home, Osa's brother causes her to "burst out crying" by telling her that Mr. Johnson has joined with cannibals in eating missionaries. When her caller arrives, Osa is still upstairs crying and, as she tells us, "With women's clothes as complicated as they were in that day, even with Mama's help, it was nearly half an hour before I could get downstairs." Later, after they are married and she has agreed to join Martin on expeditions into the realm of the cannibals, he describes to her the sort of clothing that they will need to take along:

> "And some denim overalls and huck shirts," Martin said, following me into the kitchen.
> "For me?" I asked.
> "For both of us," he replied.

The identical outfits in which Bishop envisions the Johnsons in her photograph, then, point emblematically toward the subversion of the hierarchical opposition of male and female, an opposition into the nature of which Osa Johnson will peer when, like Lévi-Strauss, she confronts the role of women in "primitive" cultures as linguistic and economic objects of circulation and exchange. The structural anthropologist's insight offers a valuable point of reference here because "Elizabeth," after perusing the picture of the Johnsons, encounters in her text disturbing images that illuminate *la pensée sauvage*. (It is important to note, moreover, if only parenthetically, that "Elizabeth," for whom reading is at once a discipline of mastery and a mode of mastering her culture, occupies herself in reading a magazine devoted to geography and ethnology— discourses that imply a troubling relationship between the reading of cultures and the assertion of an ethnocentric form of cultural mastery.)

Bishop now presents the young "Elizabeth" with a textual impasse that resists appropriation by her system of reading as mastery and in so doing challenges her confidence in the very readability of texts: "A dead man slung on a pole /—'Long Pig,' the caption said." Dividing image and caption, picture and text not only by means of the linear break, but also by the dash—a mark of punctuation that dialectically connects and separates at once—Bishop emphasizes the apparently absolute undecidability of the relationship here. Some element of error seems necessarily to have entered into the working of the text. Has "Elizabeth" mistakenly interpreted the photograph of a pig as that of a human corpse? Has an editor carelessly transposed captions so that the photograph of a corpse has been identified as that of a pig? What "Elizabeth" faces here, of course, is the fundamental "error" of figurative language that creates the difficulty in trying to locate the literal as the ground from which the figural can be construed. The pole on which the dead object—be it corpse or pig—is slung serves as the axis of meaning on which the trope itself seems to turn. Like a dash, or like the slash that marks a fraction or a mathematical ratio, the pole establishes the polarities that it also brings together. For "Elizabeth" only the discrepancy matters, the difference that cannot be mastered or read. But anthropologists—or those familiar with Osa Johnson's autobiography—will be able to read this figural relationship more easily than does "Elizabeth," since they will recognize what the phrase "Long Pig" metaphorically connotes.

Describing her first expedition into a "savage" society, Osa recalls that she and her husband were warned that " 'those fellows on Vao still bury their old people alive and eat long pig'.'' And later, remembering the dismay of the captain who, at their insistence, ferried her husband and herself to Vao despite such admonitions, Osa writes, ''If we were reckless enough to risk being served up as 'long pig' by the savages of Malekula, that was our lookout, not his.'' ''Long Pig,'' then, names man when he ceases to be human, when he enters into a system of signification which he no longer masters from an external position of privileged subjectivity, but into which he himself enters as an object of circulation. The metaphoric labelling of a ''dead man'' as ''long pig'' has the effect of exposing the metaphoricity of the apparently literal or natural category of humanity itself. Far from being a presence controlling language from without, humanity is understood to be figural, another product of the linguistic system.

Though Bishop's text, then, has challenged the stability of distinctions between inside and outside, male and female, literal and figurative, human and bestial, young ''Elizabeth'' reads on from her own position of liminality in the waiting room until she confronts, at last, an image of women and their infants:

> Babies with pointed heads
> wound round and round with string;
> black, naked women with necks
> wound round and round with wire
> like the necks of light bulbs.

Osa Johnson may again have provided Bishop with the material that she incorporates here into their imagined magazine. In her autobiography Mrs. Johnson refers to the Malekulan practice of elongating the head: ''This was done by binding soft, oiled coconut fiber around the skulls of infants shortly after birth and leaving them there for something over a year. The narrower and longer the head when the basket contrivance was removed, the greater the pride of the mother. That her baby had cried almost without ceasing during this period of distortion was of no concern whatsoever.'' The autobiography, however, does not refer to the elongation of the women's necks, and in the photograph that Osa Johnson includes of a Malekulan woman and her infant—a photograph in which the child's head is indeed ''wound round and round with string''—the mother does not wear the rings of wire that are used to stretch women's necks in some tribal cultures. Bishop willfully introduces the symmetry that characterizes her images of women and children so that both here suffer physical distortion by objects ''wound round and round'' their bodies. This assimilation of women to the status of children takes place simultaneously with the recognition made by the young ''Elizabeth'' of her own destined status as a woman, of her own inevitable role, therefore, in the sexual economy of her culture. She reads the burden of female sexuality here as the inescapability of distortion, as the enforced awareness of one's body as a malleable object. Anatomy itself loses the authority of any natural or literal grounding; instead, it becomes one more figure in the language of the culture.

As woman is reduced to a figure trapped in the linguistic circuit, so her body becomes a text on which her figural status is inscribed. The culturally sanctioned, which is to say, the patriarchally determined, markings of female sexuality are thus understood as diacritical marks, and Bishop, significantly, evokes these linguistic markings, these metonyms of woman as erotic signifier, specifically in terms of constraint. Moreover, her particular vision of constriction as the patriarchal writing of woman's sexuality on her body takes the form of a wire wound about the woman's neck, an image that conjures the garrote—an instrument of strangulation that prevents the victim from uttering any cry at all. If the necks of the women in the photograph are bound by these wires "like the necks of light bulbs," then what they illuminate for "Elizabeth" is her fate as a woman, her necessary implication in the system of signs she had thought to master by being able to read. Now, for the first time, she reacts to the text, acknowledging an emotional response to the naked women: "Their breasts," she says, "were horrifying."

The horror that "Elizabeth" feels betokens her perception of the monstrosity, the abnormality that informs the given or "norm" of sexuality. Sexuality itself, she has discovered, is always constituted as a system of signs that must operate through the substitution of figures; consequently, it is neither a "natural" system nor an inevitable one. Yet within the patriarchal system the "normal" figurations of female sexuality take the form of literal disfigurations. Woman herself becomes a creation of man since, as Simone de Beauvoir recognized years ago, one is not born a woman: as a linguistic construct who figures through disfiguration, woman is the monstrous creation of the patriarchy. And what most horrifies "Elizabeth" as she focuses on the breasts of these disfigured or monstrous women is her recognition of the fundamental affinity she shares with them. In a sense they speak to her in the words that Mary Shelley gave to the monster that she imagined as the product of a wholly masculine gestation: "my form is a filthy type of yours, more horrid even from the very resemblance." It is finally this resemblance, which is to say, the relationship of metaphoric interchangeability, that horrifies "Elizabeth." At last she must recognize fully what is at stake in the dismantling of binary oppositions, for the reader and what she reads collapse into one another as "Elizabeth" finds herself located *by* the text, *inside* the text, and *as* a text.

Yet in neutral, uninflected tones she continues:

> I read it right straight through.
> I was too shy to stop.
> And then I looked at the cover:
> the yellow margins, the date.

The very blandness of this account, following her admission of horror, testifies to an effort of denial or repression as "Elizabeth" seeks to master herself by affirming her difference from the text and, thus, her ability to master *it* through reading. She studies the cover, the margins, and the date in order to construct a frame for her reading experience that will circumscribe or contain it. The burden of her task here is the desperate need to contextualize the text so as to prevent her suffocation, her strangulation within it. The "yellow margins" that she focuses on represent her margin of security to the extent that they define a border, a yellow or cautionary zone distinguishing the inside from the outside. But the security of such a reading of the margin falls within the margin of error as soon as one recognizes the complex dynamic involved in the positing of such a frame. In a brilliant analysis of these problems in her essay "The Frame of Reference: Poe, Lacan, Derrida," Barbara Johnson cites Derrida's contention that "frames are always framed." What this means in terms of "Elizabeth" and her reading of the *National Geographic* is that the act of framing arises as a response to her disturbing recognition that the text refuses to be delimited or framed. Thus her framing of the text is itself framed by her terrifying awareness of the text's unframability. As Barbara Johnson comments in her analysis of Derrida, therefore, "the frame thus becomes not the borderline between the inside and the outside, but precisely what subverts the applicability of the inside/outside polarity to the act of interpretation."

One subversive aspect of "Elizabeth" 's response to the photograph of the women remains to be considered. The breasts that "Elizabeth" describes as horrifying may horrify not only because they link her to the disfigurations and constraint that mark female sexuality in patriarchal cultures; they may horrify as well because they evoke an eroticism that undermines the institution of heterosexuality—the institution that determines sexual difference as well as its inscriptions. Adrienne Rich has recently discussed Bishop in terms of "the lesbian writing under the false universal of heterosexuality," but here in "In the Waiting Room," and at the other crucial points throughout her career, Bishop covertly discredits that "false universal" and its ideology. After acknowledging her emotional reaction to the breasts of the naked women—in an earlier draft they are said not to horrify her, but rather to fill her with awe—"Elizabeth" explains that she continued reading because she was "too shy to stop." This shyness surely corresponds to the fearful embarrassment that expresses desire in the very act of trying to veil it. Too shy, then—which is to say, too inhibited or constrained—to stop or to linger over these pictures, "Elizabeth" reads the magazine "straight through" because doing so, in a sense, marks her reading as "straight." It prevents the embarrassing discovery of her emotional investment in the "naked women" and of her unsettling response to their breasts—a response that shifts between horror and awe.

But by silencing the voice of her own sexuality, by succumbing to the constraint of shyness and framing the text in order to distance herself from the desire that it unleashes, she locates herself, paradoxically, inside the text once more. For her constraining shyness merely reenacts the cultural inscriptions of female sexuality that the magazine has presented to her in terms of silencing and constraint. Because her reading has alerted her to the patriarchal and heterosexual foundation on which the ideology of binary oppositions rests, and because it has suggested to her the inevitability of her reduction to the status of a figure in that cultural system or text, "Elizabeth" directs her attention to the magazine's cover in an obvious effort to cover up, to deny or suppress the insights that her reading has uncovered. In the act of foregrounding the cover she undertakes to frame the text as a literary object, to reduce its provenance by underscoring the literary status of its discourse. Such a framing has the same effect as the framing achieved by the bracketing of a word or phrase by quotation marks: it produces the detachment of irony. But the irony of "Elizabeth" 's attempt here to position herself ironically with relation to the text is that irony introduces once more the elements of subversion and indeterminacy that are precisely the elements of the text that she fears and from which she seeks to detach herself.

This, then, is "Elizabeth" 's situation after her exercise in reading: sitting in the dentist's office while her aunt receives treatment inside, she looks at the cover of the *National Geographic* and tries to hold on to the solid ground of literality outside the abyss of textuality she has discovered within it. In doing so, she silences the voice of her own internal desire and conforms to the socially determined role that her shyness forces her to play. At the same time, however, she recognizes, as a result of her reading, the inadequacy of the inside/outside polarity that underlies each of her tensions—tensions that mount until they no longer admit of repression or constraint: "Suddenly, from inside, / came an oh! of pain."

With this we come back to where we began—back to the question of the voice and the question of the place from which the voice originates. But we return with a difference to the extent that the critical desire to locate or to define or to frame any literal "inside" for that voice to emerge from has been discredited as an ideological blindness, a hierarchical gesture. There is no inside in this poem that can be distinguished from its outside: the cry emanates from inside the dentist's office, and from inside the waiting room, and from inside the *National Geographic,* and from inside "In the Waiting Room." It is a cry that cries out against any attempt to clarify its confusions because it is a female cry—a cry of the female—that recognizes the attempts to clarify it as attempts to put it in its place. It is an *"oh!"* that refuses to be readily deciphered because it knows that if it is read it must always be read as a cipher—as a zero, a void, or a figure in some predetermined social text. Those critics, then, who read the poem by trying to place the cry, effect, instead, a denial of that cry which is a cry of displacement—a cry of the female refusal of position in favor of dis-position. As a figural subversion, it wages war against the reduction of woman to the status of a literal figure, an oxymoronic entity constrained to be interpreted within the patriarchal text. It is against that text that the cry wages war, becomes a war cry to unleash the textuality that rips the fabric of the cultural text. To conclude, then, is only to urge a beginning, to urge that we attend to this cry as a cry of female textuality, a cry that links "Elizabeth" to her "foolish" aunt and to the tormented mother in Bishop's story, "In the Village." In this way we can approach the poem's cry, in Stevens's words, as the "cry of its occasion" and begin to engage the issues of gender and constraint that are so deeply involved in Bishop's story of *"oh!"*

May Swenson:
"Turned Back to the Wild by Love"

Richard Howard

When May Swenson, speaking in her thaumaturgical fashion of poetry, says that "attention to the silence in between is the amulet that makes it work," we are reminded, while on other occasions in her work we are reassured, that there is a kind of poetry, as there used to be a kind of love, which dares not speak its name. Indeed, it was in the latter's heyday (1891, when Mallarmé thanked Oscar Wilde for *The Picture of Dorian Gray*, "one of the only books that can move me, for its commotion proceeds from an essential reverie, and from the strangest silences of the soul"), that the former's program was devised, by the thanker: "to *name* an object is to suppress three-quarters of our pleasure in the poem, a pleasure which consists in gradually divining . . . ; to *suggest*, that is the ideal. That is making perfect use of the kind of mystery which constitutes the symbol." Of course, there is a complementary impulse to *identify* in this reluctance to call a spade a spade; it is an impulse implicit in the very paradox supported by the word *identification*, which we use both to select an object in all its singularity, and to dissolve that "identical" object into its likeness with another. The refusal, or the reluctance, to *name* in order that she may the more truly *identify* is what we notice first about May Swenson's poetry—though she does not proceed so strictly with the enterprise as Mallarmé, for whom the designation of a flower enforced its *absence* from any bouquet. When Miss Swenson says:

> beautiful each Shape
> to see
> wonderful each Thing
> to name

she means the kind of ascertaining of Existence Hölderlin meant when he

From *Alone with America: Essays on the Art of Poetry in the United States since 1950*. © 1980 by Richard Howard. Enlarged edition, Atheneum, 1980.

said that poetry was a naming of the Gods—and for such an appeal (such an appellation), the ordinary labels do not suffice. Miss Swenson would not be so extreme about her magic as the symbolists, but she is plainly aware of the numbing power of proper names; as the story of Rumpelstiltskin demonstrates, there is an awful mastery in knowing what a being is called, and in so calling him—indeed such mastery suggests, to May Swenson at least, a corresponding lack of attention to the quality of being itself, a failure, by the wielding of nomination's "mace petrific," to encounter, to espouse form as it *becomes* what it is.

It is an old kind of poetry, then, that this poet resumes in her quest for "my face in the rock, my name on the wildest tree," a poetry that goes back to Orpheus, probably, and moves forward through Blake and Emily Dickinson, whom May Swenson specifically echoes, I think, in her eagerness to see Being wherever she looks:

> Any Object before the Eye
> can fill the space can occupy
> the supple frame of eternity
>
> my Hand before me such
> tangents reaches into Much
> root and twig extremes can touch
>
> any Hour can be the all
> expanding like a cunning Ball
> to a Vast from very small
>
> any Single becomes the More
> multiples sprout from alpha's core
> from Vase of legend vessels of lore . . .

It is the poetry which comes into existence whenever the need is felt (as by Valéry most recently, most magisterially) to *charm*, to *enchant*, to *bind by spells* an existence otherwise apprehended as inaccessibly other. For as Valéry says of Orpheus, it was only by his songs that trees knew the full horror of dancing. Similarly, in May Swenson's kennings, their method "a parliament of overlappings" and their goal "an assuaging singleness," we find that the hand in her lap, the cat on the sill, the cloud in the sky become, before we have a chance to adjust our sights and to enslave our other senses as well to what we *know*, fables of unlabelled Being:

> For each path leads both out and in
> I come while going   No to and from
> There is only here   And here
> is as well as there   Wherever
> I am led I move within the care
> of the season
> hidden in the creases of her skirts
> of green or brown or beaded red

> And when they are white
> I am not lost   I am not lost then
> only covered for the night

Evidently, Miss Swenson's effort has been to discover runes, the conjurations by which she cannot only apostrophize the hand, the cat and the cloud in their innominate otherness, but by which she can, in some essential and relieving way, *become them*, leave her own impinging selfhood in the paralyzed region where names are assigned, and assume instead the energies of natural process.

From the first—in 1954 came *her* first collection, the significantly titled *Another Animal*—May Swenson has practiced, in riddles, chants, hex-signs and a whole panoply of invented *sortilege* unwonted in Western poetry since the Witch of Endor brought up Samuel, the ways not only of summoning Being into her grasp, but of getting herself out of that grasp and into alien shapes, into those emblems of power most often identified with the sexual:

> on this ball   oh to Endure
> half dark   like the stone
> half light   sufficient
> i walk Upright   to itself alone
> i lie Prone
> within the night   or Reincarnate
>   like the tree
> the longing   be born each spring
> that i know   to greenery
> is in the Stone also
> it must be   or like the lion
> the same that rises   without law
> in the Tree   to roam the Wild
> the longing   on velvet paw . . .
> in the Lion's call
> speaks for all

Consider the array of instruments in this fragment of the first poem from that first book, "Evolution": the incantatory use of rhyme; the rhythms of the spell; the typography that lines up the first column to stand not only pat but put, as it were, against the outer verticality of the second column, so that the poem on the page articulates, by the space it leaves as by the form it takes, a regular *passage* through which the forces can move to their completion; the lower-casing of the first-person pronoun, and the capitalization of the three Entities addressed, then their relegation to lower-case too, and the assumption of capital status by the two crucial verbs, "Reincarnate" and "Endure," and by the hypostatized adjective "Wild"; the irregular little stanzas content to exhibit, in loving complacency, a single word as an entire line; the rejection of punctuation as an unnecessary artifice in this organum of being. Evidently, this poet is engaged, and more than engaged, is elated, by the responsibilities of form. In subsequent poems in *Another Animal*, as in her other books, Miss Swenson exhibits a very determined attitude toward *contrivance;* aware, I suppose, of the danger inherent in her own siren-songs, with their obsessive reliance on the devices of incantation, she is more than eager to cast off the blasphemies of "Satanic Form":

> Things metallic or glass
> frozen twisted flattened
> stretched to agonized bubbles
> bricks beams receptacles vehicles
> forced through fire hatched to unwilling form

—and to assume in their place the "blessed" and organic avatars it is her art to invoke, not so much to counterfeit as to conjure:

> flower and stone not cursed with symmetry
> cloud and shadow not doomed to shape and fixity
> the intricate body of many without rivet or nail
> O love the juice in the green stem growing . . .

Contraption, like naming, is seen as the wrong version of experience. The paradox of the riddling poet is that she must identify without naming, make without artifice, "a model of time, a map of space." Miss Swenson is engaged in the Higher Fabrication, that *poesis* which is the true baptism; when she fails to devise charms that capture Being in their toils, she becomes, like Dickinson, again, merely charming; the appeal is no more, at times, than appealing, when it needed to be a summons:

> I lived by magic
> A little bag in my chest held a whirling stone
> so hot it was past burning
> so radiant it was blinding
>
> When the moon rose worn and broken
> her face like a coin endlessly exchanged
> in the hands of the sea
> her ray fell upon the doors which opened
> and I walked in the living wood . . .

Throughout this book, as the title itself suggests, and in the course of the collections to come, May Swenson has found a figure which allows her to escape the difficulties of both nomination and mechanism; it is the figure of the centaur, which cannot be merely named for it is imaginary, and which cannot be merely artificial for it is alive. She begins, in the title poem:

> Another animal imagine moving
> in his rippling hide
> down the track of the centaur . . .

the shaped verses undulate down the page in a first presentment of "dappled animals with hooves and human knees"; in "To Confirm a Thing," the figure is moralized a little:

> In the equal Night where oracular beasts
>   the planets depose
> and our Selves assume their orbits . . .
> My thighs made marble-hard
>   uncouple only to the Archer
> with his diametrical bow
>   who prances in the South
> himself a part of his horse . . .
> Then let me by these signs
>   maintain my magnitude
> as the candid Centaur his dynasty upholds
>   And in the Ecliptic Year
> our sweet rebellions
>   shall not be occulted but remain
> coronals in heaven's Wheel.

And finally, in "Question," the same figure, which has become perhaps too cosmic, too "mechanical" in its astronomic implications, is returned to its erotic energies, the self addressed in that animal form where, by a certain incantation, Miss Swenson best finds her being in its highest range:

> Body my house
> my horse my hound
> what will I do
> when you are fallen
>
> Where will I sleep
> How will I ride
> What will I hunt
> Where can I go
> without my mount
> all eager and quick . . .
>
> With cloud for shift
> how will I hide?

May Swenson's second book was published in 1958; *A Cage of Spines*, garlanded with praise by Elizabeth Bishop, Richard Wilbur and Robert Lowell, among others; of these, only Howard Moss seems taken with the notion that in Swenson's "world," Being is illuminated so that "whatever she describes is not only more itself but more than itself." The strategies and devices, the shamanism and sorcery this poet deploys have become, in this larger, luminous collection, more elaborate, more convinced, and deserve further attention; their accommodation of the mystery that only when a thing is apprehended as something else can it be known as itself is fierce and full in *A Cage of Spines*. But we must note, first, an interesting development, from implication to statement, of the Centaur theme, the projection of energies and erotics into animal form, so that the poet may ask, "to what beast's intent / are we the fodder and nourishment?" The new note sounded occurs at the very start of the book, in a poem explicit enough to be called "The Centaur." For the first time, Swenson evokes life—her life—in the chatty, novelistic mode previously judged "too effusive in design for our analyses":

> The summer that I was ten—
> Can it be there was only one
> summer that I was ten? It must
>
> have been a long one then—

Looking down the prospect of her imagination, the poet reports how she would ride her willow branch all morning:

> I was the horse and the rider,
> and the leather I slapped to his rump
> spanked my own behind . . .

and come inside, after an exhausting morning's riding (and being ridden):

> *Where have you been?* said my mother.
> *Been riding,* I said from the sink,
> and filled me a glass of water . . .
> *Go tie back your hair,* said my mother,
> and *Why is your mouth all green?*
> *Rob Roy, he pulled some clover
> as we crossed the field,* I told her.

Here not by incantation but by exactitude in narrative, Miss Swenson gets across the doubleness in being she strives for throughout. It is a method she will resume in the book after this one, but the rest of *A Cage of Spines* is dedicated to the means of witchcraft. By riddles and charms, the poet aspires to a more resonant being than the life grudgingly acknowledged in her own body:

> I would be inheritor
> of the lamb's way and the deer's,
> my thrust take from the ground
> I tread or lie on. In thighs of trees,
> in recumbent stones, in the loins
> of beasts is found
> that line my own nakedness carried.
> Here, in an Eden of the mind,
> I would remain among my kind,
> to lake and hill, to tree and beast married.

Not only the shaped poems, the compulsive rhymes and puns ("what seams is only art"), the riddles and agnominations ("the shape of this box keels me oval / Heels feel its bottom / Nape knocks its top"—from the conundrum about eggs), but the discovery of the secret messages hidden within ordinary speech, as Being is concealed by Labels, excite Miss Swenson to poems of an almost frantic hermeticism: in two homages to writers, she extends her method to a kind of esoteric dalliance. First in "Frontispiece," which appears to describe a picture of Virginia Woolf in terms of the circumstances that led her to suicide, we realize from an odd, ominous resonance the lines have, that not only the names of the writer herself ("your chaste-fierce name") but the titles of all her books have been braided into the verse; thus the "frontis-piece" is a compendium of names indeed, only disguised, worked back into the texture of Being and used not as nominations but proof:

> The waves carve your hearse and tomb
> and toll your voyage out again again.

The second poem of dedication is even more curious, for in it not merely names but all words are susceptible of disintegration into their secret content; what we are offered is ostensibly a description of Frost ("R. F., His Hand Against a Tree") but the account is continually breaking down as Miss Swenson discovers, like Nabokov (whose English is so often a matter of perpetual inside jokes), that she can say more about her subject by letting the language speak for itself, merely doing a little pruning and spacing to let the sense in:

> Lots of trees in the fo
>   rest but this one's an O
>   a K that's plan
>   ted hims elf and nob
>   oddy has k nots of that hand
>   some polish or the knarl
>   edge of ear th or the obs
>   tiny ate servation his blueyes
>   make or the tr easures his sent
>   ient t humb les find.

These are, as she calls them, "glyphs of a daring alphabet" indeed, and "hide what they depend on." There are other diableries in this book likely to exasperate as well as to exalt; chiefly a poem called "Parade of Painters" in which 36 painters are "assigned" first a characteristic color, then a texture ("Manet porcelain, Matisse thistles," etc.), then a shape. Then the whole thing is assembled in a litany of 36 lines which reads something like a dada catalogue, save that Swenson has shown us her method and its underlying logic: we cannot fault it, but we may fail to be *charmed* by the procession, as it passes, of painter, shape, texture and color:

> Delacroix mouth viscera iris
> Degas witchmoth birch clay
> Pissaro dhow privet marble
> Seurat hourglass linen popular
> Dufy glove pearl azure
> Rouault mummy serge blood . . .

Much more characteristic of Swenson's excellence, I think, is "News from the Cabin," in which all her impulses congregate joyously around a less arbitrary theme: visits from four creatures, none named but all identified by the characteristic textures, rhythms, and vocabulary we should associate with a woodpecker, a squirrel, a jay, and a snake, if we were to *become* them by the power of our *recital* (rather like the interludes young Arthur experiences, in T. H. White's books, as he serves his apprenticeship to fish, hawks, even hedgehogs in order to learn how to be a man). Consider the sound of this from "Hairy":

> Cried *peek!* Beaked it—chiselled the drupe.
> His nostril I saw, slit in a slate whistle,
> White-black dominoes clicked in his wings.
> Bunched beneath the dangle he heckled with holes,
>   bellysack soft, eye a brad, a red-flecked
>   mallet his ball-peen head, his neck its haft.

and the movement of the end of "Scurry":

> Sat put, pert, neat, in his suit and his seat, for a minute,
>   a frown between snub ears, bulb-eyed head
>   toward me sideways, chewed.
> Rocked, squeaked. Stored the stone in his cheek.
> Finished, fell to all fours, a little roan couch;
>   flurried paws loped him off, prone-bodied,
>   tail turned torch, sail, scarf.

In these extraordinary poems, animal life is invoked, is actually *acquired* for the conjurer's purposes (extended energy, a generalized erotic awareness) by the haptic qualities of language itself, even more than by the riddling process so programmatically set up in the other pieces. The generosity, the abundance of Swenson's means may allow her, on the one hand, to speak somewhat sentimentally in "East River" of Brooklyn seen across the water as "a shelf of old shoes, needing repair, but clean knots of smoke are being tied and untied," and thereby we see, though both are patronized, Brooklyn *and* the shoes; but in "News from the Cabin," on the other, she also commands, as in the last section, "Supple," an utterance whose imagery is assimilated without condescension to its very movement, a diction so wedded to appearances that the speaker "leaves the spot" enriched with an access of being, an increment which comes only when life has been enchanted to its own understanding:

I followed that elastic: loose
   unicolored knot, a noose he made as if unconscious.
Until my shadow touched him; half his curd
   shuddered, the rest lay chill.
I stirred: the ribbon raised a loop;
    its end stretched, then cringed like an udder;
    a bifid tongue, his only rapid, whirred
    in the vent; vertical pupils lit his hood.
That part, a groping finger, hinged, stayed upright.
Indicated what? That I stood
   in his light? I left the spot.

In 1963, a large group of poems from Miss Swenson's first two volumes, with some fifty new poems, was published under the general title *To Mix with Time*, a phrase which in its own context reiterates her project: "One must work a magic to mix with time / in order to become old." Here the very compression, the proliferation *inward* of the new abracadabras seem to have enabled the poet to be elsewhere quite explicit about her undertaking:

        There unraveled
from a file in my mind a magic motion
I, too, used to play with: from chosen words a potion
could be wrung; pickings of them, eaten, could make
                you fly, walk
on water, be somebody else, do or undo anything, go back
or forward on belts of time . . .

It is good to have it spelled out, for there are here many poems of a specifically esoteric quality, whose organization on the page, as in the ear, suggests the location of a mystery in Being which the poet would attain to only by a ritual, a litany of participles and lattices of space:

There is a	Swaddled Thing
There is a	*Swaddled Thing*
There is a	Rocking Box
There is a	*Covered Box*
The	Unwrapping
the	Ripening
Then the	Loosening
the	Spoiling
The	Stiffening
then the	Wrapping
The	Softening
but the long long	Drying
The	Wrapping
the	Wrapping

the	Straightening
and	Wrapping
The rigid	Rolling
the gilded	Scrolling
The	Wrapping
and	Wrapping
and careful	Rewrapping
The	Thinning
and	Drying
but the	Wrapping
and	Fattening
There is the worm	Coiled
and the straw	Straightened
There is the	Plank
and the glaucous	Bundle
the paper	Skull
and the charred	Hair
the linen	Lip
and the leather	Eyelid
There is a	Person
of flesh that is *a rocking*	*Box*
There is a	Box
of wood that is *a painted*	*Person*

To which the poet, her own exegete, adds this "Note from a diary: I remembered Giotto's fresco, 'Birth of the Virgin' in a cloister in Florence: the 'Mother of God' was a swaddled infant held upright, like a board or plaque, by her nurse . . . and I remembered a mummy in the Vatican Museum in Rome; in her sarcophagus shaped and painted like herself, an Egyptian girl 2000 years old lay unwrapped to the waist." The notation, in the poem, of identities between the infant and the mummy, and the enactment of vital, or mortal, differences that reaches the climax of the last four lines, with their paradoxical reversals, dramatizes the kind of formal extremes May Swenson is ready to risk. "The idea," she says in "Out of my Head," the first poem in this book, "is to make a vehicle out of it." To employ, that is, the spell in order to be taken somewhere; or as she says in another place, and in her most orphic cadences:

> we weave asleep
> a body
> and awake unravel
> the same veins
> we travel

The unravelling of those travelled veins is undertaken, of course, in other ways besides such necromantic ones. There is a group of poems, in *To Mix with Time*, written in France, Italy and Spain and concerned with the reporting of surfaces, not the casting of spells. As in the earlier "Centaur," the poet appears sufficiently possessed of her identity to feel no need of commanding her surround by voodoo. She can trust her sensibility, in these new old places, to do its work, and oblige the *genius loci* to give up its own ghost:

> Gondola-slim
> above the bridge, a new moon held a dim
> circle of charcoal between its points.
> Bats played in the greenish air,
> their wing-joints
> soft as moths' against the bone-gray palazzi where
> not a window was alight . . .

These are secular poems, then, rarely moralized or magicked, but left to speak for themselves, in the descriptive mode of Elizabeth Bishop, though there are exceptions, occurring (as we might expect) in the case of the "Fountains of Aix," where the word "water" is disjoined fifteen times from the lines and made to slide down the side of a stanza:

> A goddess is driving a chariot through   water.
>   Her reins and whips are tight white   water.
>   Bronze hooves of horses wrangle with   water.
>   Faces with mossy lips unlocked
>   always uttering   water
>   Water
>   wearing their features blank,
>   their ears deaf, their eyes mad
>   or patient or blind or astonished at   water
>   always uttered out of their mouths . . .

and again in a poem about death, "The Alyscamps at Arles," in which the words "bodies," "bones," "died," "stones," and "flesh" are isolated in a central column, set off like tombs in each line, and recurring some two dozen times. Europe, we take it, is sacred ground, and the mere fact of treading it is enough, almost, for Miss Swenson's genius to speak low to her. The conjugation, in this book, of a temporal response to earth and a runic riddling of it is indeed "to mix with time;" there is a relaxation of need, somehow, as if the poet had come to find things enthralling enough in themselves:

> In any random, sprawling, decomposing thing
> is the charming string
> of its history—and what it will be next . . .

Like "Evolution," her first poem in her first book, her last one here, "The Exchange," recapitulates her enterprise—to get out of herself and into those larger, warmer energies of earth, and to do so by liturgical means ("Words? Let their / mutations work / toward the escape / of object into the nearest next / shape, motion, assembly, temporal context"):

Populous and mixed is mind.
Earth take thought,
my mouth be moss . . .
Wind be motion,
birds be passion,
water invite me to your bed.

Things Taking Place was the working title May Swenson had originally given *To Mix with Time,* and its suggestion of a larger interest in a secular world where events occur, where life "happens," and a lessening concern with the cosmic energies of "mere" Being, is even more applicable to the poet's latest work, published in 1967 in a long book called *Half Sun Half Sleep.* Not that Miss Swenson is any less interested in the energies, the powers that drive the stars in their courses, or in the measurements and movements responsible for that formal echo of dune and wave, beach and tide—rather, the largest impulses which often she could *handle,* precisely, as abstractions only, are now accommodated into the observed intercourse of her body and its environment, her life and its limits. There are charms here too, but they are *secular* charms, and the fact that so many of the rhyme words are tucked away in the "wrong" parts of the line suggests the profane intentions of these cunning incantations—if Miss Swenson has designs on life, they are subordinated to a surface she prefers unruly:

Well, do they sing? If so, I *expect* their
note is extreme. Not something one *hears,*
but must watch the cat's *ears* to *detect* . . . [emphasis mine]

she furthers, too, her old mistrust, even her outright distaste for the exemplars of "Satanic Form," which she finds in most of our modern enclosures, elevator cages, Pullman cars and airplane bellies, and specifically in our satellites and space missiles. One of the most brilliant pieces in the new book is "August 19, Pad 19," a jeering, nerve-end journal of an astronaut "positioned for either breach birth / or urn burial." Reminiscent of her other entrapped forms—the mummy and the swaddled infant—the astronaut is prepared:

. . . Never so helpless, so choked with power.
Never so impotent, so important.
So naked, wrapped, equipped, and immobile,
cared for by 5000 nurses.
Let them siphon my urine to the nearest star.
Let it flare and spin like a Catherine.

. . . T minus 10 . . . The click of countdown stops.
My pram and mummy case, this trap's
tumescent tube's still locked to wet,
magnetic, unpredictable earth.
All my system's go, but oh,

an anger of the air won't let me go.
On the screen the blip is MISSION SCRUBBED . . .

and the poem's ultimate irony is to oblige this sequestered consciousness, furious in its failure, to feel "out on the dome some innocent drops of rain." The titles suggest the poet's preferences: "On Handling Some Small Shells from the Windward Islands," "A Basin of Eggs," "Drawing the Cat," "On Seeing Rocks Cropping out of a Hill in Central Park" and—quintessentially— "Things in Common." There is of course a certain trust in her old ways of working, call them weapons even, the sharp-edged, riddling means of tricking us into the poem; the book itself is arranged with the titles in alphabetical order, and there are a number of shaped poems, of spells and counting-rhymes, for as she says in "The Truth," a poem about a snake that is snake-shaped,

> Speculations about shape amount to a counting
> of the coils.

But there is a moving away from the kind of hermetic indication that cannot show loss as well as gain. There is the sense, recorded in a poem about two trees leaning together, "All That Time," that our interpretations of phenomena may be cruelly aberrant:

> And where their tops tangled
> it looked like he was crying
> on her shoulder.
> On the other hand, maybe he
>
> had been trying to weaken her,
> break her, or at least
> make her bend
> over backwards for him . . .

and that we must devise a form that will account for "strange abrasions / zodiacal wounds." The important thing, she says, is

> To be the instrument
> and the wound of feeling.

As the book's title suggests, the balance between sacred and profane, ritual and report, with its implication of the balance between seeing and dreaming, speech and somnambulism, is carefully tended:

> The tug of the void
> the will of the world
> together . . .

These poems are exuberant in their hocus-pocus, surely, but they are also a little rueful about the facility to which one can trust in the hope of getting out of the self ("One must be a cloud to occupy a house of cloud . . . refusing the fixture of a solid soul"); also they are not so explicit in exploring "the suck of the sea's dark mind": if Swenson still asks, in a poem called "The Lightning" through which a diagonal gutter of space jabs through her twenty lines to the word "entrails," "When will I grope my way clear of the entrails of intellect?" she is nonetheless prepared to use the mementoes of that gutted intellect to deal with the sea's dark mind, referring to the "ancient diary the waves are murmuring" and accounting in terms of gains as well as losses for her existence as a rational animal:

> When I was a sea worm
> I never saw the sun,
>
> but flowed, a salty germ,
> in the bloodstream of the sea.
> There I left an alphabet
>
> but it grew dim to me.
> Something caught me in its net,
> took me from the deep
>
> book of the ocean, weaned me,
> put fin and wing to sleep,
> made me stand and made me
>
> face the sun's dry eye.
> On the shore of intellect
> I forgot how to fly . . .
>
> In brightness I lost track
> of my underworld
> of ultraviolet wisdom.
>
> My fiery head furled
> up its cool kingdom
> and put night away.

These are no longer nor even want to be the poems of a small furry animal ("the page my acre") nor of a selfless demiurge ("They founded the sun./ When the sun found them / it undertook its path and aim . . . / The air first heard itself / called glory in their lungs"); they are the witty resigned poems of a woman "hunting clarities of Being," asking

> Have I arrived from
>   left or
>   right to hover here
> in the clear permission of my
>   temperature? Is my
>   flow a fading
>   up or
>   down—my glow
>   going? Or is my flush

> rushing to a rose of ripe
> explosion?

a woman eager still to manipulate the phenomenal world by magic, but so possessed, now, of the means of her identity that the ritual, spellbinding, litaneutical elements of her art have grown consistent, even coincident, with her temporal, conditioned, suffering experience and seem—to pay her the highest compliment May Swenson could care to receive—no more than natural.

Gwendolyn Brooks's *A Street in Bronzeville*, the Harlem Renaissance and the Mythologies of Black Women

Gary Smith

When Gwendolyn Brooks published her first collection of poetry *A Street in Bronzeville* (1945) with Harper and Brothers, she already enjoyed a substantial reputation in the literary circles of Chicago. Nearly a decade earlier, her mother Keziah Brooks, had arranged meetings between her daughter and James Weldon Johnson and Langston Hughes, two of the most distinguished Black writers of America's Harlem Renaissance. Determined to mold Gwendolyn into a *lady Paul Laurence Dunbar*, Mrs. Brooks proffered poems for the famous writers to read. While Johnson's advice to the young poet was abrupt, eventually he exerted an incisive influence on her later work. In a letter and a marginal note included on the returned poems, addressed to her on 30 August 1937, Johnson praised Brooks's obvious talent and pointed her in the direction of Modernist poetry:

> My dear Miss Brooks: I have read the poems you sent me last. Of them I especially liked *Reunion* and *Myself*. Reunion is very good, and *Myself* is good. You should, by all means, continue you[r] study and work. I shall always be glad to give you any assistance that I can. Sincerely yours. James Weldon Johnson.

> Dear Miss Brooks—You have an unquestionable talent and feeling for poetry. Continue to write—at the same time, study carefully the work of the best modern poets—not to imitate them, but to help cultivate the highest possible standards of self-criticism. Sincerely, James Weldon Johnson.

Of course, the irony in Johnson's advice, addressed as it is to the future *lady* Dunbar, is that he actually began his own career by conspicuously

From *MELUS: The Journal of the Society for the Study of the Multi-Ethnic Literature of the United States* 10, no. 3 (Fall 1983). © 1983 by MELUS.

imitating Dunbar's dialect poems, *Lyrics of a Lowly Life;* yet he encourages Brooks to study the work of the "best Modern poets." He was, perhaps, reacting to the latent elements of modernism already found in her poetry; but the effect was to turn Brooks momentarily away from the Black aesthetic of Hughes's *Weary Blues* (1926) and Countee Cullen's *Color* (1925) toward the Modernist aesthetics of T. S. Eliot, Ezra Pound, and e. e. cummings. It is interesting to note, however, that, even though Johnson's second letter admonishes Brooks to study the Modernist poets, he cautions her "not to imitate them," but to read them with the intent of cultivating the "highest possible standards of self-criticism." Flattered by the older poet's attention and advice, Brooks embarked upon a serious attempt to absorb as much Modernist poetry as she could carry from the public library.

If Johnson played the part of literary mentor, Brooks's relationship with Hughes was more personal, warmer, and longer lasting. She was already on familiar terms with *Weary Blues,* so their first meeting was particularly inspirational. Brooks showed Hughes a packet of her poems, and he praised her talent and encouraged her to continue to write. Years later, after Brooks's reputation was firmly established by a Pulitzer Prize for *Annie Allen* (1949), her relationship with Hughes blossomed into mutual admiration. Hughes dedicated his collection of short stories, *Something in Common* (1963), to her. While Hughes's poetic style had an immeasurable influence on Brooks's poetry, she also respected his personal values and lifestyle. As she noted in her autobiography [*Report*], Hughes was her idol:

> Langston Hughes! The words and deeds of Langston Hughes were rooted in kindness, and in pride. His point of departure was always a clear pride in his race. Race pride may be craft, art, or a music that combines the best of jazz and hymn. Langston frolicked and chanted to the measure of his own race-reverence.
>
> He was an easy man. You could rest in his company. No one possessed a more serious understanding of life's immensities. No one was firmer in recognition of the horrors man imposes upon man, in hardy insistence on reckonings. But when those who knew him remember him the memory inevitably will include laughter of an unusually warm and tender kind. The wise man, he knew, will take some juice out of this one life that is his gift.
>
> Mightily did he use the street. He found its multiple heart, its tastes, smells, alarms, formulas, flowers, garbage and convulsions. He brought them all to his table-top. He crushed them to a writing paste. He himself became the pen.

In other words, while Johnson encouraged Brooks to find "standards for self-criticism" in Modernism, Hughes underscored the value of cultivating the ground upon which she stood. In Hughes, in both the poet and man, Brooks found standards for living: he was a model of witty candor and friendly unpretentiousness and, most importantly, a literary success.

Hughes convinced Brooks that a Black poet need not travel outside the realm of his own experiences to create a poetic vision and write successful poetry. Unlike the Modernist Eliot who gathered much of his poetic material from the drawingrooms and salons of London, Hughes found his material in the coldwater flats and backstreets of Harlem. And Brooks, as is self-evident in nearly all her poetry, learned Hughes's example by heart.

II

The critical reception of *A Street in Bronzeville* contained, in embryo, many of the central issues in the scholarly debate that continues to engage Brooks's poetry. As in the following quotation from *The New York Times Book Review*, most reviewers were able to recognize Brooks's versatility and craft as a poet:

> If the idiom is colloquial, the language is universal. Brooks commands both the colloquial and more austere rhythms. She can vary manner and tone. In form, she demonstrates a wide range: quatrains, free verse, ballads, and sonnets—all appropriately controlled. The longer line suits her better than the short, but she is not verbose. In some of the sonnets, she uses an abruptness of address that is highly individual.

Yet, while noting her stylistic successes, not many critics fully understood her achievement in her first book. This difficulty was not only characteristic of critics who examined the formal aspects of prosody in her work, but also of critics who addressed themselves to the social realism in her poetry. Moreover, what Brooks gained at the hands of critics who focused on her technique, she lost to critics who chose to emphasize the exotic, Negro features of the book, as the following quote illustrates:

> *A Street in Bronzeville* ranges from blues ballads and funeral chants to verse in high humor. With both clarity and insight, it mirrors the impressions of life in an urban Negro community. The best poem is "The Sundays of Satin-Legs Smith," a poignant and hour-by-hour page out of a zoot-suiter's life. A subtle change of pace proves Brooks' facility in a variety of poetic forms.

The poems in *A Street in Bronzeville* actually served notice that Brooks had learned her craft well enough to combine successfully themes and styles from both the Harlem Renaissance and Modernist poetry. She even achieves some of her more interesting effects in the book by parodying the two traditions. She juggles the pessimism of Modernist poetry with the general optimism of the Harlem Renaissance. Three of her more notable achievements, "kitchenette building," "the mother," and "Sundays of Satin-Legs Smith," are parodic challenges to T. S. Eliot's dispirited anti-hero J. Alfred Prufrock. "[K]itchenette building" begins with Eliot-like emphasis on the dry infertility of modern life: "We are things of dry hours and the involuntary plan." The poem concludes with the humored optimism that "Since Number

5 is out of the bathroom / we think of lukewarm water, we hope to get in it." Another example is the alienated, seemingly disaffected narrator of "the mother" who laments the loss of her children but with the resurgent, hopeful voice that closes the poem: "Believe me, I loved you all." Finally a comparison could be made between the elaborate, self-assertive manner with which Satin-legs Smith dresses himself for his largely purposeless Sunday outing and the tentative efforts of his counterpart, J. Alfred Prufrock.

Because of the affinities *A Street in Bronzeville* shares with Modernist poetry and the Harlem Renaissance, Brooks was initiated not only into the vanguard of American literature, but also into what had been the inner circle of Harlem writers. Two of the Renaissance's leading poets, Claude McKay and Countee Cullen, addressed letters to her to mark the publication of *A Street in Bronzeville*. McKay welcomed her into a dubious but potentially rewarding career:

> I want to congratulate you again on the publication of 'A Street in Bronzeville' [sic] and welcome you among the band of hard working poets who do have something to say. It is a pretty rough road we have to travel, but I suppose much compensation is derived from the joy of being able to sing. Yours sincerely, Claude McKay. (October 10, 1945.)

Cullen pinpointed her dual place in American literature:

> I have just finished reading, 'A Street in Bronzeville' [sic] and want you to know that I enjoyed it thoroughly. There can be no doubt that you are a poet, a good one, with every indication of becoming a better. I am glad to be able to say 'welcome' to you to that too small group of Negro poets, and to the larger group of American ones. No one can deny you your place there. (August 24, 1945.)

The immediate interest in these letters is how both poets touch upon the nerve ends of the critical debate that surrounded *A Street in Bronzeville*. For McKay, while Brooks has "something to say," she can also "sing"; and for Cullen, she belongs not only to the minority of Negro poets, but also to the majority of American ones. Nonetheless, the critical question for both poets might well have been Brooks's relationship to the Harlem Renaissance. What had she absorbed of the important tenets of the Black aesthetic as expressed during the New Negro Movement? And how had she addressed herself, as a poet, to the literary movement's assertion of the folk and African culture, and its promotion of the arts as the agent to define racial integrity and to fuse racial harmony?

Aside from its historical importance, the Harlem Renaissance—as a literary movement—is rather difficult to define. There is, for example, no fixed or generally agreed upon date or event that serves as a point of origin for the movement. One might easily assign this date to the publication of McKay's poems *Harlem Shadows* (1922), Alaine Locke's anthology *The New*

Negro (1925), or Cullen's anthology *Caroling Dusk* (1927). Likewise, the general description of the movement as a Harlem Renaissance is often questioned, since most of the major writers, with the notable exceptions of Hughes and Cullen, actually did not live and work in Harlem. Finally, many of the themes and literary conventions defy definition in terms of what was and what was not a New Negro poet. Nonetheless, there was a common ground of purpose and meaning in the works of the individual writers that permits a broad definition of the spirit and intent of the Harlem Renaissance. Indeed, the New Negro poets expressed a deep pride in being Black; they found reasons for this pride in ethnic identity and heritage; and they shared a common faith in the fine arts as a means of defining and reinforcing racial pride. But in the literal expression of these artistic impulses, the poets were either romantics or realists and, quite often within a single poem, both. The realistic impulse, as defined best in the poems of McKay's *Harlem Shadows,* was a sober reflection upon Blacks as second class citizens, segregated from the mainstream of American socio-economic life, and largely unable to realize the wealth and opportunity that America promised. The romantic impulse, on the other hand, as defined in the poems of Sterling Browns's *Southern Road* (1932), often found these unrealized dreams in the collective strength and will of the folk masses. In comparing the poems in *A Street in Bronzeville* with various poems from the Renaissance, it becomes apparent that Brooks agrees, for the most part, with their prescriptions for the New Negro. Yet the unique contributions she brings to bear upon this tradition are extensive: 1) the biting ironies of intraracial discrimination, 2) the devaluation of love in heterosexual relationships between Blacks, and 3) the primacy of suffering in the lives of poor Black women.

III

The first clue that *A Street in Bronzeville* was, at the time of its publication, unlike any other book of poems by a Black American is its insistent emphasis on demystifying romantic love between Black men and women. The "old marrieds," the first couple encountered on the walking tour of Bronzeville, are nothing like the youthful archetype that the Renaissance poets often portrayed:

> But in the crowding darkness not a word did they say.
> Though the pretty-coated birds had piped so lightly all the day.
> And he had seen the lovers in the little side-streets.
> And she had heard the morning stories clogged with sweets.
> It was quite a time for loving. It was midnight. It was May.
> But in the crowding darkness not a word did they say.

In this short, introductory poem, Brooks, in a manner reminiscent of Eliot's alienated *Waste Land* characters, looks not toward a glorified African past or limitless future, but rather at a stifled present. Her old lovers ponder not an image of their racial past or some symbolized possibility of self-renewal, but rather the overwhelming question of what to do in the here-and-now. Moreover, their world, circumscribed by the incantatory line that opens and closes the poem, "But in the crowding darkness not a word did they say," is one that is distinctly at odds with their lives. They move timidly through the crowded darkness of their neighborhood largely ignorant of the season, "May," the lateness of the hour, "midnight," and a particular *raison d'être*, "a time for loving." Their attention, we infer, centers upon the implicit need to escape any peril that might consume what remains of their lives. The tempered optimism in the poem, as the title indicates, is the fact that they are "old-marrieds": a social designation that suggests the longevity of their lives and the solidity of their marital bond in what is, otherwise, an ephemeral world of change. Indeed, as the prefatory poem in *A Street in Bronzeville*, the "old marrieds," on the whole debunks one of the prevalent motifs of Harlem Renaissance poetry: its general optimism about the future.

As much as the Harlem Renaissance was noted for its optimism, an important corollary motif was that of ethnic or racial pride. This pride—often thought a reaction to the minstrel stereotypes in the Dunbar tradition—usually focused with romantic idealization upon the Black woman. A casual streetwalker in Hughes's poem, "When Sue Wears Red," for example, is magically transformed into an Egyptian queen:

> When Susanna Jones wears red
> Her face is like an ancient cameo
> Turned brown by the ages.
> Come with a blast of trumpets,
>   Jesus!
>
> When Susanna Jones wears red
> A queen from some time-dead Egyptian night
> Walks once again.

Similarly, six of the first seven poems in Cullen's first published work, *Color* (1925), celebrate the romanticized virtues of Black women. The second poem in the volume, "A Song of Praise," is particularly noteworthy in its treatment of the theme:

> You have not heard my love's dark throat,
>   Slow-fluting like a reed,
> Release the perfect golden note
>   She caged there for my need.
> Her walk is like the replica
>   Of some barbaric dance
> Wherein the soul of Africa
>   Is winged with arrogance.

In the same manner, McKay's sonnet, "The Harlem Dancer," extolls the misunderstood virtue of a cabaret dancer:

> Applauding youths laughed with young prostitutes
> And watched her perfect, half-clothed body sway;
> Her voice was like the sound of blended flutes
> Blown by black players upon a picnic day.
> She sang and danced on gracefully and calm,
> The light gauze hanging loose about her form;
> To me she seemed a proudly-swaying palm
> Grown lovelier for passing through a storm.

In *A Street in Bronzeville*, this romantic impulse for idealizing the Black woman runs headlong into the biting ironies of intraracial discrimination. In poem after poem in *A Street in Bronzeville*, within the well-observed caste lines of skin color, the consequences of dark pigmentation are revealed in drastic terms. One of the more popular of these poems, "The Ballad of Chocolate Mabbie," explores the tragic ordeal of Mabbie, the Black female heroine, who is victimized by her dark skin and her "saucily bold" lover, Willie Boone:

> It was Mabbie without the grammar school gates.
> And Mabbie was all of seven.
> And Mabbie was cut from a chocolate bar.
> And Mabbie thought life was heaven.

Mabbie's life, of course, is one of unrelieved monotony; her social contacts are limited to those who, like her, are dark skinned, rather than "lemon-hued" or light skinned. But as Brooks makes clear, the larger tragedy of Mabbie's life is the human potential that is squandered:

> Oh, warm is the waiting for joys, my dears!
> And it cannot be too long.
> O, pity the little poor chocolate lips
> That carry the bubble of song!

But if Mabbie is Brooks's parodic victim of romantic love, her counterpart in "Ballad of Pearl May Lee" realizes a measure of sweet revenge. In outline, Brooks's poem is reminiscent of Cullen's *The Ballad of the Brown Girl* (1927). There are, however, several important differences. The first is the poem's narrative structure: Pearl May Lee is betrayed in her love for a Black man who "couldn't abide dark meat," who subsequently makes love to a white girl and is lynched for his crime of passion, whereas Cullen's "Brown Girl" is betrayed in her love for a white man, Lord Thomas, who violates explicit social taboo by marrying her rather than Fair London, a white girl. Moreover, Cullen's poem, "a ballad retold," is traditional in its approach to the ballad form:

> Oh, this is the tale that grandams tell
> In the land where the grass is blue,

> And some there are who say 'tis false,
> And some that hold it true.

Brooks's ballad, on the other hand, dispenses with the rhetorical invocation of the traditional ballad and begins *in medias res*:

> Then off they took you, off to the jail,
> A hundred hooting after.
> An you should have heard me at my house.
> I cut my lungs with my laughter,
>   Laughter,
>   Laughter.
> I cut my lungs with my laughter.

This mocking tone is sustained throughout the poem, even as Sammy, Pearl May Lee's lover, is lynched:

> You paid for your dinner, Sammy boy,
> And you didn't pay with money.
> You paid with your hide and my heart, Sammy
> boy,
> For your taste of pink and white honey,
>   Honey,
>   Honey,
> For your taste of pink and white honey.

Here, one possible motif in the poem is the price that Pearl May Lee pays for her measure of sweet revenge: the diminution of her own capacity to express love and compassion for another—however ill-fated—human being. But the element of realism that Brooks injects into her ballad by showing Pearl May Lee's mocking detachment from her lover's fate is a conscious effort to devalue the romantic idealization of Black love. Furthermore, Pearl May Lee's macabre humor undermines the racial pride and harmony that was an important tenet in the Renaissance prescription for the New Negro. And, lastly, Pearl May Lee's predicament belies the social myth of the Black woman as *objective correlative* of the Renaissance's romanticism.

   In another poem that uses the Blues tradition as its thematic structure, Brooks takes the reader backstage, inside the dressing room of Mame, "The Queen of the Blues." As the central figure in the poem, Mame is similar to Sterling Brown's Ma Rainey, "Mother of the Blues":

> When Ma Rainey
> Comes to town,
> Folks from anyplace
> Miles aroun'
> From Cape Girardeau,
> Poplar Bluff,
> Flocks in to hear
> Ma do her stuff.

But where Ma Rainey is realized as a mythic goddess within Black folk culture, Mame is shown to be the double victim of sexual and racial exploitation. Her social role is that of a less-than-willing performer:

> Mame was singing
> At the Midnight Club.
> And the place was red
> With blues.
> She could shake her body
> Across the floor.
> For what did she have
> To lose?

The question of loss in the poem becomes a chilling, moral refrain: "For what did she have / To lose?" This question is literally answered by the other losses in Mame's private life: her mother, father, relatives, and children. Indeed, unlike the celebrated public performances of Ma Rainey that transformed private griefs into public theatre:

> O Ma Rainey,
> Sing yo' song;
> Now you's back
> Whah you belong,
> Git way inside us,
> Keep us strong. . . .

Mame sings primarily to exorcise herself of the frustrations of unrequited love and intraracial discrimination:

> I loved my daddy.
> But what did my daddy
> Do?
> I loved my daddy.
> But what did my daddy
> Do?
> Found him a brown-skin chicken
> What's gonna be
> Black and blue.

Nonetheless, Mame's problem, as the "Queen of the Blues," might well be her lack of conformity within the blues tradition. Her questioning rebuke of her profession suggests misplaced values: "But when has a man / Tipped his hat to me?" The most obvious answer, as more than one critic of the poem has suggested, is that the pinches and slaps Mame receives are part of the time-honored rituals of a blues performance. But as a Black woman whose frustrated life compares with Mabbie and Pearl May Lee, Mame is authentic. Her complaint is not about her demeaning social role as a nightclub performer who is paid to flesh-out the dreams and sexual aspirations of her largely male audience, but more substantially about her dignity as a human being. The real price Mame pays is the loss of her female identity. What she laments is the blurred distinction between her stagelife as a romantic prop and her real life as a Black woman.

IV

To be sure, the Harlem Renaissance poets were not solely romantic in their portrayal of Black women; there was, within their poetry, an equally strong impulse towards realism. In "Harlem Shadows," for example, McKay shows the seamier side of Harlem nightlife, wherein "little dark girls" prowl the streets as prostitutes:

> I hear the halting footsteps of a lass
>   In Negro Harlem when the night lets fall
> Its veil. I see the shapes of girls who pass
>   To bend and barter at desire's call.
> Ah, little dark girls who in slippered feet
> Go prowling through the night from street to street!

And Sterling Brown, although he is less dramatic than McKay in his poem "Bessie," nonetheless recognizes the realistic underside of urban life for Black women:

> Who will know Bessie now of these who loved her;
>   Who of her gawky pals could recognize
> Bess in this woman, gaunt of flesh and painted,
>   Despair deep bitten in her soft brown eyes?
>
> Would the lads who walked with her in dusk-cooled byways
>   Know Bessie now should they meet her again?
> Would knowing men of Fifth St. think that Bessie ever
>   Was happy-hearted, brave-eyed as she was then?

For Hughes, too, the Black woman in "Young Prostitute" is described not as an Egyptian cameo, but rather as a "withered flower":

> Her dark brown face
> Is like a withered flower
> On a broken stem.
> Those kind come cheap in Harlem
> So they say.

In each of the above poems, the impulse toward romantic idealism of Black women gives way to critical realism; the mythic disguises that mask the harsh realities of social and economic deprivations are stripped away, and poor Black women are revealed as the most likely victims of racism within American society.

For Brooks, unlike the Renaissance poets, the victimization of poor Black women becomes not simply a minor chord but a predominant theme of *A Street in Bronzeville*. Few, if any, of her female characters are able to free themselves from the web of poverty and racism that threatens to strangle their lives. The Black heroine in "obituary for a living lady" was "decently wild / As a child," but as a victim of society's hypocritical, puritan standards, she

> fell in love with a man who didn't know
> That even if she wouldn't let him touch her breasts she
> was still worth his hours.

In another example of the complex life-choices confronting Brooks's women, the two sisters of "Sadie and Maude" must choose between death-in-life and life-in-death. Maude, who went to college, becomes a "thin brown mouse," presumably resigned to spinsterhood, "living all alone / In this old house," while Sadie who "scraped life / With a fine-tooth comb" bears two illegitimate children and dies, leaving as a heritage for her children her "fine-tooth comb." What is noticeable in the lives of these Black women is a mutual identity that is inextricably linked with race and poverty.

For Hattie Scott, Brooks's protagonist in a series of vignettes that chronicle the life of a Black domestic worker, the struggle to assert a female identity begins with the first poem, "the end of day." Hattie's life, measured by the sun's rising and setting, is described as a ceaseless cycle of menial tasks. The second poem in the series, "the date," details Hattie's attempt to free herself from the drudgery of domestic work:

> Whatcha mean talkin' about cleanin' silver?
> It's eight o'clock now, you fool.
> I'm leavin'. Got somethin' interestin' on my mind.
> Don't mean night school.

Hattie's "date" in the third poem, an appointment "at the hairdresser's" turns out to be a rather farcical attempt to have her hair done in an "upsweep" with "humpteen baby curls." Like Sadie's comb, Hattie's "upsweep" becomes symbolic of her persistent efforts to assert a positive identity. The reader senses, though, that her cosmetic changes, like her previous efforts with "Madam C. J. Walker" and "Poro Grower" (two hairdressers that promise instant beauty), will end in marginal success. Indeed, in the poem that follows, "when I die," Hattie imagines her funeral as a solitary affair attended by "one lone short man / Dressed all shabbily."

The final poem in the series, "the battle," ends not on a note of personal triumph for Hattie, but rather resignation and defeat. Hattie's neighbor and spiritual counterpart, Moe Belle Jackson, is routinely beaten by her husband:

> Moe Belle Jackson's husband
> Whipped her good last night.
> Her landlady told my ma they had
> A knock-down-drag-out fight.

Hattie's perception of the beating is charged with the anger and indignation of a *secret sharer* who, perhaps, realizes her own life in Moe Belle's predicament:

> I like to think
> Of how I'd of took a knife
> And slashed all the quickenin'
> Out of his lowly life.

Nonetheless, in what is surely one of the finest examples of macabre humor in Brooks's poetry, Hattie combines psychological insight and laconic understatement in her final musings about Moe Belle's fate:

> But if I know Moe Belle,
> Most like, she shed a tear,
> And this mornin' it was probably,
> "More grits, dear?"

Brooks's relationship with the Harlem Renaissance poets, as *A Street in Bronzeville* ably demonstrates, was hardly imitative. As one of the important links with the Black poetic tradition of the 1920s and 1930s, she enlarged the element of realism that was an important part of the Renaissance worldview. Although her poetry is often conditioned by the optimism that was also a legacy of the period, Brooks rejects outright their romantic prescriptions for the lives of Black women. And in this regard, she serves as a vital link with the Black Arts Movement of the 1960s that, while it witnessed the flowering of Black women as poets and social activists as well as the rise of Black feminist aesthetics in the 1970s, brought about a curious revival of romanticism in the Renaissance mode.

However, since the publication of *A Street in Bronzeville*, Brooks has not eschewed the traditional roles and values of Black women in American society; on the contrary, in her subsequent works, *Annie Allen* (1949), *The Bean Eaters* (1960), and *In the Mecca* (1968), she has been remarkably consistent in identifying the root cause of intraracial problems within the Black community as white racism and its pervasive socio-economic effects. Furthermore, as one of the chief voices of the Black Arts Movement, she has developed a social vision, in such works as *Riot* (1969), *Family Pictures* (1970), and *Beckonings* (1975), that describes Black women and men as equally integral parts of the struggle for social and economic justice.

Denise Levertov:
A Poetry of Exploration

Paul A. Lacey

In her "Statement on Poetics" in 1959 Denise Levertov wrote:

> I believe poets are instruments on which the power of poetry plays.
> But they are also makers, craftsmen: It is given to the seer to see, but
> it is then his responsibility to communicate what he sees, that they
> who cannot see may see, since we are "members one of another."

A poem is a living thing, not merely by courtesy of metaphor, but
literally. And it is a mystery not to be solved but to be approached reverently,
meditated upon, and affirmed. Both her critical writing and her poetry insist
on such an approach to poetry and, behind it, to life. Poems should evidence
an "inner harmony" which is in "utter contrast to the chaos" of life, but not a
manufactured harmony or a fantasy compensation for the way things really
are. "For me, back of the idea of organic form is the concept that there is a
form in all things (and in our experience) which the poet can discover and
reveal." As the lines from "The Artist" put it, "The true artist: capable,
practicing skillful, / maintains dialogue with his heart, meets things with his
mind." The act of writing poetry is first an act of opening oneself to experience in such a way that its *inscape* becomes revealed to us.

As her critical writings testify, the language of mystery—though not
mystification—most appropriately expresses how poems are "given" to and
received by the poet. Sense experiences, memories, the unconscious, some
image or word come together, constellate for the poet. In order to *have* or
grasp and *interpret* this complex of experiences, the poet must discover some
"expressive and unifying act," some form, "an inscape that relates the
apparently unrelated." This he does through meditation and contemplation,
opening up to or centering down upon this constellation of elements. Denise
Levertov deliberately uses words from the religious vocabulary and ac-

From *The Inner War: Forms and Themes in Recent American Poetry.* © 1972 by Fortress Press.

knowledges their source. "The act of art evokes a spirit, and in assuming the existence of a spirit, and the possibility of a transformation by means of that spirit, it is an act of prayer. It is a testimony of that *participation mystique,* that involvement of the individual in a life beyond himself, which is a basic element of religion in the broadest and deepest sense."

The poet "muses," which she defines literally as standing open-mouthed, waiting for "inspiration." As things fall together into a pattern, a correspondence between those things and words occurs. The poet is "brought to speech." "Correspondence," "counterparts," "analogies," "resemblances," "natural allegories," are all words which Denise Levertov uses to speak of poetic forms in relation to reality. "Such a poetry is exploratory."

> All trivial parts of
> world-about-us speak in the forms
> of themselves and their counterparts!
>   ("A Straw Swan at Christmas")

General discussions of methods of poetic composition are notoriously unhelpful when used to gloss particular poems, and this would be especially true for Denise Levertov's poetry, for she is telling us neither "how-to-write-an-organic-poem" nor even "how-I-write." Discourse cannot teach us how to intuit, but we may catch from her tone and attitude in her critical writings some ways in which our reading may be exploratory, as her poetry is. A good test case is her poem "Illustrious Ancestors," from *Overland to the Islands* (1958).

> The Rav
> of Northern White Russia declined,
> in his youth, to learn the
> language of birds, because
> the extraneous did not interest him; nevertheless
> when he grew old it was found
> he understood them anyway, having
> listened well, and as it is said, "prayed
>   with the bench and the floor." He used
> what was at hand—as did
> Angel Jones of Mold, whose meditations
> were sewn into coats and britches.
>   Well, I would like to make,
> thinking some line still taut between me and them,
> poems direct as what the birds said,
> hard as a floor, sound as a bench,
> mysterious as the silence when the tailor
> would pause with his needle in the air.

The poem opens with an artless telling of a family tale. If we are used to looking to the ends of lines for strong words or active verbs to carry the energy of the poem, we are disappointed: "the, " "because," "nevertheless," do not drive us forward. The flat tone and matter-of-fact handling of details seem, in fact, to undercut the promise of the title. But the anecdote engages us deeply, for it resonates like a good Hasidic tale. The words and details invite meditation by their very simplicity and artlessness. For what strikes us first is that the miraculous itself is being treated matter-of-factly. And from that simple contrast others become clear: youth and age, ignorance and wisdom, the extraneous and what lies at hand. The Rav, caught up in one understanding of the spiritual life in his youth, declines to learn what is extraneous, the language of the birds. But in his old age, because he attended to the unmysterious and everyday disciplines of Hasidism, that other capacity has come as an additional gift. The implications of the tale are rich. On the one hand, there might be the danger of pride in the Rav's decision that the language of the birds was uninteresting and extraneous; but he may also have avoided a temptation to greater pride in the piling up of *power*. In refusing to study what is a secret to man, he skirts the temptations of the magical—often associated with the demonic in Martin Buber's *Tales of the Hasidim* and his historical chronicle *For the Sake of Heaven*. The Rav did not focus on achieving powers, but on "listening well" and "praying *with*" the tools and furniture of his workaday life, "He used what was at hand." Because he had ears, he heard, as Jesus' parable in the Gospel of Mark puts it; because he learned how to listen well, he discovered in the wisdom of old age that nothing is extraneous.

The Hasidic tale of the Rav could be complete in itself, but this poem concerns inheritance and keeping faith with one's gifts, so the poet tells about an ancestor from the other side of the family and another tradition. Angel Jones also used what was at hand in such a way as to spiritualize its nature. We know of him only that he *sewed* his meditations into everyday garments, "Coats and britches." The matter-of-fact becomes a bearer of the miraculous without ceasing to preserve its original nature. Both ancestors were *makers*, and the poet affirms that some line is "still taut between me and them." She meditates on them, as they did on what was around them, and discovers what kind of poems she wants to make. Here she gathers up the threads which have run through the poem and weaves them together into the fabric she wants for her poems: concretion, precision, and through them the mysterious and the silent.

Such a reading of the poem seems to rest primarily on the idea-content, but what has made the ideas available to us, and filled them with their peculiar value, has much more to do with tone and rhythm, the movement along that taut line which connects the illustrious ancestors to the poet and the poet to the reader, than with the ideas themselves.

The poem does not call attention to itself; but its quiet stateliness leads us to those qualities of directness, hardness, and soundness, and finally to the suspension at the end of the poem, the slowing down which leaves us silent and still in the presence of mystery. The poem is like the ancestors, ordinary and yet illustrious, filled with light.

Both the subject matter and the treatment of "Illustrious Ancestors" lead a critic to ask what values of Hasidism have affected Denis Levertov's poetry. *The Jacob's Ladder* is introduced by one of the *Tales of the Hasidism: Later Masters* which throws light on both the form of that book and on all her poetry. Rabbi Moshe of Kobryn, meditating on the story of Jacob's ladder, sees Jacob as everyman. The ladder stands on the earth but reaches the heavens; man is one of countless shards of clay, but his soul reaches to heaven. " 'And behold the angels of God ascending and descending on it'—even the ascent and descent of the angels depend on my deeds."

We may note, first of all, that the particular way Rabbi Moshe breaks open the story tells us a great deal. He speaks out of the tradition of exegesis found in the Talmud—text and commentary on it which combines the most profound respect for every word with the greatest freedom for the imagination to play on the text. The rabbi, like the artist, "maintains dialogue with his heart, meets things with his mind." Jacob and what befell him is history, but it is also allegory; it has meaning in itself and in the correspondences it reveals in all human lives. Behind this exegetical method is a specific anthropology, expressed by Denise Levertov in Saint Paul's words from the Epistle to the Romans, "we are members one of another." One finds in Hasidism a deep-rooted humanism and ethical concern. One also finds an equally deep-rooted respect for the creation, this world, as an abode of holiness. Another tale of Rabbi Moshe of Kobryn, which immediately follows the one quoted in *The Jacob's Ladder*, in *Tales of the Hasidim: Later Masters*, brings all these elements together:

> The rabbi of Kobryn taught:
> God says to man, as he said to Moses: "Put off thy shoes from thy feet"—put off the habitual which encloses your foot, and you will know that the place on which you are now standing is holy ground. For there is no rung of human life on which we cannot find the holiness of God everywhere and at all times.

One *puts off* the habitual but does not repudiate it; when the habitual is seen afresh it testifies to the holy. Such a view worked out in the writing of poetry necessarily carries with it a distinct perception of the role of the poet. He can be neither the seer nor the maker as those two models have been understood by many poets since the Romantic movement; the poet is neither God who makes all things nor Adam who names all things. He is not the rebel or outcast defying God and making a contemptuous, magical fantasy world. If we do not become too enamored of the image, we might say that the poet is like Jacob in Rabbi Moshe's tale, who sees *in a dream*, the ladder between heaven and earth, who puts off the habitual and perceives the holy, and for whom seeing carries an imperative to act.

One would expect, from Denise Levertov's affinities for other poets and for her illustrious ancestors, that her poetry would be marked by delight in shapes and textures, strange, evocative words, clearly delineated scenes. She is always interested by *inwardness,* what gives meaning to shape, texture, and scene, but much of the music of her poetry comes from her delight in the details of things themselves.

The religious response to a mystery is celebration, not explanation. At her best, Denise Levertov communicates both the holiness in a scene and the "greeting of the spirit," in John Keats's phrase, which makes it real to man. "She has no superior in this clarification of a scene," says Robert Duncan, ". . . that crossing of the inner and the outer reality, where we have our wholeness of feeling in the universe."

If her poetry has its typical excellences, it has its typical weaknesses, as well. A number of the early poems fail to engage our deeper interest precisely because they assert what they do not persuade us of—a meaningful correspondence between scene and an inner reality. One person's celebration can be another's dull party, after all; and though the capacity to celebrate is valuable, it does not necessarily lead to a broader range of experience or insight. Where the poems fail, they do so typically for one of two reasons: they inflate or sentimentalize an experience, or they grasp for counterparts too hastily and produce false analogies.

No method of meditation can guarantee success, and a poetry of exploration must be valued for the quality of its exploring, not merely for its success in finding, but there are inherent problems in Denise Levertov's poetic method. To wish poems to be a counterforce, to have an inner harmony "in utter contrast to the chaos in which they exist," can lead to filtering out too much of the chaos too soon. Musing, meditating, recollecting emotion in tranquility—which is a particular form of poetic meditation—can flatten out the highs and lows of a life and produce " 'common speech' / a dead level," in place of poetry. Those who have practiced the art of meditation testify how hard it is to break away from familiar ideas and stock responses; the tendency is to graft the new onto the familiar, rather than to launch forward into the threatening and the unexpected.

In "Notes of a Scale" Denise Levertov refers to one of the *Tales of the Hasidim: The Early Masters*, which might serve as a gloss on her poetry. Rabbi Elimelekh distinguishes between two kinds of wonders, those produced by magicians as illusions to surprise others, and those he calls wonders "from the true world" which God enables one to perform. The latter take the performer by surprise—they are given, not learned.

> A wonder
> from the true world,'
> he who accomplished it
>   'overwhelmed with the wonder
> which arises out of his doing,' . . .

Magic is a learned skill, which depends on drawing from one's stock with facility. The true wonders come when the learned response, the stereotypes, the methods of meditation are broken open. One may also distinguish two kinds of poems in the same way. The first rests almost entirely on the associative process taking place in the poet's mind.

The second kind of poem, the true wonder, must be difficult to describe or it would not be what it is. Some common characteristics may be suggested, however. The darker side of experience and the unconscious have more play. Things go more deeply into the poet. The poem proceeds both associatively and dialogically, in Buber's sense. Things are *themselves* first, with their own clarity and individuality; they do not lose their natures in a divine All or gain value because we perceive their symbolic meaning. Buber insists, when he speaks of the *I-Thou* relationship, that it be called *meeting* or *witnessing*. We are addressed and we answer. He speaks of the "complete relational event" which is knowing the *Thou*. ". . . No 'going beyond sense-experience' is necessary; for every experience, even the most spiritual, would yield us only an *It*. Nor is any recourse necessary to a world of ideas and values, for they cannot become presentness to us."

> From the shrivelling gray
> silk of its cocoon
> a creature slowly
>   is pushing out
> to stand clear—
>
>   not a butterfly,
>   petal that floats at will across
>   the summer breeze
>   not a furred
>   moth of the night
>   crusted with indecipherable
>   gold—
>
> some primal-shaped, plain-winged, day-flying thing.

Nothing has to be said of the relational event; it requires no predicate. It need not suggest counterparts or archetypes to speak to us. This event, rightly called "The Disclosure," stands in its own radiance, and to attach qualities to it, even the quality of holiness, would lessen its value. We know someone observes what is happening, but the perceptions pursue the *via negativa*, "not a butterfly, . . . not a furred moth," [negative way] until the "thing" stands clear as itself. It does not come for naming; in fact the poet never gains even that degree of power over it which comes with knowing something's name.

Louis Martz, speaking of the meditative poem in English, says that it records the creation of " . . . a self that is, ideally, one with itself, with other human beings, with created nature, and with the supernatural." The typical meditative poem begins with the fact of separation, at least the distinction of subject and object, and by processes of association, memory, imagination, and "conversation" between subject and object, it creates that self which is at one with itself and everything not-itself.

But there is another kind of meditation, found in the poetry of Robert Bly, James Wright, and Gary Snyder as well as in Denise Levertov, where the discovery or creation of the self is unimportant, and only *seeing* matters.

> Zaddik, you showed me
> the Stations of the Cross

and I saw
not what the almost abstract

tiles held—world upon world—
but at least

a shadow of what
might be seen there if mind and heart

gave themselves to meditation,
deeper

and deeper into Imagination's
holy forest. . . .

("Letter to William Kintner")

The three books, *With Eyes at the Back of Our Heads, The Jacob's Ladder,* and *O Taste and See,* impress us with her serene delight in the world and pleasure in making poems which celebrate the world, "all that lives / to the imagination's tongue."

In the presence of so much which is good, one feels misanthropic to complain at what is lacking, but the poems are weakened from lack of a serious treatment of evil. The world in which "doubleness," suffering, and evil must be fought, if only to a draw, every day, is not taken very seriously in the poems.

Evil has no existence in itself but is only good "in abeyance," apparently. In "The Necessity" she takes the Hasidic image of the divine sparks encased in all things waiting for the *Teshuvah,* man's act of repentance which sets in motion God's redemption of His creation. But she uses this image to describe the making of poetry.

each part
of speech a spark
awaiting redemption, each
a virtue, a power

in abeyance unless we
give it care
our need designs in us. Then
all we have led away returns to us.

Even "During the Eichmann Trial," from *The Jacob's Ladder,* and "A March," from *O Taste and See,* two poems which take their subjects directly from contemporary social issues, both center on the appropriate inner response to the issue rather than on arguing a course of action.

Not until *The Sorrow Dance* (1967) and *Relearning the Alphabet* (1970) does she pursue the vision of evil any farther. With *The Sorrow Dance* she has broadened and deepened the range of her poetry to correspond to the degree of involvement she now has in social concerns. The dominant tone in the book is grief; not just in the larger occasions for grief, the death of the poet's older sister and the war in Vietnam, but even in the poems rejoicing in the natural world, where joy and the awareness of mortality support one another. In place of what Ralph Mills, Jr. called "poetry of the Immediate," we find poetry of the absent, of the hard-won insight or confirmation. The poetry is characterized by reassessment of the past and a reaching after new experiences in order to consolidate them within the self.

In grieving we prolong the pain of loss by *recollecting* both what gave us joy and what made us guilty in the relationship. The process is analogous to artistic creation in that memory and imagination work together to apprehend the significant form which makes available to us the ongoing meaning of a life or a cluster of events. Recollection leads on to incorporation of the other, forgiven and forgiving, into ourselves, and we take up life again, strengthened by the virtues and spirit of those we have lost. The whole dynamic is beautifully imaged in Denise Levertov's phrase, "The Sorrow Dance."

"The Wings" strikes the dominant note immediately. Something "heavy," "black," hangs hidden from view on the speaker's back. "I can't see it, can't move it." Is it "pure energy I store" or "black / inimical power, cold"? Is it to be identified with "terror, stupidity / of cold rage" or is it black only because it is pent up? The very simplest contrasts begin to bear complex implications. "Black" and its echo or rhyme words play off against "white," "flight," and "light." Similarly, "humped and heavy" plays off against "a fountain of light," "the power of flight." But potency must always be ambiguous.

> could I go
> on one wing,
>
> the white one?

The poems abide in the ambiguity of potency. They trace its dark roots and speak of the testing which so often precedes the receiving of new power: emptiness, incapacity, frustration, and incoherence. The poet recognizes in "The Mutes" that the groans of lust a woman hears from men in the subway are "grief-language," "language stricken, sickened, cast down / in decrepitude." They are sounds of impotence but they translate into other languages—into a wordless tribute to her grace, into a changed pace, into understanding of life around her. She feels their truth on her pulse: the sounds of impotence become sounds of power as the subway train comes echoing through the tunnel to jar to a halt,

> while her understanding
>
> keeps on translating:
> 'life after life after life goes by
>
> without poetry,
> without seemliness,
> without love.'

In *O Taste and See* her metaphor for the artist was the All-Day Bird, "striving / in hope and / good faith to make his notes / ever more precise." Now it is the earthworm, "out of soil by passage / of himself / constructing / castles of metaphor!" Whereas the All-Day Bird sang full-heartedly of "Sun / light. / Light / light light light," the worm "throws off" his artifacts by contracting and expanding the "muscle of his being." The images speak of hard labor, being closed in, tilling oneself, but not for the purpose of making art. The artifacts are thrown off as a by-product of the real work, which is aerating "the ground of his living." The artist humbly makes his soul, brings vitality to the ground of living—which sounds so close to Tillich's "ground of being"—and becomes a completed self.

Descent and ascent, from the periphery to the center and out again, renewed—the patterns of the elegy shape "The Sorrow Dance." From generalized despair, the perception of formlessness and incoherence, we move to the particular cause of grief and guilt memorialized in the "Olga Poems," which are the heart of the book. Through grief, the opening up to sorrow, the return from emotional death, we reach a provisional affirmation, the beginnings of new strength. The poet recognizes the world of "The Mutes," where language is "stricken, sickened." In "The Whisper" is a world of terror "filling up fast with / unintelligible signs, . . . arhythmic." Only after the self has been reconstituted by internalizing or incorporating the object of grief within itself, confirming the worthiness of this grief, can the poet recognize that "The Closed World" was the inner world. She quotes from Blake, "If the Perceptive Organs close, their Objects seem to close also."

"Incorporation" or internalization requires facing the threatening *otherness*, the shadow side of one's existence represented by the characteristics of another person, particularly one with whom there has been an unhealed breach. In "A Lamentation" the poet translates all her sister's negative qualities into her own betrayals and denials. She has denied all grief, at the cost of the vitality of love: "Grief dismissed, / and Eros along with grief."

> That robe or tunic, black gauze
> over black and silver my sister wore
> to dance *Sorrow,* hung so long
> in my closet. I have never tried it on.
>   And my dance
> was *Summer*—

To dance *Summer* betrayed her "autumn birthright" in order to please others. Sorrow always characterized Olga; denial of sorrow characterized herself, she now believes. She has betrayed not only her sister—the kind of betrayal the "easy" child feels for profiting by the sibling's difficulties—but she has betrayed her own nature as well.

She has lost definition, as has her world. "Pink sunstripes," "spaces of blue timidly steady" are her colors, not black and silver, the emblems and plumes of her sister. "There are hidden corners of sky / choked with the swept shreds, with pain and ashes." The poem achieves no resolution, but the process of opening up has begun. Blackness, darkness, shadow contend with pink and blue. Sentence fragments image the disconnectedness of her experience, the devaluing of the "I" which should be their subject.

The method of the "Olga Poems" is recollection, the calling back together of a person now "bones and tatters of flesh in earth." To recollect is also to comprehend—to grasp, to assemble in coherent form. Naturally enough, what we did not comprehend in the living person will engage us most in recollecting him. The "Olga Poems" explore the differences between the sisters, from the differences in age and physical maturation to the deep spiritual breaks between them. Olga is always the dark one, both physically and spiritually. At nine she was swept with rage and shame at seeing a slum; where her sister at the same age sees "pride in the whitened doorsteps." At an early age, *"Everything flows,"* the Heraclitean doctrine, strikes her consciousness as a counsel of despair. Her sister links the phrase to the hymn "O God, Our Help in Ages Past," *"Time / like an everlasting stream / bears all its sons away."* She therefoe puts it in the context of Christian hope.

The contrasts begin to stand clear. Olga never perceives order in her life or in the world, but she longs to impose it. She wants "to brow-beat / the poor into joy's / socialist republic," to label the disorder on her desk, base her verses on Keble's *Christian Year,* "To change, / to change the course of the river!"

> But dread
> was in her, a bloodbeat, it was against the rolling dark
> oncoming river she raised bulwarks, . . .

Energy and will characterize Olga, as her sister recalls her; she pits her strength *against* the flow. "What rage for order / disordered her pilgrimage." Olga is a pilgrim—a seeker after holiness—but also a "Black one, incubus," unable to be led along a peaceful path. The tension between these two makes her the cause of disaster to herself and others, "disasters bred of love."

The poet, the easy child, who trusted order and flow, must salvage from her sister's life some principle to give it meaning. She finds it in the "candle of compassion" which shone through the darkness.

> Black one, black one,
> there was a white
> candle in your heart.

"That kind candle" alone remains when the "comet's tail" of hatred, the disasters, even history had "burned down." A definition of Olga's life grows out of the images of natural force—the flame and the river—associated with her. They can represent meaningless flux—the disorder which Olga feared—but they can also image pattern, a cycle of fulfillment in which life and death have deeper meaning. Retracing her sister's life is more than an act of reconciliation, for Olga has not only been an *opposite* to come to terms with, she has also been a forerunner. Accordingly, she is example and warning.

Since we must all trace some of the same steps through life to death, what must be learned is in what spirit to make the trip.

Only when we have internalized the values, or come to terms with the threats, which the loved one represented to us, can we pronounce a final benediction over him. So, in the "Olga Poems" Denise Levertov opens herself to the painful and fragmentary memories until they begin to cohere around a few images and impressions: the pilgrim, the river and the sea, the "everlasting arms," the candle, music. These she gathers up for a final re-creation of her sister's life and an affirmation of its continuing value for her. Finally, the poet remembers her sister's eyes, and the effect is as if she looks her fully in the face for the first time.

> Your eyes were the brown gold of pebbles under water.
> I never crossed the bridge over the Roding, dividing
> the open field of the present from the mysteries,
> the wraiths and shifts of time sense Wanstead Park held
>   suspended,
> without remembering your eyes. Even when we were estranged
> And my own eyes smarted with pain and anger at the thought of
>   you.
> And by other streams in other countries, anywhere where the
>   light
> reaches down through shallows to gold gravel. Olga's
> brown eyes. . . .

Here is no argument, but by the subtlest associations past and present, change and permanence, the specific and the universal come together— freighted with the most personal meaning and made available to us by that loving recollection, "Olga's brown eyes." In a fashion which recalls but does not imitate the "turn" of traditional elegy, the announcement that the loved one lives in a new form, Denise Levertov brings together those "other streams in other countries," the light reaching down to gold gravel, to create a mood of unity with the world and with her sister. In this context she can speak of their estrangement and face frankly the most terrible facts about her sister's life, not because they are now explained but because the mystery of this other life has been taken into her own, to enlarge and nourish it.

> Through the years of humiliation,
> of paranoia and blackmail and near starvation, losing
> the love of those you loved, one after another,
> parents, lovers, children, idolized friends, what kept
> compassion's candle alight in you, that lit you
> clear into another chapter (but the same book) 'a clearing
> in the selva oscura,
> a house whose door
> swings open, a hand beckons
> in welcome'?

I cross
so many brooks in the world, there is so much light
dancing on so many stones, so many questions my eyes
smart to ask of your eyes, gold brown eyes,
the lashes short but the lids
arched as if carved out of olivewood, eyes with some vision
of festive goodness in back of their hard, or veiled, or shining,
unknowable gaze . . .

The final poem of "The Sorrow Dance" section, "To Speak," moves from lamentation to speech, from darkness to light, from the closed world to a new opening, from underground to the surface. Gathering up the themes and key words of the whole section, it confirms passage through a time of testing to a new endurance.

The disjunction of inner and outer life of which she speaks here she shows us, with authority, in these poems. She does not repudiate one of those worlds to live without tension in the other; she acknowledges the anguish of knowing both of them out of synchronization.

I have seen
not behind but within, within the
dull grief, blown grit, hideous
concrete facades, another grief, a gleam
as of dew, an abode of mercy,
have heard not behind but within noise
a humming that drifted into a quiet smile.

("City Psalm")

The insight stands by itself, not to be doubted, not expected to transform the horror and grief of life. Everything becomes transparent, revealing "an otherness that was blessed, that was bliss. / *I saw Paradise in the dust of the street.*" The valuing of holiness and the capacity to abide with a mystery, qualities which marked Denise Levertov's earliest poetry, run much deeper as influences in the poetry of *The Sorrow Dance*. Emotions and words are tough and knotty; the poetry shows a distrust of aestheticizing raw emotions.

The images for the inner world in "Life at War" reveal some of the changes which the poet is undergoing in understanding the holy. One inner world is that of the "Didactic Poem," a world of dark, vampire-like spirits. Another represented by body fluids, "the mucous membrane of our dreams," "husky phlegm," struggles to throw off the corruption of the first. The war is the outward sign of this inner depravity, it is "the knowledge that jostles for space / in our bodies. . . . "

We have breathed the grits of it in, all our lives,
our lungs are pocked with it,
the mucous membrane of our dreams
coated with it, the imagination
filmed over with the grey filth of it: . . .

"Life at War" refers not only to what it feels like to be alive when a war is going on, in Denise Levertov's hands that experience broadens out to describe what it means when the self is at war *with* itself. The Closed World becomes an encysted world. She emphasizes the point in "Second Didactic Poem" by describing our task as making "the honey of the human." Again biological action symbolizes the activity of a healthy inner life. The honey of man is being " 'more ourselves' / in the making," a process of "selving," in Hopkins's fine word. Corruption, dirt, virulence, the extraneous can all be turned to "Nectar, / the makings of the incorruptible," if the creature itself is healthy.

> enclosed and capped
> with wax, the excretion
> of bees' abdominal glands.
> Beespittle, droppings,hairs
> of beefur: all become honey.
> Virulent micro-organisms cannot
> survive in honey.
> The taste,
> the odor of honey:
> each has no analogue but itself.

Our gathering, containing, working, "active in ourselves," creates that honey which has no analogues. In this extended metaphor, Denise Levertov has given us an image of individuation—the more powerful because it plays off against so many other images of life at war.

The decay of language and vision which operates as a major thematic thread in *The Sorrow Dance* finds expression both explicitly and in the montagelike, deliberately unfinished forms she employs in *Relearning the Alphabet*. Particularly in "An Interim" and "From a Notebook: October '68–May '69," two long poems which, with "Relearning the Alphabet," dominate the book, she borrows heavily from newspaper stories, letters, journal entries to give a documentary—and fragmentary—quality.

The titles tell a story: "Despair," "Tenebrae," "Wanting the Moon," "Not to Have," "A Defeat," "Craving," "Mad Song," "A Hunger." So do fragments and clipped sentences which make up stanzas and whole poems. "If I should find my poem is deathsongs. / If I should find it has ended, when I looked for the next step."

The vision of unity rests on a kind of innocence, but in these poems both innocence and knowledge are a kind of damnation. She pictures a Black boy grabbing armfuls of gladioli in the Detroit Riots of 1967, but her imagination can do nothing with the picture, so the boy stands there, like a daydream whose action we cannot control, "useless knowledge in my mind's eye." She repeats "Biafra, Biafra, Biafra," to enlarge the "small stock of compassion / grown in us by the imagination," "trying to make room for more knowledge in my bonemarrow," but again the imagination fails, for she can find nothing to do.

In place of the easy inspiration of her earlier poems, that assurance of the connectedness of things, the unity between life and poems, there is now hunger, "a longing silent at song's core." Useless knowledge is guilty knowledge, what the traditional phrase means by "knowledge of sin." It presents itself as burden, loss of motive, existential distrust, "useless longing." The organic relationship between language and reality—so important to Denise Levertov—can no longer be assumed.

> O language, mother of thought,
> are you rejecting us as we reject you?
>
> Language, coral island
> accrued from human comprehensions,
> human dreams,
>
> you are eroded as war erodes us.

In place of the old singleness of vision—which allowed "nakedness" of language and innocent inspiration—the poet sees with fractured vision, "multiple vision." "Advent 1966" speaks out of that multiple vision, contrasting Southwell's vision of the Burning Babe, "prefiguring / the Passion upon the Eve of Christmas," with our vision of the burned children of Vietnam, "as off a beltline, more, more senseless figures aflame." Christ's suffering redeems—"furnace in which souls are wrought into new life"—but the multiple, repeated suffering of the children damns.

> Because in Vietnam the vision of a Burning Babe
> is multiplied, multiplied,
> the flesh on fire
> not Christ's, as Southwell saw it, prefiguring
> the passion upon the Eve of Christmas,
>
> but wholly human and repeated, repeated,
> infant after infant, their names forgotten,
> their sex unknown in the ashes,
> set alight, flaming but not vanishing,
> not vanishing as his vision but lingering,
>
> cinders upon the earth or living on
> moaning and stinking in hosptals three abed;
>
> because of this my strong sight,
> my clear caressive sight, my poet's sight I was given
> that it might stir me to song,
> is blurred.

The suspended phrases, lingering over the gift of sight, fall to the harshness of "blurred." Nightmare images follow: a cataract filming over the inner eyes, a monstrous insect possessing one and looking out through the eye-sockets "with multiple vision." Sight remains strong and clear—"the insect / is not there, what I see is there"—but there is nothing for the sight to caress.

Her vision is still single, then, in that it perceives an inherent order in things, but it has enlarged to include a profound awareness of evil. In the seven-part poem, "An Interim," she contrasts the harmony of the natural world with the disorder of America and the tensions surrounding her husband's acts of resistance to the Vietnam War. "An Interim" is one exercise of several in the book probing the deepest psychological and moral problem of the radical dissenter—how to translate resistance to what he perceives as all-pervasive evil into a positive peace. Many things may support the dissenter—adherence to a clear moral code, companionship with like-minded people, outrage, but also paranoia and hatred. The poem evolves around two definitions of peace, peace represented by nature—"Peace as grandeur. Energy / serene and noble,"—and peace defined by the spiritual effect of its opposite—"The soul dwindles sometimes to an ant / rapid upon a cracked surface."

Inner peace cannot come to the resister unless he has first experienced that soul-dwindling. Like the poet, his work is to repossess the soul, but that can only be done by larger acts of restoration, including restoring virtue to language by making words accord with deeds. So the poet tests her way from one to another model of resistance, counterpointing passages praising the grandeur of ocean and sun with news accounts of a noncooperator's prison fast, reflections on the self-immolation of "the great savage saints of outrage" who burned themselves, diary entries and excerpts from the poet's letters concerning her husband's impending trial. She rejects none of the models, but affirms as her own, working "to make from outrage / islands of compassion others could build on." Of such resisters she says, "Their word if good, / language draws breath again in their *yes* and *no*, / true testimony of love and resistance."

The poem represents an attempt to regain organic form—in life more than in literary creation—not a successful discovery of form. Overcoming her "cramp of fury" leads her into diffuse and flat writing. Yet we feel behind what is more a sketch for a poem than a finished work the regaining of perspective, a renewed trust in the virtue of language and the virtue of men.

"From a Notebook: October '68–May '69" pursues the same impressionistic method, gathering up phrases of poetry, fragments from reading, distant and recent memories, intense experiences into a notebook-poem which explores the choice, "Revolution or death." This exploration proceeds on several levels—the political and social are the most obvious, but the deepest and most influential is the personal, signaled by the weaving of nineteenth-century poems about death into the fabric of her reflections. Moving into middle age has been an important theme in both *The Sorrow Dance* and *Relearning the Alphabet*; in "From a Notebook" the question of the old labor song, *"Which side are you on?"* refers not only to the choice indicated by "Revolution or death" but also by the contrast between the world of the young and that of the aging. At stake is learning how to live the second half of a life, how to grow as a poet.

The poem circles its subjects, exemplifying in its method what it "discovers" as its conclusion: that revolution must not be merely circular and life not merely linear, but that both must radiate from a center.

The rhythm of the opening section is set by the repeated phrase "Revolution or death," which acts on us as though the throb of train wheels repeated it. Working into that rhythm are those suggested by *"Which side are you on?"* and the biblical question "What makes this night different from all other nights?" Everything speaks of choice: choosing a side, being of the chosen people, choosing life with the young, because "Death is Mayor Daley," Death is also *"Unlived life / of which one can die."* Revolution is identified with "prismatic radiance pulsing from live tissue," and with resisters "blowing angel horns at the imagined corners," pronouncing a benediction over the world in an image borrowed from John Donne.

A counterstatement follows in the second section. Death is not only "the obscene sellout," it is also lovely and soothing. Over against this, the image of the pulsing brain:

>   The will to live
> pulses.   Radiant emanations
> of living tissue, visible only
> to some photo-eye we know
> sees true because mind's dream-eye,
> inward gage, confirms it.
>   Confirmation,
> a sacrament.

"How to live and the will to live," "revolution or death," objects, events, memories cluster around an unknown, shifting center which gives them "a character that throughout all transformations / reveals them connatural." Her life, seen as the tension of opposites, is also centered around something to which the opposites relate.

Enantiodromia, the being torn apart by opposites, which Jung speaks of as the problem of the mature person, aptly describes both the polarization one sees in American society and the conflicts within the self that Denise Levertov has explored since *The Sorrow Dance*; "Revolution or death" speaks simultaneously of the political and the psychic life.

Language again serves as a symbol for what is happening to the poet. Her roots are in the nineteenth century, so she is out of touch with those she most wants to know. Though she chooses revolution her words do not reach forward into it. "Language itself is my one home, my Jerusalem," but in this age of refugees she too has been uprooted.

> My diction marks me
> untrue to my time;
> change it, I'd be
> untrue to myself.

Part II is not "a going beyond" but a return and reexamination of themes. It is a meditation on revolution itself, which she describes as a new life, as like the secret uprising of the moon, as pervasive as "odor of snow, / freshwater, / stink of dank / vegetation recomposing."

Her husband, an intransigent pacifist friend, A. J. Muste become human symbols of resistance, revolution, and peace-making, both because of their own individual integrity and because the fullest human life is only a beginning.

What people can do together, as in the making of the People's Park in Berkeley, also symbolizes the revolution. "The War / comes home to us . . . " she says, when the People's Park is seized by the police. In the action of clearing the land, however, she has seen "poets and dreamers studying / joy together," finding in the cleared land a New World,

> each leaf of
> the new grass near us
> a new testament. . . .

The revolution she finally affirms is like a force of nature: a tree rising out of a flood, a sea full of swimmers, islands—like the islands of compassion in "In the Interim"—"which step out of the waves on rock feet."

"Relearning the Alphabet" recapitulates the book, gathering up its dominant themes, words, and images and making them the milestones of a journey from anguish back to "the ah! of praise." The device which shapes the poem, patterning it on the ABC books of childhood, allows many rich influences to operate. The organization is, on the surface, simple and arbitrary, since the sequence in which we learn the letters of the alphabet has no significance in itself, yet it is as absolute as numeral order. This is a quest-poem, however, and quests also move from point to point in what first appears to be an arbitrary sequence but eventually stands out as a necessary order where each test prepares us for the next. To relearn the alphabet requires going back to first things, to childhood.

"Relearning the Alphabet" is a poem of exploration, retracing an inner landscape which corresponds to the outward landscape—Vietnam, Biafra, Boston, Milwaukee, Berkeley, Maine—over which the other poems have ranged. What has been sought, or mourned, in those poems—joy, the moon, inspiration—is sought here.

It is also a recapitulation of her poetic life, gathering phrases and references from several of her own poems and from other poets, Hasidic tales, and fairy tales. In form the poem is also a recapitulation; she has relearned the alphabet by trying its sounds.

The poem begins in broken phrases, words displayed together kaleidescopically, but they touch on the stages of the quest; joy to be found in the extremes of anguish and ardor; to be relearned as unthinking knowledge; to be protected and fed with anguish and ashes.

> Joy—a beginning. Anguish, ardor.
> To relearn the ah! of knowing in unthinking
> joy: the beloved stranger lives.

> Sweep up anguish as with a wing-tip,
> brushing the ashes back to the fire's core.

"The fire's core" runs through the poem as a signature for the contrarieties of joy, changing and enlarging in meaning as the poet appropriates more of her experiences and insights into the framework offered by alphabetical order.

Hoping and wanting are important, but they make nothing happen. Being open, following the leading, are all the questor has. She has guides on her quest, but they lead by misdirection and by making her stumble. When she is "called forth" by a question, she only knows what she was unable to find:

> Lost in the alphabet
> I was looking for
> the word I can't now say

(love)

But the calling forth occurred through the love in a question, and suddenly she finds herself home again, back from the false quests.

> I am trusted, I trust
> the real that transforms me.
> And relinquish
> in grief
> *the seeing that burns through, comes through*
> *to fire's core;*   transformation, continuance,
> as acts of magic I would perform, are no longer
> articles of faith.

False quests are those we will ourselves to make—wanting the moon. Being "called forth" depends on letting go, relinquishing what is most precious to the will. The whole book has been concerned with holding onto or recapturing vision and joy, or satisfying hunger and longing. It has been marked by distrust of former innocence, near-repudiation of former simplicity and easy inspiration. But always she has wanted confirmation of her past, "transformation, continuance," and many of the poems have fought through to magnificently enlarged vision, still rooted in "imagination's holy forest" as she had known it. In "Relearning the Alphabet" the final relinquishment occurs, the recognition that "acts of magic" and "articles of faith" are "rules of the will—graceless / faithless," and that she must yield all desire, all yearning for vision or wisdom, before the treasure will disclose itself. And the treasure is a new trust, a recognition that holiness *is*, both in the world and in the self.

> Relearn the alphabet,
> relearn the world, the world
> understood anew only in doing, under-
> stood only as
> looked-up-into out of earth,

the heart an eye looking,
the heart a root
planted in earth.
Transmutation is not
under the will's rule.

Everything the poet wanted has been given, but neither in the form nor with the meaning she had willed. Confirmation, joy, the fire's core—she has gained each through the making of poetry. *Relearning the Alphabet* represents a completion and a new beginning. In her "Statement on Poetics" in 1959, Denise Levertov had said, "Insofar as poetry has a social function it is to awaken sleepers by other means than shock." In her last two books we are aware of the terrible shocks she has sustained and the struggle she has passed through to regain or earn her eloquence.

All utterance
takes me step by hesitant step towards
—yes, to continuance: into
that life beyond the dead-end where
. . . I was lost.

We find a new sophistication in her understanding of what it means to be "members one of another." It has consequences for political action, from making a people's park to conspiring against "illegitimate authority." That enlarged understanding has brought new subjects to her poetry and an enlarged practice in writing "organic" poetry. The inherent form behind things, the truth, has been sought through montage and documentary. The poetry which results sometimes seems extravagant, rough, or unfinished. But we trust it because we trust the life it comes out of and the sense of holiness which inspires Denise Levertov to write.

Anne Sexton: Somehow to Endure

J. D. McClatchy

Even the covers of an Anne Sexton book are contradictory. The poet posed demurely on their jackets: a sun-streaked porch, white wicker, the beads and pleated skirt, the casual cigarette. Their tame titles—literary or allusive: *To Bedlam and Part Way Back, All My Pretty Ones, Love Poems, Transformations, The Book of Folly*. And yet beyond, inside, are extraordinary revelations of pain and loss, an intensely private record of a life hungering for madness and stalked by great loves, the getting and spending of privileged moments and suffered years. The terrible urgency of the poems, in fact, seems to invite another sort of contradiction, the kind we feel only with strong poets: disappointments. Occasionally there are poems which frankly misfire for being awkward or repetitious, stilted or prosaic. [A. Alvarez] has caught it:

> So her work veers between good and terrible almost indiscriminately. It is not a question of her writing bad poems from time to time, like everybody else; she also prints them cheek by jowl with her purest work. The reason, I suppose, is that the bad poems are bad in much the same way as her good ones are good: in their head-on intimacy and their persistence in exploring whatever is most painful to the author.

The influences on her poetry—ranging from Rilke, Lawrence, Rimbaud and Smart, to Jarrell, Roethke, Lowell, Plath, and C. K. Williams—were easily acquired, obviously displayed, and often quickly discarded, while a few deeper influences—like that of Neruda—were absorbed and recast. She described herself as "a primitive," yet was master of intricate formal techniques. Her voice steadily evolved and varied and, at times, sought to escape

From *Anne Sexton: The Artist and Her Critics*. © 1978 by J. D. McClatchy. Indiana University Press, 1978.

speaking of the self, but her strongest poems consistently return to her narrow thematic range and the open voice of familiar feelings. *Do I contradict myself? Very well then I contradict myself.* For the source of her first fame continued as the focus of her work: she was the most persistent and daring of the confessionalists. Her peers have their covers: Lowell's allusiveness, Snodgrass's lyricism, Berryman's dazzle, Plath's expressionism. More than the others, Sexton resisted the temptations to dodge or distort, and the continuity and strength of her achievement remain the primary witness to the ability of confessional art to render a life into poems with all the intimacy and complexity of feeling and response with which that life has been endured.

Endurance was always her concern: why must we? how can we? why we must, how we do: "to endure,/somehow to endure." It is a theme which reenacts not only the sustained source of her poetry but its original impulse as well. At the age of twenty-eight, while recovering from a psychotic break-down and suicide attempt, she began writing poems on the advice of her psychiatrist: "In the beginning, the doctor said, 'Write down your feelings because someday they might mean something to somebody. No matter how despairing you are, there are other people going through this who can't express it, and if they should read it they would feel less alone.' And so he gave me my little reason to go on; it shifted around, but that was always a driving, driving force." . . .

Surprisingly little has been written with any authority on the subject of confessionalism, which has become, under the rubric of "sincerity," an impulse behind many of the significant social movements and styles since 1960.

One of the few studies available is Theodor Reik's *The Compulsion to Confess,* a work which, while hardly exhaustive, at least opens up a few theoretical approaches toward an understanding of the "compulsion" and its results. Broadly, Reik defines a confession as "a statement about impulses or drives which are felt or recognized as forbidden," and their expression involves both the repressed tendency and the repressing forces. If this secular interpretation seems to exclude the usual religious (and even legal) sense of the term as narrowed to facts and intentions, they can easily be added to Reik's definition without any loss to the force of his point. . . .

To some extent, then, the poetry is therapeutic; or as D. H. Lawrence said, "One sheds one's sicknesses in books—repeats and presents again one's emotions, to be master of them." Eric Erikson underscores this aspect of the situation by reminding that "the individual's mastery over his neuro-sis begins where he is put in a position to accept the historical necessity which made him what he is." Acceptance becomes survival. Anne Sexton: "writing, and especially having written, is evidence of survival—the books accumulate ego-strength." And so confessional poets are driven back to their losses, to that alienation—from self and others, from sanity and love—which is the thematic center of their vision and work. The betrayals in childhood, the family romance, the divorces and madnesses, the suicide attempts, the self-defeat and longing—the poets pursue them in their most intimate and painful detail. . . .

We learn what we are by relearning what we have become. But what is important to note now is the essentially narrative structure of the process, of one's experiences recounted in this time as remembered in their own past time. And narrative is likewise the most distinctive structural device in confessional poetry. The importance and integrity of chronology affect both the way in which individual poems are composed and the way they are collected into sequences and volumes, and these arrangements, in turn, are of thematic importance as facts or memories, shifting desires or needs or anxieties or gratifications change the landscape of personality. Sexton's poem "The Double Image," for instance, is a closely written and carefully parted account of her hospitalization and her necessary separation from her mother's shame and her daughter's innocence. The poem opens with the specificity of the achieved present—"I am thirty this November. . . . We stand watching the yellow leaves go queer"—and then drifts back through three yeers of madness and bitter history, to Bedlam and part way back, its larger thematic concerns held in precise details—dates, objects, places, names—among which are studded still smaller stories that memory associates with the main narrative. The destructions that survival implies in the poem are given their haunting force and authenticity by the history which the narrative leads the reader through so that he himself experiences the dramatic life of events and feelings. . . .

The rhetorical importance of confessional subject matter—especially insofar as it involves a characteristically Freudian epistemology—leads, in turn, to another consideration. In his most important gloss on the mediation of art, Freud wrote: "The essential *ars poetica* lies in the technique of overcoming the feeling of repulsion in us which is undoubtedly connected with the barriers that rise between each single ego and the others." Or between the single ego and its history, he might have added. And among the barriers the self constructs are the familiar defense mechanisms: repression, displacement, suppression, screen memories, condensation, projection, and so on. Such psychological techniques, in turn, have their rhetorical analogues, not surprisingly those most favored by modernist poets and their New Critics: paradox, ambiguity, ellipsis, allusion, wit, and the other "tensions" that correspond to the neurotic symptoms by which the self is obscured. And in order to write with greater directness and honesty about their own experiences, Sexton and the other confessional poets have tended to avoid the poetic strategies of modernism—to de-repress poetry, so to speak—and have sought to achieve their effects by other means. Sexton's turn toward open forms, as though in trust, is an example. In general, it can be said of Sexton's poems, as of other confessional poems, that the patterns they assume and by which they manage their meanings are those which more closely follow the actual experiences they are recreating—forms that can include and reflect direct, personal experience; a human, rather than a disembodied voice; the dramatic presentation of the flux of time and personality; and the drive toward sincerity. By this last concept is meant not an ethical imperative, but the willed and willing openness of the poet to her experience and to the character of the language by which her discoveries are revealed and shared. Not that the structures of sincerity abandon every measure of artifice. While she may have associated the imagination so strongly with memory, Sexton realized as well that the self's past experiences are neither provisional nor final, that even as they shape the art that describes them, so too they are modified by that very art. The flux of experience, rather than its absolute truth, determines which concerns or wounds are returned to in poem after poem, either because they have not yet been understood or because the understanding of them has changed. And Sexton is sharply aware, in her work, of the difference between factual truth and poetic truth—of the need to "edit" out, while trying not to distort, redundant or inessential "facts" in the service of cleaner, sharper poems. In a crucial sense, confessional art is a means of *realizing* the poet.

As the poet realizes himself, inevitably he catches up the way we live now: especially the personal life, since our marriages are more difficult than our wars, our private nightmares more terrifying than our public horrors. In addition, then, to our sense of the confessional poet as a survivor, he or she functions as a kind of witness. What may have begun as a strictly private need is transformed, once it is published, into a more inclusive focus—and here one recalls Whitman's "attempt, from first to last, to put a *Person*, a human being (myself, in the latter half of the Nineteenth Century, in America) freely, fully, and truly on record." The more naked and directly emotional nature of confessional poems heightens the integrity and force of their witness to the inner lives of both poets and readers; or, as Sexton has remarked, "poems of the inner life can reach the inner lives of readers in a way that anti-war poems can never stop a war." The final privatism of poetry itself, in other words, affords the confessional poet a certain confidence in using the details of intimate experience in ways that earlier would have been considered either arrogant or obscure. And the ends to which those details are put are not merely self-indulgent or self-therapeutic—or, in Robert Lowell's phrase, "a brave heart drowned on monologue." Of her own work, Anne Sexton once reminisced: "I began to think that if one life, somehow made into art, were recorded—not all of it, but like the testimony on an old tombstone—wouldn't that be worth something? Just one life—a poor middle-class life, nothing extraordinary (except maybe madness, but that's so common nowadays)—that seems worth putting down. It's the thing I have to do, the thing I want to do—I'm not sure why." And she went on to describe a reader's response to this "testimony": "I think, I hope, a reader's response is: 'My God, this has happened. And in some real sense it has happened to me too.' This has been my reaction to other poems, and my readers have responded to my poems in just this way."

Perhaps the most telling evidence of this sort of response are the countless letters that anonymous readers sent to Sexton, explaining how her poetry revealed their own troubled lives to them and often making impossible demands on the poet, so strong was the readers' sense of the real, suffering person in the poetry. It is no wonder that, with bitter wit, Sexton once described herself in a poem as "mother of the insane." But at a deeper level, there is some dark part in any one of us which her work illuminated, often distressingly. Like Wordsworth, who wished to allow his audience "new compositions of feeling," Sexton's response to her own experience becomes a model for a reader's response to his or her own. The poems function as instruments of discovery for the reader as well as for the poet, and the process of discovery—ongoing through poems and collections, as through life—is as important as the products, the poems which the poet has drawn directly out of her experience, often as isolated stays against confusion. The immediacy of impact and response, and the mutual intimacy between poet and reader, correspond with an observation by Ernst Kris on aesthetic distance: "When psychic distance is maximal, the response is philistine or intellectualistic. At best, the experience is one of passive receptivity rather than active participation of the self. . . . [But] when distance is minimal the reaction to works of art is pragmatic rather than aesthetic." To emphasize the "pragmatic" response of readers to this poetry—even though the term describes the response of most poets to their experience, however the subsequent poem may inform it—may be viewed as an effort to minimize the "art" of the poems. I hope my subsequent remarks will describe that art sufficiently, or at least with more attention to real questions than most critics have so far paid Sexton.

Despite the authority and abundance in *To Bedlam and Part Way Back,* Sexton was careful, perhaps compelled, to include an apologia, a poem called "For John, Who Begs Me Not to Enquire Further"—addressed to her discouraging teacher John Holmes, and so finally to the critic in herself. The poem's title echoes the book's epigraph, from a letter of Schopenhauer to Goethe concerning the courage necessary for a philosopher: "He must be like Sophocles's Oedipus, who, seeking enlightenment concerning his terrible fate, pursues his indefatigable enquiry, even when he divines that appalling horror awaits him in the answer. But most of us carry in our heart the Jocasta who begs Oedipus for God's sake not to inquire further. . . ." The sympathy she can afford for Homes—"although your fear is anyone's fear,/like an invisible veil between us all"—recalls Freud's sense of the repulsion with the self and others which art overcomes. Her cautious justification is modeled on her psychiatrist's plea: "that the worst of anyone/can be, finally,/an accident of hope." And the standard she sets herself is simply making sense:

> Not that it was beautiful,
> but that, in the end, there was
> a certain sense of order there;
> something worth learning
> in that narrow diary of my mind,
> in the commonplaces of the asylum

> where the cracked mirror
> or my own selfish death
> outstared me.

Part of that order is substantive and thematic, the urge to recover and understand the past: "I have this great need somehow to keep that time of my life, that feeling. I want to imprison it in a poem, to keep it. It's almost in a way like keeping a scrapbook to make life mean something as it goes by, to rescue it from chaos—to make 'now' last." But if the ability to extend the past and present into each other further depends upon the orders of art, that art cannot succeed without a prior commitment to honesty—or, to use Sexton's peculiar term, as a confessional poet she must start with a wise passivity, with being "still." That word occurs in her poem about the tradition, "Portrait of an Old Woman on the College Tavern Wall," where the poets sit "singing and lying/around their round table/and around me still." "Why do these poets lie?" the poem goes on to question, and leaves them with mortal irony "singing/around their round table/until they are still." Whether death or silence, this "stillness" is the view of experience, both prior to and beyond language, from which her ordering proceeds. The difficulty, as she knows in another poem, "Said The Poet to The Analyst," is that "My business is words":

> I must always forget how one word is able to pick
> out another, to manner another, until I have got
> something I might have said . . .
> but did not.

The business of the Analyst—again, an internal figure, a sort of artistic conscience—is "watching my words," guarding against the Jocasta who would settle for "something I might have said" instead of what must be revealed.

Sexton's business with words—the ordering of statement and instinct—is the adjustment of their demands to her experience: in her figure, to make a tree out of used furniture. Though her attitudes toward form evolved, from the beginning there was an uneasy ambivalence: the poet insisting on control, the person pleading, "Take out rules and leave the instant," as she said in one interview. Her solution was to use the metaphor of deceit, but to reverse it into a very personally inflected version of form:

> I think all form is a trick to get at the truth. Sometimes in my hardest poems, the ones that are difficult to write, I might make an impossible scheme, a syllabic count that is so involved, that it then allows me to be truthful. It works as a kind of super-ego. It says, "You may now face it, because it will be impossible ever to get out" . . . But you see how I say this not to deceive you, but to deceive me. I deceive myself, saying to myself you can't do it, and then if I can get it, then I have deceived myself, then I can change it and do what I want. I can even change and rearrange it so no one can see my trick. It won't change what's real. It's there on paper.

Though her early work occasionally forces itself with inversions and stolid High Style, her concern for the precisions of voice and pace reveal her care in indulging a lyric impulse only to heighten the dramatic. What Richard Howard has said of her use of rhyme is indicative of her larger sense of form: "invariably it is Sexton's practice to use rhyme to bind the poem, irregularly invoked, abandoned when inconvenient, psychologically convincing." The truth-getting tricks, in other words, serve as a method of conviction for both poet and reader. For the poet, form functions to articulate the details and thrust of her actual experience, while for the reader it guides his dramatic involvement in the re-creation: both convictions converging on authenticity, on realization. And so the voice is kept conversational, understated by plain-speech slang or homely detail—its imagery drawn from the same sources it counterpoints, its force centered in the pressure of events it contours, the states of mind it maps. This is clearly the case with the poems of madness in the first section of *To Bedlam and Part Way Back*. . . .

M. L. Rosenthal has seen in these poems "the self reduced to almost infantile regression," but more often the voice is that of an older child, which implies a consciousness that can experience the arbitrariness of authority and the sufferings of loss without understanding either chance or cause. The inferno of insanity opens, appropriately, with the poet lost in the dark wood of her "night mind":

> And opening my eyes, I am afraid of course
> to look—this inward look that society scorns—
> Still I search in these woods and find nothing worse
> than myself, caught between the grapes and the thorns.
>
> > ("Kind Sir: These Woods")

The disorientation necessitates the search: here, the descent into her own underworld, as later she will ascend part way back. Likewise, the figure of the child—so important in Part Two, where it subsumes both the poet and her daughter—introduces the themes of growth and discovery, of the growth into self by discovering its extremes, as in the poem addressed to her psychiatrist:

> And we are magic talking to itself,
> noisy and alone. I am queen of all my sins
> forgotten. Am I still lost?
> Once I was beautiful. Now I am myself,
> counting this row and that row of moccasins
> waiting on the silent shelf.
>
> > ("You, Dr. Martin")

The struggle to find "which way is home" involves the dissociation and resumption of different personalities ("Her Kind," "The Expatriates," "What's That"), the limits of paranoia and mania ("Noon Walk on the Asylum Lawn," "Lullaby"), and the dilemma of memory that drives pain toward exorcism ("You, Dr. Martin," "Music Swims Back to Me," "The Bells," "Said the Poet to the Analyst").

Though, as she says, there is finally "no word for time," the need to restore it is the essential aspect of the ordering process:

> Today is made of yesterday, each time I steal
> toward rites I do not know, waiting for the lost
> ingredient, as if salt or money or even lust
> would keep us calm and prove us whole at last.
>
> ("The Lost Ingredient")

What has been lost, along with sanity, is the meaning of those who made her, and this first book introduces us to the cast she will reassemble and rehearse in all her subsequent work, even through "Talking to Sheep" and "Divorce, Thy Name is Woman" in *45 Mercy Street:* the hapless boozy father, the helpless cancer-swollen bitch of a mother, the daughters as both victims and purifiers, the shadowy presence of her husband, the analyst as dark daddy and muse, the clutching company of doomed poets—and most touchingly, the great-aunt whom she calls Nana. Sexton's obsession with her Nana—the "Nana-hex" she calls it later—results from both sympathy and guilt. "She was, during the years she lived with us, my best friend, my teacher, my confidante and my comforter. I never thought of her as being young. She was an extension of myself and was my world." For this very reason, when her great-aunt, after a sudden deafness, had a nervous breakdown from which she never recovered, the poet could find her both an emblem of her own suffering and a source of guilt for fear she had somehow caused it. Nana is brought on tenderly in the lyrical elegy "Elizabeth Gone," but in the next poem, "Some Foreign Letters," her life is used as the focus of the poet's own anxieties as she sits reading the letters her great-aunt had sent to her family as a young woman on her Victorian Grand Tour. The poem proceeds by verse and refrain—Nana's letters of her youth, the poet's images of the same woman different—to point up the disjunction between memories: Nana's diaried ones, which have trapped her youth in an irretrievable past, and the poet's own memories of Nana trapped in age and lost to death:

> Tonight your letters reduce
> history to a guess. The Count had a wife.
> You were the old maid aunt who lived with us.
> Tonight I read how the winter howled around
> the towers of Schloss Schwöbber, how the tedious
> language grew in your jaw, how you loved the sound
> of the music of the rats tapping on the stone
> floors. When you were mine you wore an earphone.

The "guilty love" with which the poem ends is the poet's own ambivalent response to her inability to have rescued her Nana—even as she realizes she will not be able to save herself—from the facts that are fate, a life that cannot be unlived or chosen. The last stanza's pathos derives from its prediction of what has already occurred, the proof that guilt is suffered again and again:

Tonight I will learn to love you twice;
learn your first days, your mid-Victorian face.
Tonight I will speak up and interrupt
your letters, warning you that wars are coming,
that the Count will die, that you will accept
your America back to live like a prim thing
on a farm in Maine. I tell you, you will come
here, to the suburbs of Boston, to see the blue-nose
world go drunk each night, to see the handsome
children jitterbug, to feel your left ear close
one Friday at Symphony. And I tell you,
you will tip your boot feet out of that hall,
rocking from its sour sound, out onto
the crowded street, letting your spectacles fall
and your hair net tangle as you stop passers-by
to mumble your guilty love while your ears die.

The poet speaks her warning here not as a suspicious Jocasta but as a knowing Tiresias, helpless before time, that most visible scar of mortality. And the family to which she resigns Nana is, of course, her own as well, and the self-recovery which the volume's arrangement of poems plots necessarily moves to recover her parents, as so much of her later work too will do.

The book's second section is The Part Way Back, in the sense of both return and history. The painful realizations of adjustment, the lessons of loss and recovery weight the book's two anchor poems—"The Double Image" and "The Division of Parts." They are long poems, explorations lengthened to accommodate their discoveries and unresolved dilemmas, and extended by subtle modulations of voice and structure to dramatize their privacies. "The Double Image," the book's strongest and most ambitious poem, is actually a sequence of seven poems tracing the terms of Sexton's dispossession—similar to Snodgrass's "Heart's Needle," which was its model. The other poem, which clearly echoes Snodgrass's voice as well, is an independent summary of her losses, and makes the subsequent poems seem to have insisted themselves on her later. If that was the case, there is reason for it, since the jagged lines of the first poem reflect the uncertain hesitancy in naming the guilt that had caused her self-hatred and her suicide attempts and breakdown. It is addressed, in retrospect, to the daughter whose infant illness released the long-held guilt:

> a fever rattled
> in your throat and I moved like a pantomime
> above your head. Ugly angels spoke to me. The blame,
> I heard them say, was mine. They tattled
> like green witches in my head, letting doom
> leak like a broken faucet;
> as if doom had flooded my belly and filled your bassinet,
> an old debt I must assume.

She tries to solve her life with death—"I let the witches take away my guilty soul"—but is forced back from the "time I did not love/myself" to face the new life she has made in her child and the old life she had made for herself. She assumes the old debts in the following narrative of her recovery. If the first poem turned on her commitment and the loss of her daughter, the second turns on her release and the loss of her mother, to whom she returns as "an angry guest," "an outgrown child." The poet had grown "well enough to tolerate/myself," but her mother cannot forgive the suicide attempt and so cannot accept her daughter: she "had my portrait/done instead," a line that refrains the tedium and repressed menace that punches out each stanza. The tension of presence begins to sort the past; the church is another Bedlam, her parents her keepers:

> There was a church where I grew up
> with its white cupboards where they locked us up,
> row by row, like puritans or shipmates
> singing together. My father passed the plate.
> Too late to be forgiven now, the witches said.
> I wasn't exactly forgiven. They had my portrait
> done instead.

The third poem opens up the deaths in and of relationships. Sexton's distance from her own daughter gains its double reference: "as if it were normal/to be a mother and be gone." As the poet gathers her strength, her mother sickens, and madness, love-loss, and death are drawn into a single figure which points again at guilt. Her mother's cancer—"as if my dying had eaten inside of her"—accuses Sexton with questions that "still I couldn't answer." The fourth poem is centered as an interlude of partial return and acceptance: Sexton back from Bedlam, her mother from the hospital, her daughter from the exile of innocence. The fact of survival converts its sterility into patience: the blank, facing portraits mirror the reversal of concern:

> During the sea blizzards
> she had her
> own portrait painted.
> A cave of a mirror
> placed on the south wall;
> matching smile, matching contour.
> And you resembled me; unacquainted
> with my face, you wore it. But you were mine
> after all.

The fifth poem begins to draw the women together into a chorus, their roles merging into a new knowledge:

> And I had to learn
> why I would rather
> die than love, how your innocence
> would hurt and how I gather

> guilt like a young intern
> his symptoms, his certain evidence. . . .
>
> We drove past the hatchery,
> the hut that sells bait,
> past Pigeon Cove, past the Yacht Club, past Squall's
> Hill, to the house that waits
> still, on the top of the sea,
> and two portraits hang on opposite walls.

The sixth is a self-study, the poet finding herself in the distanced image of her mother, as in the next poem she discovers how selfish are the maternal motives of love. But in this poem, it is the process of life that learns from *la nature morte:*

> And this was the cave of the mirror,
> that double woman who stares
> at herself, as if she were petrified
> in time—two ladies sitting in umber chairs.
> You kissed your grandmother
> and she cried.

The final poem, again addressed to the poet's daughter, summarizes her learning:

> You learn my name,
> wobbling up the sidewalk, calling and crying.
> You call me *mother* and I remember my mother again,
> somewhere in greater Boston, dying.

But the last stanza unwinds into a tentative resumption of guilt—its last line speaking, with an odd irony, the voice of Jocasta: "And this was my worst guilt; you could not cure/ nor soothe it. I made you to find me."

In "The Division of Parts," Sexton carries the account past her mother's death, which has left her, on Good Friday, with "gifts I did not choose." The last hospital days are retold, and the numbness with which they stun her implies the larger truth of the poem:

> But you turned old,
> all your fifty-eight years sliding
> like masks from your skull;
> and at the end
> I packed your nightgowns in suitcases,
> paid the nurses, came riding
> home as if I'd been told
> I could pretend
> people live in places.

But people live not in space or places, but in time and in others, and their demands puzzle the poet's guilt: "Time, that rearranger/ of estates, equips/

me with your garments, but not with grief." Her inheritance steals on her "like a debt," and she cannot expiate her loss: "I planned to suffer/and I cannot." Unlike "Jesus, *my stranger*," who assumed "old debts" and knew how and why to suffer, Sexton is emptied of belief by need:

> Fool! I fumble my lost childhood
> for a mother and lounge in sad stuff
> with love to catch and catch as catch can.
>
> And Christ still waits. I have tried
> to exorcise the memory of each event
> and remain still, a mixed child,
> heavy with cloths of you.
> Sweet witch, you are my worried guide.

In this book Sexton realizes the motive of her subsequent books: "For all the way I've come/I'll have to go again." Only ever part way back, she tries her art against her mind—"I would still curse/ you in my rhyming words/ and bring you flapping back, old love"—but her litany of incantatory adjectives cannot lose loss, and if she cannot love it, she has learned to live it.

The religious note introduced at the end of *To Bedlam and Part Way Back*, evoked by the death which aligns it with other needs and losses, is even more apparent in her next book, *All My Pretty Ones* (1962). Two of its best-known poems—"For God While Sleeping" and "In the Deep Museum"—are really part of a much larger group that threads through all her collections, on through "The Jesus Papers" in *The Book of Folly* and into "Jesus Walking" in *The Death Notebooks* and the major poems in *The Awful Rowing Toward God*, whose title best describes the project. Though she herself referred to these poems as "mystical," they are more obviously religious since their concerns are always the human intricacies of need and belief, and their context is Sexton's need for belief and her inability to believe as that dilemma interacts with her relationships to herself and others, the dead and dying. This explains too why her religious poetry centers almost exclusively on the person of Jesus, the central figure of belief who himself despaired at the end, who brought love and found none, who gave life and was nailed to a tree. But her relationship to Jesus, as it develops through the books, is an ambivalent one. On the one hand, he serves as a sympathetic emblem of her own experience: "That ragged Christ, that sufferer, performed the greatest act of confession, and I mean with his body. And I try to do that with words." This is the force of the poems in *All My Pretty Ones*. To touch a crucifix—"I touch its tender hips, its dark jawed face,/ its solid neck, its brown sleep"—is to remind herself of poetry's work for salvation:

> My friend, my friend, I was born
> doing reference work in sin, and born
> confessing it. This is what poems are:
> with mercy
> for the greedy,

> they are the tongue's wrangle,
> the world's pottage, the rat's star.
>> ("With Mercy for the Greedy")

The Christ who is "somebody's fault," like the poet, is "hooked to your own weight,/jolting toward death under your nameplate" ("For God While Sleeping"). But at the same time, Sexton is fascinated by another Jesus: "Perhaps it's because he can forgive sins."Like her psychiatrist, Jesus is a man who can take on her guilt, a man who suffers with her and for her. This is the Jesus "In the Deep Museum," where gnawing rats are the "hairy angels who take my gift," as he blesses "this other death": "Far below The Cross, I correct its flaws. Her purest statement of this sense of Christ comes in *The Death Notebooks*, in "Jesus Walking": "To pray, Jesus knew,/is to be a man carrying a man." It is the simplicity of such strength which takes the measure of weaker men in her life, especially her father, whose death brings him into the poetry of *All My Pretty Ones*. . . .

[But her] decisive book, *Live or Die* (1966), announces [important changes.] With its longer poems in open forms which more subtly accommodate a greater range of experience, and with a voice pitched higher to intensify that experience, *Live or Die* represents not a departure from her earlier strengths but the breakthrough into her distinctive style. Perhaps the most immediate aspect of that style is its more extravagant use of imagery:

> I sat all day
> stuffing my heart into a shoe box,
> avoiding the precious window
> as if it were an ugly eye
> through which birds coughed,
> chained to the heaving trees;
> avoiding the wallpaper of the room
> where tongues bloomed over and over,
> bursting from lips like sea flowers. . . .
>> ("Those Times . . .")

This is the sort of imagery that will be even more exploited in later books where "like" becomes the most frequently encountered word. It is a technique that risks arbitrary excesses and embarassing crudities, that at its best can seem but a slangy American equivalent of Apollinaire's surrealism: *Les nuages coulaient comme un flux menstruel.* But it is crucial to remember, with Gaston Bachelard, that "we live images synthetically in their initial complexity, often giving them our unreasoned allegiance." And Sexton's use of images is primarily psychotropic—used less for literary effect than as a means to pry deeper into her psychic history, to float her findings and model her experience. As she said, "The poetry is often more advanced, in terms of my unconscious, than I am. Poetry, after all, milks the unconscious. . . . "Images are the heart of poetry. And this is not tricks. Images come from the unconscious. Imagination and the unconscious are one and the same. . . ."

And if Rimbaud was right to demand of such associative poetry a *"dérèglement de tous les sens,"* it can be seen as Sexton's necessary road of excess through her experiences of madness and the disorientation of her past, so that her metaphors are a method not to display similarities but to discover identities.

Although *Live or Die* shows, for this reason, the influence of her readings in Roethke and Neruda, a more important factor was the new analyst she began seeing while at work on this book. He was more interested in dreams than her earlier doctors had been, and Sexton found herself dealing more directly with her unconscious: "You taught me/to believe in dreams;/ thus I was the dredger" ("Flee on Your Donkey"). Several poems in *Live or Die* are direct dream-songs—"Three Green Windows," "Imitations of Drowning," "Consorting with Angels," "In the Beach House," and "To Lose the Earth." The latent content in these poems—such as the primal scene of "the royal strapping" in "In the Beach House"—is expressive but abandoned to its own independence, unlike more conscious fantasies such as "Menstruation at Forty," in which themes of death and incest are projected onto the imagined birth of a son. The insistence of the unconscious also draws up the poems of her childhood—"Love Song," "Protestant Easter," and especially "Those Times . . .," one of the book's triumphs. Robert Boyers has described *Live or Die* as "a poetry of victimization, in which she is at once victim and tormentor," and "Those Times . . ." torments the poet with her earliest memories of victimization: "being the unwanted, the mistake/that Mother used to keep Father/from his divorce." Her suffering was as silent as her envy of a doll's perfection:

> I did not question the bedtime ritual
> where, on the cold bathroom tiles,
> I was spread out daily
> and examined for flaws.

But her felt exclusion was assumed and rehearsed in a closet's dark escape, where she sat with her hurts and dreams, as later she would sit in madness and poetry:

> I did not know that my life, in the end,
> would run over my mother's like a truck
> and all that would remain
> from the year I was six
> was a small hole in my heart, a deaf spot,
> so that I might hear
> the unsaid more clearly.

The other crucial influence on *Live or Die* is the play she wrote at the time—first titled *Tell Me Your Answer True* and eventually produced in 1969 as *Mercy Street*—sections of which were carried over as poems into *Live or Die* and lend the book its character of psychodrama. Sexton's description of herself during a poetry reading could apply to her presence in this book as well: "I am an actress in my own autobiographical play." The vitality, even the violence, of the book's drama of adaptation recall Emily Dickinson's sly lines:

> Men die—externally—
> It is a truth—of Blood—
> But we—are dying in Drama—
> And Drama—is never dead.

To match the expansive forms and intense imagery of these poems, the voice that speaks them grows more various in its effects, matching a strident aggression or hovering tenderness with the mood and matter evoked. Above all, there is energy, whether of mania or nostalgia. And it is more expressly vocative here, as her cast is introduced separately and her relationship to each is reworked: her father ("And One for My Dame"), mother ("Christmas Eve"), daughters ("Little Girl, My Stringbean, My Lovely Woman," "A Little Uncomplicated Hymn," "Pain for a Daughter"), husband ("And One for My Dame," "Man and Wife," "Your Face on the Dog's Neck"), and Nana ("Crossing the Atlantic," "Walking in Paris"). There is a very conscious sense about these poems of the times since her first book that she has spent with her living and her dead. "A Little Uncomplicated Hymn," for instance, alludes directly to "The Double Image" to catch at a perspective for the interval; the new poem, according to Sexton, was the "attempt to master that experience in light of the new experience of her life and how it might have affected her and how it affects me still; she wasn't just an emblem for me any longer. Every book, every poem, is an attempt to master things that aren't ever quite mastered." And so one watches her recircling her experiences to define and refine her understanding of them. Her parents are written of more sharply, and her regret is less for what she has lost than for what she never had. Her great-aunt's account of her youth in Europe, which structures "Some Foreign Letters," was the motive for Sexton's attempt to retrace in person Nana's journey—"I'd peel your life back to its start"—both to solve the riddle of Other People ("I come back to your youth, my Nana,/ as if I might clean off/ the mad woman you became,/ withered and constipated,/ howling into your own earphone"), and so to solve her own origins ("You are my history (that stealer of children)/ and I have entered you"). But the attempt is not only abandoned, it is impossible, she cannot walk off her history, the past cannot be toured, only endured: where I am is hell. . . .

The demand for release into life, as the title *Live or Die* balances her options, is the counterweight to the measure of death in the book, scaled from suicide attempts ("Wanting to Die," "The Addict") to the deaths of past figures who were part of her—John Holmes ("Somewhere in Africa") and Sylvia Plath ("Sylvia's Death"). "Flee on Your Donkey" struggles with the ambiguous impatience, introducing it first as weariness with "allowing myself the wasted life": "I have come back/ but disorder is not what it was./ I have lost the trick of it!/ the innocence of it!" Her desire for communion—"In this place everyone talks to his own mouth"—reverses her earlier escape inward: "Anne, Anne,/ flee on your donkey,/ flee this sad hotel." And by the time she can write the simple title "Live" over the book's last poem, the "mutilation" that previous poems had struck off is renounced. The evidence of survival is enough: "Even so,/ I kept right on going,/ a sort of human statement" that says finally: "I am not what I expected." If her guilt has not been solved, it has at least been soothed by her acceptance of and by her "dearest three"—her husband and daughters. And if the resolution of "Live" sounds unconvinced, unconvincing, it is because of Sexton's dependence on others, lulling the self into a passive tense.

The survival achieved, the rebirth delivered, is then praised in *Love Poems* (1969), in many ways her weakest collection. . . . The masks she wears in *Love Poems* don't hide Sexton's confessional impulse, they avoid it. Her motive may well have been to search out new voices. Certainly this is the case with her next work, *Transformations* (1971). She began these versions of Grimms' tales on the advice of her daughter after an extended dry spell in her work, and when, five poems later, she had written "Snow White and the Seven Dwarfs," she felt she should continue the experiment into a book which would release a more playful aspect of her personality that her earlier books had neglected. . . .

The book's Ovidian title points to Sexton's first fascination with Grimm—one which Randall Jarrell spoke of in his poem "The Märchen":

> Had you not learned—have we not learned, from tales
> Neither of beasts nor kingdoms nor their Lord,
> But of our own hearts, the realm of death—
> Neither to rule nor die? to change, to change!

The power of fairy tales has always resided in their "changed" dream-landscapes, and Freud discussed them as "screen memories," survivals of persistent human conflicts and desires, narratives whose characters and situations are symbolic of the unconscious dramas in any individual's psyche. With this in mind, the psychoanalytical uses of the word "transformations" bear on Sexton's work. It can refer both to the variations of the same thematic material represented in a patient's dreams of experience and to the process by which unconscious material is brought to consciousness. So too Sexton's poems are variations on themes familiar from her earlier work—at one point she says, "My guilts are what/ we catalogue"—transformed into fantasies or dreams discovered in the Grimm tales, which are anyone's first "literature" and become bound up with the child's psyche. The introductions that precede each story—replacing the analogous moral pointing in the fairy tale—usually isolate her more private concern in each, and the tales which elaborate them include subjects ranging from adultery ("The Little Peasant") to despair ("Rumpelstiltskin") to deception ("Red Riding Hood") to parents' devouring their children ("Hansel and Gretel"). . . .

The fabular impulse behind *Transformations* is resumed in *The Book of Folly* (1972), both in the three short stories included among the poems and in "The Jesus Papers" sequence, which is a taunting, Black-mass transformation of the salvation story. The entire book, in fact, has a summary quality to it. The forged stylization of *Love Poems* returns in "Angels of the Love Affair," six sonnets on love's seasons. The angel in each is the "gull that grows out of my back in the dreams I prefer," and those dreams are hushed, flamboyant, touching memories of certain sheets, bits of dried blood, lemony woodwork, a peace march—all the abstracted details of moments that are warm only in her darknesses. But what is more important is her return to the fully confessional mode:"I struck out memory with an X/ but it came back./ I tied down time with a rope/ but it came back" ("Killing the Spring"). On the simplest level, the detritus of time has clustered new collisions or crises: the death of her sister—"her slim neck/ snapped like a piece of celery" in a car crash—or the national disasters ("The Firebombers," "The Assassin"). Generally, the subjects she recircles are familiar, but her angle of attack and attitude is new: more self-conscious, often more strident and defiant, more searching. . . .

It is [the] sense of what still remains to be lost that occasions [a] tonal shift. In contrast with "You, Dr. Martin" or "Cripples and Other Stories," a new poem to her psychiatrist, "The Doctor of the Heart," is scornfully reductive, resentful of the soothing instead of solving, challenging the doctor with her history and her art:

> But take away my mother's carcinoma
> for I have only one cup of fetus tears.
>
> Take away my father's cerebral hemorrhage
> for I have only a jigger of blood in my hand.
>
> Take away my sister's broken neck
> for I have only my schoolroom ruler for a cure.
>
> Is there such a device for my heart?
> I have only a gimmick called magic fingers.

Whether the mind is too strong or not strong enough to adjust to the violent changes that death forces on us no longer seems to matter to the poem's manic finale:

> I am at the ship's prow.
> I am no longer the suicide
>
> with her raft and paddle.
> Herr Doktor! I'll no longer die
>
> to spite you, you wallowing
> seasick grounded man.

This defiance of death demands, first of all, that the tyranny of her own impulse toward suicide be fully evoked: she must "lie down/ with them and lift my madness/ off like a wig," since "Death is here. There is no/ other settlement" ("Oh"). And for this reason she returns, in "The Other," to what has always terrified her poetry: the alien self she cannot escape, who insanely possesses her and can keep her from the self that makes poems and love and children:

When the child is soothed and resting on the breast
it is my other who swallows Lysol.
When someone kisses someone or flushes the toilet
it is my other who sits in a ball and cries.
My other beats a tin drum in my heart.
My other hangs up laundry as I try to sleep.
My other cries and cries and cries
when I put on a cocktail dress.
It cries when I prick a potato.
It cries when I kiss someone hello.
It cries and cries and cries
until I put on a painted mask
and leer at Jesus in His passion.

As in *Live or Die*, these are the dreams that confront endurance. Reformulated, death and madness, which had once seemed her only innocence, come to the silence she is writing against:

The silence is death.
It comes each day with its shock
to sit on my shoulder, a white bird,
and peck at the black eyes
and the vibrating muscle
of my mouth.

("The Silence")

The *Book of Folly*'s remembrance of things past is likewise more direct when it turns to her family. "Anna Who Was Mad"—Anna, the anagram for the Nana whose namesake Sexton is—alternates interrogative and imperative lines to force the guilt of cause and effect: "Am I some sort of infection?/ Did I make you go insane?" . . .

The book's centering six-poem sequence, "The Death of the Fathers" [is] surely one of Sexton's triumphs, daring in its explorations and revelations, its verse superbly controlled as the voice of each poem is modulated to its experience, now shifting to the declaratives of a child, now heightening to involved regrets and prayers. While watching Sexton trace memories of her father mixed with sexual fantasies, one must recall Freud's sense of the origin of childhood memories:

Quite unlike conscious memories from the time of maturity, they are not fixed at the moment of being experienced and afterwards repeated, but are only elicited at a later age when childhood is already past; in the process they are altered and falsified, and are put into the service of later trends, so that generally speaking they cannot be sharply distinguished from phantasies.

Similarly, since fantasies become memories, it becomes impossible and useless beyond a certain point to distinguish between "events" that happened and fears or desires imagined so strongly that they might as well have happened. And further, Freud writes that the "screen memories" made of childhood traumas "relate to impressions of a sexual and aggressive nature, and no doubt also to early injuries to the ego (narcissistic mortifications). In this connection it should be remarked that such young children make no sharp distinction between sexual and aggressive acts, as they do later."

Sexton's sequence divides naturally into two parts of three poems each, the first set in childhood to evoke her father, and the second set in the present to focus his double death and the "later trends" that have occasioned the fantasies in the first. The opening poem, "Oysters," is her initiation, at once a fantasy of self-begetting and a memory of desire that, once conscious, defeats innocence. She is Daddy's Girl having lunch with her father at a restaurant, and fearfully eats her oysters—"this father-food," his semen. "It was a soft medicine/ that came from the sea into my mouth,/ moist and plump./ I swallowed." Then they laugh through this "death of childhood"— "the child was defeated./ The woman won." The second poem, "How We Danced," continues the fantasy in an Oedipal round:

> The champagne breathed like a skin diver
> and the glasses were crystal and the bride
> and groom gripped each other in sleep
> like nineteen-thirty marathon dancers.
> Mother was a belle and danced with twenty men.
> You danced with me never saying a word.
> Instead the serpent spoke as you held me close.
> The serpent, that mocker, woke up and pressed against me
> like a great god and we bent together
> like two lonely swans.

And the third poem, "The Boat," though it reverts to an earlier time, is a kind of coital coda to her subconscious victory. This time Leda's swan is her godlike captain, out in the same sea from which the oysters came, "out past Cuckold's Light," where "the three of us" ride through a storm that her father masters, but at its height there is the moment which both resolves her fantasies and predicts their destruction, in a memory of violence both sexual and aggressive:

> Now the waves are higher;
> they are round buildings.
> We start to go through them
> and the boat shudders.
> Father is going faster.
> I am wet.
> I am tumbling on my seat
> like a loose kumquat.
> Suddenly
> a wave that we go under.

> Under. Under. Under.
> We are daring the sea.
> We have parted it.
> We are scissors.
> Here in the green room
> the dead are very close.

The second part narrates the death of the fathers. In "Santa," the child's mythic sense of her father is killed: "Father,/ the Santa Claus suit/ you bought from Wolff Fording Theatrical Supplies,/ back before I was born,/ is dead." After describing how her father dressed up her childhood—when "Mother would kiss you/ for she was that tall"—she comes to liquor's reality principle: "The year I ceased to believe in you/ is the year you were drunk." And by the time her father, in turn, dressed up for her own children, the emptiness of having replaced her mother is apparent: "We were conspirators,/ secret actors,/ and I kissed you/ because I was tall enough./ But that is over." "Friends" details another death, as her father is distanced by doubt. The Stranger in her childhood could have been any of the men who would come to steal her from her father, but this family friend is more ominous:

> He was bald as a hump.
> His ears stuck out like teacups
> and his tongue, my God, his tongue,
> like a red worm and when he kissed
> it crawled right in.
>
> Oh Father, Father,
> who was that stranger
> who knew Mother too well?

The question this poem ends on—"Oh God,/ he was a stranger,/ was he not?"—is answered brutally in the last poem, "Begat," a kind of family romance in reverse:

> Today someone else lurks in the wings
> with your dear lines in his mouth
> and your crown on his head.
> Oh Father, Father-sorrow,
> where has time brought us?
>
> Today someone called.
> "Merry Christmas," said the stranger.
> "I am your real father."
> That was a knife.
> That was a grave.

The father she had called hers dies again—the stranger takes "the *you* out of the *me*"—and the poems end with a pathetic elegy on the distance she has come since childhood and the first poem of this sequence, since the understood desire. The end rises to a last regret with the simple details of intimacy's allowances and sadnesses, and the memory of her father dressed as Santa turns as raw as the blood they no longer share, the "two lonely swans" who danced in fantasy are now fired by betrayal and loss:

> Those times I smelled the Vitalis on his pajamas.
> Those times I mussed his curly black hair
> and touched his ten tar-fingers
> and swallowed down his whiskey breath.
> Red. Red. Father, you are blood red.
> Father,
> we are two birds on fire.

The blend of memory and fantasy in "The Death of the Fathers," each sharpening and supporting the effect of the other, is the culmination of Sexton's confessional style. Her next book, *The Death Notebooks* (1974), develops this technique still further. . . .

[Clearly] the most significant and successful poem in *The Death Notebooks* is "Hurry Up Please It's Time," a sort of long, hallucinatory diary-entry: "Today is November 14th, 1972./ I live in Weston, Mass., Middlesex County,/ U.S.A., and it rains steadily/ in the pond like white puppy eyes." The style is pure pastiche, mixing dialect and dialogue, nursery rhymes and New Testament, references ranging from Goethe to Thurber, attitudes veering between arrogance and abasement. At times she is "Anne," at times "Ms. Dog"—becoming her own mock-God. She can sneer at herself ("Middle-class lady,/ you make me smile"), or shiver at what "my heart, that witness" remembers. The recaptured spots of time—say, a quiet summer interlude with her husband and friends—are run into projected blotches spread toward the death to come. And though its expansive free form dilutes all but its cumulative force, the poem is an advance on the way "The Death of the Fathers" had whispered its confessions.

Sexton's two posthumously published collections—*The Awful Rowing Toward God* (1975) and *45 Mercy Street* (1976)—are largely disappointing and anticlimactic, except when isolated poems in either book echo earlier successes. . . . Still, they remain as flawed evidence of Sexton's steady boldness, her readiness to risk new experiments in verse to record renewed perceptions of her experience in life, in the manner Emerson claimed that art is the effort to indemnify ourselves for the wrongs of our condition. There is, as one critic has said of her, "something awesome, even sublime in a woman who is not afraid to sound crude or shrill so long as she is honest, who in her best work sounds neither shrill nor crude precisely because she is honest." Her courage in coming true not only made Sexton one of the most distinctive voices in this generation's literature, and a figure of permanent importance to the development of American poetry, but has revealed in its art and its honesty a life in which we can discover our own.

Adrienne Rich:
A Feminine Tradition

Margaret Homans

Association with nature and exclusion from speaking subjectivity amount to two different ways of placing the woman in dualistic culture on the side of the other and the object. Although the configurations of Mother Nature and Romantic egotism create problems specific to the nineteenth century, and although society and literature have undergone enormous changes since then, our language is still what it was and it continues to create for the woman poet many of the same impediments encountered by nineteenth-century women, if in different forms. Returning these specifically nineteenth-century problems to their context in a general and continuing tradition of the objectification of women, I should like to suggest in this chapter that poetry by women is still and is likely to remain conditioned by its response to various manifestations of masculine authority, and that women poets today might learn from the nineteenth century's range of failed and successful strategies for writing within the same tradition. The women poets then and now must distinguish the advantageous from the detrimental in their inheritance from Eve. Eve as she is read by masculine culture is interchangeable with Mother Nature: the object of men's conversation, beautiful but amoral, the "mother of all living" (Genesis 3:20), and best kept under control and silent. Eve as Dickinson reads her and as she might be read by others is the first human speaker to learn a non-literal language, and therefore the most suitable prototype for poetic subjectivity. Dorothy Wordsworth is a docile daughter of nature, hoping that her docility will make up for the fall; Brontë is like a guilty Eve, repeating over and over a violation of male authority for which she believes the punishment is death; Dickinson celebrates Eve's duplicity, her invention of the art of concealment. To become poets, women must shift from agreeing to see themselves as daughters of

From *Women Writers and Poetic Identity: Dorothy Wordsworth, Emily Brontë, and Emily Dickinson.*
© 1980 by Princeton University Press.

nature and as parts of the world of objects to seeing themselves as daughters of an Eve reclaimed for their poetry.

With the aim of countering the traditional illusions about femininity, the prevailing feminist opinion is that poetry by women must report on the poet's experience as a woman, and that it must be true. Although it is appropriate that readers learn to expand their notions of what constitutes acceptable poetic subject matter—motherhood is as universal and as potentially imaginative an experience as, say, romantic love—this emphasis on truth implies a mistaken, or at least naïve, belief about language's capacity not just for precise mimesis but for literal duplication of experience. [Elsewhere], I cited the use of Muriel Rukeyser's phrase "No more masks!" to call for a feminist poetry that would resolve women's difficult position within a dualistic culture simply be declaring an end to dualism; another anthology's title, *The World Split Open*, refers to the consequence of "one woman's" telling "the truth about her life" in Rukeyser's "Kathë Kollwitz." Whether or not these borrowings represent Rukeyser fairly, they assume that telling the truth without any sort of mask is both possible and desirable. Patriarchal culture may have particularly misused language in its perceptions of women, as feminist arguments maintain, but language is inherently fictive and creates masks whether or not the speaker or writer wishes it. The hope that language can gradually be released from a heritage of untruths about women may not be entirely deluded, but when those lies reinforce and are reinforced by the inherently fictive structure of language, it is chasing phantoms to expect that language will suddenly work for the expression of women's truth. This aim is fundamentally antithetical to the aims of poetry, and doom itself by denying itself the power that poetry genuinely offers.

Dickinson's discovery that to depart from dualistic language is to risk becoming either silent or incomprehensible was prompted by conditions that still prevail. Since her day writers and readers have become even more aware of the way dualism pervades language, in part through semiology, which has made a science of the necessary discrepancy between a word and its referent. Though Dickinson made a private and relatively early revolution in challenging herself and her future readers to imagine alternatives to dualistic thinking, no self-conscious writer today can believe in the goal of a unitary language such as Dickinson's contemporaries could still have imagined. The call for a women's language that, on the model of a single-sex society, would be free of masculine fictions about women is just such an anachronistic dream. A close reading of Dickinson demonstrates that the best course is to embrace and exploit language's inherent fictiveness, rather than to fight against it. Almost nothing would remain after the excision from language of undesirable fictions and the hierarchical structures that support them. Luce Irigaray arrives by way of psychoanalysis at a position quite close to Dickinson's poetic sense of language's limits, a hundred years later, when she says that there may well be woman's language, but that it sounds like babbling; free from dualism, it does not make any of even the rudimentary distinctions upon which ordinary comprehensibility rests. Because the very notion of a sign is based on dualism, the words of this language bear indeterminate and non-repeating relations to their referents, and its syntax, lacking the ordinary relationship between subject and object, excludes logic and any possibility of linear reading. Impracticable as it may be, this projected non-dualistic language is at least more genuinely revolutionary and poetically suggestive than the goal of a feminist literal language in which words and their referents would be exactly determinate—language, furthermore, whose original is Adam's speech.

The naïve wish for a literal language and the belief in poetry's capacity for the duplication of experience foster a conception of the feminine self in poetry that is, paradoxically, even more egotistical than some of the masculine paradigms from which it intends to free itself. In the poetics of "female experience," the poet's own female "I" must be unabashedly present in the poem, in order for the poem to be true. The poet must not hide behind a mask of convention or let her modesty exclude her from the poem altogether. This emphasis on self sounds at first like the answer to Dorothy's evasions of self, or to Brontë's uncertainty about the external sources of her power, as if these impediments to poetry had been removed by twentieth-century women's increasing self-confidence. But when Rich says ". . . I am Adrienne alone" or when Alta names herself in a poem ("my name is Alta. / I am a woman."), that particular, personal "I" differs greatly from the sense of self that underlies much of Romantic poetry. Wordsworth, egotist though he is, does not name himself Wordsworth; "creative soul" and "Poet" are names that enlarge the self, where explicit naming would diminish it. Claiming one's own subjectivity seems, from the example of the nineteenth-century poets, a necessary precondition of writing poetry, but the unmasked and reductive "I" is only a further function of that belief in the literal, that it can be expressed and have literal effects. The new "I" has nothing to do with creative power; its purpose is to make poetry approximate as closely as possible a personal, spoken communication. It will not do simply to perform a poor imitation of the masculine "I" for the sake of asserting equality, because true equality is inconceivable within the conceptual framework of dualism. Dickinson's poems in which the self is composed of two identical, self-regarding parts point to a sense of self that undermines dualism far more effectively than the self-centered, single "I" of feminist poetry.

To place an exclusive valuation on the literal, especially to identify the self as literal, is simply to ratify women's age-old and disadvantageous position as the other and the object. Contemporary poetry by women that takes up this self-defeating strategy risks encounters with death that are destructive both poetically and actually. The current belief in a literal "I" present in poetry is responsible for the popular superstition that Sylvia Plath's death was the purposeful completion of her poetry's project, the assumption being that if the speaker is precisely the same as the biographical Plath, the poetry's self-destructive violence is directed toward Plath herself, not toward an imagined speaker. This reading of Plath is unfair to the woman and, by calling it merely unmediated self-expression, obscures her poetry's real power. In poem after poem depicting or wishing for physical violence, the imagery of violence is part of a symmetrical figurative system, and death is figured as a way of achieving rebirth or some other transcendence. Plath's project may not thus be very different from that of Dickinson, who speaks quite often from beyond the grave, reimagining and repossessing death as her own in order to dispel the terrors of literal death. However, within that figurative system the poet embraces a self-destructive program that must soon have been poetically terminal, even if it did not bring about the actual death. . . .

A mask, however despised by those who call for an end to them in women's poetry, provides for any poet a necessary separation between the self and the poem, just as the knowledge of language's fictiveness, the origin of masks, can mediate between a woman poet and the cultural dictate that women are objects. To embrace a belief in the literal means to embrace death, not death transformed but actual death. Rich's poem "Diving into the Wreck" became for many readers in the early 1970s a manifesto of feminist poetry, because of its androgynous collectivity and because of its polemic about discarding our old myths about the sexes in order to see "the wreck and not the story of the wreck / the thing itself and not the myth." And yet even here, the diver depends on the mask that permits her to see these things under water and that in fact stands between her and death: "my mask is powerful / it pumps my blood with power." The poem thus qualifies its own wish for total revelation, knowing that such qualification is not an evasion but a necessity if the poet is to go on writing. The poem, further, makes its point about discarding myths in the highly figurative framework of a miniature allegory, demonstrating as part of its polemic that the mask that figuration provides is not incompatible with feminist rhetoric. A belief in figuration is life-giving.

The dangerous acceptance of literalization appears also in poems bearing on the idea of the mother, making a point of contact between the [nineteenth-century] poets and their recent inheritors. None of the nineteenth-century poets were themselves mothers, but all the modern poets mentioned here were or are mothers. The nineteenth-century poets could consider motherhood from the removed viewpoints of tradition and of their remembered daughterhoods; even so, the subject was troubling. Whatever difficulties they experienced in relation to the concept of motherhood are multiplied for the women for whom it is not a concept but a consuming reality. Motherhood is literal creativity. It must be difficult for a woman to choose as her vocation poetry or figurative creativity, perhaps to the detriment of the maternal vocation with which she is expected to be contented, because the values associated with motherhood and with poetry are so very different. It may be that developing a poetics of literal truth, however impossible an aim, is the most logical response to this situation, the only poetics that might be expected to compete with motherhood on motherhood's untranslatable terms. When Rich turns her attention to motherhood, she writes in non-fiction prose rather than in verse, explaining, analyzing, and arguing rather than inventing. The term "non-fiction" helps to account for the switch: the subject of motherhood calls forth a desire to avoid fictions and to approximate the truth. Motherhood resists incorporation into the traditional values of poetry.

The entrance of psychoanalytic insights into common language has made it possible for a woman's identity with her mother to be openly accepted and for her struggles with this relationship to become appropriate topics for poetry. Relative to the covert mentions of the mother in works by Dorothy and Brontë, the mother's inhibiting influence is all on the surface in Sexton's poetry, perhaps fulfilling Irigaray's aim to have women reclaim their maternal origins. Yet because motherhood still represents the same group of values and qualities that it represented in the nineteenth century, this greater certainty about identity between mother and daughter does nothing to relieve what was threatening about the suggestions of that identity for Dorothy and Brontë, but instead intensifies it enormously. "I see around me tombstones grey" presents an extreme case of earth as the devouring mother identified with death; the speaker cannot allow herself to imagine transcendence for herself after death, in spite of her dislike for the idea of a final mortality, because of her closing non-ironic acknowledgment that she is identified with that maternal earth. The figure of the mother in Dorothy's "Irregular Verses" ("To Julia Marshall—A Fragment") and the implicit figure of Mother Nature in other poems block her efforts and even her desire to become a poet. These maternal figures seem ominous enough; but compared with Sexton's and Plath's the nineteenth-century image permits at least an illusion of freedom. There is now no possibility of plausibly imagining an alternative transcendence.

Plath's late poem on the mother, "Medusa," uses with even greater intensity the same counterproductive or suicidal strategy that informs the poems about the father: the poem implicates the speaker herself in the attack on the mother, not because she must die in order to get rid of her, as in the case of the father, but because the two women are too much alike. The mother's love is expressed as a grotesque sucking (she is pictured as having tentacles that grasp with suckers) that causes mother and child to exchange places. What the speaker is trying to deny is an identification with her mother that is mediated by the Christian myth of transubstantiation:

> Who do you think you are?
> A communion wafer? Blubbery Mary?
> I shall take no bite of your body.

The refusal to identify with the mother also means a refusal of nourishment, past and present, so that to deny the mother is also to deny the self. The mother is identified with physical properties of motherhood that are seen here horrifically: "Fat and red, a placenta / Paralyzing the kicking lovers," "Bottle in which I live, / Ghastly Vatican"; and although these belong to the mother, the poem's concern with identity between daughter and mother implies the speaker's fear that they are hers too. The final line is ambiguous:

"There is nothing between us" suggests both that the "Old barnacled umbilicus" has been severed and that there is nothing separating them.

Two of Sexton's farewells to her mother, written after her mother's death, endeavor to free themselves of the mother's presence, but both poems are weighted with the tug of origins back to death. The memory of the mother is at least restrictive, often fatal. In "The Division of Parts" the poet as daughter is loaded with guilt at her mother's death, so much so that she cannot "shed my daughterhood," and is haunted in sleep by her mother's image. She is able to shift this burden somewhat, from herself as daughter to the more neutral position of "inheritor" (the occasion of the poem is the division of the mother's property between three sisters) by reducing the mother to an aspect of language. A torrent of words descriptively naming the mother closes with "my Lady of my first words," so that the inheritance is of language; this gift alone can be accepted without guilt. In "The Double Image" the portraits of mother and daughter hang opposite each other, so similar that they seem instead one portrait and its reflection in a mirror. The poet's closing guilty address to her own daughter, "I made you to find me," echoes the implied words of the poet's mother earlier in the poem, "I made you to kill me":

> She turned from me, as if death were catching,
> as if death transferred,
> as if my dying had eaten inside of her.
>
> . . . .
> On the first of September she looked at me
> and said I gave her cancer.
> They carved her sweet hills out
> and still I couldn't answer.

In Plath's "Edge" one of the ways of figuring death is that the "perfected" woman has reincorporated her dead children back into her body. Sexton, making an even more explicit relation between death and maternity, makes pregancy grotesquely the metaphor for her mother's death from cancer:

> That was the winter
> that my mother died,
> half mad on morphine,
> blown up, at last,
> like a pregnant pig.

Later in the same poem she puns on the word "deliver," having it refer both to childbirth and to deliverance from suffering. If her mother gives birth to death, then the poet herself is death's twin. In "The Death Baby" the poet imagines her own babyhood as "an ice baby"; then, exactly repeating her mother, she pictures her death—assumed her to be a voluntary act—as the taking up of the death baby, "my stone child/with still eyes like marbles."

When she holds the death baby, death itself "will be / that final rocking," where rocking also means turning into rock.

"That final rocking:" Adrienne Rich ends *The Dream of a Common Language,* so far her most didactically feminist book, in a highly affirmative mood, with a woman who turns into a rock. "Transcendental Etude" (1977), the book's closing poem, bewilderingly celebrates a number of male visions of femininity that have always restricted women, both humanly and poetically, and yet this celebration is made in the name of a revolutionary feminism. To overturn Freud's views on femininity is the twentieth-century woman's equivalent for the nineteenth century's objections to patriarchal religion, and a poem of a year earlier, "Sibling Mysteries," introduces the grounds for anti-Freudian sentiment with textbook clarity:

> The daughters never were
> true brides of the father
>
> the daughters were to begin with
> brides of the mother
>
> then brides of each other
> under a different law

"Transcendental Etude" enlarges experiential Lesbianism into an aesthetic project, at the same time enacting a program for recovering lost maternal origins. "A whole new poetry" will spring from the identity of self, lover, and mother, through the enlarging and consoling of the self:

> Birth stripped our birthright from us,
> tore us from a woman, from women, from ourselves
> so early on
> and the whole chorus throbbing at our ears
> like midges, told us nothing, nothing
> of origins, . . .
> . . . .
> Only: that it is unnatural,
> the homesickness for a woman, for ourselves,
> for that acute joy at the shadow her head and arms
> cast on a wall, her heavy or slender
> thighs on which we lay, flesh against flesh,
> . . . .
> *This is what she was to me, and this*
> *is how I can love myself—*
> *as only a woman can love me.*

The reader scarcely has a chance to consider whether this love that obliterates difference can be productive poetically, because before going on the poem enacts the promised return to the mother, in a final passage that is ostentatiously old-fashioned both in its imagery and in its import for poetry.

> Vision begins to happen in such a life
> as if a woman quietly walked away
> from the argument and jargon in a room
> and sitting down in the kitchen, began turning in her lap
> bits of yarn, calico and velvet scraps,
> laying them out absently on the scrubbed boards
> in the lamplight, . . .

More little objects, domestic and natural, all with traditional feminine associations, are described for ten further lines. It is implied that the woman is arranging them, but we see only the objects, while she has faded from view. This description is followed by a polemic against the traditional values of art:

> Such a composition has nothing to do with eternity,
> the striving for greatness, brilliance—
> only with the musing of a mind
> one with her body, . . .

The poems in *The Dream of a Common Language* are presumably something more than this and it is misleading for the poet to celebrate such absent musings as a paradigm for poetry, even though the poem keeps on being seductively lovely. The woman is passive and stereotypically lacking in an identity of her own:

> with no mere will to mastery,
> only care for the many-lived, unending
> forms in which she finds herself, . . .

She becomes both a dangerous object and the cure for the wound it inflicts (the traditional types for the woman as whore and as saint), becoming at last (but not finally, the poem suggests)

> the stone foundation, rockshelf further
> forming underneath everything that grows.

This ending may not be literally suicidal, as identity with the mother is for Sexton, but it is poetically terminal. Instead of "a whole new poetry beginning here," as promised, both poem and book end here with a return to the mother, to mothers of the past. Earlier the poem seemed to be proposing to take a detour into the past in order to reincorporate the past into the present, but the return never takes place. What happens in this poem is uncannily like the process of Dorothy's "A Winter's Ramble in Grasmere Vale," even to the point of the similarity of the closing images. Rich's "rockshelf" if uncomfortably close to the beautiful rock Dorothy encounters on a walk originally undertaken, as Rich's poem is, in a spirit of searching for newness; the rock is the emissary from Mother Nature that prevents her from continuing both her search and her poem. (Plath's mother in "Medusa" too may turn her into stone.) Rich's rock is an image of mother as nature, the chthonic feminine object whose existence as the valorized image of womanhood has impeded and continues to impede the ability of women to choose, among many other things, the vocation of poet. The great difference between Dorothy and Rich is that Rich is fully conscious of all the cultural implications of her exhortation, and willfully propounds this image when she could have chosen any other, whereas Dorothy can scarcely see around the impressive bulk of her brother's views. Dorothy has no polemical purpose; Rich knows her language is lovely enough to persuade us that she embraces inarticulateness, and that we should, too. Rich's lovely woman in the lamplight, turning her back on "argument and jargon," is as much a threat to the life of the female mind as Dickinson's Mother Nature, who "Wills Silence—Everywhere—." The poem exhorts a twin impossibility; the literal in a poem, and this sort of woman as poet.

Two earlier poems in the same volume take a different position relative to the literal, and although Rich does not grant them the polemical force of standing last and of announcing themselves as models for a new poetry, they do suggest possibilities for poetry somewhere between total acquiescence to male paradigms of femininity and an unimaginable revolution in language. Like "Transcendental Etude" they look back at tradition, but not only do they avoid the trap of femininst literalism that that poem endorses, they also endeavor to find positive value in tradition. "To a Poet" (1974) is at once a critique of the poetics of the literal and a positive revision of Romantic egotism. Quoting, with significant changes, the first two lines of Keats' sonnet "When I have fears," Rich invites Keats to leave the solitude produced by his fear of mortality ("—then on the shore / Of the wide world I stand alone") and join a collectivity of poets. Gently correcting Keats' sorrowing inwardness, she carries Keats' special capacity for generous sympathy into this poem and beyond the point where Keats took it himself, to an actual address to other poets who might share Keats' own anxieties. Here are Keats' lines:

> When I have fears that I may cease to be
> Before my pen has gleaned my teeming brain

and here is Rich's version:

> *and I have fears that you will cease to be*
> *before your pen has glean'd your teeming brain*

In addition to having Keats turn from addressing himself to addressing someone else, the poet fuses her "I" with his in an even subtler sympathy. The lines come in the middle of an address to a woman poet who is "dragged down" by the confining vocation of impoverished motherhood but for whom poetry is still somehow just possible:

> Language floats at the vanishing-point
> *incarnate*   breathes the fluorescent bulb
> *primary*   states the scarred grain of the floor
> and on the ceiling in torn plaster laughs   *imago*

The grand and abstract poetic language that his woman finds (in the traditional location of the sublime, "the vanishing-point") transcends her circumstances. The speaker then describes a different woman who lives

> where language floats and spins
> *abortion*   in
> the bowl

At the opposite pole from the first woman's chance at a saving transcendence, for this woman word and object are one in a way that fully realizes the worst connotations of the closing of "Transcendental Etude." In a literalization of Keats' metaphor of the fertility of the mind, which he fears to lose, this woman must forgo her literal fertility and, because of this, any mental fertility she might have. This word that literally floats and then vanishes literalizes the transcendent language that figuratively floats at the vanishing-point for the first woman. Could this second woman write at all, she would be able only to repeat in a language close to literal a horrifying "female experience." While the poem corrects Keats in order to direct his and the poet's sympathy toward the suffering woman, it also endorses Keats as a way of correcting the idea of a reductive poetry of female literalism. Keats has already started the imaginative process he seeks when he chooses the word "gleaning" as a figure for writing poetry: layering Keats' poem with her own, Rich reminds us of the powerful transport figuration offers.

"To a Poet" makes its peace with tradition through a high degree of selectivity: Keats' sympathy and relative lack of self-centeredness are exceptional among the Romantics. "Phantasia for Elvira Shatayev" (1974) takes on, in order to revise, a much larger and more difficult portion of tradition. The poem admits and inserts itself into a dualistic system and makes its mark not by undermining it—as in Dickinson's more radical project—but by claiming to meet its challenge—to cross the various boundaries it sets up— through a feminist rhetoric. At the same time, the poem undermines the same literalism that "To a Poet" decries. It at once accepts and stretches beyond its limits the notion of a poetry of female experience: although the poem's pretext is an actual event, the deaths of the members of a women's mountain-climbing team, the experience is utterly unlike what is usually meant by "female experience," and the poem is in any case about transcending experience. The poem escapes the likelihood of its readers confusing its "I" with the author by having an overtly fictive persona, Elvira Shatayev imagined as speaking from beyond her death, but as when the poet fuses her own "I" with Keats' in "To a Poet," titling the poem "Phantasia for . . ." makes it clear that the poet is speaking here too. This layered persona is, furthermore, ready to take up other personae:

> If in this sleep I speak
> it's with a voice no longer personal
> (I want to say   *with voices*)

This collectivizing of the self is central to the poem's revision of Romantic egotism, and to its effort to find an explicitly feminist transcendence. Instead of a poet-hero solitary in his self-consciousness, the poem presents a group, heroic in its mutuality: *"I have never seen / my own forces so taken up and shared / and given back."* The poem solves for itself the nineteenth-century women's fear that poetic power may be located only outside the self: poetic voice and power are here in an everywhere that is not other.

The poem asserts that transcendence need not belong exclusively to the masculine imagination. The poem's setting crowds it with memories of Romantic poetry's strivings after sublimity and of its assertions of imaginative power—Wordsworth's mountain visions in Books VI and XIV of *The Prelude*, Shelley's "Mont Blanc" and Promethean scenarios in Shelley and Byron—and of the Miltonic and Biblical mountains of vision that precede these. But having joined this company, the speaker and her companions, women of power and vision of their own, pass into the universal in a way that is overtly feminist. The poem harmoniously pairs what might be viewed as a traditionally masculine form of transcendence with a new and self-consciously feminist one:

> Every cell's core of heat   pulsed out of us
> into the thin air   of the universe
> the armature of rock beneath these snows
> this mountain   which has taken   the imprint of our minds
> through changes elemental and minute
> as those we underwent
> to bring each other here
> choosing ourselves   each other   and this life
> whose every breath   and grasp   and further foothold
> is somewhere   still enacted   and continuing

The first two lines of this passage represent a literal or physical transcendence of the body in death, which shifts imperceptibly into the major Romantic project of having the mind transcend its boundaries to imprint nature with its power. The last two lines reach another Romantic goal, to transcend the limits of death and find beyond it power and sublimity. Between these two Romantic projects and linking them syntactically is a transcendence of the individual self that identifies itself here and elsewhere as explicitly feminist. Not content simply to find for this feminist transcendence a place alongside them, the poem's extraordinary claim is that these Romantic projects are fulfilled only through it. It holds that the transcendence the Romantics sought was impossible under the conditions of Romantic egotism and is only possible through collectivity. The subordinate clauses that begin in the transitions between the pivotal lines, "changes elemental and minute / as those we underwent" and "this life / whose every breath . . .," cause the first of the Romantic projects to be measured by and the second to be dependent upon the feminist project's achievement; only by first crediting the power of collectivity can the reader then enter into the feeling that neither the mountain nor death create insuperable barriers to consciousness. The passage makes these transcendences occur, and it makes them a totality.

The speaker's grieving husband is portrayed at first as finite and other, somewhat stereotypically and unfairly as women often are portrayed where the self is male. Climbing the mountain to bury her, his boots leave "their geometric bite / colossally embossed" on the snow; compared to the limitless women, he is enclosed in selfhood:

> You come (I know this)   with your love   your loss
> strapped to your body   with your tape-recorder   camera
> ice-pick

He will bury them "in the snow   and in your mind / While my body lies out here." The poem enters into the nineteenth-century problem of the woman dying into nature, but here it is the universe—"the possible," not chthonic nature—of which she has become a part, and death generates speech rather than curtailing it. The husband is put in the position of the male poet who gains his central speaking self from the silent otherness of the women he buries, but unlike Lucy and Margaret, these women cannot be buried in nature, nor can they be silenced:

> When you have buried us   told your story
> ours does not end   we stream
> into the unfinished   the unbegun
> the possible

But this man is engaged in a generous and loving action that atones for the speaker's memory of having "trailed" him on previous climbs when the old relations between the sexes still obtained. Through him, the poet forgives the male poets their limitations and accepts with grace what they have to offer; the poem is beyond anger.

Where "Transcendental Etude" foils its own feminist program by uncritically accepting what amounts to the male paradigm of the woman who merges with nature, "Phantasia" makes stronger claims for its feminism by revising and incorporating another traditional paradigm. Rather than the woman's becoming a rock, "the armature of rock" of the snow-covered mountain takes "the imprint of our minds." To imprint a rock is to re-engage a strategy like Dickinson's, to ask language's difference to reopen an apparent closure. By so beautifully having the dead climber speak, "Phantasia" performs (as do many of Dickinson's poems) one of the highest and most traditional imaginative functions: it calls the dead back to life. Having made outrageous claims for its fiction-making power, the poem closes with a final, powerful act of figuration:

> *What does love mean*
> *what does it mean   "to survive"*
> *A cable of blue fire ropes our bodies*

> *burning together in the snow   We will not live*
> *to settle for less   We have dreamed of this*
> *all of our lives*

Like Dickinson's "long, big shining fibre," this cable of blue fire is both infinitely suggestive, and irreducible and untranslatable. It joins the bodies together simultaneously as it joins them to sublime regions; and it makes the necessity for figuration inseparable from the necessity for collectivity and for transcendence.

"Phantasia for Elvira Shatayev" makes figuration necessary; "Transcendental Etude" ends by trying to make an end to figuration. The woman who becomes a rock begins her figurative life quite neutrally, as a metaphor for the manner in which vision takes place in the new life of women loving women: "Vision begins to happen in such a life / as if a woman quietly walked away . . . ." In other words, the poet can now write poetry that does not engage in abstract preludes to action, but that instead takes action itself. The woman is a figure for vision, or for poetry. But what begins to happen in such a poem is that the figure for vision becomes the vision itself; not only is this how vision occurs, but also this is the sort of vision that occurs. To prove that exhortations are over and that practice has begun, the poem stops using abstract terms like "spirit" and "poetry," and does something very practical: it gives us a concrete image. The image is at once tenor and vehicle, both a figure for vision and the vision itself. This collapse of the usual structure of rhetoric is repeated at the close of the passage, where it is said that the woman becomes the broken glass and the soothing leaf and the rockshelf, rather than, conventionally, that she is like these things. This is an undoing of rhetoric that can never be an undoing of language, in the manner of Dickinson's very different kind of undoing, because what it points toward is an impossible conflation of word and referent, or signifier and signified. This conflation is also the aim of that other tenet of contemporary women's poetry, to speak literally and to be true. A woman, fortunately, can be a rock only in a poem; language's difference saves this poetics from itself.

Sylvia Plath: Enlargement or Derangement?

Barbara Hardy

Passions of hate and horror prevail in the poetry of Sylvia Plath, running strongly counter to the affirmative and life-enhancing quality of most great English poetry, even in this century. We cannot reconcile her despairing and painful protest with the usual ideological demands of Christian, Marxist,and humanist writers,whether nobly and sympathetically eloquent, like Wordsworth, breezily simplified, like Dylan Thomas, or cunning in ethical and psychological argument, like W. H. Auden or F. R. Leavis. Her poetry rejects instead of accepting, despairs instead of glorying, turns its face with steady consistency toward death, not life. But these hating and horrified passions are rooted in love, are rational as well as irrational, lucid as well as bewildered, so humane and honorable that they are constantly enlarged and expanded. We are never enclosed in private sickness here, and if derangement is a feature of the poetry, it works to enlarge and generalize, not to create an enclosure. Moreover, its enlargement works through passionate reasoning, argument, and wit. Its judgment is equal to its genius.

The personal presence in the poetry, though dynamic and shifting, makes itself felt in a full and large sense, in feeling, thinking, and language. In view of certain tendencies to admire or reject her so-called derangement as a revelatory or an enclosed self-exploration, I want to stress this breadth and completeness. The poetry constantly breaks beyond its own personal cries of pain and horror, in ways more sane than mad, enlarging and generalizing the particulars, attaching its maladies to a profoundly moved and moving sense of human ills. Working through a number of individual poems, I should like to describe this poetry as a poetry of enlargement, not derangement. In much of the poetry the derangement is scarcely present, but where it is, it is out-turned, working through reason and love.

From *The Survival of Poetry*, edited by Martin Dodsworth. © 1970 by Barbara Hardy. Faber and Faber, 1970.

I want to begin by looking at a poem from *Ariel* which shows how dangerous it is to talk about the "typical" Sylvia Plath poem, or even the "typical" late poem. I must make it clear that I do not want to rest my case on the occasional presence of life-enhancing poems, but to use one to explain what I mean by imaginative enlargement. "Nick and the Candlestick" (written October 1962) is not only a remarkable poem of love, but that much rarer thing—are there any others?—a fine poem of maternal love. It is a poem which moves toward two high points of feeling, strongly personal and particular, deeply eloquent of maternal feeling, and lucidly open to a Christian mythical enlargement. The first peak comes in the tenth stanza, and can perhaps be identified at its highest point in one word, the endearment "ruby," which is novel, surprising, resonant, and beautiful:

> Remembering, even in sleep,
> Your crossed position.
> The blood blooms clean
>
> In you, ruby.
> The pain
> You wake to is not yours.

The second peak comes at the end, in a strongly transforming conclusion, a climax in the very last line. It comes right out of all that has been happening in the poem but transforms what has gone before, carrying a great weight and responsibility, powerfully charged and completing a process, like an explosion or a blossoming:

> You are the one
> Solid the spaces lean on, envious.
> You are the baby in the barn.

The final enlargement is daring, both in the shock of expansion and in the actual claim it makes. She dares to call her baby Christ and in doing so makes the utmost claim of her personal love, but so that the enlargement does not take us away from this mother, this child, this feeling. This most personally present mother-love moves from the customary hyperbole of endearment in "ruby" to the vast claim. When we look back, when we read again, the whole poem is pushing toward that last line, "You are the baby in the barn." The symbol holds good, though at first invisibly, for the cold, the exposure, the dark, the child, the mother, the protection, and the redemption from share of pain. Each sensuous and emotional step holds for the mother in the poem and for Mary: this is the warmth of the mother nursing her child in the cold night; this is a proud claim for the child's beauty and the mother's tenderness; this is love and praise qualified by pain. Any mother loving her child in a full awareness of the world's horror—especially seeing it and feeling it—vulnerable and momentarily safe in sleep—is reenacting the feeling in the Nativity, has a right to call the child the "baby in the barn."

"Ruby" is a flash of strong feeling. It treasures, values, praises, admires, measures, contemplates, compares, rewards. Its full stretch of passion is only apparent when the whole poem is read, but even on first encounter it makes a powerful moment, and strikes us as thoroughly formed and justified at that stage. Like every part of the poem, even the less urgent-sounding ones, it refers backward and forward, and has also continuity not only within the poem but with larger traditions of amorous and religious language, in medieval poetry (especially *The Pearl*), in the Bible, in Hopkins. The fusion of the new and the old is moving. This baby has to be newly named, like every baby, and has its christening in a poem, which bestows a unique name, in creative energy, as ordinary christening cannot, but with something too of the ritual sense of an old and common feeling. Sylvia Plath is a master of timing and placing, and the naming endearment comes after the physically live sense of the sleeping child, in the cold air, in the candlelight, in its healthy color. The mildly touched Christian reference in "crossed position" prepares for the poem's future. Its gentleness contrasts strongly, by the way, with the violence of very similar puns in Dylan Thomas, and confirms my general feeling that Sylvia Plath is one of the very few poets to assimilate Thomas without injury, in an entirely benign influence. Her sensuous precision is miles away from Thomas: "ruby" is established by the observation, "The blood blooms clean/In you," and the comparison works absolutely, within the poem, though it has an especially poignant interest when we think of the usual aggressiveness and disturbance of redness in her other poems, where the blooming red of tulips or poppies are exhausting life-demands, associated with the pain of red wounds, or the heavy urgency of a surviving beating heart. Here it is a beloved color, because it is the child's, so in fact there is a constancy of symbolism, if we are interested. "Clean," like "crossed" and "ruby" has the same perfectly balanced attachment to the particularity of the situation—this mother, this baby—and to the Christian extension. "The pain / You wake to is not yours" works in the same way, pointing out and in, though the words "out" and "in" do less than justice to the fusion here.

The perfected fusion is the more remarkable for being worked out in a various tone, which includes joking. Like the medieval church, or the Nativity play, it can be irreverent, can make jokes about what it holds sacred, is sufficiently inclusive and sufficiently certain. So we are carried from the fanciful rueful joke about "A piranha/Religion, drinking//Its first communion out of my live toes" to the final awe. Or from the casual profane protest, "Christ! they are panes of ice" to the crossed position, the pain not his, the baby in the barn. An ancient and audacious range.

If this is a love poem, it is one which exists in the context of the other *Ariel* poems, keeping a sense of terrors as well as glories, in imagery which is vast and vague: "the stars/Plummet to their dark address"; and topically precise and scientific: "the mercuric/Atoms that cripple drip/Into the terrible well." It is a poisoned world that nourishes and threatens that clean blood. Perhaps only a child can present an image of the uncontaminated body, as well as soul, and there is also present the sense of a mother's fear of physical contamination. The mercuric atoms are presumably a reference to the organo-mercury compounds used in agriculture, and the well seems to be a real well.

The poet loves and praises, but in no innocent or ideal glorying. This is a cold air in which the candle burns blue before yellow, nearly goes out, reminds us of the radiance in so many paintings of Mother and Child, but also of a real cold night, and of the miner's cold, his dark, his cave, his nightwork, his poisoned breathing. The intimacies and protections and colors are particular too: "roses," "the last of Victoriana," "soft rugs." The expansion moves firmly into and out of a twentieth-century world, a medieval poetry, ritual, and painting, and the earliest Christ-story, and this holds for its pains and its loving. It moves from light to dark, from love to fear. It moves beyond the images of mother-love, indeed begins outside in the first line's serious wit, "I am a miner." It uses—or, better, feels for—the myth of Redemption not in order to idealize the particulars but rather to revise and qualify the myth, to transplant it again cheerfully, to praise only after a long hard look at the worst. The love and faith and praise are there, wrung out and achieved against the grain, against the odds. She said of the poem, in a BBC broadcast: "A mother nurses her baby son by candlelight and finds in him a beauty which, while it may not ward off the world's ill, does redeem her share of it."

True, it is not typical. There are two other very loving poems of maternal feeling, "Riddle" and "You're," happy peals of conceits, but nothing else moves so, between these two extremities of love and pain, striking spark from such poles. "Nick and the Candlestick" is not proffered as an instance of togetherness, but as a lucid model of the enlargement I want to discuss.

At the heart of her poetry lies the comment that she herself made about this enlargement:

> I think my poems come immediately out of the sensuous and emotional experiences I have, but I must say I cannot sympathize with these cries from the heart that are informed by nothing except a needle or a knife or whatever it is. I believe that one should be able to control and manipulate experiences, even the most terrifying— like madness, being tortured, this kind of experience—and one should be able to manipulate theses experiences with an informed and intelligent mind. I think that personal experience shouldn't be a kind of shut-box and mirror-looking narcissistic experience. I believe it should be generally relevant, to such things as Hiroshima and Dachau, and so on.

A mere explicit statement that the poet believes personal experience of pain should not be a mirror or a shut box but should be relevant to Hiroshima and Dachau is plainly not an answer to the question of appropriateness. Nor would a mere listing of such references do much: the intelligent poet can after all attempt but fail to break open the shut box, may impose intellectually schematic associations with the larger world. Alain Resnais in *Hiroshima Mon Amour* seems to be open to the charge of using the larger pain of atomic war to illuminate his personal center, so that the movement is not that of enlargement but of diminution. Something similar seems to happen in a good many Victorian attempts to enlarge the personal problem, to combine the personal and social pain, and we may well object that the endings of *Bleak House* and *Crime and Punishment* are unsuccessful attempts to solve the large pain by the lesser reconciliation. I have spent what may seem an excessive time on "Nick and the Candlestick" in order to establish not so much a typical feeling, but a form: the particularity and the generalization run together in equal balance, asking questions of each other, eroding each other, unifying in true imaginative modification. I want to suggest that this is the mode of Sylvia Plath's major poetry, and that it succeeds exactly where Resnais failed. But it should be said, perhaps, that this problem of combination or enlargement works in a special way, involving artists working from experience of personal pain, depression, despair. The optimist, like Dickens and Dostoevsky, may well find it easy to join his larger pain and his smaller triumph. For the tragic artist like Sylvia Plath it is more the problem of competitive pains: how to dwell in and on the knives and needles of the personal life without shutting off the knives and needles in Biafra, Vietnam, Dachau, and Hiroshima. It is almost a problem of competing sensibilities, and the tragic artist's temptation in our time is probably to combine indecorously, like Resnais, to make the Hiroshima a metaphor for an adultery, to move from outer to inner and confirm an especially terrible shut box.

Before I move from "Nick and the Candlestick" to the more terrible fusions elsewhere in *Ariel*, I want to look at some of the earlier attempts in *The Colossus* (1960). Many of the poems here show a fairly familiar and conventional tension and control. In some poems there is a narrow sensuous or social image of something painful, something dying: the dryness, unpleasant fruition, hard and yellow starlight, and difficult "borning" of "The Manor Garden" have nothing to say for nature; the inhuman boom and monotony of "Night Shift" show men reduced to tend the machine; "Hardcastle Crags" defeats the walker's energy by massive indifference and hard labor. Such poems accumulate the sense of unreward, ugliness, labor, repulsion, hostility, but each makes only its individual assertion, proffering no generalization.

In another group of poems in this volume, there is an attempt to break up such hardness, though scarcely to redeem or transform. Such poems as "Two Views of a Cadaver Room," "Watercolor of Grantchester Meadows," "The Eye-mote," or "Black Rook in Rainy Weather" show a darkening, rather than a darkened, vision. Affirmation is there, is valued, but is unstable. The destructive eye-mote is there for good, enlarged and confirmed as more than temporary by the move towards Oedipus, so we know that the sight cannot return, that the "Horses fluent in the wind" are gone. In "Black Rook in Rainy Weather" the poem sets out a belief in meaningful experience, but the belief rocks unsteadily, the experience is erratic and unguaranteed, can only bring "A brief respite from fear/Of total neutrality." The vigor of the meaningful moment is certainly there, "hauling up eyelids," but in most of these poems that weight gain against loss, there is less vigor, or a final movement toward the loss. "Black Rook" ends with the naming of the spasmodic trick, the random rare descent, but "The Eye-mote" moves more characteristically away from the balance between easy fluid harmony, and the pained, blurred distorted vision, to tip the scales. We move over into blindness, guilt, loss of more than a small beauty. "Watercolor of Grantchester Meadows" has a dark landscape, uses the spring idyll ambiguously, and sharpens one point to drive it hard against our senses and sense. It creates a swimmy swoony dream of spring, water, love, in the impressionist blurring and the little nursery-plate brightness, to build a bridge from the world of (superficial) sweetness to destructiveness. In "Two Views of a Cadaver Room" the movement from death to love is deceptive: the poem allows only a tiny ambiguous space for "the little country" where the lovers can be "blind to the carrion army." No redeeming corner, this, because "Foolish, delicate" and "not for long," stalled only "in paint," and responding in true Brueghel disproportionateness to the earlier apparent redemption, in the first half of the poem, where after the dissection, "He hands her a cut-out heart like a cracked heirloom." All these poems, with the possible exception of "Black Rook," fall out of love with the world of love, yearn for it but know what they are up against. They share a certain static quality: the pastoral term, for instance, in the Grantchester poem, is decorously but very carefully planning its own erosion, right from the start, and the poet's stance seems to be well outside the poem. Even in "The Eye-mote," where there is an expansion into the Oedipus myth, it is told rather than enacted: "I dream that I am Oedipus." Though "the brooch-pin and the salve" effectively revise the splinter and the eyebath, they do so by a movement of literary reference, very different from the total resonance in "Nick" where the poem is plainly gathering its strengths and meanings, like all the best art, from conscious and unconscious assembling. The brilliant stroke of wit in "Before the brooch-pin and the salve/Fixed me in this parenthesis" is perhaps a limited one: the pun is dazzling in the light of the Oedipal situation, and plainly relates to all those other poems about parent relationships. But after a little reflection one begins to wonder if "parenthesis" is quite the best word, after all, for either the Oedipal blindness or a loss of innocence. A spurt of wit remains on the superficial level. As a pun, it is not quite up to Mercutio's or Lady Macbeth's.

Ted Hughes tells us that the personality of Oedipus and others were important persons in her life, but he is right to say that in this poem, and elsewhere, they may seem literary. It is not a matter of artificiality but of a certain thinness of feeling: the enlargement does not quite come off. Similarly, in the Grantchester poem, which strikes me perhaps as a subdued answer to Dylan Thomas's "Sir John's Hill" (just as "Nick" seems like a subdued answer to Hopkins's "The Starlight Night"), the movement from the human situation to the animal world seems relaxed, cool, insufficiently felt—or rather, felt to be felt in the poem. Her feelings for Greek tragedy and animal life were evidently far from thinly literary, but in some of these poems they were not yet getting sufficiently incorporated and expressed.

There are a number of poems in *The Colossus*, however, where a different stance and structure achieves something much more imaginatively substantial: "Lorelei," "All the Dead Dears," "Suicide off Egg Rock," "Full Fathom Five," "Medallion," "The Burnt-out Spa," and "Mussel Hunter at Rock Harbor" are most impressive poems of a dying fall. Each moves slowly and lucidly into a death or a longing for a death or a blessing of death. They are, if you like, perverse love poems. Instead of working by the usual kind of enlargement, from the personal to the larger world, they attempt an empathetic drama, where a kind of death is explored, imagined, justified. If I list the last lines, a common quality in the conclusions can be my starting point:

> Stone, stone, ferry me down there.
> ("Lorelei")

> Deadlocked with them, taking root as cradles rock.
> ("All the Dead Dears")

> The forgetful surf creaming on those ledges.
> ("Suicide off Egg Rock")

> I would breathe water.
> ("Full Fathom Five")

> The yardman's/Flung brick perfected his laugh.
> ("Medallion")

> The stream that hustles us

> Neither nourishes nor heals.
> ("The Burnt-out Spa")

> this relic saved/Face, to face the bald-faced sun.
> ("Mussel Hunter at Rock Harbor")

Each poem is dramatized, individualized. Each constructs a different feeling for death. These conclusions, which all settle for death, are earned in separate and solidly substantial ways, emotionally intense and rationally argued, each working through a distinct human experience which ends by wanting death.

In "Lorelei" it is the peace of death that lures, which is why the sirens' song and their silence are both maddening. The sense of "maddening" is both superficial and profound, for the listener knows that what the sirens offer is illusion, cannot be a solicitation except in nightmare or when "deranged by harmony." The images are fully responsive: "descant from borders/Of hebetude, from the ledge//Also of high windows" and "Drunkenness of the great depths"; and "your ice-hearted calling." It is the earlier "Sisters, your song/Bears a burden too weighty/For the whorled ear's listening" that earns the sense of inevitability in the final weight of "Stone, stone."

The same can be said of all the other poems in this group. Each makes its individual movement to death, each is a dying. In "All the Dead Dears" death is repulsive, but none the less urgent for that. The dead pull us, willy-nilly, into our graves and the three skeletons in the Archaeological Museum are suitably and grotesquely "unmasked" and "dry" witnesses to life's (death's?) eating game. The poem moves step by step from the first instance, from the stranger-in-blood to the sense of ancestral pull, to the father's death, through the family feasts, into a coffin as inevitable as a cradle. The whole poem takes color from the first grotesque image, so that her father's death (of course a recurring image) is seen in the right bizarre fashion: "Where the daft father went down/With orange duckfeet winnowing his hair," and the right, though typically very mild (it strengthens terribly once we see through it, though, this mildness) sense of the animal and human, and the live and dead, overlapping. The final Gulliver image completes the grotesque line and the imagery of a trap.

The image of clarity and cleanness at the end of "Suicide off Egg Rock" finishes off the man who walks away from the debris of the beach and the muck of living—"that landscape/Of imperfections his bowels were part of." Each poem is a separate dying, thoroughly imagined. The apparently stoical image of the crab's face at the end of that very fine poem "Mussel Hunter at Rock Harbor" may look like an emblem proffered to the human world by the animals, but must take on the color of all that goes before. It is only a crab-face saved, a crab death, a scrupulous rejection of symbol made at the end of a poem that has slowly forced the human being to feel itself reduced in and by the seabeast world. The terrible "Full Fathom Five" creates an oceanic image with human features, and the real drowned father colors the terror and makes possible a childlike plea for water rather than thick and murderous air. "The Burnt-out Spa" establishes, rather like "Suicide off Egg Rock," a rubbishy land in contrast to a pure water, and this is reinforced in the final yearning for the purified human reflection: "It is not I, it is not I, it is not I," whose sad wail is explained by all that has gone before.

These are individuated dramas of dying. The obsession is evident: the poetic flexibility, the inventive enlargements, and the self-explanatory structures show the control and the unenclosed sensibility. The actual mythological or literary symbols are part of such enlargement: the Lorelei, the drowned father in Ariel's song, the museum skeletons, Gulliver, the Oriental crab-face are all part of a dense formation of feeling, not tenuous-seeming annexes, like the Oedipus of "The Eye-mote." It is such density that may take them to the verge of allegory, but keeps them substantially on its right side. Like much good poetry, it is tempted to be allegory, but refuses.

Moving to the *Ariel* poems, one recognizes that such inventiveness has become more powerful, and sometimes less lucid. In a poem of pain and delirium, "Fever 103°," the wildness and fast movement of the conceits are excused by the feverishness they dramatize. They cover a wide range. They jerk from Isadora's scarves to Hiroshima ash to lemon water and chicken water; from the bizarre conceit to the simple groping, "whatever these pink things are"; glimpses of horrors to lucidity, self-description, affectionateness, childishness: the range and the confusion establish the state of sickness. There are the other well-known poems of sickness, "Tulips," "In Plaster," and "Paralytic," which dramatize individual, and different, sick states, all of them appropriately formed, in process and style. Each of these four poems is personal (which is not to say that the persona is not imaginary: in "In Plaster" and "Paralytic" it seems to be so, judging from external and internal evidence) but each is a complete and controlled drama of sick mind and body. Because it is sickness that is overtly dramatized, there is no sense of an improperly won competition with the world's ills. They are brought in, by a species of decorous hallucinations. But the plainness of the act of hallucination, the lucid proffering of a febrile, convalescent, enclosed or paralyzed state, allows the larger world to make its presence properly felt. The burning in "Fever 103°" reminds us of atomic ash, while keeping the separation clear. The plaster cast in "In Plaster" reminds us of the other imprisonments and near-successful relationships: "I used to think we might make a go of it together—/After all, it was a kind of marriage, being so close." This is not an allegory about marriage: these poems of sickness allow her to suggest a whole number of identifications which move toward and back from allegory. This is not a sick poem but a poem about being sick. Quite different. Of course it is a sick person who is drawn to poems about sickness, but the physical sickness makes up actual chunks of her existence, and sometimes the poems are about chilblains, cuts, influenza, and appendicitis. She is drawn to sickness, mutilation, attacks, and dying, but each poem is a controlled and dynamic image with windows, not a lining of mirrors. In "Fever 103°" and "In Plaster" the dramatized act of hallucination holds the personal and the social in stable and substantial mutual relationships, neither absorbing the other.

In "Tulips," there is a slow, reluctant acceptance of the tulips, which means a slow, reluctant acceptance of a return to life. The poem dramatizes a sick state, making it clear that it is sickness. The flowers are hateful, as emblems of cruel spring, as presents from the healthy world that wants her back, as suspect, like all presents. They are also emblems of irrational fear: science is brilliantly misused (as indeed in feeble and deranged states of many kinds) and phototropism and photosynthesis are used to argue the fear: the flowers really do move toward the light, do open out, do take up oxygen. The tulips are also inhabitants of the bizarre world of private irrational fantasy, even beyond the bridge of distorted science: they contrast with the whiteness of nullity and death, are like a baby, an African cat, are like her wound (a real red physical wound, stitched so as to heal, not to gape like opened tulips) and, finally, like her heart. The end of the poem is transforming, opens up the poem. The poem, like the tulips, has really been opening from the beginning, but all is not plain until the end, as in "Nick." Moreover, in the end the tulips win, and that is the point. It is a painful victory for life. We move from the verge of hallucination, which can hear them as noisy, or see them as dangerous animals, to a proper rationality, which accepts recovery. The poems hinges on this paradox: while most scientific, it is most deranged; while most surreal, it is most healthy:

> And I am aware of my heart: it opens and closes
> Its bowl of red blooms out of sheer love of me.
> The water I taste is warm and salt, like the sea,
> And comes from a country far away as health.

It is the country she has to return to, reluctant though she is: the identification of the breathing, opened, red, springlike tulips with her heart makes this plain. She wanted death, certainly, as one may want it in illness or, moving back from the poem to the other poems and to her real death, as she wanted it in life. But the poem enacts the movement from the peace and purity of anaesthesia and feebleness to the calls of life. Once more, the controlled conceits; and the movement from one state to another creates expansion. The poem opens out to our experience of sickness and health, to the overwhelming demands of love, which we sometimes have to meet. The symbolism of present giving and spring flowers makes a bridge from a personal death-longing to common experience: something very similar can be found in the short poem "Poppies in October" which uses a similar symbolism and situation for a different conclusion and feeling; and in the magnificent bee poems, where the solid facts and documentations of bee-keeping act as a symbolic base for irrational and frightening fantasy *and* as a bridge into the everyday and ordinary explanations and existences.

The concept of explicit hallucination seems useful. In the bee poems we move away from the poetry of sickness to another kind of rejected allegory. These poems stress technical mysteries. The craft and ritual of beekeeping are described with a Kafkaesque suggestiveness, and can take off into a larger terror and come back after all into the common and solid world. In "The Bee Meeting," her lack of protective clothing, her feeling of being an outsider, then an initiate, the account of the disguised villagers and the final removal of disguise, the queen bee, the spiky gorse, the box—all are literal facts which suggest paranoiac images but remain literal facts. The poem constantly moves between the two poles of actuality and symbolic dimension, right up to and including the end. A related poem, "The Arrival of the Bee Box," works in the same way, but instead of suggesting paranoiac fear and victimization, puts the beekeeper into an unstable allegorical God-position. The casual slangy "but my god" unobtrusively works toward the religious enlargement:

> I am no source of honey
> So why should they turn on me?
> Tomorrow I will be sweet God, I will set them free.
>
> The box is only temporary.

After the suggestiveness comes the last line, belonging more to the literal beekeeping facts, but pulled at least briefly into the symbolic orbit. These are poems of fear, a fear which seems mysterious, too large for its occasion. They allow for a sinister question to raise itself, between the interpretation and the substance. The enlargement which is inseparable from this derangement is morally vital and viable: these poems are about power and fear, killing and living, and the ordinariness and the factual detail work both to reassure us and to establish that most sinister of fears, the fear of the familiar world. Perhaps the most powerful bee poem is "The Swarm." Here the enlargement is total and constant, for the poem equates the destruction of the swarm with a Napoleonic attack, and presents a familiar argument for offensive action: "They would have killed *me*." It presents two objective correlatives, the bees and Napoleon, in an unfailing grim humor:

> Stings big as drawing pins!
> It seems bees have a notion of honor,
> A black, intractable mind.
> Napoleon is pleased, he is pleased with everything.
> O Europe! O ton of honey!

The humor comes out of the very act of derangement: imagine comparing this with that, just imagine. It depends on the same kind of rationally alert intelligence that controls "Fever 103°."

It is present in the great *Ariel* poems: "Lady Lazarus," "Daddy," "Death & Co.," "A Birthday Present," and "The Applicant," which are very outgoing, very deranged, very enlarged. In "Lady Lazarus" the persona is split, and deranged. The split allows the poem to peel off the personal, to impersonate suicidal feeling and generalize it. It is a skill, it is a show, something to look at. The poem seems to be admitting the exhibitionism of suicide (and death poetry?) as well as the voyeurism of spectators (and readers?). It is also a foul resurrection, stinking of death. This image allows her to horrify us, to complain of being revived, to attack God and confuse him with a doctor, any doctor (bringing round a suicide) and a Doktor in a concentration camp, experimenting in life and death. It moves from Herr Doktor to Herr Enemy and to miracle makers, scientists, the torturer who may be a scientist, to Christ, Herr God, and Herr Lucifer (the last two after all collaborated in experiments on Adam, Eve, and Job). They poke and nose around in the ashes, and this is the last indignity, forcing the final threat: "I eat men like air." It is a threat that can intelligibly be made by martyred victims (she has red hair, is Jewish), by phoenixes, by fire, by women. The fusion and dispersal, once more rational and irrational, makes the pattern of controlled derangement, creating not one mirror but a hall of mirrors, all differently distorting, and revealing many horrors. Such complexity of reference, such enactment of desperation, hysteria and hate, permits at times the utterly bare cry, like the endearment in "Nick": "I turn and burn." Again, the range of tone is considerable. There is the dry irony, only capable of life in such surroundings of hysteria: "Do not think I underestimate your great concern," and the slangy humor, "I guess you could say I've a call," which, like the communion tablet in "Tulips" is an antireligious joke, not a solemn allusion, though you do not see the joke unless you feel the solemnity. There is the sensuous particularity, extremely unpleasant. It is tactual, visual, and olfactory: "Pick the worms off me like sticky pearls," "full set of teeth" and "sour breath." The sheer active hostility of the poem works through the constant shift from one mode to another, one tone to another, one persona to another. It races violently and spasmodically toward the climax.

This kind of structural derangement of structure, which allows for collision, a complex expansion, and a turn in several directions, sometimes becomes very surrealist in dislocation. It fragments into opaque parts, as in that most baffling poem, "The Couriers," and in "The Applicant." We might be tempted to see the enlargement in "The Applicant" as an allegory of marriage, relationship, dependence, were it not for the violent twist with which the poem shuffles off such suggestion:

> First, are you our sort of a person?
> Do you wear
> A glass eye, false teeth or a crutch,
> A brace or a hook,
> Rubber breasts or a rubber crotch,
>
> Switches to show something's missing? No, no? Then
> How can we give you a thing?
> Stop crying.
> Open your hand.
> Empty? Empty. Here is a hand
>
> To fill it and willing
> To bring teacups and roll away headaches
> And do whatever you tell it.
> Will you marry it?
> It is guaranteed
>
> To thumb shut your eyes at the end
> And dissolve of sorrow.
> We make new stock from the salt.
> I notice you are stark naked.
> How about this suit—
>
> Black and stiff, but not a bad fit.
> Will you marry it?
> It is waterproof, shatterproof, proof
> Against fire and bombs through the roof.
> Believe me, they'll bury you in it.

The hand to fill the empty hand and shut the eyes, or (later) the naked doll that can sew, cook, talk, move toward this allegory, but the black stiff suit "waterproof, shatterproof" in which "they'll bury you" moves away toward any kind of panacea or protection. What holds the poem together, controlling such opacities of derangement, is the violent statement of deficiency hurled out in the first stanza, and the whole violent imitation of the language of salesmanship, the brisk patter of question, observation, suggestion, and recommendation. The enlargement works not just through the ill-assembled fragments—hand, suit, and in the later stanza, doll—but through the satirized speech, which relates needs, deficiencies, dependence, and stupid panaceas to the larger world. Life (or love) speaks in the cheap-jack voice, as well it may, considering what it may seem to have to offer. This is an applicant not just for relationship, for marriage, for love, for healing, but for life and death.

This brilliant linguistic impersonation works more generally in these poems, as a source of black humor, as satiric enlargement, as a link with ordinariness, as unselfpitying speech. It is present in small doses but with large effect in the massive, rushing, terrible poem, "Getting There." Here the death train is also the painful dying, the dragging life, also wars, machines, labor. The poem questions, and the questions stagger: "How far is it? / How far is it now?" It dwells painfully and slowly in the present tense: "I am dragging my body," "And now detonations," "The train is dragging itself." Its derangements present animals and machines in a mangling confusion: the interior of the wheels is "a gorrila interior," the wheels eat, the machines are brains and muzzles, the train breathes, has teeth, drags and screams like an animal. There is a painful sense of the body's involvement in the machine, the body made to be a wheel. The image creates an entanglement, involves what Sartre calls the "dilapidation" of surrealism. There is the horror of a hybrid monster, a surrealist crossing of animal with machine. The rational arguments and logical connections are frightening in their precision. The wheel and the gorilla's face can be confused into one image, big, round, dark, powerful. Krupp's "brains" is almost literally correct. The train noise can sound like a human scream, the front of a train can look like a face.

The method of combination as well as the content, as in all good poetry, generates the passions. The sense of strain, of hallucination, of doing violence to the human imagery is a consequence of the derangements. The rational excuses simply play into the hands of such sense of strain, by making it work visually, bringing it close, giving it substance and connection with the real European world. The movement is a double one, it creates a trope and a form for unbearable pain, and intolerable need for release. It enlarges the personal horror and suggests a social context and interpretation, in Krupp, in the train, in Russia, in the marvelously true and fatigued "some war or other," in the nurses, men, hospital, in Adam's side and the woman's body "Mourned by religious figures, by garlanded children." And finally, in Lethe. Its end and climax is as good as that in "Nick":

> And I, stepping from this skin
> Of old bandages, boredoms, old faces
>
> Step to you from the black car of Lethe,
> Pure as a baby.

There is the naked appearance of the myth new made, the feeling that Lethe has had to wait till now to be truly explained, as the Nativity had to wait for "Nick." After such pain of living and dying, after so many bewildered identifications, after such pressure and grotesque confusion, we must step right out of the skin. And when we do, the action reflects back, and the body seems to have been the train. This adds another extension of the derangement of human, animal, and mechanical. After this, only Lethe. The poem then begins to look like a nightmare of dying, the beginning of forgetting, the lurching derangements working as they do in dreams.

Once more, the expansion permits the naked cry. This happens more quietly and sadly in "The Moon and the Yew Tree" where the movement outward is against the Christian myth, but works so as to generalize, to show the active seeking mind in the exercise of knowledge and comparison. This movement explains, permits, and holds up the bare, dreadful admission, "I simply cannot see where there is to get to." The feeling throughout is one of deep and tried depression. The moon is no light, no door:

> It is a face in its own right,
> White as a knuckle and terribly upset.

The oddity and childishness of the funny little analogy and the simple bare statement "terribly upset" all contribute to the tiredness. So does the science of "drags the sea after it like a dark crime" and the conceit "the O-gape of complete despair," which have a slight archness and flickering humor, like someone very tired and wretched who tries to smile. Nature is all too simply interpreted, colored by "the light of the mind," is cold, planetary, black, blue. The moon is quite separate from the consolations of religion, though there are echoes of other myths which emphasize this, of Hecate and witchcraft, as in "The Disquieting Muses." Such sinister suggestions, like the remote and decorative images of the saints, "all blue,/Floating on their delicate feet over the cold pews,/Their hands and faces stiff with holiness" are made in a matter-of-fact, slightly arch way. These are Stanley Spencer-like visions, made in a childish, tired voice: "The moon is my mother. She is not sweet like Mary./Her blue garments unloose small bats and owls." The very quietness, compared with her more violent poems of fear, has its own stamp of acceptance. The several bald statements in the poem belong to the quiet, tired prevailing tone: "How I would like to believe in tenderness" and "the message of the yew tree is blackness—blackness and silence."

The poem of deep depression still enlarges, still knows about the larger world, still tries a tired but personal humor:

> Eight great tongues affirming the Resurrection.
> At the end, they soberly bong out their names.

The poem's empathy is powerful, but it is perhaps most powerful when it is dropped. The end returns to the explicit act of interpretation—what do the moon and the yew tree mean?—of the beginning. The poem moves heavily into the meditation, then out of it. There has been an attempt at enlargement, but the colors here are the colors of the mind, and the attempts at mythical explanation or extension all fail. It seems like a poem about making the effort to write out of depression, where the act of enlargement is difficult, the distance that can be covered is short.

In "A Birthday Present" the same process shapes a different passion. The enlargement in this poem is again a movement toward Christian myth, this time a perverted annunciation. The poem longs for release, like so many others, but in its individual mood. This time she pleads and reasons carefully, patiently, with humility, is willing to take a long time over it. The pace of her poems varies tremendously, and while "Daddy," "Lady Lazarus," and "Getting There" move with sickening speed, "A Birthday Present" is appallingly slow. Its slowness is right for its patience and its feeling of painful burden. It is created by the pleas, "Let it not . . . Let it not," and the repetitions which here put the brakes on, though in other poems they can act as accelerators. Its questioning slows up, and so does its vagueness, and its unwillingness to argue endlessly—or almost endlessly. The humilities are piteously dramatized: "I would not mind," "I do not want much of a present," "Can you not," "If you only knew," "only you can give it to me," "Let it not." There is the childishness, horrifying in the solemn pleasure of "there would be a birthday." From time to time there is the full, adult, knowing, reasoning voice, that can diagnose: "I know why you will not"; reassure: "Do not be afraid"; and be ironic: "O adding machine—/Is it impossible for you to let something go and have it whole?/Must you stamp each piece in purple."

It is not surprising that Sylvia Plath felt constrained to speak these late poems: they are dramatized, voiced, often opaque but always personalized. Their enlargements are made within the personal voice: groping for the resemblance to some war, some annunciation, some relationship, some institution, some gothic shape, some prayer, some faith. Even where there is a movement toward the larger world, as in "The Moon and the Yew Tree" or "A Birthday Present," it has a self-consciousness, a deployment of knowledge, a reasoning, a sense of human justice, that keeps it from being sick or private. The woman who measures the flour and cuts off the surplus, adhering "to rules, to rules, to rules," and the mind that sees the shortcomings of adding machines is a persona resisting narcissism and closure, right to the death.

Audre Lorde: The Severed Daughter

R. B. Stepto

Throughout the years, Afro-American poets and the New York publishing houses have had a both peculiar and predictable relationship. The "peculiar" aspect has been much the same as that which has branded so many other social and business relations as "peculiar": the dominance of race ritual in matters where "pure" human contact should prevail. What has been "predictable" is that the publishing of these poets, when it has occurred, has been in rushes or spates and usually in response to some kind of socio-cultural movement or outburst—a "Negro renaissance" in the 1920s, a "Black revolution in the 1960s—which to no small degree soon becomes, in the world of letters, as much a publisher's hype as a genuine aesthetic upheaval. All this demonstrates (as if we needed further demonstration) that, as institutions, the trade houses are as undeniably American as, say, a department store, an automobile corporation, or the U.S. Army; and that, as American businesses, they are no different from the rest when it comes to the art of making a buck.

But somehow we continue to expect the publishing houses to operate on a plane above that of race ritual and money-making because they are, to an astonishing degree, the discoverers of talent, arbiters of taste, and guardians of the written word. To be sure, many non-Afro-American poets fall into the trough, as it were, either because they are overlooked or because they couldn't or wouldn't ride the crest of a wave. But rarely have they been subjected to the kind of immorality and illiteracy that lies behind the stories too many good Afro-American poets often tell—stories which almost always seem to begin, "they rejected my poems because they weren't 'political,' " or worse, "they wouldn't take my manuscript because it wasn't 'black.' " These "readings" (of a market, perhaps, but not of poetry) from outwardly intelli-

From *Parnassus: Poetry in Review* 8, no. 1 (Fall/Winter 1979). © 1980 by Poetry in Review Foundation.

gent people linger and assault the poet and the poet's reviewer alike. While the poet is prompted to ask, "Shall I try again?" the reviewer cannot help wondering if a given book has been published because it has merit or because it has been construed to be part of yet another socio-cultural "event." These latter queries are especially pertinent when the poet in question is offering (up?) his or her first book, but they pertain as well to the conditions of authorship concocted for or imposed upon the seasoned writer. The publication of [a] new [book] of poems, Audre Lorde's *The Black Unicorn* allows us to pursue these questions in several interesting ways, and to observe in particular how major publishing houses, perhaps with some assistance from an author, market a "black book" of poems in what is ostensibly a pause between "renaissances" or "revolutions." . . .

Audre Lorde's seventh volume of poems, *The Black Unicorn*, is a big, rich book of some sixty-seven poems. While *The Black Unicorn* is "packaged" (the prominent half-column of authenticating commentary from Adrienne Rich constitutes much of the wrapping), it really does not need this promoting and protecting shell. Perhaps a full dozen—an incredibly high percentage— of these poems are searingly strong and unforgettable. Those readers who recall the clear light and promise of early Lorde poems such as "The Woman Thing" and "Bloodbirth," and recall as well the great shape and energy of certain mid-1970s poems including "To My Daughter the Junkie on a Train," "Cables to Rage," and "Blackstudies," will find in *The Black Unicorn* new poems which reconfirm Lorde's talent while reseeding gardens and fields traversed before. There are other poems which do not so much reseed as repeople, and these new persons, names, ghosts, lovers, voices—these new I's, we's, real and imagined kin—give us something fresh, beyond the cycle of Lorde's previously recorded seasons and solstices.

While *The Black Unicorn* is unquestionably a personal triumph for Lorde in terms of the development of her canon, it is also an event in contemporary letters. This is a bold claim but one worth making precisely because, as we see in the first nine poems, Lorde appears to be the only North American poet other than Jay Wright who is sufficiently immersed in West African religion, culture, and art (and blessed with poetic talent!) to reach beyond a kind of middling poem that merely quantifies "blackness" through offhand reference to African gods and traditions. What Lorde and Wright share, beyond their abilities to create a fresh, New World out of ancient Old World lore, is a voice or an *idea* of a voice that is essentially African in that it is communal, historiographical, archival, and prophetic *as well as* personal in ways that we commonly associate with the African *griot, dyēli,* and tellers of *nganos* and other oral tales. However, while Wright's voice may be said to embody what is masculine in various West African cultures and cosmologies, Lorde's voice is decidedly and magnificently feminine. The goal of *The Black Unicorn* is then to present this fresh and powerful voice, and to explore the modulations within that voice between feminine and feminist timbres. As the volume unfolds, this exploration charts history and geography as well as voice, and with the confluence of these patterns the volume takes shape and Lorde's particular envisioning of a black transatlantic tradition is accessible.

All this begins, as suggested before, in the first nine poems in which we encounter the legendary women and goddesses—the sisters and especially the mothers—who inaugurate Lorde's genealogy of timbres and visages. In poems such as "From the House of Yemanjá," "Dahomey," and "125th Street and Abomey,"mothers including Yemanjá (goddess of oceans, mother of the other *Orisha* or Yoruba goddesses and gods) and Seboulisa ("The goddess of Abomey—'The Mother of us all' ") appear, often in new renderings of the legends that surround them:

> My mother has two faces and a frying pot
> where she cooked up her daughters
> into girls
> before she fixed our dinner.
> My mother has two faces and a broken pot
> where she hid out a perfect daughter
> who was not me
> I am the sun and moon and forever hungry
> for her eyes

Much of this would be little more than mere reference of the sort alluded to before were the poems not galvanized and bound by the persona's unrelenting quest for freedom, voice, and women kin. At the beginning of the quest, the persona is a black unicorn, a protean figure who, in one manifestation, is a Dahomean woman with attached phallus dancing the part of Eshu-Elegba (Yemanjá's messenger son of many tongues) in religious ritual. At the end, she is a "severed daughter"—"severed" in that she is in a new but tethered geography ("125th Street and Abomey") and has cut away an imposed ritual tongue—who has found a voice of her own that can utter "Whatever language is needed" (a skill allowed before only to Yemanjá's *son*) and can even laugh.

> Half earth and time splits us apart
> like struck rock,
> A piece lives elegant stories
> too simply put
> while a dream on the edge of summer
> of brown rain in nim trees
> snail shells from the dooryard
> of King Toffah
> bring me where my blood moves
> Seboulisa mother goddess with one breast
> eaten away by worms of sorrow and loss
> see me now
> your severed daughter
> laughing our name into echo
> all the world shall remember.

As we move from the first set of poems about black mothers, daughters, and sisters—women who can "wear flesh like war," conjoin "dying cloth," and "mock Eshu's iron quiver"—to those which come in the remaining three sections, there is a subtle shift in poetic form that appears to signal, in turn, a shift in focus from acquisition of voice to that of art. In the first set, in stanzas such as

> The black unicorn is restless
> the black unicorn is unrelenting
> the black unicorn is not
> free.

and

> Mother I need
> mother I need
> mother I need your blackness now
> as the august earth needs rain.

Lorde makes effective use of the principle of repetition that is at the heart of oral composition in all "pre-literate" cultures, and at the heart as well of such conspicuous Afro-American art forms as the blues. (Indeed, each of the stanzas just presented may be said to be a modified but identifiable blues verse.) In the remaining sections of the volume, repetition and other devices which are, in this context, referents in written art to oral forms, are largely forsaken in favor of the kind of taut free verse Lorde usually employs. What is fascinating about this, as suggested before, is that while the declarative voice forged in the first group of poems remains, that voice speaks less of discovering language and of moving, perhaps, from speech to laughter, and more of poems—of written art readily assuming the posture of a healing force.

This is true even of the poems about social unrest and injustice. In "Chain," for example, a poem prompted by a news item describing two teenage girls who had borne children by their natural fathers, there is the cry,

> Oh write me a poem mother
> here, over my flesh
> get your words upon me
> as he got his child upon me

Similarly, in "Eulogy for Alvin Frost" we find,

> I am tired of writing memorials to black men
> whom I was on the brink of knowing
>
> Dear Danny who does not know me
> I am
> writing to you for your father
> whom I barely knew
> except at meetings where he was

> distinguished
> by his genuine laughter
> and his kind bright words

In the final section, "Power" begins with yet another suggested distinction between poetry and speech,

> The difference between poetry and rhetoric
> is being
> ready to kill
> yourself
> instead of your children.

and ends with a very particular statement of confession and self-instruction,

> I have not been able to touch the destruction within me.
> But unless I learn to use
> the difference between poetry and rhetoric
> my power too will run corrupt as poisonous mold
> or lie limp and useless as an unconnected wire

As the latent sexuality in the final line suggests, the shift in *The Black Unicorn* in poetic concern from acquisition of voice to that of art concerns as well the articulation of a homosexual love that was only barely alluded to before in the many figurations of tongue as women-warriors' sword and speech. Indeed, the pulsing love poems, in which tongue finally becomes most explicitly an erotic tool and goal—

> I am tempted
> to take you apart
> and reconstruct your orifices
> your tongue your truths your fleshy altars
> into my own forgotten image
>
> > ("Fog Report")

—and in which sex and art most explicitly meet—

> I do not even know
> who looks like you
> of all the sisters who come to me
> at nightfall
> we touch each other in secret places
> draw old signs and stories
> upon each other's back and proofread
> each other's ancient copy.

—consummate the volume in a rich if not altogether unexpected manner.

Whether or not the subject at hand is love, children under assault, people in prison, childhood "wars," or the quest for a certain rare literacy, the poet in *The Black Unicorn* steadily pursues (and defines in that pursuit) a viable heroic posture and voice for womankind. The success of the volume may be seen in the fact that when the poet declares in the final poem,

> I will eat the last signs of my weakness
> remove the scars of old childhood wars
> and dare to enter the forest whistling

we believe her. In this period between renaissance and/or revolutions, Lorde's verse may need promotion in order to sell, but that doesn't mean that the verse is thin or insignificant. *The Black Unicorn* offers contemporary poetry of a high order, and in doing so may be a smoldering renaissance and revolution unto itself.

Amy Clampitt: "The Hazardous Definition of Structures"

Richard Howard

Of [the] 50 poems [in Amy Clampitt's *The Kingfisher*,] 14 have appeared in *The New Yorker*, consecrated there by the most fastidious editorial taste now (and for the last 25 years) operative in the world of commercial periodicals; in her own high middle ages, Amy Clampitt has had her first book published ninth in the Knopf Poetry Series, consecrated there by the most fastidious editorial taste now (and for the last four years) operative in the world of commercial publishing; embellished with commendations from Richard Wilbur and Helen Vendler, who has since reviewed the book at length in *The New York Review of Books* ("to enter a Clampitt poem is to enter a distinguished mind that then goes on an unpredictable journey of memory, association, musing, description, judgment, pining, correction and imagining"), this poetry is doomed to success.

Of course, success is perhaps the showiest way we have of ignoring our poets—thrusting them into the neglectful limelight where they can writhe—as if the sound were turned off on a brilliant screen—until someone rescues them from the pillory of acclaim. "A century from now," Vendler prophecies, "someone" will read Clampitt to find out "what, in the twentieth century, made up the stuff of culture." Pathetically, I can only add to this syndrome of camouflaging celebrity, for I too enjoy and admire these poems at just that pitch of enthusiasm which sets them beyond the pale—or the murk—where poems usually *take*. It seems to me that *The Kingfisher* has given me more delight (what Roland Barthes calls *jouissance*, not *plaisir*) than any first book of poems since the first book of poems I read by A. R. Ammons. Amy Clampitt does things in her own way, but of course unless we can say what that way is, it is not perhaps really doing them. I shall try.

It has to do with some readily identifiable devices. Syntax, for one thing

From *Parnassus: Poetry in Review* 11, no. 1 (Spring/Summer 1983). © 1984 by Poetry in Review Foundation.

("in Clampitt, one thing is sure to lead to another"—Vendler): the poem is wreathed around its grammar, often being one very long sentence, submissive to the voice, observant of the local inflections, but governing the weight of the lines on the page, *down* the page, so that we know throughout that we are within a governance, the thrall of grammar, which is the same word, if you trace it far enough "back," as glamour. When the man protesting against witches in the *Malleus Malleficarum* claims he knows he has been ensorceled because "she cast a glamor about my member," we may pre-empt his phrase and apply it to the elements of a Clampitt poem in its articulation: she casts a glamour about *its* members which are not, here, phallic but fraternal, participating agencies of subordination, because she wields a pertinent grammar upon and within them. In this she brings to mind not her immediate lineage (that matriarchal mass we begin to perceive: Moore, Swenson—who also commends Clampitt's "keen mind" on the jacket—Bishop, Van Duyn; we shall end by perceiving the connection these poets have with certain lyric prose-writers: Paley, Ozick, most recently Marilyn Robinson), but the incremental redundances of Robert Browning, whose music is syntactical, not a matter of chiming. Consider these parallel stanzas:

Wheeling, the careening
winds arrive with lariats
and tambourines of rain.
Torn-to-pieces, mud-dark
flounces of Caribbean

cumulus keep passing,
keep passing. By afternoon
rinsed transparencies begin
to open overhead, Mediterranean
windowpanes of clearness

crossed by young gusts'
vaporous fripperies, liquid
footprints flying, lacewing
leaf-shade brightening
and fading. Sibling

gales stand up on point
in twirling fouettés
of debris. The day ends
bright-cloud-wardrobe
packed away. Nightfall

hangs up a single moon
bleached white as laundry,
serving notice yet again how
levity can also trample,
drench, wring and mangle.

All I believed is true!
   I am able yet
   All I want, to get
By a method as strange as new:
Dare I trust the same to you?

If at night, when doors are shut,
   And the wood-worm picks,
   And the death-watch ticks
And the bar has a flag of smut,
And a cat's in the water-butt—

And the socket floats and flares,
   And the house-beams groan,
   And a foot unknown
I surmised on the garrett-stairs,
And the locks slip unawares—

And the spider, to serve his ends,
   By a sudden thread,
   Arms and legs outspread,
On the table's midst descends,
Comes to find, God knows what friends!—

If since eve drew in, I say,
   I have sat and brought
   (so to speak) my thought
To bear on the woman away,
Till I felt my hair turn gray . . .

There is a parallel confidence as well in the thread of syntax—except, of course, that Browning's sentence (on the right) will go on for eleven more stanzas: he is the more difficult poet, determinedly so. But as my little exhibition makes plain, Clampitt's other main device, or at least one you can collect for yourself by merely glancing at her page, is her science of enjambment (replacing rhyme by unwonted suspensions). This is probably the most arduous weapon in the armory of the regiment of women poets I have invoked—and on their discoveries we are still, as it were, banking. Clampitt ends her lines—breaks them open—in such a way as to show meanings not otherwise evident. The sense strikes against the ends of lines and their beginnings like a river defining itself by its entertainment now of one bank, now of the other, and this axiological enclosure becomes her signature, Clampitt's way of ensuring the meaning of every method that comes to hand.

The book's title, we may note, comes from Hopkins's famous sonnet: "As kingfishers catch fire, dragonflies draw flame"—something to do with the analogies, across realms of being, of comparable, exchangeable energies. In Hopkins as in Clampitt, any object, by fulfilling its distinctive nature, gives glory back to the energy which brought it into being—the energy which Hopkins calls God. For him (and for Him), the object cries: *what I do is me, for that I came;* for her, the glory is less clamorous: *"there being no past to speak of/ other than setbacks."*

In Clampitt, we discover that the objects are likely to be broken, discarded, or ruined ones—a leak in the brickwork beside a stairway in the Times Square Subway: "as though we watched the hairline fracture/ of the quotidian widen to a geomorphic fissure"; and again the residue of junk on the littoral, "Beach Glass":

> I keep a lookout for beach glass—
> amber of Budweiser, chrysoprase
> of Almadén and Gallo, lapis
> by way of (no getting around it,
> I'm afraid) Phillips'
> Milk of Magnesia, with now and then a rare
> translucent turquoise or blurred amethyst
> of no known origin.
>
>   The process
> goes on forever: they came from sand,
> they go back to gravel,
> along with the treasuries
> of Murano, the buttressed
> astonishments of Chartres,
> which even now are readying
> for being turned over and over as gravely
> and gradually as an intellect
> engaged in the hazardous

> redefinition of structures
> no one has yet looked at.

This transformation of discard into value is what we can listen for first in the poems of Amy Clampitt. In a poem like "Salvage" she will reach as far back as she writes forward,

> re-establishing
> with each arcane
> trash-basket dig
> the pleasures of the ruined.

In a culture like ours, near to drowning in its own garbage, she functions with a certain ecological security: waste not, want not, especially when it is out of others' waste that you can make up your own wants. Not surprisingly, there are fifteen pages of notes—not teasing, as in Eliot or Empson; not merely identifying, as in Moore; but midwifely: "the scheme may be clearer if this poem is thought of as a meditation in the form of a travelogue." One advantage about publishing your poems when you are so evidently a grown-up (which means, of course: uncertain, as no adolescent can afford to be, about what being a grown-up means) is that you don't have to be nervous about being hard, obscure, or even just complicated. You just go ahead and tell how to get on with it. These poems are enormously allusive (nor does she reveal that we need to remember "milk of Magnesia" is a classical reference as willingly as she explains her Catholic ones: "clean as a crucifix—a thrift . . . that looks like waste"), and they are expansive too—from Iowa to Greece by way of Italy, France, and England, with flying visits to Africa and Tenochtitlán. I suppose that is one way of saying (not claiming) that the poet is "major," "strong," "relevant"—whatever the current cant for the poet who shoulders others out of the way: Clampitt expects you to be prepared to deal with *anything* in her poems, and if you are not, she will help you. What she calls the "hazardous redefinition of structures/ no one has yet looked at" is what we can listen for, look to initially, in her poems. They will reward us as only the new poet can, by making us re-order the old poets, and adding herself to what it is we can do to the world ("everything that is the case") by perceiving it. I shall praise *The Kingfisher* best by saying that its poet jeopardizes her second book extravagantly: I have never waited for *the next installment* with greater qualms, yet with greater confidence.

Tremors of Exactitude:
Vicki Hearne's *Nervous Horses*

John Hollander

Vicki Hearne's first collection of poems is the work of a writer who trains horses and reads Wittgenstein. [This book will not] satisfy easy expectations. Hearne's *Nervous Horses* are both sinewy and agitated, as they are both actual and figurative—the horses of modernity. Her poems, largely in supple and controlled syllabic verse, are meditative but taut. In "Genuine and Poignant", she shows she has learned Wallace Stevens's first lessons in poetic *dressage*:

> Just that once, not to grieve, and the hill
> To stand suddenly bare and pure
> Confidently shaking its dust
> Through the warm window.

But she moves in other poems to the more animated subject of her horses and her dogs. Aware of the philosophical problem of other minds, of how (and even what) we know of others' thoughts and feelings, she treats the otherness of animals as intimate and terrifying. The consciousness of those animals, a beautifully hypothetical entity which keeps flickering in and out of interest, the more we know and are with them, is among the things this book so beautifully explores. The poems form a kind of romance in which our theories about how we ought sensibly to talk, and what the skilled experience of training animals leads one to say, are engaged in a dialectical sparring-match.

But she writes neither mock training-manuals, nor the journal notes of a self-conscious rider. Her poems often puzzle and are puzzled themselves; she is particularly concerned to avoid the way in which so much contemporary verse sets up and relates crude concepts of subject and object, experience and image, in an unacknowledged and unexplored realm of thought.

From *Times Literary Supplement*, no. 4061 (January 30, 1981). © 1981 by John Hollander.

The book's final, splendid "The Metaphysical Horse" is a poem about coming to terms with one's own metaphors—in this case, conceptions which are like mirror-images but which, having been lived with, allow her to end as follows:

> Circling elegantly we
> Glimpse the always receding
> True proposal in the glass
> And join the horses, who dance,
> Tremors of exactitude
> Flaring, still fresh on their limbs.

Hearne's practical experience of horses is at one with her interest in their mythologies. Plato's fable of horse and rider, Renaissance training manuals, the folklore of handlers, fall like shadows over her actual animals. She herself has what she calls in the title of one poem "The fastidiousness of the Musician"; exercises, lessons, set problems and puzzles are her typical occasions. The longest poem here, the penultimate "St. George and the Dragon" has a quasi-narrative line, but records the quest not *of* the mounted knight, but rather *for* him, in the fragmentations of a picture-puzzle. The problem of piecing together an imaginative construction that will hold harks back to James Merrill's jigsaw puzzle of memory in "Lost in Translation". Hearne's poem modulates this into an amusingly domesticated metaphor in which friends and teachers help the poet cope with the epistemological puzzles, trials and errors which occupy the whole of this distinguished first book.

Jay Macpherson: Poetry in Canada, 1957

Northrop Frye

This is an unusually thin year: one good book, two promising ones, and a miscellaneous assortment of what the Elizabethans might politely have called a paradise of dainty devices, though it would be more accurate to speak of an amusement park of rhythmical gadgets. Some of these latter are pleasant and readable enough: with others, one is strongly tempted to take the plangent tone of a couplet which appears on the opening page of one of the year's few published volumes:

> Last of the mighty oaks nurtured in freedom!
> Brambles and briars now supersede treedom.

However, here goes. The good book, of course, as the Governor-General's committee has this time recognized, is Jay Macpherson's *The Boatman.* . . . The book itself is one of the few physically attractive objects on my Canadian poetry shelves, and the fact is an appropriate tribute to its contents, for *The Boatman* is the most carefully planned and unified book of poems that has yet appeared in these surveys. It is divided into six parts. The first, "Poor Child," contains poems that appeared in a small pamphlet reviewed here some years ago: they form a series of tentative explorations of poetic experience, ranging in tone from the macabre "The Ill Wind" to the plaintive "The Third Eye." The next two sections are called "O Earth Return" and "The Plowman in Darkness." The titles come from two poems of Blake that deal with "Earth" as the whole of fallen nature in female form, and the subjects are chiefly the more common mythical figures connected with this "Earth," including Eve, Eurynome, the Cumaean Sibyl, Mary Magdalene, and the bride of the Song of Songs, identified with the Queen of Sheba. Hence the subtitle, "A Speculum for Fallen Women." The two parts are, like Blake's lyrics, matched by contrast against each other, the relation often

From *University of Toronto Quarterly* 27, no. 4 (July 1958). © 1958 by University of Toronto Press.

being marked by identical titles. The contrast is not so much Blake's innocence and experience, though related to it, as a contrast between a theme
idealized by a kind of aesthetic distance and the same theme made colloquial
and familiar. "Sibylla," whose fate is described in the motto to Eliot's *The
Waste Land*, appears in "O Earth Return" thus:

> Silence: the bat-clogged cave
> Lacks breath to sigh.
> Sibylla, hung between earth and sky,
> Sways with the wind in her pendant grave.

and in "The Plowman in Darkness" thus:

> I'm mercifully rid of youth.
> No callers plague me ever;
> I'm virtuous, I tell the truth—
> And you can see I'm clever!

In the last two sections the corresponding male figures appear. "The
Sleepers," intensely pastoral in tone, is focussed on Endymion and his
moon-loved daze, with overtones of Adonis and Adam. Then the figures of
Noah and his ark emerge, expanding until they become identified with God
and his creation respectively. The creation is inside its creator, and the ark
similarly attempts to explain to Noah, in a series of epigrams in double
quatrains, that it is really inside him, as Eve was once inside Adam:

> When the four quarters shall
> Turn in and make one whole,
> then I who wall your body,
> Which is to me a soul,
>
> Shall swim circled by you
> And cradled on your tide,
> Who was not even, not ever,
> Taken from your side.

As the ark expands into the flooded world, the body of the Biblical leviathan,
and the order of nature, the design of the whole book begins to take shape.
The Boatman begins with a poem called "Ordinary People in the Last Days," a
wistful poem about an apocalypse that happens to everyone except the poet,
and ends with a vision of a "Fisherman" who, more enterprising than Eliot's
gloomy and luckless shore-sitter, catches a "myriad forms," eats them,
drinks the lake they are in, and is caught in his turn by God.

Such myths as the flood and the apocalypse appear less for religious
than for poetic reasons: the book moves from a "poor child" at the centre of a
hostile and mysterious world to an adult child who has regained the para-
disal innocent vision and is at the circumference of a world of identical forms.
In the title poem the reader is urged to follow this process as best he may:

> Then you take the tender creature
> —You remember, that's the reader—
> And you pull him through his navel inside out.

The wonderland of this Noah's ark inside Noah, where the phoenix and the abominable snowman have equal rights with books and eggs and the sun and moon, is explored in the final section: "The Fisherman: A Book of Riddles." The riddles are not difficult, the solutions being thoughtfully provided in the title, and, like so many of the Anglo-Saxon riddles, they are circumferential rather than simply elliptical descriptions, hence the riddle on "Egg" symbolizes the poet's relation to her reader as well:

> Reader, in your hand you hold
> A silver case, a box of gold.
> I have no door, however small,
> Unless you pierce my tender wall,
> And there's no skill in healing then
> Shall ever make me whole again.
> Show pity, Reader, for my plight:
> Let be, or else consume me quite.

Miss Macpherson chooses strict metres and small frames: she is, as the blurb says, melodious, but her melody is of that shaped and epigrammatic quality which in music is called tune. Within her self-imposed limits there is an extraordinary tonal variety, from the delicate *ritardando* of "The Caverned Woman" to the punning *knittelvers* of "The Boatman," and from the whispered *pianissimo* of "Aiaia" (the island of Circe) to the alliterative thundering of "Storm." She can—a noticeable feat in Canada—write a sexual poem without breaking into adolescent pimples and cackles; she can deal with religious themes without making any reed-organ wheezes about the dilemma of modern man; she has a wit and an erudition that are free of wisecracks and pedantry; she can modulate in eight lines from "Philomel's unmeasured grief" to the human jay who

> Chatters, gabbles, all the day,
> Raises both Cain and Babel.

The elegiac poems are the most resonant, and they make the strongest initial impression, though the lighter ones have equal staying power. There are few dying falls: usually a poem ends with a quiet authority that has a ring of finality about it, leaving the reader nothing to do but accept the poem— "Reader, take," as the riddle on "Book" says.

There is little use looking for bad lines or lapses in taste: *The Boatman* is completely successful within the conventions it adopts, and anyone dissatisfied with the book must quarrel with the conventions. Among these are the use of a great variety of echoes, some of them direct quotations from other poems, and an interest in myth, both Biblical and Classical, that may make some readers wonder uneasily if they should not be reading it with a mythological handbook.

One should notice in the first place that the echoes are almost invariably from the simplest and most popular types of poetry. They include Elizabethan lyrics ("While Philomel's unmeasured grief" sounds like the opening of a madrigal); the lyrics of Blake; hymns ("Take not that Spirit from me"); Anglo-Saxon riddles; Christmas carols ("The Natural Mother"); nursery rhymes ("Sheba"); ballads and newspaper verse ("Mary of Egypt" and the second "Sibylla"). The use made of these echoes is to create a kind of timeless style, in which everything from the tags of mediaeval ballad to modern slang can fit. One has a sense of rereading as well as reading, of meeting new poems with a recognition that is integrally and specifically linked with the rest of one's poetic experience. The echoes also enable the poet to achieve the most transparent simplicity of diction. There is little of the "density" of more intellectualized poetry, and ambiguities and ironies are carried very lightly:

> In a far-off former time
> And a green and gentle clime,
> Mamma was a lively lass,
> Liked to watch the tall ships pass,
> Loved to hear the sailors sing
> Of sun and wind and voyaging,
> Felt a wild desire to be
> On the bleak and unplowed sea.

The flat conventional phrases here, including the Homeric tag in the last line, would seem commonplace or affected if their context had not been so skillfully worked out for them. It is true that for many readers there is nothing so baffling as simplicity, but Miss Macpherson's simplicity is uncompromising.

As for mythology, that is one of poetry's indispensable languages: most of the major English poets, including the best poets of today, demand and expect a considerable knowledge of myth, and although Douglas LePan calls Canada a country without a mythology, the same thing is increasingly true even of Canadian poets. Miss Macpherson's myths, like her allusions, flow into the poems: the poems do not point to them. Knowing who Adam and Eve and Noah are will get one through most of the book, and although a glance at the opening page of Robert Graves's Penguin book on Greek myth might help with Eurynome, I find no poem that has the key to its meaning outside itself.

> Oh wake him not until he please,
> Lest he should rise to weep:
> For flocks and birds and streams and trees
> Are golden in his silver sleep.

For thousands of years poetry has been ringing the changes on a sleeper whom it is dangerous to waken, and the myths of Endymion, of the bridegroom in the Song of Songs, of Adam, of Blake's Albion, of Joyce's Finnegan, are a few of the by-products. Such myths in the background enrich the suggestiveness of the above four lines, but the lines are not dependent on the echoes, either for their meaning or for their poetic value. Or again:

> The woman meanwhile sits apart and weaves
> Red rosy garlands to dress her joy and fear.
> But all to no purpose; for petals and leaves
> Fall everlastingly, and the small swords stands clear.

The reader who remembers his Milton, however vaguely, will see how the fall of sex from love to lust belongs in a complex which includes the first efforts at clothing, the appearance of thorns on the rose, the coming of winter after fall, the angelic swords over Paradise, and the aggressive use of sex which the phallic image of "small swords" suggests. But none of this would have any point if the quatrain itself did not carry its own meaning.

I have glanced at the critical issues raised by *The Boatman* because it seems to me a conspicuous example of a tendency that I have seen growing since I began this survey eight years ago. With the proviso that "professional" in this context has nothing to do with earning a living, the younger Canadian poets have become steadily more professional in the last few years, more concerned with poetry as a craft with its own traditions and discipline. The babble of unshaped free verse and the obscurities of private association are inseparable from amateurish poetry, but they are emphatically not "modern" qualities: serious modern poets in Canada struggle hard for clarity of expression and tightness of structure. The second volumes of Douglas LePan, P. K. Page, and James Reaney (of whom more next year) show this markedly, as do the first volumes of Wilfred Watson and Anne Wilkinson, and all the volumes of Irving Layton since *In the Midst of My Fever*. It is consistent with this that the more amateurish approach which tries to write up emotional experiences as they arise in life or memory has given way to an emphasis on the formal elements of poetry, on myth, metaphor, symbol, image, even metrics. The development is precisely parallel to the development in Canadian painting from deliberately naïve landscape to abstraction and concentration on pictorial form. As in 1890 with the Scott-Lampman-Roberts group, and again in the *New Provinces* generation, there seems to be once more in Canadian poetry, on a much bigger scale, a "school" in its proper sense of a number of poets united only by a common respect for poetry.

Jay Macpherson: *Poems Twice Told*

Margaret Atwood

When I was young, poetry reviewing in Canada was very ingrown. Poets reviewed the work of their friends and enemies then, partly because few others were interested in reviewing poetry at all, partly because the poetry world was so small that everyone in it was either a friend or an enemy. However, it was understood that anyone likely to read the review would know which was which.

Writers still occasionally review their friends and enemies, but it can no longer be assumed that the average reader knows it. So I feel it necessary to state by way of prelude that Jay Macpherson not only taught me Victorian literature back in 1960—like all good teachers, she behaved as if it mattered, thus converting my surly contempt for the subject into fascinated admiration—but is one of my oldest and most appreciated friends. Having said that, I will retreat to the middle distance, from which the reviewer's voice should issue impartial as God's (though it rarely does) and try to deal with the subject at hand.

Impossible, of course. Re-reading *The Boatman*, the first of the two books included in this volume, makes me remember Jay Macpherson as I first knew her. I was enormously impressed, not just by the fact that here in front of me was a real poet, and a woman at that, who had actually had a book published—no mean feat in the Canada of those days—but by her wardrobe. She always wore clothes that were by no means "fashionable," clothes in fact that nobody else could get away with, but which seemed exactly right for *her*.

It's the same with the poetry. No one else writes like this. In fact, looking back, it seems that no one else ever did, and that all the fuss about a "mythopoeic school" of poetry was simply misguided criticism. If "mythopoeic" means that the poet lets on she knows about mythologies, the most

From *Second Words*. © 1982 by O. W. Toad Ltd. House of Anansi Press Ltd. and Beacon Press, 1982.

unlikely among us would have to accept the label. (Daphne Marlatt, George Bowering and Frank Davey, for example.) Although a critic intent on the usual version of this theory might make a case for *The Boatman* and its involvement with the shapes of traditional stories, *Welcoming Disaster* would probably defeat him. Its personal and indeed sometimes notably eccentric voice carries the reader far beyond any notions of "school." Macpherson's poetry is one-of-a-kind, not in defiance of current convention so much as apart from it. It's a world unto itself, and from *The Boatman's* poem called "Egg" comes the best advice for approaching it: "Let be, or else consume me quite."

The Boatman has been much written about, but for the sake of those who may not be familiar with it I'll say a little about it. It appears to be a "sequence" of very short, condensed lyric poems. (I say "appears," because it was not planned that way; Macpherson is not a programmatic writer, and her work, when it falls into sequences, does so because her imagination is working with a certain body of material, not because she thinks she needs a poem of a certain kind to fill a gap and then composes it.) They are not all of the same kind: some are straight-faced lyrics, some are sinister or comic parodies on the same subjects (*pace* Blake's two sets of *Songs*) and some are puzzle-poems, or riddles. I tend to get on a little better with the straight lyrics. The others are adroit and clever, though they seem to me to exist, as many kinds of jokes do, for the purpose of defusing a profound uneasiness.

The central voice of *The Boatman* is one of a complex and powerful grief, and its central symbols revolve around separation and loss. Like all hermetic poetry, *The Boatman* offers the reader multiple choices about its true "subject." Is it "about" the relationship between two lovers, the relationship between Creator and fallen world, the relationship between author, book and reader, or dreamer and dream, or man and his imaginative world? Why not all? The most potent poems in the book, for me, are those in the small sequence-within-a-sequence, "The Ark," eight eight-line lyrics that are astonishing for their simplicity and grace, and for the amount of emotional force they can pack into sixty-four lines. They are "about" all of the above, and after more than twenty years of reading them I still find them devastating.

One of Macpherson's most exquisite poems is in the small section entitled "Other Poems"—post-*Boatman*, pre-*Disaster*. It's called "The Beauty of Job's Daughters," and I won't quote from it because you need to read the whole thing, but it's an excellent example of what an outwardly-formal, flexibly-handled lyricism can do. It also epitomizes one of the main themes of *The Boatman*: the "real" world, that of the imagination, is inward.

Between *The Boatman* and "Other Poems," and *Welcoming Disaster*, came a long pause. Macpherson's total output has been minute compared with that of most other Canadian poets of her stature, and she's about the farthest thing from a "professional" poet you could imagine. A young novelist said to me recently, "Poetry isn't an art, it's a circuit." For Macpherson, never a circuit-rider, poetry isn't a "profession" but a gift, which is either there or not there but can't be made to be there by exercise of will. In fact, the first poems in *Welcoming Disaster* are about the loss or absence of the imaginative world so beautifully evoked in "Job's Daughters," the failure of inspiration, and the futility of trying to conjure it up. As well as its redemptive qualities: "Breathing too is a simple trick, and most of us learn it. / Still, to lose it is bad, though no-one regrets it long." When the Muse finally shows up, what she reveals this time is not paradise regained.

If *The Boatman* is "classical" (which, in purity of line, simplicity of rhythms, and choice of myths and symbols, it is), then *Welcoming Disaster* is, by the same lights, "romantic": more personal, more convoluted, darker and more grotesque, its rhythms more complex, its main symbol-groupings drawn not only from Classical and Biblical mythology but from all kinds of odd corners: nineteenth-century Gothic novels (and their twentieth-century avatars, such as *Nosferatu* and Karloff movies), the Grimms' Goose Girl story ("What Falada Said"), Babylonian mythology ("First and Last Things"), lore of magicians, ghouls, mazes and crossroads. The main movement of the book concerns a descent to the underworld; and, as everyone knows, the most successful recipes for this include a plan for getting not only there but back, usually by means of the advice or actual company of a sybil, spirit guide or boatman. (The boatman in *The Boatman* is mainly Noah; in *Welcoming Disaster* it's his upside-down counterpart, Charon, who takes you not to the world renewed but to the world dead.) In this case the fetish-cum-spirit guide-cum-God-cum-sinister ferryman is a teddy bear, which—again—only Macpherson could get away with.

What's in the underworld? In Egyptian mythology it's the place where the soul is weighed; for Orpheus, it's the place where the lost love is finally lost; in Jackson Knight's book on Virgil (cited in Macpherson's notes) the underground maze leads to the king and queen of the dead, especially the queen: it's a place of lost mothers. There are echoes too of all those nineteenth-century ghosts, from Catherine Earnshaw on down, who come to the window at night, of vampiristic or sinister-double relationships which recall Blake's Shadow and Emanation figures; of Faustian pacts with darkness. Jungians will revel in this book, though it is hardly orthodox Jungianism. But the important thing is that in the process some poems emerge that would more than satisfy Houseman: they do make the hair stand up on the back of your neck. "They Return," for instance, or "Hecate Trivia," or "Some Ghosts and Some Ghouls."

Welcoming Disaster, like *The Boatman*, has its more playful moments, but on the whole its tone ranges between the eerie and the ruthless: poems of invocation or rigorous and sometimes bloody-minded self-analysis. Macpherson was never much of a meditative Wordsworthian, if such labels apply. She's much more like Coleridge: inner magic, not outer-world description or social comment, is her *forte*.

When I was asked to write this review it was suggested that I include an "appreciation" of Macpherson's "career." But what do we mean by a poet's "career," apart from the poems? Do poets even have "careers?" Some do, but it's a word that seems more appropriate when applied to politicians: something pursued, worked at, having to do with leverage and personal advancement and the media-created persona. Jay Macpherson is simply not career-minded in this way. There's nowhere she wants to get, in the sense of "getting somewhere." She reminds us that poetry is not a career but a vocation, something to which one is called, or not, as the case may be. She's still the best example I know of someone who lives as if literature, and especially the writing of poetry, were to be served, not used.

Atwood's Haunted Sequences:
The Circle Game, The Journals of Susanna Moodie, and *Power Politics*

Judith McCombs

> *It was the addiction*
> *to stories . . .*
> *Stories that could be told*
> *on nights like these to account for the losses,*
> *litanies of escapes, bad novels, thrillers*
> *deficient in villains . . .*
> *Who knows what stories*
> *would ever satisfy her*
> *who knows what savageries*
> *have been inflicted on her*
> *and others by herself and others. . . .*
> —MARGARET ATWOOD, "Gothic Letter on a Hot Night,"
>   *You Are Happy*

RETURN OF THE GOTHIC: ATWOOD'S GHOSTS

In Margaret Atwood's work generally, but especially in her three long poetry sequences, the neglected and long outcast stepchild of literature, the Gothic, comes to life again. An obviously Gothic terror haunts *The Circle Game* (1966), *The Journals of Susanna Moodie* (1970), and *Power Politics* (1971). Although this Gothic inheritance was spelled out in 1968, in Atwood's "Speeches for Dr. Frankenstein" and in the Gothic "Revenant" poem, which complains of the ghosts from *Wuthering Heights* that inhabit

> the skull's noplace, where in me
> refusing to be buried, cured,
> the trite dead walk

still Atwood's Gothic voices were not widely recognized until her satiric, anti-Gothic novel, *Lady Oracle* (1976), brought the old tradition into daylight focus. Nor was this Gothic inheritance much valued by contemporary critics until Robert D. Hume, Peter Haining, Ellen Moers, and others began to reclaim the Gothic and the female Gothic tradition for serious literature.

The original Gothic inhabits that body of British literature which begins in 1765 with Horace Walpole's *The Castle of Otranto*, and flourishes in William Beckford, Ann Radcliffe, Matthew Lewis, Charles Maturin; in the nineteenth century, in *Frankenstein, Wuthering Heights, Jane Eyre, Dracula*; and, crossing the Atlantic water, in certain Poe tales, etc. The Gothic aims at terror or horror as a dominant effect; it customarily invokes the feudal past and the weird supernatural. The usual elements of the Gothic were the haunted setting—customarily a castle or forest—whose supernatural powers, be they real or deceptive, menaced and dwarfed the human characters; the hero-villain, who often goes back to the demon-lover of the ballads; the female victim or, in Radcliffe especially, the female hero-victim; and an overall reality that is either negative or, at best, deeply split between good and evil. In the twentieth century, the Gothic comes to life in (for example) certain works of William Faulkner and Flannery O'Connor, in Jean Rhys' *Wide Sargasso Sea*, Sylvia Plath's *Bell Jar* and death poems—and in much of Atwood's lyric poetry, in many of the interior monologues of her fiction, and especially in her first three poetry sequences, *The Circle Game*, *The Journals of Susanna Moodie*, and *Power Politics*.

These three sequences resurrect the Gothic spirit of terror in the female hero-victim, a terror emanating from the major elements of the original British Gothic literature—or from their direct descendants. Beginning with *The Circle Game*, this terror inhabits a female *I* who is, like Ann Radcliffe's heroines "simultaneously persecuted victim and courageous heroine." As the earlier Gothic heroine (Walpole's Maddalena, Radcliffe's Emily) was trapped in chamber and cell, so Atwood's *I* is trapped in a chamber of horrors inside her skull. As the traditional female hero-victims confronted a haunted, menacing castle or a monstrous, threatening forest, so Atwood's *I*'s are menaced by an inhuman universe, grim and icy wastes, entangled and haunted wilderness. As the elder female heroes were tempted by what Atwood's recent creator of costume Gothics calls "the hero in the mask of a villain, the villain in the mask of a hero," a man who offers an exciting but threatening escape from the boredom and constraints of ordinary female life, and who might reveal himself as demon, killer, monster; so Atwood's female *I*'s are tempted by male Others whose power animates and captivates, whose guises enthrall, whose love spells death. As Mary Shelley's unique Gothic, *Frankenstein*, divides and links the creator-villain to his monster-creature, so Atwood's creating *I* is author-victim to her lover-Other. Lastly, as the elder Gothic terror fed on divided and doubled realities—the hero-victim, the escape-trap, the villain-hero, the Frankensteinian monster-creature, the demonic or vampirish love-death—so Atwood's divided and redoubled images, lies in the mask of truth and truth in the mask of lies, permute and magnify the Gothic terror that her work creates.

This essay will focus first on the interior Gothic that dominates *The Circle Game*; next on the wilderness Gothic of *The Journals of Susanna Moodie*; and finally on the Frankensteinian mirrored and remirrored Other of *Power Politics*. Because, in all three books, this Gothic terror emanates from female *I*'s who are both hero and victim—and behind these *I*'s, from a female author—Atwood's work belongs to the genre Moers calls female Gothic; this essay will consider, as Moers does in *Literary Women*, how femaleness feeds or shapes this Gothic.

INTERIOR GOTHIC: THE CIRCLING *I*

The Circle Game is apparently the least sequential of Atwood's first three sequences, and yet its effect is the most claustrophobically and terrifyingly Gothic. It lacks the signposts of place and time that segment Moodie's *Journals*, the epigraphs that categorize *Power Politics*. But it has a center—the short title sequence—and framing poems at start and end; it has concurrent and encircling images, and a recurring flight from man to nature, self to Other, threat to death.

Most important, the *Circle* has throughout a single *I* and single setting in which the Gothic terrors gather. The female *I* is herself the setting of this Gothic; the chamber of horrors is interior to her consciousness. Though the horrors she sees are always possible—in nature, myth, or man—still no other character confirms her terror; no other agent sets loose the menaces. What is visible to other characters is ordinary and harmless; only her vision opens into horror. She is simultaneously the hero and the victim of the Gothic horrors that unreel inside her skull; the author who conceives these torments and their imperiled sufferer. Like a witch or sibyl, a Faust or Dr. Frankenstein, she summons up the menaces, the villains and the shambling monster-shapes: and yet she is the corpse, the prisoner, the target in the stories that she tells.

Like a stoic hero—or a greedy adventurer—in the midst of terrors, this *I* will not cry out; like a helpless victim—or enthralled addict—she dare not voice her terror. In *The Circle Game* as in the *Journals* and in *Power Politics*, only the reader and the *I* witness the terror. Literally or psychically, the *I* is isolated, a silenced scream, a paralyzed Cassandra. If an Other is present, he seems oblivious to the cause or fact of terror; at best he ignores it; at worst, he may *be* the cause. Even in *Power Politics*, which is ostensibly addressed to an Other, there are hardly any poems in which the *I* really speaks so that the *you* really hears. For to tell an Other (where he is present) would be to test the spell, to risk his confirming and thereby aggravating the terror—or to risk his denying and thereby aggravating the isolation.

Thus, in the opening poem, only the *I* can see her body lost in nature, invisible, distorted, drowned beneath the lake. In the second poem (which reruns Ovid's Flood), only the *I* perceives, as they stroll through an apparent mist, the underlying Diluvian Flood and slowly forming brutal faces. In "A Descent through the Carpet," only this Alice adventures below the surface harbours, descending in her mind's eye to the icy, voracious, prehistoric depths that bred her mammal life, the Darwinian seas of starved dream creatures where

> to be aware is
> to know total
>   fear.

In the title poem, only the *I* senses the prisoning rhythms of nature and myth, children and lover, *I* and *you*. In the following camera man poem, only the *I* sees how nature shifts and dissolves, beyond his lense's range. Only the *I* witnesses her own flight from him into nature, her dissolution into a hurricane speck. In the northern ice poems, only the *I* sees how glaciers, winter, and breakup menace self and Other. In the paired ending poems, only the *I* witnesses their future skeletons, gone back to nature, cannibalized by one of them, now fields where children play.

The natural universe, then, is in *The Circle Game* a modern version of the Gothic setting that surrounds and menaces the hero-victim *I*; here nature, in her mind's eye, drowns, obliterates, shocks, freezes, buries the self, and sometimes the Other as well. The traditional claustrophobic cells and passageways have narrowed to the smaller circle of the *I*'s skull; but have simultaneously metamorphosed into a modern, northern, and inhuman universe, where floe and flood, shifting time and expanding space, conspire against the *I*. The fictions of this universe are scientific rather than literary. The terms are modern rather than romantic or sacred. The scene is cold and vast Canadian (overlaying Frankenstein's final Arctic flight) rather than the picturesque Mediterranean landscape of much Gothic of the eighteenth and nineteenth centuries. But the effect of this universe, this nature—where to be aware is to know total fear—is the same pervasive and animating terror that galvanized the elder Gothics.

This deadly nature in a deadly universe is the coldest, vastest, and least human of the three concurrent horrors that encircle the summoning *I*. The second sort of horrors are the monster-ghosts from myth and history that come alive inside her skull; and the third sort are her menacing familiars, the joyless circling children and the imprisoning lover of the title sequence.

These second, specific monsters are still interior Gothic, and they haunt the *I*'s vision in the midst of ordinary, harmless scenes: walking beside him, only she can see beneath apparent mist the Diluvian Flood and shambling, brutal life; outside her window, the random face of the Hanged Man (her Muse?) disintegrates,

> shouting at me
> (specific) me
> desperate messages with his
> obliterated mouth
>
> in a silent language.

As she pauses between trains, the scream-toppled lady and the razor man who travel like voodoo dolls in her suitcase come to life. Her powers summon them even as her emptiness attracts their forms, and their terror is the edge that she inhabits:

> I move
> and live on the edges
> (what edges)

> I live
> on all the edges there are.

Only the *I* sees that the billboard lady is a vampire, and the grey flannel man is food for ghouls; and that the *you* and *I* may also be those Frankensteinian

> scraps glued together
> waiting for a chance
> to come to life.

The same interior emptiness that attracts and feeds these smaller Gothic monsters is what binds the hero to the villain-lover, the empty *you* of the central title sequence:

> You refuse to be
> (and I)
> an exact reflection, yet
> will not walk from the glass,
> be separate.

Like a clinging double, an empty Alice or a science-fiction pod, she looks to him, and he to others, in a travesty of Victorian sex roles: he for images alone, she for images in him:

> You look past me, listening
> to them, perhaps, or
> watching
> your own reflection somewhere.

It is he who commands the tranced and joyless children who play at circling: "You make them/turn and turn, according to/the closed rules of your games." The power is his, the dependency hers; it is she who is caught in his indifferent gaze, "transfixed/by your eyes'/cold blue thumbtacks." Lover and double, villain and fellow victim and Muse, his incarnations are multiple, and his powers therefore inescapable. Like an evil wizard or magician he rings her with his spells: "your observations change me/to a spineless woman in/a cage of bones."

But does the real danger come from Gothic spell or outer world, from him or them?

> (of course there is always
> danger but where
> would you locate it).

Sheltered by his dangerous games, caught in female dependency and female powerlessness, she crumples in his eyes. At the end of the sequence, she is still half-paralyzed and half-enthralled, able only to want "the circle/ broken."

After this nadir the whole book is transformed: the *I* breaks out and flees to nature; a male Other alternately pursues or accompanies her. Though these continuing flights, escapes, and deaths are her metaphors and her nightmares—therefore an interior Gothic still—yet in overview these repeated escapes and deaths, this continuing flight of the female *I* to/from/with a male Other, to/from a nature that is both refuge and death, evoke the fleeing Isabellas and Maddalenas of the elder Gothics. Or the Arctic ice chase of wretched creator and wretched being that ends Shelley's *Frankenstein*: for after the central sequence, nature becomes far vaster and far icier; deaths are constantly foreseen; the hero-villain lover-Other is skull and skeletal; rescuer or not, he brings death. At book's end, deadly nature and deadly man have triumphed: the *you* and *I* are buried, and her bones gnawed, apparently by him.

The Circle Game, then, creates a spell of female Gothic terror, centered in a hero-victim *I* who flees from man to nature, from self to Other, from threat to death. Remove the spell, and what would be left? A plot where nothing happens: a flat enclosing circle, inside which a modern female *I* languishes, discontent and bored. Passive, she passes for normal—i.e., normal for a female. Powerless, she feels herself surrounded by powers that she cannot control or become—powers that belong to men, her sexual Others. Childless, she fears and avoids children. Menaced, she does not venture on her own; she follows or goes escorted—or else becomes a target. Dependent, she divides herself between herself and her sexual Other, and assigns to him the stronger role. Empty, circling and encircled, she is her victim and her jailor, bored with her own plight.

Return the Gothic terror, and this plot, this character, come to life. Like a vampire lover, this terror calls forth the wilder powers of the *I*, and rescues her from stagnant female "normalcy." Because this Gothic terror stays hidden, silent and interior, it is with her everywhere; it animates and inwardly subverts—but does not overtly challenge—the patriarchial status quo. Like a vampire lover, this terror carries its own punishment; for she is victim, target, paralyzed and drained.

WILDERNESS GOTHIC: THE VICTIM AND THE WITCH

The Journals of Susanna Moodie, Atwood's dream-conceived account of what the actual nineteenth-century Ontario pioneer and commercial writer, Susanna Moodie, witnessed but did not in her lifetime reveal, is the most Gothic of the poetry sequences to date. *The Circle Game*, as we have seen, creates the spirit of female Gothic terror, but reruns tradition in another century, another universe; *Power Politics* has a wealth of Gothic elements and exemplifies the Gothic doubleness of Atwood's thought; but in *Power Politics* the female Gothic terror is undercut by other, non-Gothic politics. Only in the *Journals* do the original Gothic spirit and elements prevail.

These three journals, which begin in the nineteenth-century backwoods of Ontario, reveal a wilderness Gothic of old patterns imported to the new continent: here the forest is menacing, invading, breeds monsters. Its inhabitants are either alien and jeering villains, or else its victims. Surrounded by its undergrowth, the hero loses her body's image and her soul's identity. The shadowy husband turns wereman; the children die and come back as brier-fingered haunts; in the last journal Moodie herself turns ghostly revenant. Like the dark woods of our foremothers' tales in Grimm and the haunted forests and castles of eighteenth- and nineteenth-century Gothic, this wilderness setting casts a spell that overpowers the humans, breaks down their civil Christian souls, and drags them deathward.

Furthermore, although this wilderness is not personified, it nonetheless tempts the hero as the Gothic Heathcliff lover tempts: for it offers Moodie an escape from the proper menfolk's rule: it provides a savage kingdom that, like a demon-lover, compels her surrender to its power. Against the forest power the menfolk dwindle, impotent as Lintons; the hero escapes from their "legitimate" order to a savagery that, as in the demon-lover ballads and Julia Anne Curtis's "Knight of the Blood-Red Plume," first excites, then takes her life. But Atwood's *Journals* does not end there: Moodie's death initiates her into a wilderness kingdom that she makes her own: at the end, like a triumphant witch or an immortal Catherine, she becomes the voice of the wilderness, the prophet of her own wild, eternal realm.

This vision of the wilderness as menace and temptor may have one other source as powerful as the Gothic, Grimm, and ballad literature: I mean the Northern forests themselves—or rather, the Northern forests as "universally" experienced by carriers of Western European culture. Moodie's terror of the wilderness, then, would not be confined to Moodie, nor to Atwood, nor to literature, nor to the literate. Fear of bodily death and spiritual disintegration may well be *the* (Western European) human response to a nature that is dark, unpeopled forest, and harsh winters. Atwood was raised in such terrain, and may know. In *Survival* she argues that Canadian literature—including the historic Moodie's work—is haunted by Nature as Monster, inhuman, anti-human, freezing, and deadly. Certainly a lot of non-literary nineteenth-century settlers and trappers were panicked, threatened, crazed, and quite literally killed by the North American wilderness.

In the *Journals*, as in *The Circle Game*, the vision of nature as monster-villain stays interior to the female *I*: no other character notices or confirms the danger. Even though the horrors that Atwood's Moodie endures in the wilderness—isolation, disintegration, death—seem genderless; and even though her first-person narration, using the generic pronoun, *I*, implies a universal human voice—still it is only the female *I* who admits—and magnifies—the danger.

Like all Atwood's female Gothic heroes, Moodie is both author and character, egotist and victim:

> I take this picture of myself
> and with my sewing scissors
> cut out the face.
>
> Now it is more accurate:

>   where my eyes were,
>   every-
>   thing appears.

The double portrait-frame ovals that follow this self-scissoring epigraph (and introduce each of Moodie's three journals) are empty, save for dates. Atwood's accompanying collages are scissored-out images of the hero, dead or alive, surrounded by emptiness, stuck like an encapsuled cyst into a wilderness she does not touch.

From epigraph on through the first of the three journals—the one which covers her seven years' trials in the wilderness—Moodie attacks her own vision, assumes guilt for distorting, sides with the non-human wilderness but against her species and herself. Disembarking at Quebec with book, knitting, and shawl, she seems outwardly a mirror image of Moers's Traveling Heroines of the Gothic—one of those "British ladies who in point of fact did set sail for Canada and India and Africa, with their bonnets, veils, and gloves, their teacups and tea cozies—ill-equipped for vicissitudes of travel, climate, and native mutiny, but well-equipped to preserve their identity as proper Englishwomen." But the heirloom image cracks as, disembarking, Moodie blames her

>   own lack
>   of conviction which makes
>   these vistas of desolation
>   . . . omens of winter.

When the water refuses to reveal her image and the rocks ignore her, she becomes in her own eyes invisible, untranslatable.

Trapped on the backwoods farm, Moodie sees the wilderness as a large darkness: "It was our own/ignorance we entered./I have not come out yet." A stranded Red Riding Hood, she needs wolf's eyes—not her human eyes—to see true: "Whether the wilderness is/real or not/depends on who lives there." If it depends on the men, it only seems real, for as planters they impose their own illusions of progress, force the tangled forest to become the straight Cartesian rows of their futile dream. If the wilderness depends on her, it may be real, but then she is not: her opened eyes are "surrounded, stormed, broken/in upon by branches, roots, tendrils."

With heroic courage, alone and unaided, Moodie faces the terror of her own disintegration. When she is finally able to look in a mirror, at the end of the first journal, she sees a body gone back to nature, an exhumed corpse, the proper lace and black rotted off, the skin "thickened/with bark and the white hairs of roots," the eyes bewildered, almost blind, budlike. The "heirloom face" she brought with her is a "crushed eggshell/among other debris" of shattered china, decayed shawl, pieces of letters—all those artifacts and emblems of the English gentlewoman she once was. Helpless, invaded—a female Gothic plight—she has been taken over by the wilderness as by an evil spell: she is the living but unrecognizable dead:

> (you find only
> the shape you already are
> but what
> if you have forgotten that
> or discover you
> have never known).

In the tradition of female Gothic, this facing of the empty self is heroic courage: but it is also a female lack of identity, a female dependency on the image to *be* the self.

Throughout the journals, while men impose their civil power on the wilderness, Moodie lets the wilderness impose its savage, Gothic power on her. The first journal, with Moodie as Gothic matron invaded by monstrous lair, builds a climactic Gothic terror. But when Moodie is unexpectedly rescued from those seven years of captive terror and is hauled back to civilization on her husband's sleigh, then she suddenly finds herself dispossessed of the wild eyes that had begun to glow within her; she feels relief but also "unlived in: they had gone."

The middle journal, of Moodie's first thirty years in Belleville, shows her recollecting in tranquility her experiences of savagery. (You can take the woman out of the wilderness, but you can't take the wilderness out of the woman.) Outwardly rescued, inwardly she rejects civilization, and dwells among danger, death, and horror. She sees her children die (literally) back into the land and return as clutching, brier-fingered ghosts. She sees the painfully built homesteads that were her composite self revert to forest. She sees the land itself as icy river and unknown ocean on which the living float; only the dead can enter its depths. Inside her head history breaks down to gibberish. The 1837 War she witnessed unravels into "those tiny ancestral figures/flickering dull white through the back of your skull,/confused, anxious," idiot faces and banana-clustered hands holding flags or guns, their advances through trees and fire no more actual than a child's crayon-scribbled fort.

Gothic victim turned celebrant of Gothic chaos and death, Moodie shows us the universal savagery beneath our civil selves:

> (Note: Never pretend this isn't
> part of the soil too, teadrinkers, and inadvertent
> victims and murderers, when we come this way
>
> again in other forms, take care
> to look behind, within
> where the skeleton face beneath
>
> the face puts on its feather mask, the arm
> within the arm lifts up the spear:

Her dreams are nightmare ghosts that claim her waking life: she is haunted by the wet and surging horror of the long-past bush garden where anything planted came up blood; by the suicidal and scar-throated hunter, Brian, who killed and felt his skin grow fur, his soul run innocent as hooves. Her dream-imagined, fear-furred night bear

> is real, heavier
> than real   I know
> even by daylight here
> in this visible kitchen
>
> it absorbs all terror

as it moves inside her skull towards her family in the lighted cabin.

By the end of the middle journal, Moodie comes to see herself not as the captive of exterior Gothic powers, but instead as the source of an interior Gothic wisdom: there are two voices inside her head, dividing reality between convention and horror. The truths she chooses are "jubilant with maggots." Atwood's accompanying collage shows Moodie scissored out, aged, hooded, staring witch-like from one baleful, deeply shrouded eye; a thin emptiness divides her, not from wilderness, but from civil, steepled Belleville.

In the last, death journal (which ranges up to the present), Moodie transcends her Gothic horrors of decay and death by joining them as, aging, she lets slip her human shapes and consciousness. In the "Daguerreotype Taken in Old Age" she accepts her image as pitted, cratered, eroded, a moon-face in the garden, a dead "being/eaten away by light." In the "Wish: Metamorphosis" she welcomes her shrinking, furred, and feather-wrinkled body, her puckered, burrowing mind, and exults at last in the animal eyes that may glow within her later, underground.

Dying, Moodie renounces flesh and custom, teacup and history. With a hero's—or a witch's—spirit of adventure, she crosses over into the wilderness and becomes its voice. Dead and underground, she prophesies against the bulldozer's silver paradise. Atwood's collage shows her buried body curving with the strata, completely touching, blending in at last, her limbs drifting or dancing with the earth. In a resurrection that is both Christian and pagan, she joins "those who have become the stone/voices of the land."

At the last Moodie appears as a ghostly old lady on a modern bus, unbanishable: "this is my kingdom still." Allied with snow and storm, she threatens her twentieth-century audience—us—with her wild, Gothic powers:

> I am the old woman
> sitting across from you on the bus,
> her shoulders drawn up like a shawl;
> out of her eyes come secret
> hatpins, destroying
> the walls, the ceiling
>
> Turn, look down:
> there is no city;

this is the centre of a forest

your place is empty.

Like a triumphant witch, or a science-fiction time traveller, or a medieval revenant, this hero haunts us with the Grimm and Gothic terrors of the elder, wilder realm that she has made her own.

DOUBLE OR NOTHING: THE VICTOR AND THE BEING

Power Politics is Atwood's most doubled and dividing sequence: even its Gothic structure is dual, for its victor/victim games (Atwood's critical terms, from *Survival*) reenact not only the invaded hero-victim *I* vs. the monstrous hero-villain *you* of *The Circle Game* and elsewhere; but also, concurrently, the Gothic nightmare of that early victor who dared create a monster being— Mary Shelley's Victor, surnamed Frankenstein.

These two sets of Gothic antagonists overlap, contrast, juxtapose, and superimpose upon each other, so that the victim of one set may simultaneously be the victor of the other pair: "How can I stop you/Why did I create you" asks the female *I*, shifting from imperilled victim to guilty author of her torments—and she is truly both. Each of these Gothic antagonists is paired to an external Other who is its double, shadow, outcast self—as Shelley's Victor and "being" (her term) were each other's alter images. Each of Atwood's antagonists is also self-split within, for evil or good, power or suffering: female and male compete for victory and victimhood; creator and created vie like Shelley's pair in enmity and wretchedness. The Gothic terror and the Gothic horror, so divided and redoubled, take place as in a hall of mirrors, where reality is instantly evaded and yet reflected, distorted and yet magnified.

Even the cover of *Power Politics* (conceived by Atwood and executed by William Kimber) forwarns us of reality within reality: for the warrior and his captive woman are sadomasochism in Gothic dress. But they are simultaneously the burdened male tied to dependent female, for his extended arm, tied to her dangling weight, would suffer excruciating pain. They are simultaneously a suit of rigid, empty armor (he has no flesh, no eyes) which props the female seer whose pose is the Hanged One of the Tarot, signifying "life in suspension," real bodily "life and not death."

Throughout *Power Politics* reality is thus triple: the Gothic sadomasochistic pair are true—so true that the book is usually read as sexist realism, women readers confirming it and men readers protesting, as Atwood has observed. But the pair are also true reversed, he victim and she heartless. And always they are characters within a third, Frankensteinian Gothic where as creator-seer she is Victor, he the hapless being.

Thus, in the first of the three sections, he enters as a cruel hook; then a three-headed monster, rising like Victor's being or a Canadian Indian monster from a snowbank, shivering "cunningly." Farcically stabbed, he inflates to a dirigible-sized Superman. Drunk, he plays Christ. Beautiful wooden General, he promises bronze rescues but delivers her blind, paralyzed, one of a slavish horde of female followers who casts flowers under his hooves. Strange and repellent growth, he thrives in darkness. A body with head attached, he collides and they both shatter. A dead starfish, he floats belly up on her. And when towards the end of the section he escapes, "nothing/ remembers you but the bruises/on my thighs and the inside of my skull."

As the above litany makes clear, his role of monstrous Gothic villain alternates with his role as pathetic Gothic monster. The Superman gets stabbed; the beautiful wooden General fixes it so he almost wins and longs to be bandaged before he is cut; the bruiser makes *his* escape. But even his sufferings smack of romantic male egotism, a demand for female sympathy as well as female submission.

Though her role of victim alternates with, and is compounded by snarl, threat, and self-denunciation, her rebellion is all an interior female Gothic, a victim's fantasy: the restaurant stabbing is farce and wish, an act that doesn't happen, unreal as his apotheosis into Superman dirigible. The next poems show him alive and dominant, fake Christ who gets her succour, fake General who literally overrides his female followers. Her perception that he is fake is but interior female hatred, a victim's curse, silent or unheard. The double victim/villain roles of each confuse and paralyze the female *I*; her horror and her guilt confound escape, for she would escape his menace and cannot escape his suffering or her guilt.

But the above litany also reveals the *you* as a projection made monstrous by the creating *I*, a Gothic Other drawn from Shelley's *Frankenstein*. As the first wretch (Shelley's term) was made outwardly hideous but inwardly humane; as he sought love from his horrified creator, fled in rain, wandered suffering and unpitied, then reappeared to his heartless creator in an Alpine sea of ice, so this monster in the opening poem "reappears" in a snowbank with needs and "cunning;" shivers, seeks love, and flees from his unloving creator, and dissolves in rain at the end of the first section. But this Victor has read *Frankenstein*, and coldly proclaims her guilt:

> I approach this love
> like a biologist
> pulling on my rubber
> gloves & white labcoat
>
> You flee from it
> like an escaped political
> prisoner, and no wonder.

As in *Frankenstein*, this creator repudiates the "body with head/ attached" that is the complement to her own divided self, the "head with/ body attached." The being's flight reveals the creator's monstrous and unloving egotism. As in Shelley, the two compete for power and victimhood. When one waxes, the Other wanes. but unlike Shelley's being, this Other is a sexual Other, and yet so close a mirror-double that his external reality is never sure. Throughout the first section, the creating *I* shapes him cruel, hideous, fake, evil, multiform; at the end she forgets his vanished, rain-dissolved shape, which, like the Cheshire Cat or Watchbird haunts her bed:

> My walls absorb
> you, breathe you forth
> again, you resume
> yourself, I do not recognize you.

Read as a Frankensteinian Gothic, then, the first section of *Power Politics* covers creation and flight of the wretch. The victor *I* projects an outwardly monstrous Other, and monstrously recoils from it. The second, central section corresponds roughly to the wretch's unsuccessful attempts to join humanity. In Atwood as in Shelley, humanity is revealed as murderous persecuters, and the wretch begins to imitate them. In this section the real monster is what the legend of Frankenstein has become for the whole world in the twentieth century: the atomic nightmare given life, the monster system that may destroy us all. Against the gigantic horrors of the war machine, the private Gothic costumes recede, quaint fakeries; the *I* and *you* struggle simply to stay alive and innocent. What does appear of private victor-victim games here is mostly defrocked; the *you* could be anyone generic and faceless, merely alive, ordinary, and "growing older, of course you'll/die but not yet, you'll outlive/even my distortions of you." At the end of the second section, she preaches mutual flight from power games, but there is no reply, perhaps no listener.

The third and final section turns from global horrors back to the personal Gothic duel where the *I* and *you* contend in sterile sadomasochism. She would go back to nature, but fears creation and refuses children; nature thereafter threatens her with death, and the literary horrors "fertilize each other/in the cold and with bulging eyes." This final section corresponds roughly to the last parts of Shelley's novel; in both books the hideous being turns from man to nature, and turns to hideous killer. The creating *I* is racked by the monster's persecutions and by guilt. Like Victor's being, Atwood's Other crosses over into nature, and flourishes there as bestial god or noble, godlike beast. The original Victor followed but died in pursuit; Atwood's creator starts to follow but, fearing death, turns back.

In Atwood's third section the Gothic sadomasochism breaks out unchecked: as in the first section, but far worse, it is she who dies, gets broken, blames herself; she who waits, dependent, for his revelation or torment; she who gets trampled in his escape; she who is the imperilled and tortured female victim; and, at the end, the human target stalked by natural monster him. The beautiful wooden General of the first section seems naïve and playful compared to this monster-villain loosed from horror film, from *Frankenstein*, from sadomasochistic tales. Now he is simultaneously the evil Rochester (see Jean Rhys' female Gothic novel, *Wide Sargasso Sea*, for how Rochester changed from lover to villain, and drove his first wife mad), King Kong, and Frankensteinian monster of the film.

Now her victim's alliance *with* her tormentor is grotesque terror and masochism:

> catastrophe, I see you
> blind and one-handed, flashing
> in the dark, trees breaking
> under your feet, you demand,
> you demand
>
> I lie mutilated beside
> you; beneath us there are
> sirens, fires, the people run
> squealing, the city
> is crushed and gutted,
> the ends of your fingers bleed
> from 1000 murders
>
> Putting on my clothes
> again, retreating, closing doors
> I am amazed/I can continue
> to think, eat, anything
>
> How can I stop you
>
> Why did I create you.

The terror is real, the sadism is real, only the Gothic costumes are false. In the next poem, as she hesitates outside the door, telling the wrong lies, she sees him as bleeding Christ and slain God, and warns him to escape her costumes. Yet the door leads to his Bluebeard's castle stairs, his Fichter's room of bloodied, dismembered wives. But the last alternative—sans costumes, sans lies—is the worse: "In the room we will find nothing/In the room we will find each other."

Now he escapes again to nature; she briefly follows, but soon pulls back to the human side of the window. Like Victor's being in the Alpine heights and Arctic wastes he goes on, allied with earth, sea, and death, lost in water and moving shadow. In the penultimate poem the *I* repudiates all costumes; the bronze man, the fragile man, the scaling fanged Dracula she made "were all inaccurate." But were they? She is still inside a mirrored and remirrored gothic horror chamber where the victim cannot know who is victim and cannot flee: the last poem shows him scaled again, and Frankenstein's monster again, rising from "the pits and starless/deep nights of the sea," unstoppable, bearing towards her "a new death/which is mine and no-one else's."

Power Politics, then, creates a mirrored Gothic of the Other where a male who is both wretch and victim, monster and villain, stalks a female who is both distorter and creator, adventurer and victim. Inside this doubly Gothic structure the horror and the terror redouble, divide, and multiply. Atwood's sequence thus reflects not only Gothic literature and modern, fragmented reality, but also the particular power politics of a society where men have outward power and women have inward pain: the female *I* is alienated from her body and her head, even from her terror; addict, she comes alive only in relation to a sexual Other who is a series of oppressive masculine poses. His power threatens her, his sufferings milk her; either way, she is his victim and yet guilty of her victimization. That she prefers the Gothic horrors to reality is not only her private addiction, but also the politics of how the dominated endure, and the aesthetics of how the bored escape. That the Gothic stays interior, and that the *I* creates only by seeing—not by speaking, leading, acting— is not only a Gothic addiction/vision, but is also the silence of the politically isolated and disabled.

Atwood's Frankensteinian *Politics*, then, brings to static climax the Other-centered and interior Gothic of the first two sequences. Here, as in *The Circle Game*, the female *I* flees in static and recurrent terror the shifting, deadly, vulnerable, monstrous lover-Other. Here, as in *The Circle Game*, the *I* is locked into a polarized victor-victim duel with her sexual Other and/or with an inhuman, icy, post-Darwinian universe that promises her death. In *Power Politics*, the terror swings inward to the mirrored and remirrored Frankensteinian Gothic; in the nineteenth-century *Journals*, the terror swings outward to the inhuman natural universe, which becomes a monstrous, haunted lair, tempting as a demon-lover, luring the hero-victim into its deadly, savage realm.

But, whether the worst danger comes from sexual Other or from inhuman Other, in all three sequences the target is the same: the female *I*. And the outward power and danger, for good or evil, is the same: the Other, be it inhuman or masculine. And, in all three sequences, the Gothic stays interior to the female *I* who is its secret author, its silenced victim: no character, but only the reader can (perhaps) be trusted to share this animating and addicting terror. The politics of this terror, invisible to patriarchs yet everywhere for those who share and identify, are female-centered: for this interior terror releases, diverts, and dangerously, narrowly channels the limits and burdens and nightmares common to the ordinary, daylit female life.

This essay, having followed the Gothic terror and its elements through Atwood's first three poetic sequences, book-by-book and theme-by-theme; having pursued the more visible ghosts of Grimm and British Gothic therein; having then, like a traveller at journey's end, gathered its memories and souvenirs into a summary display (a simple one, but with a dangerous two-way metaphor of female Gothic life and literature saved for the last)— this essay could well stop here. But that summary display, which appears complete but gathers only some parts into a convenient and deceptive whole, misrepresents the protean nature and effects of Atwood's Gothic: these sequences, these Gothic elements and terrors, should not be left to fall by default into such a whole.

For Atwood's poetic work, here and elsewhere, is multifaceted as the fly's eye: to fix one aspect in one light is to turn away to darkness the other facets. These three poetic sequences reflect, refract, and like a lens distill from/to reality (whatever that appears to be) and Atwood's other work, made and not yet made; from Grimm, *Frankenstein*, the Brontës; from science fiction, comic books, horror films; from the *Bible*, scientific fictions, modern politics and sexist realism, Canadian literature and North American Indian myth; from the Lord Knows What. Though Atwood's best work, in these sequences and elsewhere, is as compellingly original as Coleridge's Xanadu, in one (misleading) sense it is not original at all, but a place in which the shapes of her culture come to life, metamorphosing like Proteus, like ghosts, like caterpillars: and among these shifting forms the Gothic is one obvious yet transient shape, one kind of voice, not simple, not stable, but resonant, echoing, drifting back and forth and sideways with the other voices that it has become and will become in other readings, other sequences.

Biographical Notes

Anne Bradstreet was born in 1612 or 1613, probably in or around Northamptonshire, England. Her father, Thomas Dudley, was steward to an earl. According to Cotton Mather, her mother, Dorothy Yorke, was "a Gentlewoman whose Extract and Estate were Considerable." After recovering from smallpox, the sixteen-year-old Anne married Simon Bradstreet, the Cambridge-educated son of a Nonconformist minister.

On March 29, 1630, the Bradstreets, the Dudleys, and other members of the Massachusetts Company set sail for the New World. They arrived in a poverty-stricken Salem on June 12. By December, the Company had settled in a place they called Newtown, site of present-day Cambridge, Massachusetts. In 1634, Anne and Simon Bradstreet and the Dudleys moved to Ipswich, where Anne Bradstreet's first child, Simon, was born and where she did most of her writing. After another move in 1640, the poet spent the remainder of her life in Andover.

Unbeknownst to her, John Woodbridge, the Minister of Andover, sailed back to England in 1647 with a copy of some of Bradstreet's poems. He arranged to have them published in London in 1650 under the title *The Tenth Muse, Lately Sprung Up in America*, making her the first published American poet. She spent the remainder of her life raising children and writing and revising her poetry. She died in Andover in September 1672.

EMILY DICKINSON

Emily Dickinson was born in Amherst, Massachusetts, on December 10, 1830. From 1847 to 1848 she attended Mount Holyoke Female Seminary in South Hadley, Massachusetts. Her first known poem, "Awake ye muses nine, sing me a strain divine," a valentine to George Gould, was published in a February 1850 Amherst College *Indicator*.

Unmarried and reticent, Dickinson traveled very infrequently and remained in her parents' house all her life. She was certainly not unaware of her literary contemporaries, however. An avid reader of British and American authors, she heard Emerson speak at Amherst in 1857. In 1862, she wrote to Thomas Wentworth Higginson, a noted poet and critic, asking for literary advice. He responded, and although he thought that her poetry was a little strange, their correspondence turned into a lifelong friendship.

In March of 1883, Thomas Nash asked Dickinson to submit a volume of poems for publication. She never filled this request, and when she died in 1886, only seven of her poems had been published. While sorting through her sister's effects, Lavinia Dickinson discovered over nine hundred poems, divided and sewn into sixty little packets or "volumes." T. W. Higginson and Mabel Loomis Todd edited, considerably altered, and published some of these poems in 1890 and 1891. For the next sixty years variously edited volumes of Dickinson's poetry were published, and the complete variorum edition, *The Poems of Emily Dickinson*, edited by Thomas H. Johnson, appeared in 1955.

GERTRUDE STEIN

Gertrude Stein was born in Allegheny, Pennsylvania, in 1874, the youngest of five children. Before she was grown up, both of her parents died, and Gertrude and her brother Leo were placed under the guardianship of their older brother, Michael, who continued to manage their father's estate and to provide for them throughout their lives.

Gertrude and Leo were very close; when he went to study at Harvard, she followed and began taking courses at Radcliffe. At the suggestion of William James, she undertook a series of experiments on automatic writing. She published her results in *The Harvard Psychological Review* in 1896 and 1898. Interested in pursuing a career in psychology, she began medical school at The Johns Hopkins University in the fall of 1898. By the end of her third year, however, she was no longer devoted to completing medical school. Searching for something to do, she joined Leo in the autumn of 1903 in Paris at 27 rue de Fleurus, the studio that became famous in the next several years for their extensive and daring collection of modern art.

Gertrude Stein began to write seriously in Paris: she completed her first novella, *Quod Erat Demonstrandum* (*Q.E.D.* or *Things As They Are*) in 1903; a year later, she finished *Fernhurst*, and the subsequent two years were spent translating Flaubert's *Trois Contes* (*Three Stories*) and writing *Three Lives*. She met Alice B. Toklas, her lifelong companion, in 1907. As her writing became more prolific and more experimental, Stein's circle of friends widened to include Matisse, Picasso, Hemingway, F. Scott Fitzgerald, Appollinaire, Gris, Marie Laurencin, Sherwood Anderson, and many other influential twentieth-century artists. Stein's early and middle works include *Tender Buttons* (1914), *The Making of Americans* (1925), *Composition as Explanation* (published posthumously), *Lucy Church Amiably* (1930), and *How to Write*

(1931). Following the great success of *The Autobiography of Alice B. Toklas*, published in 1933, Stein returned to the United States on a speaking tour. Her lectures are collected in *Lectures in America* and *Narration*. Upon her return to Paris, she wrote *The Geographical History of America* (1936) and *Everybody's Autobiography* (1937). She continued to write throughout World War II and up until her death, of cancer, in 1946. Much of her work was published posthumously by Yale University Press in the 1950s.

H. D. (HILDA DOOLITTLE)

Hilda Doolittle was born on September 10, 1886, in Bethlehem, Pennsylvania. She entered Bryn Mawr College in 1904, but within two years withdrew because of poor health. For the next five years she wrote and lived with her family. In 1911, she traveled abroad and remained in England. Two years later she married Richard Aldington, a British Imagist poet.

H. D.'s first book, *Sea Garden*, was published in 1916, along with *Choruses from Iphigenia in Aulis*, a translation. She also became assistant editor of *The Egoist*, a post she later relinquished to T. S. Eliot. In 1918, she met Winifred Ellerman, a historical novelist who wrote under the name Bryher. Bryher remained a lifelong friend, benefactor, and companion. H. D.'s daughter, Perdita, was born in 1919; she also separated from her husband that year. For the next several years, she traveled extensively with Bryher—to Greece, the United States, then Egypt and Switzerland. From the mid-1920s to the early 1930s, H. D. wrote and published at a furious pace. *Heliodora and Other Poems* appeared in 1924, her *Collected Poems* in 1925, *Palimpsest*, a novel, in 1926, *Hippolytus Temporizes*, a verse drama, in 1927, *Hedylus*, a novel, in 1928, and *Red Roses for Bronze* in 1931.

From 1933 through 1934, H. D. was under analysis by Freud; she wrote about this experience in *Tribute to Freud*, published in 1956. Between the late 1930s and her death on September 28, 1961, H. D. wrote ten more books, including *The Hedgehog* (1936), a children's story, *The Walls Do Not Fall* (1944), the first of her *War Trilogy*, *Bid Me To Live* (1960), a novel, and *Helen in Egypt* (1961). In 1959 she received the Brandeis University Creative Arts Award for Poetry and in 1960 she was the first woman to receive the Award of Merit Medal for Poetry from the American Academy of Arts and Letters.

MARIANNE MOORE

Marianne Moore was born on November 15, 1887, in Kirkwood, Missouri. She graduated from Bryn Mawr College in 1909 and from Carlisle Commercial College a year later. In 1911, she began to teach business classes at the United States Industrial Indian School. Her first poems appeared in 1915, in *The Egoist*, *Poetry*, and *Others*. Moore and her mother moved to New York City in 1918, and three years later *Poems* was published by Egoist Press. That same year, she began part-time work as a librarian in the Hudson Park branch of the New York Public Library. *Observations* was published by Dial

Press in 1924; the publisher also gave Moore a $2,000 award for "unusual literary value." The following year she became editor of *The Dial* magazine, a post she retained until the magazine ceased publication in 1929. *Selected Poems* was published in 1935, and ten years later Moore received a Guggenheim Fellowship. In 1947 she was elected to The National Institute of Arts and Letters, and in 1949 she received an honorary degree from Wilson College, the first of sixteen such degrees that she received from American institutions.

Collected Poems*, published in 1951, won the Pulitzer Prize, a National Book Award, and a Bollingen Prize. Moore was a visiting lecturer at Bryn Mawr College in 1953, and the following year her translation of *The Fables of La Fontaine* appeared, winning the Croix de Chevalier des Arts et Lettres. *Predilections*, a collection of essays and reviews, was published in 1955, and six years later *A Marianne Moore Reader* became available. As Marianne Moore aged, various festivities were held in her honor: The National Institute of Arts and Letters celebrated her seventy-fifth birthday, and in 1964 *Festschrift for Marianne Moore's Seventy-Seventh Birthday* and *Omaggio a Marianne Moore* were published. Her *Complete Poems* appeared in 1967, winning the Edward McDowell Medal and the Poetry Society of America's Gold Medal. The year 1968 brought Moore a National Medal for Literature and the opportunity for the long-time baseball fan to pitch the first ball of the season at Yankee Stadium. Named Senior Citizen of the Year by the New York Conference on Aging in 1969, Marianne Moore also received her last honorary degree, from Harvard University, in that year. She died on February 5, 1972, and the second edition of *The Complete Poems of Marianne Moore*, with her final revisions, was published in 1981.

LOUISE BOGAN

Louise Bogan was born on August 11, 1897, in Livermore Falls, Maine. She grew up in New England and entered Boston University in 1915. A year later, however, she left school and married Curt Alexander, an Army career man. In 1917, they moved to the Panama Canal Zone, where their daughter was born. Two of Bogan's poems, "Betrothed," and "The Young Wife," were published that year in the magazine *Others*. In 1918, she returned to the United States with her daughter; her marriage broke up soon afterward.

Bogan continued to write and she held a number of jobs, including work at various branches of the New York Public Library. Her first book, *Body of This Death*, was published in 1923. A year later she began writing book reviews and accepted the managing editorship of *The Measure*. Her second book, *Dark Summer*, was published in 1929, and in 1930 she received the John Reed Memorial Prize from *Poetry*. A year later, close to a nervous breakdown, she entered the New York Neurological Institute. Her recovery was speedy, and a month later she resumed her normal life.

In 1933, Bogan received a Guggenheim Fellowship for writing abroad, went to Europe, and, upon her return, had another brief breakdown. Her third book, *The Sleeping Fury*, was published in 1937, and *Poems and New Poems* appeared in 1941.

From 1948 through 1968, Bogan taught at seven different universities ranging from the University of Washington to New York University. She continued to write poetry and criticism, which was collected and published in 1955 as *Selected Criticism: Poetry and Prose*, and she made several collaborative translations: Goethe's *Elective Affinities* with Elizabeth Mayer, poems by Paul Valéry with May Sarton, and *The Journals of Jules Renard* with Elizabeth Roget. Bogan also continued to receive awards: she won the Bollingen Prize in 1955, a $5,000 prize from The American Academy of Poets in 1959, the Senior Creative Arts Award from Brandeis in 1962, and a $10,000 prize from the National Endowment for the Arts. Her last book of poetry, *The Blue Estuaries: Poems 1923–1968*, was published in 1969. A year later, on February 4, 1970, Louise Bogan died. *A Poet's Alphabet: Reflections on the Literary Art and Vocation* was published posthumously.

ELIZABETH BISHOP

Elizabeth Bishop was born on February 8, 1911, in Worcester, Massachusetts. Her father died eight months after her birth, and her mother was hospitalized for mental disorders several times in Bishop's very early life, and then from 1916 until her death in 1934. She grew up in the homes of various relatives: with her mother's parents in Nova Scotia, with her father's parents in Worcester, and finally with her Aunt Maud in Boston.

In 1934, during her senior year at Vassar, Bishop met Marianne Moore, and the two poets became very close friends. Bishop's first poems were published in 1935 in an anthology entitled *Trial Balances*. Her first book, *North & South*, was published in 1946; a year later she received a Guggenheim Fellowship. Other awards followed, from Bryn Mawr and the American Academy of Arts and Letters, and Bishop decided in 1951 to use some of her prize money to travel in South America and through the Strait of Magellan. She came to a halt in Brazil because of illness, but, after she recovered, decided to stay there. For the next twenty-three years she lived with her friend Lota Constenat de Macedo Soares in Rio de Janeiro and Ouro Prêto, Brazil.

Bishop's poems *North & South—A Cold Spring* appeared in 1955 and won the 1956 Pulitzer Prize, a *Partisan Review* Fellowship, and an Amy Lowell Traveling Fellowship. Her next book, *Questions of Travel*, was published in 1965. *Complete Poems* followed in 1969, winning a National Book Award. In the fall of 1970, she began a yearly one-semester appointment at Harvard, and when Lota died, Bishop moved to Boston. Coincident with the publication of her *Geography III* in 1976, she received the Neustadt International Prize for Literature. Three years later she died, and the last collection of her poetry, *The Complete Poems: 1927–1979*, was published posthumously.

MAY SWENSON

May Swenson was born in Logan Utah, in 1919, to Swedish Mormon parents. She graduated from Utah State Agricultural College with a B.A. degree in English, and went to work as a reporter for various newspapers in and around Logan. In 1937 she went to New York, where she worked as a secretary. She later became editor for New Directions Press. Her first poems were published by the *Saturday Review of Literature*; appearances in *The Nation, Poetry, The Hudson Review, Partisan Review*, and *Contact* followed. Her first book, *Another Animal: Poems*, was published in 1954. *A Cage of Spines* appeared in 1958, and she won an Amy Lowell Traveling Fellowship in 1961. *To Mix with Time* (1963) followed this journey, and in 1965 Swenson became the poet in residence at Purdue University. *Poems to Solve* was published in 1966, *Half Sun, Half Sleep* in 1967, and *Iconographs* and *More Poems To Solve* appeared in 1971. Her most acclaimed book, *New and Selected Things Taking Place*, was published in 1978 and nominated for the National Book Award in 1979. Swenson also won a $10,000 fellowship from The Academy of American Poets in 1979.

GWENDOLYN BROOKS

Gwendolyn Brooks was born on June 7, 1917, in Topeka, Kansas. She grew up on the South Side of Chicago, however, where she lives today. Strongly encouraged by her parents, she wrote poetry throughout her childhood, and, at sixteen, published her first poem in *The Defender*. She met her husband, aspiring writer Henry Blakely, at an NAACP Youth Council meeting, and they were married in 1939. Their son, Henry Jr., was born in 1940, and their daughter, Nora, in 1953.

Brooks's first book, *A Street in Bronzeville*, was published in 1945, and she received a grant from The National Institute of Arts and Letters, *Mademoiselle's* Merit Award, and a Guggenheim Fellowship. With the publication of *Annie Allen* in 1949, Gwendolyn Brooks became the first black woman to win a Pulitzer Poetry Prize. *Maud Martha* appeared in 1953, followed by *Bean Eaters* in 1960, *Selected Poems* in 1963, *In the Mecca* in 1968, and *The World of Gwendolyn Brooks* in 1971.

Brooks taught at various colleges in Illinois in the 1960s and in 1968 was named Poet Laureate of Illinois. Late in the 1960s, she became active in the Black Arts Movement; along with other black poets, she began to organize "neighborhood cultural events"—art exhibits, music festivals, and poetry readings—in Chicago's black neighborhoods. She also began to publish her books with black-owned and -operated presses. *Riot* (1969), *Family Pictures* (1970), *Aloneness* (1971), a children's book, and *Beckonings* (1975) were all published with the Broadside Press. Brooks was awarded her first honorary degree in 1970 from Northwestern University; it has been followed by more than forty such degrees. She has received two Guggenheim Fellowships since 1970 and the Shelley Award from the Poetry Society of America. She continues to publish with black presses: *Primer for Blacks* (1980) and *To Disembark* (1981) were published by The Third World Press.

DENISE LEVERTOV

Denise Levertov was born on October 24, 1923, in Ilford, Essex, England. She began writing poetry as a child, and at twelve had the audacity to send a sample of poetry to T. S. Eliot. He responded, advising her to continue writing. "Listening to Distant Guns" was published in *Poetry Quarterly* in 1940, and thereafter, her work was frequently accepted by British literary magazines. Her first book, *The Double Image*, was published in late 1946.

While traveling in Switzerland after the war, Levertov met the American writer Mitchell Goodman and married him. They moved to the United States in 1948, when she was pregnant with their son, Nikolai Gregory. She became a citizen of the United States in 1955, and her first American book, *Here and Now*, was published in 1957 by City Lights Press. Other volumes followed quickly: *Overland to the Islands* appeared in 1958, and *With Eyes at the Back of Our Heads*, a collection that won the Bess Hopkin Prize from *Poetry* magazine, in 1960. In 1962, Levertov received a Guggenheim Fellowship; in the early 1960s she was also poetry editor of *The Nation*. From 1964 to 1966 she was an associate scholar at the Radcliffe Institute for Independent Studies in Boston. In 1965 she received a medal from the American Institute of Arts and Letters and, with Muriel Rukeyser and other poets, established an activist group called Writers and Artists Protest against the War in Vietnam. *The Sorrow Dance*, published in 1967, shows signs of this activism and the death of Levertov's sister, Olga. Other books, *To Stay Alive* and *The Freeing of the Dust*, written during the war years, are also strongly marked by these experiences of war and protest.

Divorced in the mid-1970s, Levertov has taught in various colleges and universities, published two more books of poetry, *Life in the Forest* (1978) and *The Collected Earlier Poems: 1940–1960* (1979), and *Light up the Cave* (1981), a collection of prose, reviews, and essays.

ANNE SEXTON

Anne Sexton was born Anne Gray Harvey on November 9, 1928, in Newton, Massachusetts. On August 16, 1948, she eloped with Alfred Muller Sexton II to North Carolina. The following year they moved to Massachusetts, where, after attending a modeling course, Anne Sexton was periodically employed as a model. Between the birth of her daughter, in 1953, and her son, in 1956, she was hospitalized for "emotional disturbance." In 1956, she was again admitted to a mental hospital, her children were sent to relatives, and she attempted to commit suicide.

With the encouragement of her psychiatrist, she began to write poetry; they both saw it as a way of allowing her unconscious to "speak." She began to take poetry classes with John Holmes at the Boston Center for Adult

Education in 1957, and in 1958 she won a scholarship to the Antioch Writers Conference, where she worked with W. D. Snodgrass. She also developed friendships with Maxine Kumin, Sylvia Plath, and George Starbuck, and was given a place in Robert Lowell's graduate writing seminar at Boston University. Her first book, *To Bedlam and Part Way Back*, was published in 1960, and in 1961 she taught poetry and writing at Harvard and Radcliffe. The following year she was hospitalized again, in a pattern that continued to repeat itself: awards and publication, followed by suicidal depression. By the end of 1963, she had published eight books and received a number of awards which included a traveling fellowship from the American Academy of Arts and Letters, election as a Fellow of the Royal Society of Literature in London, a Pulitzer Prize for *Live or Die*, the Shelley Award from the Poetry Society of America, a Guggenheim Fellowship, and honorary degrees from Tufts and Fairfield Universities and Regis College. On October 4, 1974, she committed suicide by carbon monoxide poisoning.

ADRIENNE RICH

Adrienne Rich was born in Baltimore on May 16, 1929. She wrote poetry throughout her childhood, and when she graduated from Radcliffe College in 1951 her first book, *A Change of World*, was published in the Yale Younger Poets series. The following year, she received a Guggenheim Fellowship, and traveled in Europe. When she returned in 1953, she married Alfred H. Conrad, a professor at Harvard. Their first son, David, was born in 1955, the same year that *Diamond Cutters and Other Poems* appeared. Two other sons were born, Paul in 1957 and Jacob in 1959. In 1960, Adrienne Rich won The National Institute of Arts and Letters Award for Poetry and was the Phi Beta Kappa poet at William and Mary College. The following year she received another Guggenheim Fellowship and took her family to live in the Netherlands. The year 1962 brought her a Bollingen Foundation Grant for the translation of Dutch poetry, and the following year an Amy Lowell Traveling Fellowship.

Snapshots of a Daughter-in-Law won The Bess Hopkin Prize from *Poetry* magazine. In 1965 Rich was the Phi Beta Kappa Poet at Swarthmore College; the following year *Necessities of Life* was published and nominated for the National Book Award. In 1966 Rich was Phi Beta Kappa poet at Harvard, and from 1966 through 1968 she taught, variously, at Swarthmore, Columbia, and in the Open Admission and SEEK programs at City College of New York. *Selected Poems* was published in England in 1967, and *Leaflets* appeared in 1969.

In 1970 her husband died. Adrienne Rich remained in New York City with her sons, continuing to teach and write with an increasingly feminist focus. *The Will to Change* was published in 1971, winning the Shelley Award of The Poetry Society of America, and *Diving into the Wreck* appeared in 1973. She accepted the National Book Award for *Diving*, along with the other nominees, Audre Lorde and Alice Walker, "in the name of all the women whose voices have gone . . . unheard." Her *Poems: Selected and New* appeared in 1974, followed by a historical work: *Of Woman Born: Motherhood as Experience and Institution* in 1976. Her most recent works have included *The Dream of a Common Language* (1978), *A Wild Patience Has Taken Me This Far* (1981), and *Sources* (1983).

SYLVIA PLATH

Sylvia Plath was born on October 27, 1932, in Boston. Her father died when she was eight years old. In August 1950, just before she entered Smith College, her short story "And Summer Will Not Come Again" appeared in *Seventeen* magazine. A poem, "Bitter Strawberries," was also published in the *Christian Science Monitor*. These small successes were followed by more short stories and reviews in *Seventeen*, and a prizewinning story published in *Mademoiselle*. At the end of her sophomore year, Plath won a guest editorship on the staff of *Mademoiselle*, and for the month of June 1952 lived in New York in what seemed a fashionable whirl of celebrities. The month culminated in the publication of an article, an editorial piece, and a poem. Later that summer, after her return home, Plath attempted to commit suicide. She was rescued, however, and after several months of hospitalization and treatment, she returned to Smith and completed her degree with honors. Funded by a Fulbright Fellowship, she began a program of studies at Cambridge, and she continued to publish poems. She also met and married the British poet Ted Hughes in 1956. A year later the couple moved to the United States, Plath to teach at Smith, and Hughes at the University of Massachusetts. After a year of teaching, the two poets moved to Boston to try to live on the earnings from their writings.

In December 1959, Ted Hughes and Sylvia Plath returned to England; the following April their daughter, Frieda, was born. Later that year, Plath's first volume of poetry, *The Colossus*, was published. In 1961 she received a Saxton Fellowship, which covered her expenses while she wrote *The Bell Jar*, published in 1963 under the pseudonym Victoria Lucas. In 1962, a son, Nicholas, was born, Sylvia Plath finished a radio play entitled *Three Women: A Monologue for Three Voices*, and discovered that her husband was having an affair. The dissolution of their marriage was explosive and catapulted Plath into a deep depression. She and the children moved to London and lived in a tiny apartment during the winter of 1962–1963, the period when she composed most of the poems which comprise the *Ariel* volume. On the morning of February 11, 1963, Sylvia Plath committed suicide by inhaling gas from her oven. Most of her work was published posthumously, and *The Collected Poems*, edited by Ted Hughes and published in 1981, won a Pulitzer Prize for poetry.

AUDRE LORDE

Audre Lorde was born on February 18, 1934, in New York. As a young adult in the 1950s, she held several jobs and attended night school at Hunter College. When her father died in 1953 and left her a small inheritance, she decided to go to Mexico, where she attended the National University of Mexico for a year. Upon her return, she was hired as an assistant to the librarian in the Welfare Department; she also continued to take classes at Hunter and completed her degree in 1959. Two years later she received a Master of Library Science from Columbia University, and began to work in New York libraries. Her first publishing success was also in 1961: Langston Hughes included some of her poems in his anthology, *New Negro Poets, USA*. Throughout the 1960s her poetry was anthologized, for the most part by editors in Holland, Italy, and England. Her poetry also began to appear in black magazines such as *Black World* and *Harlem Writers Quarterly*.

Although Lorde has identified herself throughout her life as a lesbian, she married Edwin Ashley Robbins in 1962. They had two children and were amicably divorced within seven years. Finally, in the late 1960s, Lorde began to receive recognition for her work. In 1968 she received an award from the National Endowment for the Arts, held a visiting professorship at Atlanta University, and was the Poet in Residence at Tougaloo College in Mississippi. Her first book of poetry, *The First Cities*, also appeared that year. *Cables to Rage* was published in 1970 by Broadside Press, and *From a Land Where Other People Live*, published in 1970, was nominated for a National Book Award in 1974.

In the 1970s, Lorde taught at Lehman College, John Jay College of Criminal Justice, and City College of New York. She was appointed a professor at Hunter College, a position which she retains today. *Coal* was published in 1976, *The Black Unicorn* in 1978, and *Chosen Poems Old and New* appeared in 1982. Lorde has also written *The Cancer Journals* and *Zami: A New Spelling of My Name*, both autobiographical prose, and *Sister Outsider*, a collection of essays.

AMY CLAMPITT

Amy Clampitt was born in the first half of the twentieth century in New Providence, Iowa, and graduated from Grinnell College. In 1978, her poems began to appear in literary magazines and periodicals, including *The New Yorker*, *The Kenyon Review*, *The New Republic*, *Prairie Schooner*, *Poetry*, and *The Yale Review*. She was awarded a Guggenheim Fellowship in 1982, and her first highly acclaimed book, *The Kingfisher*, was published in 1983. Her second collection of poems, *What the Light Was Like*, was published in 1985.

VICKI HEARNE

Vicki Hearne was born in 1946. A horse and dog trainer for some years, she also wrote poetry. Her first book, *Nervous Horses*, was published in 1980, and in 1982 she coauthored *Horse Breaking: The Obedience Method*. She has taught poetry and fiction at the University of California at Riverside and is currently teaching English at Yale University. Her second volume of poetry, *In the Absence of Horses*, was published in 1983. She has also written several articles on animals and language.

JAY MACPHERSON

Jay Macpherson, born in 1931, is a Canadian, reportedly descended from the 18th-century Scottish poet Macpherson who wrote under the name Ossian. She is a poet and professor of English at Victoria College in the University of Toronto. Her critical work includes a major study of the nineteenth-century prose romance, *The Spirit of Solitude*, and her poetry has appeared in three volumes: *The Boatman* (1957), *Welcoming Disaster* (1976), and *Poems Twice Told* (1981). She has also written on mythology for children.

MARGARET ATWOOD

Margaret Atwood was born on November 18, 1939, in Ottawa, Ontario, Canada. Much of her childhood was spent writing stories and poems. In 1957, she enrolled in Victoria College, University of Toronto, where she studied with Jay Macpherson and continued to write. Her first book, *Double Persephone*, was published in 1961 and awarded the E. J. Pratt Medal for Poetry. Throughout the 1960s, she sporadically attended graduate school at Harvard and in 1967 began a dissertation on the English metaphysical romance. She received the President's Medal for Poetry from the University of Western Toronto in 1966, and her first major collection of poems, *The Circle Game*, was published. A year later, she won the Governor-General's Poetry Award for *The Circle Game*, and first prize in the Centennial Commission Poetry Competition for *The Animals in That Country*.

Between 1967 and 1983, Margaret Atwood taught literature and creative writing at four different Canadian Universities, and wrote a number of novels—including *The Edible Woman* (1969), *Surfacing* (1972), *Lady Oracle* (1976), and *Life Before Man* (1979)—and volumes of poetry—*The Journals of Susanna Moodie* (1970), *Power Politics* (1971), *You Are Happy* (1974), *Two-Headed Poems* (1978), and *Murder in the Dark* (1983). Her awards from that period include a D. Litt. from Trent University in 1973, another honorary degree from Queen's University in 1974, the City of Toronto Book Award and the Canadian Bookseller's Association Award in 1977, a Litt. D. from Concordia University and a Radcliffe Medal in 1980. Following the birth of her daughter, Eleanor, in 1976, Atwood also began writing children's books.

Contributors

HAROLD BLOOM, Sterling Professor of the Humanities at Yale University, is the author of *The Anxiety of Influence*, *Poetry and Repression*, and many other volumes of literary criticism. His forthcoming study, *Freud: Transference and Authority*, attempts a full-scale reading of all of Freud's major writings. A MacArthur Prize Fellow, he is general editor of five series of literary criticism published by Chelsea House.

JANE DONAHUE EBERWEIN is a professor of English at Oakland University in Rochester, Michigan.

SHIRA WOLOSKY teaches English at Yale University. She is the author of *Emily Dickinson: A Voice of War*.

JOANNE FEIT DIEHL teaches English at the University of California at Davis. She is the author of *Dickinson and the Romantic Imagination*.

SHARON CAMERON is a professor of English at The Johns Hopkins University. Her most recent book is *The Corporeal Self: Allegories of the Body in Melville and Hawthorne*.

RANDA K. DUBNICK teaches English at the University of Kansas.

ADALAIDE MORRIS teaches English at the University of Iowa. She has written many articles on American women poets, is the author of *Wallace Stevens: Imagination and Faith*, and coeditor of *Extended Outlooks: The Iowa Review Collection of Contemporary Women Writers*.

BONNIE COSTELLO is an assistant professor of English at Boston University. She is the author of *Marianne Moore: Imaginary Possessions*.

DAVID BROMWICH is a professor of English at Princeton University.

DIANE WOOD MIDDLEBROOK is a professor of English at Stanford University.

SANDRA COOKSON is a poet and critic. She has taught at the University of Connecticut, Storrs.

HELEN VENDLER is a professor of English at Boston University and at Harvard University. President of the Modern Language Association in 1980, she is also a prolific critic; some of her work is collected in *Part of Nature, Part of Us.*

LEE EDELMAN is an assistant professor of English at Tufts University. He writes poetry and has published criticism on Hart Crane, John Ashbery, and Elizabeth Bishop.

RICHARD HOWARD is a poet, critic of poetry, and translator. He has written eight books of poetry, including *Fellow Feelings*, *Misgivings*, and *Lining Up*, and translated Baudelaire's *Les Fleurs du Mal*, as well as many books by Roland Barthes.

GARY SMITH teaches English at Southern Illinois University at Carbondale.

PAUL A. LACEY is provost and professor of English at Earlham College in Richmond, Indiana.

J. D. McCLATCHY is both a poet and a critic of poetry. His works include *Anne Sexton: The Artist and Her Critics* (1978), *Scenes from Another Life: Poems* (1981), and *Stars Principal* (1986). He is currently teaching in the Creative Writing Program at Princeton University.

MARGARET HOMANS is a professor of English at Yale University and the author of *Women Writers and Poetic Identity: Dorothy Wordsworth, Emily Brontë, and Emily Dickinson.*

BARBARA HARDY teaches in the History and Literature Program at Harvard University.

R. B. STEPTO teaches English and Afro-American Studies at Yale University. He has written *Behind the Veil* and coedited *Chant of Saints*, an anthology of Afro-American literature.

JOHN HOLLANDER is a poet, critic, and professor of English at Yale University. His numerous books include *Blue Wine and Other Poems*, *Power of Thirteen*, *Rhyme's Reason: A Guide to English Literature*, *Twelfth Night and the Morality of Indulgence*, and *Vision and Resonance: Two Senses of Poetic Form.* He has also edited *The Oxford Anthology of English Literature* with Frank Kermode.

NORTHROP FRYE is a professor of English at the University of Toronto. Through his writing and speaking, he has done much to contribute to and encourage Canadian letters. Several of his many books are *Fearful Symmetry: A Study of William Blake*, *The Secular Scripture:A Study of the Structure of Romance*, *The Bush Garden*, and *Anatomy of Criticism.*

MARGARET ATWOOD is a Canadian writer. She is the author of numerous books of poetry, several novels, and a book of criticism.

JUDITH McCOMBS teaches at the Center for Creative Studies, College of Art and Design in Detroit. In addition to her work on Margaret Atwood, she has written two books of poetry, *Sisters and Other Selves* and *Against Nature: Wilderness Poems*.

Bibliography

Abel, Elizabeth, ed. *Writing and Sexual Difference.* Chicago: The University of Chicago Press, 1982.

Evans, Mari, ed. *Black Women Writers (1950–1980): A Critical Evaluation.* New York: Anchor Press/Doubleday, 1984.

Gilbert, Sandra M., and Susan Gubar, eds. *Shakespeare's Sisters: Feminist Essays on Women Poets.* Bloomington: Indiana University Press, 1979.

Jacobus, Mary, ed. *Women Writing and Writing About Women.* London: Croom Helm in association with The Oxford Women's Studies Committee, 1979.

McConnell-Ginet, Sally, Ruth Barker, and Nelly Furman, eds. *Women and Language in Literature and Society.* New York: Praeger Publishers, 1980.

Moers, Ellen. *Literary Women.* Garden City, N.Y.: Doubleday and Company, 1979.

Rich, Adrienne. *On Lies, Secrets and Silence.* New York: W. W. Norton and Company, 1979.

Vendler, Helen. *Part of Nature, Part of Us.* Cambridge: Harvard University Press, 1980.

ANNE BRADSTREET

Ball, Kenneth R. "Puritan Humility in Anne Bradstreet's Poetry." *Cithera* 13 (November 1973): 29–41.

McCay, Mary A. "Anne Hutchinson and Anne Bradstreet: Two New England Women." *Dutch Quarterly Review* 11, no. 1 (1981): 2–21.

Mawer, Randall R. " 'Farewel Dear Babe': Bradstreet's Elegy for Elizabeth." *Early American Literature* 15, no. 1 (Spring 1980): 29–41.

Rosenmeier, Rosamund. "Divine Translation: A Contribution to the Study of Anne Bradstreet's Method in the Marriage Poems." *Early American Literature* 12, no. 2 (Fall 1977): 121–34.

343

Salska, Agnieszka. "Puritan Poetry: Its Public and Private Strain." *Early American Literature* 19, no. 2 (Fall 1984): 107–21.

Stanford, Ann. *Anne Bradstreet: The Wordly Puritan: An Introduction to Her Poetry*. New York: Burt Franklin and Company, 1974.

EMILY DICKINSON

Beauchamp, William. "Riffaterre's *Semiotics of Poetry* with an Illustration in the Poetry of Emily Dickinson." *CENTRUM* 1, no. 1 (Spring 1981): 36–47.

Blake, Caesar R., and Carlton F. Wells, eds. *The Recognition of Emily Dickinson*. Ann Arbor: University of Michigan Press, 1968.

Burbick, Joan. "Emily Dickinson and the Revenge of the Nerves." *Women's Studies* 7, nos. 1 and 2 (1980): 95–110.

Cameron, Sharon. *Lyric Time: Dickinson and the Limits of Genre*. Baltimore: The Johns Hopkins University Press, 1979.

Diehl, Joanne Feit. "Dickinson and Bloom: An Antithetical Reading of Romanticism." *Texas Studies in Literature and Language* 23 (1981): 418–41.

Frye, Northrop. "Emily Dickinson." In *Major Writers of America*, edited by Perry Miller. New York: Harcourt, Brace and World, Inc., 1962.

Gilbert, Sandra M., and Susan Gubar. "A Woman-White: Emily Dickinson's Yarn of Pearl." In *The Madwoman in the Attic*. New Haven: Yale University Press, 1979.

Homans, Margaret. *Women Writers and Poetic Identity*. Princeton: Princeton University Press, 1980.

Juhasz, Suzanne, ed. *Feminist Critics Read Emily Dickinson*. Bloomington: Indiana University Press, 1983.

Keller, Karl. *The Only Kangaroo among the Beauty: Emily Dickinson's America*. Baltimore: The Johns Hopkins University Press, 1979.

Knox, Helene. "Metaphor and Metonymy in Emily Dickinson's Figurative Thinking." *Massachusetts Studies in English* 7/8 (1981): 49–56.

Wolosky, Shira. *Emily Dickinson: A Voice of War*. New Haven: Yale University Press, 1984.

GERTRUDE STEIN

Bridgeman, Richard. *Gertrude Stein in Pieces*. New York: Oxford University Press, 1970.

DeKoven, Marianne. "Gertrude Stein and Modern Painting: Beyond Literary Cubism." *Contemporary Literature* 22, no. 1 (Winter 1981): 81–95.

Delta, a review of the Centre d'Etude et de Recherches sur les écrivains du sud aux Etats-Unis (Center of Studies and Research on Writers of the Southern United States). Special issue on Gertrude Stein, no. 10 (May 1980).

Dubnick, Randa. *The Structure of Obscurity: Gertrude Stein, Language and Cubism*. Bloomington: Indiana University Press, 1984.

Liston, Maureen R. *Gertrude Stein: An Annotated Critical Bibliography*. Kent: Kent State University Press, 1979.

Perloff, Marjorie. "Poetry As Word System: The Art of Gertrude Stein." *American Poetry Review* 10 (1979): 33–43.

Steiner, Wendy. *Exact Resemblance to Exact Resemblance: The Literary Portraiture of Gertrude Stein*. New Haven: Yale University Press, 1978.

Sutherland, Donald. *Gertrude Stein: A Biography of Her Work*. New Haven: Yale University Press, 1951.

Walker, Jayne L. *The Making of a Modernist: Gertrude Stein from* Three Lives *to* Tender Buttons. Amherst: University of Massachusetts Press, 1984.

Weinstein, Norman. *Gertrude Stein and the Literature of Modern Consciousness*. New York: Frederick Ungar Publishing Company, 1970.

H. D. (HILDA DOOLITTLE)

DuPlessis, Rachel Blau. "Romantic Thralldom in H. D." *Contemporary Literature* 20, no. 2 (Spring 1979): 178–203.

DuPlessis, Rachel Blau, and Susan Stanford. "Woman is Perfect: H. D.'s Debate With Freud." *Feminist Studies* 7, no. 3 (Fall 1981): 417–30.

Friedman, Susan. "Creating a Woman's Mythology: H. D.'s *Helen in Egypt*." *Women's Studies* 5, no. 2 (1977): 163–97.

Gelpi, Albert. "Hilda in Egypt." *The Southern Review* 18, no. 2 (Summer 1982): 233–50.

Gilbert, Sandra M. "H. D.? Who Was She?" *Contemporary Literature* 24, no. 4 (Winter 1983): 496–511.

Gubar, Susan. "The Echoing Spell of H. D.'s *Trilogy*." *Contemporary Literature* 19, no. 2 (Spring 1978): 196–218.

———. "Sapphistries." *Signs* 10, no. 1 (Autumn 1984): 43–62.

Morris, Adalaide. "Reading H. D.'s 'Helios and Athene.'" *Iowa Review* 12, no. 2/3 (Spring/Summer 1981): 155–63.

MARIANNE MOORE

Abbott, Craig S. *Marianne Moore: A Descriptive Bibliography*. Pittsburgh: University of Pittsburgh Press, 1977.

Boroff, Marie. *Language and the Poet: Verbal Artistry in Frost, Stevens and Moore*. Chicago: The University of Chicago Press, 1979.

Costello, Bonnie. "Marianne Moore and Elizabeth Bishop: Friendship and Influence." *Twentieth Century Literature* (Marianne Moore issue) 30, no. 2/3 (Summer/Fall 1984): 130–49.

———. *Marianne Moore: Imaginary Possessions*. Cambridge: Harvard University Press, 1981.

Glatstein, Jacob. "Marianne Moore." Translated by Doris Vidaver. *Yiddish* 6, no. 1 (Spring 1985): 67–73.

Newlin, Margaret. "'Unhelpful Hymen!': Marianne Moore and Hilda Doolittle." *Essays in Criticism* 27, no. 3 (July 1977): 216–30.

Phillips, Elizabeth. *Marianne Moore.* New York: Frederick Ungar Publishing Company, 1982.

LOUISE BOGAN

Bowles, Gloria. "Louise Bogan: To be (or not to be?) a Woman Poet." *Women's Studies* 5, no. 2 (1977): 131–35.

Collins, Martha, ed. *Critical Essays on Louise Bogan.* Boston: G. K. Hall and Company, 1984.

Moore, Patrick. "Symbol, Mask and Meter in the Poetry of Louise Bogan." In *Gender and Literary Voice.* New York: Holmes and Meier Publishers, Inc., 1980.

Ridgeway, Jacqueline. "The Necessity of Form to the Poetry of Louise Bogan." *Women's Studies* 5, no. 2 (1977): 137–49.

ELIZABETH BISHOP

Blasing, M. Konuck. "Mont d'Espoir or Mount Despair, The Re-Verses of Elizabeth Bishop." *Contemporary Literature* 25, no. 3 (Fall 1984): 341–53.

Bromwich, David. "Elizabeth Bishop's Dream Houses." *Raritan* 4, no. 1 (Summer 1984): 77–94.

Costello, Bonnie. "Vision and Mastery in Elizabeth Bishop." *Twentieth Century Literature* 28 (Winter 1982): 351–70.

Doreski, Carole. "Elizabeth Bishop: 'All the Conditions of Existence.' " *Literary Review* 27 (Winter 1984): 262–71.

Handa, Carolyn. "Elizabeth Bishop and Women's Poetry." *South Atlantic Quarterly* 82 (Summer 1983): 269–81.

Schwartz, Lloyd, and Sybil P. Estess, eds. *Elizabeth Bishop and Her Art.* Ann Arbor: University of Michigan Press, 1983.

World Literature Today. Special issue on Elizabeth Bishop (Winter 1977).

MAY SWENSON

Smith, Dave. "Perpetual Worlds Taking Place." *Poetry* 135, no. 5 (1980): 291–96.

Stanford, Anne. "May Swenson: The Art of Perceiving." *The Southern Review* 5, no. 1 (January 1969): 58–75.

Stepanchev, Stephen. "May Swenson." *American Poetry since 1945.* New York: Harper and Row, 1965.

GWENDOLYN BROOKS

Furman, Marva Riley. "Gwendolyn Brooks: The 'Unconditioned' Poet." *College Language Association Journal* 17, no. 1 (September 1973): 1–10.

Hansell, William H. "Aestheticism versus Political Militancy in Gwendolyn Brooks's 'The Chicago Picasso' and 'The Wall.' " *College Language Association Journal* 17, no. 1 (September 1973): 11–15.

Hudson, Clenora F. "Racial Themes in the Poetry of Gwendolyn Brooks." *College Language Association Journal* 17, no. 1 (September 1973): 16–20.

Hull, Gloria T. "A Note on the Poetic Technique of Gwendolyn Brooks." *College Language Association Journal* 19, no. 2 (December 1975): 280–85.

Smith, Gary. "The Black Protest Sonnet." *American Poetry* 2, no. 1 (Fall 1984): 2–21.

Stetson, Erlene. "*Songs After Sunset* (1935–1936): The Unpublished Poetry of Gwendolyn Elizabeth Brooks." *College Language Association Journal* 24, no. 1 (September 1980): 87–96.

Werner, Craig. "Gwendolyn Brooks: Tradition in Black and White." *Minority Voices* 1, no. 2 (Fall 1977): 27–38.

DENISE LEVERTOV

Howard, Richard. "Denise Levertov." In *Alone with America*. New York: Atheneum, 1980.

Ostriker, Alicia. "In Mind: The Divided Self and Women's Poetry." *The Midwest Quarterly* 24, no. 4 (Summer 1983): 351–65.

Sautter, Diane. "Tacit and Explicit Tulips." *Pre/Text: Interdisciplinary Journal of Rhetoric* 1, no. 1/2 (1982): 45–59.

ANNE SEXTON

Hartman, Geoffrey. "Les Belles Dames Sans Merci." *Kenyon Review* 22, no. 4 (Autumn 1960): 691–94.

McClatchy, J. D., ed. *Anne Sexton: The Artist and Her Critics*. Bloomington: Indiana University Press, 1978.

Zollman, Sol. "Criticism, Self-Criticism, No Transformation: The Poetry of Robert Lowell and Anne Sexton." *Literature and Ideology* 9 (1971): 29–36.

ADRIENNE RICH

Altieri, Charles. "Self-Reflection as Action." In *Self and Sensibility in Contemporary American Poetry*. Cambridge: Cambridge University Press, 1984.

Atwood, Margaret. "Adrienne Rich: *Poems, Selected and New*." In *Second Words*. Toronto: House of Anansi Press, 1982.

Gelpi, Barbara Charlesworth, and Albert Gelpi, eds. *Adrienne Rich's Poetry*. New York: W. W. Norton and Company, 1975.

Howard, Richard. "Adrienne Rich." In *Alone with America*. New York: Atheneum, 1980.

Hudgins, Andrew. " 'The Burn Has Settled In': A Reading of Adrienne Rich's *Diving into the Wreck*." *The Texas Review* 2, no. 1 (Spring 1981): 49–65.

Kalstone, David. *Five Temperaments*. New York: Oxford University Press, 1977.

McDaniel, Judith. *Reconstituting the World: The Poetry and Vision of Adrienne Rich*. Argyle, N.Y.: Spinsters Ink, 1978.

Vivley, Sherry Lute. "Adrienne Rich's Contemporary Metaphysical Conceit." *Notes on Contemporary Literature* 12, no. 3 (May 1982): 6–8.

SYLVIA PLATH

Alexander, Paul, ed. *Ariel Ascending: Writings About Sylvia Plath.* New York: Harper and Row, 1985.

Broe, Mary Lynn. "Recovering the Complex Self: Sylvia Plath's Beeline." *Centennial Review* 24 (Winter 1980): 1–24.

Dickie, Margaret. "Sylvia Plath's Narrative Strategies." *Iowa Review* 13, no. 2 (Spring 1982): 1–14.

Newman, Charles, ed. *The Art of Sylvia Plath: A Symposium.* Bloomington: Indiana University Press, 1970.

Perloff, Marjorie. "Sylvia Plath's *Collected Poems:* A Review Essay." *Resources for American Literary Study* 11 (Autumn 1983): 304–13.

Simpson, Louis. *A Revolution in Taste.* New York: Macmillan Publishing Company, 1978.

VanDyne, Susan. "Fueling the Phoenix Fire: The Manuscripts of Sylvia Plath's 'Lady Lazarus.' " *Massachusetts Review* 24 (Summer 1983): 395–410.

AUDRE LORDE

Lorde, Audre, and Adrienne Rich. "An Interview." In *Sister Outsider.* Trumansburg, N.Y.: The Crossing Press, 1984.

AMY CLAMPITT

Fenton, James. "*The Kingfisher* by Amy Clampitt." *Poetry Review* 74, no. 1 (April 1984): 27–29.

McClatchy, J. D. Review of *The Kingfisher* by Amy Clampitt. *Poetry* 143, no. 3 (December 1983): 165–67.

Vendler, Helen. "On the Thread of Language." *The New York Review of Books,* March 3, 1985, 19–22.

White, Edmund. "Poetry As Alchemy." *The Nation,* April 16, 1983, 485–86.

JAY MACPHERSON

Bromwich, David. "Engulfing Darkness, Penetrating Light." *Poetry* 127, no. 4 (January 1976): 236–39.

Djawa, Sandra. "Letters in Canada 1981." *University of Toronto Quarterly* 51, no. 4 (Summer 1982): 344–45.

MARGARET ATWOOD

Allen, Carolyn. "Failures of Word, Uses of Silence: Djuna Barnes, Adrienne

Rich and Margaret Atwood." *Regionalism and the Female Imagination* 4, no. 1 (Spring 1978): 1–8.

Davidson, A. E., and C. N. Davidson, eds. *The Art of Margaret Atwood.* Toronto: House of Anansi Press, 1981.

Grace, Sherill. *Violent Duality: A Study of Margaret Atwood.* Montreal: Véhicule Press, 1980.

Grace, Sherill, and Lorraine Weir, eds. *Margaret Atwood: Language, Text, and System.* Vancouver: University of British Columbia, 1983.

Sandler, Linda, ed. *Margaret Atwood: A Symposium.* Victoria: University of Victoria, 1977.

Acknowledgments

" 'No rhet'ric we expect': Argumentation in Bradstreet's 'The Prologue' " by Jane Donahue Eberwein from *Early American Literature* 16, no. 1 (Spring 1981), © 1981 by University of Massachusetts. Reprinted by permission of the journal editor.

"Emily Dickinson: A Voice of War" (originally entitled "Introduction") by Shira Wolosky from *Emily Dickinson: A Voice of War* by Shira Wolosky, © 1984 by Yale University. Reprinted by permission of Yale University Press.

" 'Ransom in a Voice': Language as Defense in Dickinson's Poetry" by Joanne Feit Diehl from *Feminist Critics Read Emily Dickinson*, edited by Suzanne Juhasz, © 1983 by Indiana University Press. Reprinted by permission.

"*Et in Arcadia Ego:* Representation, Death, and the Problem of Boundary in Emily Dickinson" (originally entitled "*Et in Arcadia Ego:* Representation, Death, and the Problem of Boundary") by Sharon Cameron from *Lyric Time: Dickinson and the Limits of Genre* by Sharon Cameron, © 1979 by The Johns Hopkins University Press. Reprinted by permission.

"Two Types of Obscurity in the Writings of Gertrude Stein" by Randa K. Dubnick from *The Emporia State Research Studies* 24, no. 3 (Winter 1976), © 1976 by Emporia Kansas State College. Reprinted by permission.

"The Concept of Projection: H. D.'s Visionary Powers" by Adalaide Morris from *Contemporary Literature* 25, no. 4 (Winter 1984), © 1984 by the Board of Regents of the University of Wisconsin System. Reprinted by permission of the University of Wisconsin Press.

"The 'Feminine' Language of Marianne Moore" by Bonnie Costello from *Women and Language in Literature and Society*, edited by Sally McConnell-

Ginet, Ruth Borker, and Nelly Furman, © 1980 by Praeger Publishers. Reprinted by permission of Praeger Publishers.

"Emphatic Reticence in Marianne Moore's Poems" (originally entitled "Marianne Moore's Poems") by David Bromwich from *Poetry* 139, no. 6 (March 1982), © 1982 by the Modern Poetry Association. Reprinted by permission of the author and *Poetry*.

"The Problem of the Woman Artist: Louise Bogan, 'The Alchemist' " by Diane Wood Middlebrook from *Critical Essays on Louise Bogan*, edited by Martha Collins, © 1984 by Martha Collins. Reprinted by permission of Twayne Publishers, a division of G. K. Hall & Co., Boston.

" 'The Repressed Becomes the Poem': Landscape and Quest in Two Poems by Louise Bogan" by Sandra Cookson from *Critical Essays on Louise Bogan,* edited by Martha Collins, © 1984 by Martha Collins. Reprinted by permission of Twayne Publishers, a division of G. K. Hall & Co., Boston.

"Elizabeth Bishop: Domestication, Domesticity, and the Otherworldly" (originally entitled "Elizabeth Bishop") by Helen Vendler from *World Literature Today* 51, no. 1 (Winter 1977), © 1977 by University of Oklahoma Press. Reprinted by permission. This essay also appeared in *Part of Nature, Part of Us: Modern American Poets* (Harvard University Press, 1980).

"The Geography of Gender: Elizabeth Bishop's 'In the Waiting Room' " by Lee Edelman from *Contemporary Literature* 26, no. 2 (Summer 1985), © 1985 by the Board of Regents of the University of Wisconsin System. Reprinted by permission of University of Wisconsin Press.

"May Swenson: 'Turned Back to the Wild by Love' " by Richard Howard from *Alone with America: Essays on the Art of Poetry in the United States since 1950* by Richard Howard, © 1980 by Richard Howard. Reprinted by permission.

"Gwendolyn Brooks's *A Street in Bronzeville*, the Harlem Renaissance and the Mythologies of Black Women" by Gary Smith from *MELUS: The Journal of the Society for the Study of the Multi-Ethnic Literature of the United States* 10, no. 3 (Fall 1983), © 1983 by MELUS. Reprinted by permission.

"Denise Levertov: A Poetry of Exploration" (originally entitled "A Poetry of Exploration") by Paul A. Lacey from *The Inner War: Forms and Themes in Recent American Poetry* by Paul A. Lacey, © 1972 by Fortress Press. Reprinted by permission.

"Anne Sexton: Somehow to Endure" by J. D. McClatchy, excerpted from a longer essay in *Anne Sexton: The Artist and Her Critics*, edited by J. D. McClatchy, © 1978 by J. D. McClatchy. Bloomington: Indiana University Press, 1978. Reprinted by permission.

"Adrienne Rich: A Feminine Tradition" (originally entitled "A Feminine Tradition") by Margaret Homans from *Women Writers and Poetic Identity:*

Dorothy Wordsworth, Emily Brontë, and Emily Dickinson by Margaret Homans, © 1980 by Princeton University Press. Reprinted by permission of Princeton University Press.

"Sylvia Plath: Enlargement or Derangement?" (originally entitled "Enlargement or Derangement") by Barbara Hardy from *The Survival of Poetry*, edited by Martin Dodsworth, © 1970 by Barbara Hardy. Reprinted by permission of the author and Faber and Faber Ltd. This essay later appeared in *Ariel Ascending: Writings about Sylvia Plath* (Harper and Row, 1985) and *The Advantage of Lyric* (Indiana University Press, 1977).

" Audre Lorde: The Severed Daughter" (originally entitled "The Phenomenal Woman and the Severed Daughter") by R. B. Stepto from *Parnassus: Poetry in Review* 8, no. 1 (Fall/Winter 1979), © 1980 by Poetry in Review Foundation. Reprinted by permission.

"Amy Clampitt: 'The Hazardous Definition of Structures' " (originally entitled "The Hazardous Definition of Structures") by Richard Howard from *Parnassus: Poetry in Review* 11, no. 1 (Spring/Summer 1983), © 1984 by Poetry in Review Foundation. Reprinted by permission.

"Tremors of Exactitude: Vicki Hearne's *Nervous Horses*" (originally entitled "Tremors of Exactitude") by John Hollander from *Times Literary Supplement*, no. 4061 (January 30, 1981), © 1981 by John Hollander. Reprinted by permission.

"Jay Macpherson: Poetry in Canada, 1957" (originally entitled "Letters in Canada: 1957") by Northrop Frye from *University of Toronto Quarterly* 27, no. 4 (July 1958), © 1958 by University of Toronto Press. Reprinted by permission of the author and University of Toronto Press.

"Jay Macpherson: *Poems Twice Told*" by Margaret Atwood from *Second Words* by Margaret Atwood, © 1982 by O. W. Toad Ltd. Reprinted by permission of House of Anansi Press Ltd. and Beacon Press.

"Atwood's Haunted Sequences: *The Circle Game, The Journals of Susanna Moodie*, and *Power Politics*" by Judith McCombs from *The Art of Margaret Atwood: Essays in Criticism*, edited by Arnold E. Davidson and Cathy N. Davidson, © 1981 by House of Anansi Press Ltd. Reprinted by permission.

Index of Names and Titles

Adams, Léonie, 145
"Ad Castitatem" (Bogan), 153–54
"Addict, The" (Sexton), 251
"Advent 1966" (Levertov), 230
"After the Persian" (Bogan), 159
"Aiaia" (Macpherson), 303
Aiken, Conrad, 118
"Alchemist, The" (Bogan), 146–47, 150
Aldington, Richard, 101, 109
All My Pretty Ones (Sexton), 237, 248, 249
"All That Time" (Swenson), 201
"All the Dead Dears" (Plath), 279, 280
Alvarez, A., 237
"Alyscamps at Arles, The" (Swenson), 199
American Imagistes, 19
American Renaissance (Matthiessen), 71
Ammons, A. R., 295
"Among School Children" (Yeats), 73–74
Anderson, Charles R., 4, 55–56, 60
"And One for My Dame" (Sexton), 251
"Angels of the Love Affair" (Sexton), 253
"An Interim" (Levertov), 229, 231
"Anna Who Was Mad" (Sexton), 254

Annie Allen (Brooks), 206, 216
"An Octopus" (Moore), 130, 133
Another Animal (Swenson), 191, 192
"Applicant, The" (Plath), 283, 284–85
Ariel (Plath), 274, 280–81, 283
"Ark, The" (Macpherson), 308
"Armor's Undermining Modesty" (Moore), 134
Arner, Robert, 9
"Arrival of the Bee Box, The" (Plath), 282–83
"Artist, The" (Levertov), 217
Ashbery, John, 176
"Assassin, The" (Sexton), 253
"At the Fishhouses" (Bishop), 137
Atwood, Margaret, 311–26
Auden, W. H., 273
Auerbach, Erich, 49, 50
"August 19, Pad 19" (Swenson), 200–201
Augustine, Saint, 62–63, 74
"Auroras of Autumn, The" (Stevens), 6
Austen, Jane, 6
Awful Rowing Toward God, The (Sexton), 248, 257

Bachelard, Gaston, 249
Bacon, Francis, 138, 141–42

"Ballad of Chocolate Mabbie, The" (Brooks), 211
"Ballad of Pearl May Lee" (Brooks), 211–12
Ballad of the Brown Girl, The (Cullen), 211–12
Barlow, Joel, 10
Barthes, Roland, 77, 78, 83, 295
"Battle, the" (Brooks), 215–16
Baudelaire, Charles, 156
Baxter, Richard, 138
Bean Eaters, The (Brooks), 216
"Beauty of Job's Daughters, The" (Macpherson), 308
Beckett, Samuel, 75
Beckford, William, 311
Beckonings (Brooks), 216
"Bee Meeting, The" (Plath), 282
Bell Jar, The (Plath), 312
"Bells, The" (Sexton), 243
Berryman, John, 238
"Bessie" (Brown), 214
"Birthday Present, A" (Plath), 283, 287
Bishop, Elizabeth, 1, 2, 6–8, 137, 161–73, 175–87, 193
Blackmur, R. P., 117
"Black Rook in Rainy Weather" (Plath), 277–78
"Blackstudies" (Lorde), 290
Black Unicorn, The (Lorde), 290, 293, 294

Blake, William, 3, 38, 140, 225, 301, 309
Bleak House (Dickens), 277
"Blessed Is the Man" (Moore), 133
"Bloodbirth" (Lorde), 290
Bloom, Harold, 32, 57
Blue Estuaries: Poems, 1923–1968, The (Bogan), 145–46, 152
Bly, Robert, 222
"Boat, The" (Sexton), 255–56
Boatman, The (Macpherson), 301, 302–5, 308
"Boatman, The" (Macpherson), 303
Body of This Death (Bogan), 153
Bogan, Louise, 145–50, 151–59
Book of Folly, The (Sexton), 237, 248, 252–53, 254
Borderline (Macpherson), 107, 108
Bowering, George, 308
Boyers, Robert, 250
Bradstreet, Anne, 2–3, 9–15
Bridgman, Richard, 96
Brinnin, John Malcolm, 86
Brooks, Gwendolyn, 205–16
Brooks, Keziah, 205
Brown, Sterling, 209, 212, 214
Browning, Robert, 296–97
Bryher (Winifred Ellerman), 97, 104, 105, 108, 109
Burke, Edmund, 138
Burke, Kenneth, 143
"Burnt-out Spa, The" (Plath), 279, 280
"By Disposition of Angels" (Moore), 133

"Cables to Rage" (Lorde), 290
Cage of Spines, A (Swenson), 193, 194
Caroling Dusk (Cullen), 209
"Cassandra" (Bogan), 146, 147
Castle of Otranto, The (Walpole), 311
"Caverned Woman, The" (Macpherson), 303
"Centaur, The" (Swenson), 194
Chadwick, Mary, 107
"Chain" (Lorde), 292

Chaucer, 6, 12
Christ and Time (Cullmann), 62
"Christmas Eve" (Sexton), 251
"Cinema and the Classics, The" (Doolittle), 105
Circle Game, The (Atwood), 311, 312, 313–16
"City Psalm" (Levertov), 228
Clampitt, Amy, 295–98
Close Up, 105, 106, 107, 108
Coleridge, Samuel Taylor, 70
Color (Cullen), 206, 210
Colossus, The (Plath), 277, 279
Compulsion to Confess, The (Reik), 238
"Consorting with Angels" (Sexton), 250
"Coriolan" (Eliot), 159
Corn, Alfred, 178–79
Cosmos and History (Eliade), 61
"Couriers, The" (Plath), 284
Course in General Linguistics (Saussure), 80
Crane, Hart, 6
Crime and Punishment (Dostoevsky), 277
"Cripples and Other Stories" (Sexton), 253
"Crossing the Atlantic" (Sexton), 251
"Crows, The" (Bogan), 147–48
"Crusoe in England" (Bishop), 168–69
Cullen, Countee, 206, 208, 209, 210, 211–12
Cullmann, Oscar, 62
Cummings, e. e., 118, 206
Cunningham, J. V., 46
Curtis, Julia Anne, 317

"Daddy" (Plath), 283, 287
"Daguerreotype Taken in Old Age" (Atwood), 320
"Dahomey" (Lorde), 291
"Date, the" (Brooks), 215
Davey, Frank, 308
"Death & Co." (Plath), 283
"Death Baby, The" (Rich), 264–65
Death Notebooks, The (Sexton), 248, 249, 257
"Death of the Fathers, The" (Sexton), 254, 257
De Man, Paul, 46, 71

Demosthenes, 11, 12, 14
"Descent through the Carpet, A" (Atwood), 313
"Design" (Frost), 31
Deutsch, Babette, 145
Development of Abstractionism in the Writing of Gertrude Stein, The (Hoffman), 86
Dickens, Charles, 277
Dickinson, Emily, 2, 3, 4–5, 6, 7, 8, 15, 17–39, 41–76, 251, 259, 260
Dickinson, Emily, poems by: (P 24), 26; (P 258), 49–51; (P 280), 45–47; (P 281), 47–48; (P 286), 53–55; (P 287), 51–53; (P 290), 3; (P 344), 56; (P 412), 55–56; (P 414), 43–44; (P 430), 35–37; (P 465), 59–65, 72, 73, 74; (P 479), 29; (P 532), 76; (P 594), 20–21; (P 615), 34, 56, 57–58, 74; (P 683), 35; (P 712), 65–71, 72, 73, 74; (P 722), 33–34; (P 742), 31–32; (P 754), 65; (P 764), 7; (P 835), 27–29; (P 855), 38; (P 1056), 26–27; (P 1088), 21–22; (P 1282), 24; (P 1651), 24–25
Diehl, Joanne Feit, 4
"Diving into the Wreck" (Rich), 262
"Division of Parts, The" (Sexton), 245, 247–48, 264
"Divorce, Thy Name is Woman" (Sexton), 244
Dobson, Silvia, 104
"Doctor of the Heart, The" (Sexton), 253
"Do I wake or sleep" (Keats), 74
Doolittle, Hilda, 97–115, 145
Dostoevsky, Fëdor, 277
"Double Image, The" (Sexton), 239, 245–47, 251, 264
Dracula (Stoker), 311
Dream of a Common Language, The (Rich), 265, 266
Drummond de Andrade, Carlos, 166
Du Bartas (Guillaume de Salluste), 11, 12, 14

Dudley, Thomas, 11
Dunbar, Paul Laurence, 206
Duncan, Robert, 102, 111, 221
"During the Eichmann Trial" (Levertov), 223

Earnshaw, Catherine, 309
"Earth" (Macpherson), 301
"Edge" (Plath), 264
"Egg" (Macpherson), 303, 308
Egoist, The, 101
Eisenstein, Sergey, 107
"Elephants" (Moore), 133, 141, 142
Eliade, Mircea, 61, 71–72
Eliot, George, 6
Eliot, T. S., 30, 95, 99, 117, 136, 143, 158, 159, 206, 207, 209, 302
"Elizabeth Gone" (Sexton), 244
Ellis, Havelock, 102, 109
Emerson, Ralph Waldo, 2, 3, 5, 19, 23
"Emperor of Ice-Cream" (Stevens), 163
"End of March, The" (Bishop), 7
"End of the day, the" (Brooks), 215
"England" (Moore), 133
Erikson, Eric, 238
"Esso" (Bishop), 162–63
Estess, Sybil, 178
"Eulogy for Alvin Frost" (Lorde), 292–93
"Evolution" (Swenson), 191–92
"Exchange, The" (Swenson), 199–200
"Expatriates, The" (Sexton), 243
"Eye-mote, The" (Plath), 277, 278

Family Pictures (Brooks), 216
Faulkner, William, 312
Fenollosa, Ernest, 99
"Fern Hill" (Thomas), 63
"Feuernacht" (Bogan), 153
"Fever 103°" (Plath), 280, 281
"Fifteenth Farewell" (Bogan), 146, 148–50
"Firebombers, The" (Sexton), 253

"First Death in Nova Scotia" (Bishop), 163–64
"Fish, The" (Moore), 133
"Fisherman: A Book of Riddles, The" (Macpherson), 302, 303
"Flee on Your Donkey" (Sexton), 250, 251
Fletcher, Angus, 70
Fletcher, John Gould, 101
Flowering of the Rod, The (Doolittle), 111, 114–15
For a New Novel (Robbe-Grillet), 63
"For God While Sleeping" (Sexton), 248, 249
"For John, Who Begs Me Not to Enquire Further" (Sexton), 241–42
45 Mercy Street (Sexton), 244, 250, 257
"Fountains of Aix" (Swenson), 199
"Four Monarchies, The" (Bradstreet), 10, 13–14
"Four Quartz Crystal Clocks" (Moore), 133, 134
"Frame of Reference: Poe, Lacan, Derridda, The" (Johnson), 186
Frankenstein (Shelley), 311, 312, 322, 323
Freud, Sigmund, 2, 6, 107, 108, 109, 110, 239, 252, 254–55, 265
Friedberg, Anne, 107
Friedman, Susan, 109
"Frigate Pelican, The" (Moore), 120, 133, 135
"Frog Report" (Lorde), 293
"From a Notebook: October '68 – May '69" (Levertov), 229, 231, 232–33
"From the House of Yemanjá" (Lorde), 291
"Frontispiece" (Swenson), 195
Frost, Robert, 6, 31, 172, 195
"Full Fathom Five" (Plath), 279, 280

Garden of Eloquence (Peacham), 10
"Genuine and Poignant" (Hearne), 299
Geography III (Bishop) 161, 177

"Gertrude Stein, William James, and Grammar" (Levinson), 79
"Getting There" (Plath), 285–86, 287
Gift, The (Doolittle), 108
Gilbert, Sandra M., 33, 176
Goblins and Pagodas (Fletcher), 101
"Grave, A" (Moore), 133, 135–37
Graves, Robert, 304
Gregg, Frances, 109
Grimm, Jacob and Wilhelm, 252, 309
Gubar, Susan, 33, 176

Haas, Robert, 80
Haining, Peter, 311
"Hairy" (Swenson), 196
Half Sun Half Sleep (Swenson), 200
"Hardcastle Crags" (Plath), 277
"Harlem Dancer, The" (McKay), 210–11
Harlem Shadows (McKay), 208, 209, 214
Harmonium (Stevens), 143
Hartman, Geoffrey, 57, 118, 122, 124–25
Hawthorne, Nathaniel, 19, 71
Hazlitt, William, 2
H.D. Book, The (Duncan), 102
Hearne, Vicki, 2, 299–300
"Heart's Needle" (Snodgrass), 245
"Hecate Trivia" (Macpherson), 309
Heidegger, Martin, 51
Helen in Egypt (Doolittle), 97, 105
"Helmsman, The" (Doolittle), 101
Hemans, Felicia, 119
Hensley, Jeannine, 11
Herbert, George, 68
"Her Kind" (Sexton), 243
"Hermes of the Ways" (Doolittle), 101
Hermetic Definition (Doolittle), 105
"Hero, The" (Moore), 133, 135, 142
"Her Shield" (Jarrell), 117
Hersland, David, 81, 82–83

Hiroshima Mon Amour (film), 277
"His Shield" (Moore), 121–22, 133
Hoffman, Daniel, 71, 82, 86
Holden, Raymond, 152, 154–55
Hölderlin, Friedrich, 189–90
Hollander, John, 176
Hopkins, Anne, 11, 278, 297
Howard, Richard, 243
"How We Danced" (Sexton), 255
Hughes, Langston, 205, 206–7, 210, 214
Hughes, Ted, 278
Hulme, T. E., 99, 100, 101
Hume, Robert D., 311
"Humility, Concentration and Gusto" (Moore), 122–23, 135
"Hurry Up Please It's Time" (Sexton), 257
Hutchinson, Anne, 11

"Illustrious Ancestors" (Levertov), 218–20
"Ill Wind, The" (Macpherson), 301
I Married Adventure (Johnson), 182
"Imitations of Drowning" (Sexton), 250
"In Distrust of Merits" (Moore), 121, 133, 143
"In Plaster" (Plath), 281
"In the Beach House" (Sexton), 250
"In the Days of Prismatic Color" (Moore), 133, 135, 139–40
"In the Deep Museum" (Sexton), 248, 249
In the Mecca (Brooks), 216
In the Midst of My Fever (Layton), 305
"In the Waiting Room" (Bishop), 165–66, 177–87
"In This Age of Hard Trying" (Moore), 119–20
Irigaray, Luce, 260

"Jabberwocky" (Carroll), 91
Jacob's Ladder, The, (Levertov), 220, 223
Jakobson, Roman, 77, 78, 79–80, 83–84, 92–93, 96

James, Henry, 145, 150
James, William, 79, 80, 93
Jane Eyre (C. Brontë), 311
Jarrell, Randall, 117, 129, 237, 252
"Jerboa, The" (Moore), 133, 135, 142
"Jesus Papers, The" (Sexton), 248, 252
"Jesus Walking" (Sexton), 248, 249
Johnson, Barbara, 186
Johnson, James Weldon, 205–6
Johnson, Osa and Martin, 182, 183, 184
Johnson, Samuel, 2, 140
Journals of Susanna Moodie, The (Atwood), 311, 312, 316–21
Joyce, James, 95
Juhasz, Suzanne, 118, 124

Kalstone, David, 176
"Kathë Kollwitz" (Rukeyser), 260
Keats, John, 74, 221, 267–68
Keller, Karl, 20
"Killing the Spring" (Sexton), 253
Kimber, William, 321
"Kind Sir: These Woods" (Sexton), 243
Kingfisher, The (Clampitt), 295, 297
"Kitchenette building" (Brooks), 207–8
Knight, Jackson, 309
"Knight of the Blood-Red Plume" (Curtis), 317
Knopf Poetry Series, 295
Kümmel, Friedrich, 52

"Labors of Hercules, The" (Moore), 133
"Lady Lazarus" (Plath), 283–84, 287
Lady Oracle (Atwood), 311
"La Figlia che Piange" (Moore), 143
La Fontaine, Jean de, 138
"Lamentation, A" (Levertov), 225–26
Lawrence, D. H., 237, 238
Layton, Irving, 305
Leavis, F. R., 273
LePan, Douglas, 304, 305
"Letter to William Kintner" (Levertov), 222–23

Levertov, Denise, 217–35
Levinson, Ronald, 79
Lewis, Janet, 145
Lewis, Matthew, 311
"Life at War" (Levertov), 228–29
"Lightning, The" (Swenson), 202
Literary Women (Moers), 312
"Little Girl, My Stringbean, My Lovely Woman" (Sexton), 251
Little Review, The, 105
"Little Uncomplicated Hymn, A" (Sexton), 251
Live or Die (Sexton), 249, 250, 251–52
Locke, Alaine, 208–9
Lorde, Audre, 289–94
"Lorelei" (Plath), 279–80
"Lost Ingredient, The" (Sexton), 244
"Lost in Translation" (Merrill), 300
Love Poems (Sexton), 237, 252, 253
"Love Song" (Sexton), 250
Low, Barbara, 107
Lowell, Amy, 101
Lowell, Robert, 176, 193, 237, 238, 240
"Lullaby" (Sexton), 243
Lyrical Ballads (Wordsworth), 171
"Lyric Present: Simple Present Verbs in English Poems, The" (Wright), 73
Lyrics of a Lowly Life (Dunbar), 206

McKay, Claude, 208, 209, 210–11, 214
Macpherson, Jay, 2, 301–5, 307–10
Macpherson, Kenneth, 105, 107, 108, 109
Madwoman in the Attic, The (Gilbert and Gubar), 20, 176
Majic Ring, The, (Doolittle), 104
Making of Americans, The (Stein), 77, 78, 80–83, 84, 85, 87, 89, 90, 96
Mallarmé, Stéphane, 189
Malloy (Beckett), 75
"Man and Wife" (Sexton), 251

"Man-Moth, The" (Bishop), 137
"Manor Garden, The" (Plath), 277
"Map, The" (Bishop), 175
"March, A" (Levertov), 223
"Märchen, The" (Jarrell), 252
"Marina" (Eliot), 159
Marlatt, Daphne, 308
"Marriage" (Moore), 133, 135, 137–39
Martin, Wendy, 2–3
Martz, Louis, 222
"Mary of Egypt" (Macpherson), 304
Matthiessen, F. O., 71
Maturin, Charles, 311
"Mauberley" (Moore), 143
Mazzaro, Jerome, 178
"Medallion" (Plath), 279
"Medusa" (Bogan), 153
"Medusa" (Plath), 263
"Melanchthon" (Moore), 133, 142
Melville, Herman, 19, 71, 74
"Menstruation at Forty" (Sexton), 250
Merrill, James, 300
"Metaphysical Horse, The" (Hearne), 300
Millay, Edna Saint Vincent, 117, 123, 145
Mills, Ralph, Jr., 224
Milton, John, 3, 63–64
Moby-Dick (Melville), 71
Modern Idiom, The (Porter), 20
Moers, Ellen, 311, 312
"Moon and the Yew Tree, The" (Plath), 286–87
Moore, Marianne, 2, 8, 117–31, 133–43, 176
"Moose, The" (Bishop), 170–73, 175
Moss, Howard, 156, 193
"Most of It, The" (Frost), 172
"Mother, the" (Brooks), 207, 208
"Mother of the Blues" (Brown), 212–13
"Mouse Island" (Doolittle), 104
"M., Singing" (Bogan), 153
"Music Swims Back to Me" (Sexton), 243
"Mussel Hunter at Rock Harbor" (Plath), 279, 280

"Mutes, The" (Levertov), 224

"Natural Mother, The" (Macpherson), 304
"Necessity, The" (Levertov), 223
Neruda, Pablo, 237
Nervous Horses (Hearne), 299
New Negro, The (Locke), 208–9
"News from the Cabin" (Swenson), 196–97
"New York" (Moore), 133, 135
New Yorker, The, 295
New York Review of Books, The, 295
New York Times Book Review, The, 207
"Nick and the Candlestick" (Plath), 274–76, 277
Nietzsche, Friedrich, 18, 21
"Night Shift" (Plath), 277
Niké (Doolittle), 104
"Noon Walk on the Asylum Lawn" (Sexton), 243
"Notes of a Scale" (Levertov), 221–22
"Notes on Recent Writing" (Doolittle), 111
Notes on Thought and Vision (Doolittle), 102–3, 106
"Novices" (Moore), 126–27

O'Connor, Flannery, 312
"O Earth Return" (Macpherson), 301, 302
"Of Bronze — and Blaze" (Dickinson), 4, 5
"Oh" (Sexton), 253
"Old marrieds" (Brooks), 209–10
"Olga Poems" (Levertov), 225, 226–28
"On Being Modern with Distinction" (Ransom), 117
"One Art" (Bishop), 168
"125th Street and Abomey" (Lorde), 291
Only Kangaroo among the Beauty, The (Keller), 20
"Ordinary People in the Last Days" (Macpherson), 302
O Taste and See (Levertov), 223, 225

"Other, The" (Sexton), 253–54
"Other Poems" (Macpherson), 308
Overland to the Islands (Levertov), 218
"Oysters" (Sexton), 255

Page, P. K., 305
"Pain for a Daughter" (Sexton), 251
"Pangolin, The" (Moore), 120, 133, 135, 142–43
Panofsky, Erwin, 53, 72
"Paper Nautilus, The" (Moore), 125–26
"Parade of Painters" (Swenson), 195–96
"Paralytic" (Plath), 281
"Past Is the Present, The" (Moore), 140
Peacham, Henry, 10
Pearce, Roy Harvey, 118, 124
Pearson, Norman Holmes, 111
"People's Surroundings" (Moore), 141
"Peter" (Moore), 133
"Peter Quince at the Clavier" (Moore), 143
"Phantasia for Elvira Shatayev" (Rich), 268–71
Picture of Dorian Gray, The (Wilde), 189
Plath, Sylvia, 2, 237, 238, 251, 261–62, 263, 264, 273–87, 312
"Plowman in Darkness, The" (Macpherson), 301, 302
"Plumet Basilisk, The" (Moore), 120, 133
"Poem" (Bishop), 166–68
"Poet, The" (Emerson), 3–4
"Poet as Woman, The" (Ransom), 117
"Poetry and Grammar" (Stein), 79
"Poetry is a Destructive Force" (Stevens), 7–8
Poetry of American Women, The (Watts), 129
POOL Productions, 105
"Poor Child" (Macpherson), 301
Pope, Alexander, 140

"Poppies in October"
(Plath), 282
Porter, David, 20
Porter, Katherine Anne, 145
"Portrait of an Old Woman
on the College Tavern
Wall" (Sexton), 242
Pound, Ezra, 30, 95, 99, 100,
101, 109, 138, 143, 206
"Poussin and the Elegiac
Tradition" (Panofsky),
53
"Power" (Lorde), 293
Power Politics (Atwood), 311,
312, 321–26
"Projector" (Doolittle), 106
"Prologue, The"
(Bradstreet), 9–15
"Protestant Easter" (Sexton),
250
"Psychiatrist's Song"
(Bogan), 152, 154,
156–59
Psychology, 79, 80
"Pull Down Thy Vanity"
(Moore), 143
"Putting to Sea" (Bogan),
152, 154–56, 158

Quarles, Francis, 2, 3
"Queen of the Blues, The"
(Brooks), 212–14
"Question" (Swenson), 193
Questions of Travel (Bishop),
161

Radcliffe, Ann, 311, 312
Raleigh, Sir Walter, 63
Ransom, John Crowe,
117–18, 123, 124
Reade, Charles, 138
Reaney, James, 305
"Redemption" (Herbert),
68–69
Reik, Theodor, 238
Relearning the Alphabet
(Levertov), 223, 229,
231, 235
"Relearning the Alphabet"
(Levertov), 233–35
Report (Brooks), 206
Resnais, Alain, 277
"Revenant" (Atwood), 311
"R. F., His Hand Against a
Tree" (Swenson), 195
Rhys, Jean, 312, 323
Rich, Adrienne, 186, 259–71
Richardson, Samuel, 6

"Riddle" (Plath), 276
Rilke, Rainer Maria, 237
Rimbaud, Arthur, 237, 250
Riot (Brooks), 216
Robbe-Grillet, Alain, 63, 64
Roberts, Elizabeth Madox,
145
Robeson, Paul, 107
Rodeck, Peter, 104, 109
Roethke, Theodore, 237
Rogers, John, 14
Room of One's Own, A
(Woolf), 128
Rosenmeier, Rosamund, 10
Rosenthal, M. L., 243
Rossetti, Christina, 117
Rukeyser, Muriel, 260

Sachs, Hanns, 107
"Said The Poet to The
Analyst" (Sexton), 242,
243
"Sailing to Byzantium"
(Yeats), 146–47, 156
"St. George and the
Dragon" (Hearne), 300
"Salvage" (Clampitt), 298
Sanford, Ann, 10, 11
"Santa" (Sexton), 256–57
"Satanic Form" (Swenson),
192
Saussure, Ferdinand de, 77,
78, 80
"Scurry" (Swenson), 196
Sea Garden (Doolittle),
100–101
"Sea Gods" (Doolittle), 101
"Sea Unicorns and Land
Unicorns" (Moore), 129
"Self-Reliance" (Emerson),
23
"Sestina" (Bishop), 161–62
Sexton, Anne, 237–57, 264
Shakespeare, William, 3, 6,
48, 138
Shaw, George Bernard, 140
"Sheba" (Macpherson), 304
Shelley, Mary, 185, 312, 321,
322, 323
"Shrine, The" (Doolittle),
101
"Sibling Mysteries" (Rich),
265
"Sibylla" (Macpherson), 302,
304
"Silence" (Moore), 133
"Silence, The" (Sexton), 254
"Sir John's Hill" (Thomas),
278

"Sleepers, The"
(Macpherson), 302
Smart, Christopher, 237
"Snakes, Mongooses, Snake
Charmers, and the
Like" (Moore), 133
Snodgrass, W. D., 238, 245
"Snowbound" (Whittier),
163
"Snow White and the Seven
Dwarfs" (Sexton), 252
Snyder, Gary, 222
"Sojourn in the Whale"
(Moore), 133, 142
"Some Foreign Letters"
(Sexton), 244–45, 251
"Some Ghosts and Some
Ghouls" (Macpherson),
309
Something in Common
(Hughes), 206
"Somewhere in Africa"
(Sexton), 251
"Song" (Bogan), 153
"Song of Praise, A"
(Cullen), 210
Sonnet 64 (Shakespeare), 48
Sorrow Dance, The
(Levertov), 223–24, 228,
229, 231
Southern Road (Brown), 209
"Speculum for Fallen
Women, A"
(Macpherson), 301
"Speeches for Dr.
Frankenstein"
(Atwood), 311
"Spenser's Ireland" (Moore),
133, 142
"Starlight Night, The"
(Hopkins), 278
Starobinski, Jean, 41
"Statement on Poetics"
(Levertov), 217, 235
"Steeple-Jack, The" (Moore),
133, 134–35
Stein, Gertrude, 2, 77–96
Stevens, Wallace, 3, 5, 6, 7,
32, 75, 143, 163, 166,
176, 299
Stevenson, Anne, 176–77
"Storm" (Macpherson), 303
Straw Swan at Christmas, A
(Levertov), 218
Street in Bronzeville, A
(Brooks), 205, 207–8,
209–10, 211, 214–16
"Student, The" (Moore),
133, 135, 142

"Suicide off Egg Rock," (Plath), 279, 280
"Sundays of Satin-Legs Smith, The" (Brooks), 207, 208
Survival (Atwood), 317, 321
Sutherland, Donald, 95
"Swarm, The" (Plath), 283
Swenson, May, 2, 189–203
"Sylvia's Death" (Sexton), 251

Taggard, Genevieve, 145
"Tale, A" (Bogan), 152–53
Tales of the Hasidism: Early Masters (Levertov), 221
Tales of the Hasidism: Later Masters (Levertov), 220
"Talking to Sheep" (Sexton), 244
Tate, Allen, 67
Tell Me Your Answer True (Sexton), 250
Tender Buttons (Stein), 77, 78, 80, 84–85, 86–87, 88, 89, 90–92, 93–95, 96
Tennyson, Alfred, Lord, 156
Tenth Muse, The (Bradstreet), 10, 12, 13, 14
"There Was a Child Went Forth" (Whitman), 165
"They Return" (Macpherson), 309
Things Taking Place (Swenson), 200
"Third Eye, The" (Macpherson), 301
Third Rose, The (Brinnin), 86
Thomas, Carey, 119
Thomas, Dylan, 63, 273, 275, 278
"Those Times . . ." (Sexton), 249, 250
"Three Green Windows" (Sexton), 250
"To a Poet" (Rich), 267, 268
"To a Snail" (Moore), 120
"To a Steam Roller" (Moore), 133, 142
To Bedlam and Part Way Back (Sexton), 237, 241, 243, 248
"To Confirm a Thing" (Swenson), 193
"To Julia Marshall — A Fragment" (D. Wordsworth), 263
"To Lose the Earth" (Sexton), 250

"To Military Progress" (Moore), 133
To Mix with Time (Swenson), 197–99
"To My Daughter the Junkie on a Train" (Lorde), 290
"To Speak" (Levertov), 228
"To Statecraft Embalmed" (Moore), 133
Tragic Muse, The (Henry James), 145
"Transcendental Etude" (Rich), 265–66, 267, 268, 270, 271
Transformations (Sexton), 237, 252
Tribute to Freud (Doolittle), 97, 98, 104, 108, 110
Tribute to the Angels (Doolittle), 111, 113–14
Trilogy (Doolittle), 97, 105, 111–15
"Truth, The" (Swenson), 201
"Tulips" (Plath), 281, 282, 284
"Two Aspects of Language and Two Types of Aphasic Disturbances" (Jakobson), 80
"Two Views of a Cadaver Room" (Plath), 277, 278

Updike, Daniel Berkeley, 123
"Upon Mrs. Anne Bradstreet Her Poems, Etc." (Rogers), 14

Valéry, Paul, 190
Van Eck, Peter, the character, 104–5
Vendler, Helen, 177–78, 295
Virgil, 11
"Virginia Britannia" (Moore), 133, 135

"Walking in Paris" (Sexton), 251
Walls Do Not Fall, The (Doolittle), 111, 113
Walpole, Horace, 311
"Wanting to Die" (Sexton), 251
Waste Land, The (Eliot), 158, 159, 209, 302

"Watercolor of Grantchester Meadows" (Plath), 277, 278
Watson, Wilfred, 305
Watts, Emily, 129
Weary Blues (Hughes), 206
Weisbuch, Robert, 57
Welcoming Disaster (Macpherson), 308, 309
"What Are Years?" (Moore), 133
"What's That" (Sexton), 243
Wheelock, John Hall, 155
"When I Buy Pictures" (Moore), 127–28, 133
"When I die" (Brooks), 215
"When Sue Wears Red" (Hughes), 210
"Whisper, The" (Levertov), 225
White, Elizabeth Wade, 9, 11, 14
Whitman, Walt, 3, 5, 19, 165, 172, 240
Wide Sargasso Sea (Rhys), 312, 323
Wilbur, Richard, 193, 295
Wilde, Oscar, 189
Wilkinson, Anne, 305
Williams, C. K., 237
Williams, William Carlos, 5, 118, 143
Wilson, Edmund, 96
Wing Beat (film), 105
"Wings, The" (Levertov), 224
Winters, Yvor, 66
"Winter's Ramble in Grasmere Vale, A" (D. Wordsworth), 266
"Wish: Metamorphosis" (Atwood), 320
With Eyes at the Back of Our Heads (Levertov), 223
"With Mercy for the Greedy" (Sexton), 248–49
"Woman Thing, The" (Lorde), 290
"Women" (Bogan), 148
Wood, Michael, 178
Woodbridge, John, 12, 13
Woolf, Virginia, 128, 195
Wordsworth, Dorothy, 259, 263, 266, 267
Wordsworth, William, 152, 171, 172, 241, 273
Wright, George, 73, 74, 75
Wright, James, 222
Wright, Jay, 290

Wuthering Heights (E. Brontë), 311
Wylie, Elinor, 145

Yeats, William Butler, 73–74, 146, 156

"You, Dr. Martin" (Sexton), 243, 253
"Young Prostitute" (Hughes), 214
"You're" (Plath), 276

"Your Face on the Dog's Neck" (Sexton), 251

Zaturenska, Marya, 145